Goals, Goal Structures, and Patterns of Adaptive Learning

Goals, Goal Structures, and Patterns of Adaptive Learning

Edited by

Carol Midgley
University of Michigan

LAWRENCE ERLBAUM ASSOCIATES, PUBLISHERS

2002   Mahwah, New Jersey   London

Lawrence Erlbaum Associates, Inc., Publishers
10 Industrial Avenue
Mahwah, NJ 07430

Cover design by Kathryn Houghtaling Lacey

Library of Congress Cataloging-in-Publication Data

Goals, goal structures, and patterns of adaptive learning / Carol
Midgley, editor.
        p.   cm.
Includes bibliographical references and index.
    ISBN 0-8058-3884-8 (Cloth : alk. paper)
    1. Learning, Psychology of. 2. Goal (Psychology). 3. Motivation
in education—United States. 4. Academic achievement—United
States. I. Midgley, Carol.
    LB1060 .G63 2002
    370.15'23—dc21   2001045107
                                                          CIP

Books published by Lawrence Erlbaum Associates are printed
on acid-free paper, and their bindings are chosen for strength
and durability.

Printed in the United States of America
10   9   8   7   6   5   4   3   2   1

For Rees

Contents

Foreword

In memory of Carol Midgley—our colleague, our mentor, and our friend—
from her students.

Over two decades ago, a perspective since labeled "goal theory," emerged
and has grown to become one of the most predominant perspectives in the
study of achievement motivation. Many researchers contributed to the emergence and pre-eminence of this position; no one more so than Carol Midgley.
While this volume is the product of multiple persons, and attends to a range of
topics reflecting different perspectives, it nevertheless emerges as a significant
testimony to her work. And, as fate would have it, exists now as Carol's legacy:
her work, the mentorship she provided, her gentle criticism, her friendship, as
well as her theoretical and practical contributions to the fields of education and
psychology. She passed away on November 23, 2001, after the manuscript was
completed, but before it was published.

Carol's guiding hand is reflected throughout the book and she has shaped it
with significant contributions that will extend far beyond the memory of her
friends and colleagues. First, there is the development and creative use of ques-
tionnaire methods designed to assess not only motivational orientations of individuals, but also the nature of contexts that might prompt, shape, and guide
these orientations. Carol recognized the role that context played in eliciting
and guiding motivation. She also recognized the practical need for educators to
understand how context could be framed so as to elicit the optimum investment
of students. Not only did she recognize such a need, she made significant attempts to meet it. Her work, as this volume attests, speaks not just to fellow researchers, but also addresses the concerns of practitioners: teachers and
childcare professionals, as well as policymakers and opinion setters. Of her it
can be truly said that she lives on in her work, including specifically the work
reflected in this volume.

But Carol herself would likely be dismayed if I made her the subject of the book and did not stress the importance of the issues that are pursued and must be earnestly dealt with by others. She would probably say, "Here's a start. Now, it's your turn!" And that in the final analysis is what this and any good book is about, especially a book in an ever-emerging field such as "motivation and achievement."

—*Martin L. Maehr*
Ann Arbor, MI
December 26, 2001

Preface

Carol Midgley
University of Michigan

During the last decade, members of a research team at the University of Michigan have been using achievement goal theory as the lens through which to examine the relations among achievement goals; the learning context; and students' and teachers' patterns of cognition, affect, and behavior. Achievement goal theory has emerged as a preeminent approach to motivation (Ames, 1992; Dweck & Leggett, 1988; Elliot, 1997; Maehr, 1989; Nicholls, 1989; Pintrich, 2000). In an invited address on the history of motivational research in education, Weiner (1990) pointed to goal orientation theory as "a major new direction, one pulling together different aspects of achievement research" (p. 629). This theory has developed within a social-cognitive framework that focuses on the purposes or goals that are pursued or perceived in an achievement setting. Rather than conceiving of individuals as possessing or lacking motivation, the focus is on how individuals think about themselves, their academic tasks, and their performance (Ames, 1987). Goals provide a framework within which individuals interpret and react to events, and result in different patterns of cognition, affect, and behavior (Dweck & Leggett, 1988). Theorists have described two achievement goals in particular: the goal to develop ability (variously labeled a mastery goal, learning goal, or task goal), and the goal to demonstrate ability or to avoid the demonstration of lack of ability (variously labeled a performance goal, ego goal, or ability goal). Although there are some differences among achievement goal

xi

theorists regarding the exact nature and functioning of these two types of goals, for the most part there is considerable overlap among these different conceptions (Ames, 1992; Heyman & Dweck, 1992).

With funding from the William T. Grant Foundation, we have been conducting a large-scale, longitudinal research study following students from the last year of elementary school to the first year of high school (the Patterns of Adaptive Learning Study). We used both quantitative and qualitative methods, collecting survey data from students, teachers, and principals; observing classrooms; and interviewing students and their parents. A large number of presentations and publications have emerged from this program of research. We are now in a position to summarize the many studies that we have conducted and to frame them in terms of the larger literature, emphasizing the contribution of this research to both motivational theory and educational practice.

We also have developed scales to assess various constructs associated with achievement goals on surveys (the Patterns of Adaptive Learning Scales—PALS). We receive requests for PALS from researchers throughout the world. We have also developed and used a protocol for observing classrooms, using a goal theory framework (Observing Patterns of Adaptive Learning—OPAL). In addition to my colleague Martin Maehr, many respected researchers have participated in this endeavor, beginning when they were graduate students in the Combined Program in Education and Psychology at the University of Michigan. Included are the following:

Eric Anderman, PhD, University of Kentucky

Lynley Hicks Anderman, PhD, University of Kentucky

Revathy Kumar (formerly Arunkumar), PhD, University of Toledo

Kimberley Edelin Freeman, PhD, F. D. Patterson Research Institute, Fairfax, Virginia

Margaret Gheen, University of Michigan

Leslie Morrison Gutman, PhD, University of Michigan

Ludmila Hruda, University of Michigan

Avi Kaplan, PhD, Ben Gurion University of the Negev, Israel

Elizabeth Linnenbrink, University of Michigan

Roxana Marachi, University of Michigan

Michael Middleton, PhD, University of New Hampshire

Helen Patrick, PhD, Purdue University

Robert Roeser, PhD, Stanford University

Allison Ryan, PhD, University of Illinois

Tim Urdan, PhD, Santa Clara University

These scholars serve as authors of the chapters in this book, along with Hunter Gehlbach, who is a graduate student at Stanford collaborating currently with Rob Roeser.

Each chapter takes a different perspective on the role of goals and goal structures, summarizing and integrating studies from the Patterns of Adaptive Learning Study within the context of the larger literature emanating from goal theory. The focus in particular is on students and teachers in classrooms and schools, and especially, though not exclusively, in schools serving adolescents.

Chapter 1 ("Methods for Studying Goals, Goal Structures, and Patterns of Adaptive Learning"), authored by Eric Anderman and Carol Midgley, describes the methods used in the Patterns of Adaptive Learning Study. In addition, the various approaches used by researchers to assess on surveys personal achievement goals and perceptions of the goal structure in the learning environment are described. Over 800 students, 500 teachers, and 37 principals in four ethnically and economically diverse school districts in southeastern Michigan participated in the survey component of this study. In addition, 10 elementary classrooms in two of the districts were observed, and interviews were conducted with subsets of students and parents.

Chapter 2 ("Achievement Goals and Goal Structures"), authored by Avi Kaplan, Mike Middleton, Tim Urdan, and Carol Midgley, presents an overview of achievement goal theory and the distinction between mastery and performance goals. The recent conceptualization of performance goals in terms of approach and avoidance components is also described. Studies that enhance our understanding of the relations among personal goals, the goal structure in the learning environment, and students' adaptive and maladaptive approaches to learning are summarized, including those that have emerged from the Patterns of Adaptive Learning Study. In addition, studies examining the antecedents and consequences of changes in goals and the perceived goal structure are discussed, because longitudinal studies within this tradition are rare.

Chapter 3 ("Goals, Goal Structures, and Avoidance Behaviors"), authored by Tim Urdan, Allison Ryan, Eric Anderman, and Margaret Gheen, considers the role of personal goals and the goal structure in the classroom in exacerbating or ameliorating the use of avoidance behaviors by students. Although avoidance motives and behaviors played a prominent role in classic motivational theory, they have, until recently, received little attention in goal theory research. Most research has focused on approach behaviors such as effort, persistence, and choice. Avoidance behaviors that are discussed in this chapter include self-handicapping, avoiding academic risk and novelty, and avoiding seeking help in the classroom when it is needed. Engaging in these behaviors is seen as a way to protect self-worth. Cheating is also a way to enhance self-worth by guaranteeing success, and is discussed in this chapter in relation to personal goals and the goal structure in the classroom.

Chapter 4 ("Social Motivation and the Classroom Social Environment"), authored by Helen Patrick, Lynley Anderman, and Allison Ryan, takes a broader look at goals and goal structures by considering students' social goals and social aspects of the learning environment. Social goals refer to students' objectives for their interactions with others, and include wanting to be socially responsible, promoting social relationships with peers, and acquiring social status. During early adolescence, social relationships and interactions escalate in importance. Parents and teachers often fear that social goals will supercede or interfere with academic goals. However, there is evidence that social goals can combine with academic goals in a way that promotes motivation and learning. In addition to social goals, students' social perceptions are considered, including their social efficacy, support from teachers, and feelings of belonging at school. Studies are described that look at correlates of these social goals and perceptions, as well as their associations with changes in students' achievement goals, task engagement, and affect over time. Furthermore, goal theory emphasizes the importance of the classroom context in influencing students' goals and the way they engage in tasks. This chapter builds on that perspective by focusing on two aspects of the social environment in classrooms, including students' perceptions that the teacher promotes mutual respect and promotes interaction among students. Studies that focus on these two dimensions, with respect to changes in students' motivation and engagement, are discussed.

Chapter 5 ("Stage–environment Fit Revisited: A Goal Theory Approach to Examining School Transitions"), authored by Carol Midgley, Michael Middleton, Margaret Gheen, and Revathy Kumar, takes a longitudinal perspective and considers the role of goals and goal structures as students move from elementary to middle school, and from middle to high school. In earlier studies we pointed to the lack of fit between students' needs at that stage of life and the opportunities afforded them in the learning environment. We use our more recent transition studies as a basis for examining the assumptions inherent in stage–environment fit. In studies conducted in schools before middle school reform was undertaken, there was evidence that the emphasis on mastery goals decreased and the emphasis on performance goals increased when students moved to middle school. This change in goal emphasis was suggested as a reason for declining motivation after the transition to middle school. In contrast, the middle schools participating in the Patterns of Adaptive Learning Study were implementing recommended reforms (e.g., Carnegie Task Force, 1989). The survey data indicated that students no longer reported an increase in the emphasis on performance goals after the transition to middle school. However, there was still a significant decline in the mastery goal emphasis. Findings regarding changes within the middle school years, and during the transition to high school, are also presented.

Chapter 6 ("Goal Structures in the Learning Environment and Students' Disaffection From Learning and School"), authored by Revathy Kumar, Margaret

Gheen, and Avi Kaplan, discusses the implications of achievement goal theory
for students who are disengaged from the schooling process. Studies are reviewed, including those from the Patterns of Adaptive Learning Study, that examine the goal structure and students' affect, use of maladaptive coping
strategies to deal with failure, lack of identification with school, skepticism
about the value of schooling, engagement in disruptive behavior, and feelings of
dissonance between their lives at home and at school. In addition, this chapter
considers the role of the recent emphasis on testing and accountability in exacerbating the performance goal emphasis in classrooms and schools. Many who
support the current emphasis on standardized testing and accountability do so in
the name of students who are not experiencing success in school. However, goal
theory research suggests that the increased emphasis on performance goals that
has accompanied the standards movement may further alienate these students.

Chapter 7 ("Can Achievement Goal Theory Enhance Our Understanding of
the Motivation and Performance of African American Young Adolescents?"),
authored by Kim Freeman, Leslie Gutman, and Carol Midgley, considers the
role of race in studies using achievement goal theory as a framework. Research
on achievement goals has been criticized for the lack of studies involving African American students. Yet goal theory may allow us to take a new perspective
on race and student motivation. Considerable research documents the negative
effects on students of an orientation to performance goals and/or an emphasis
on performance goals in classrooms. Cultural minority students may be particularly vulnerable to the negative effects of performance goals, in that this goal
emphasis may exacerbate their sense of "differentness," because it results in
undue attention to the self. Using data from students in the Patterns of Adaptive
Learning Study, interactions between race and achievement goals, including
extrinsic goals, in predicting academic self-efficacy, grade point average,
self-handicapping, the avoidance of help seeking in the classroom, and
self-regulated learning are examined. In addition, a qualitative study based on
interviews conducted with a subsample of African American middle school
students from an impoverished neighborhood is described in detail. Students
describe in their own words both their personal goals and the goals they perceive in the classroom. These studies raise issues about the role of extrinsic
goals for African American students.

Chapter 8 ("A Goal Theory Perspective on Teachers' Professional Identities
and the Contexts of Teaching"), authored by Rob Roeser, Roxana Marachi, and
Hunter Gehlbach, focuses in particular on teachers. Research on the contexts of
teaching and teachers' goal-related approaches to instruction is considerably
less well developed than research on the contexts of learning and students' adaptive and maladaptive approaches to learning. Using a systems approach, both
variable-centered and person-centered results from the Patterns of Adaptive
Learning Study are described that examine teachers' beliefs about teaching, their

perceptions of the school goal structure, and their goal-related approaches to instruction. Data from principals are also included as another, more "objective" assessment of the goal structure in schools. In addition, the complex pathways by which aspects of teachers' work environments and professional identities relate to students' motivation in the classroom are discussed.

Chapter 9 ("Observing Classroom Goal Structures to Clarify and Expand Goal Theory") authored by Lynley Anderman, Helen Patrick, Lidi Hruda, and Elizabeth Linnenbrink, focuses on the results of the classroom observation component of the Achievement Goals Project. Most of the research using an achievement goal perspective has been quantitative and has utilized survey methodology. The relatively few studies that have used observational methods to examine goals and goal structures are discussed, along with the rationale for expanding goal theory research through observational methods. In the Patterns of Adaptive Learning Study, 10 fifth-grade classrooms were observed on each of the first 3 days of the school year, for five additional sessions during the first 3 weeks of school, and again for 3 days during the spring semester. Observers wrote continuous running records recording details about behaviors and speech that related to the following classroom features: the nature of tasks; the locus of authority in the classroom; methods of recognition, grouping, and evaluation; the use of time; social interactions; and students' approaches to seeking help when needed. In this chapter, three empirical studies that draw from observational data, in combination with the students' survey data are described. Information about the development of the protocol used to observe classrooms (OPAL) is also included.

Chapter 10 ("Patterns of Adaptive Learning Study: Where Do We Go From Here?"), authored by Martin Covington, provides a perspective on the chapters in this book and on the Patterns of Adaptive Learning Study from someone who has not been a participant, but whose research and writings have informed our thinking. He describes the contributions of the study to our understanding of the dynamics of school achievement and suggests how best to capitalize on the insights and knowledge that have been generated. He also proposes an agenda for future research that builds on the research conducted by the Patterns of Adaptive Learning Study group as well as by others who share a vision of what school can and should become.

We do not believe that goal theory provides the only motivational framework for considering the issues covered in this book, or the "best" framework. We do believe that educational research has suffered from a lack of attention to theory. As Entwisle and others have pointed out, our knowledge of adolescents' schooling is seriously undermined by the lack of a theoretical foundation. "The dearth of theory contributes to problems at every level; in the absence of theory it is difficult to integrate findings from different studies, to reconcile those that disagree, or to set research priorities" (Entwisle, 1990, p. 222). Goal theory provides a the-

oretical and empirical foundation upon which to build a science of adolescent schooling. Theory-based principles and models can be tested and revised, using both quantitative and qualitative methods. Their applicability to different groups also can be tested and can lead to the refinement of theory. We find goal theory to be particularly useful in that it acknowledges the importance of context, and of considering the individual-in-context. We also find that goal theory works well in real-life settings, and translates into specific recommendations for providing a more facilitative learning environment. It can and has been used to provide a guide for school reform (Ames, 1990; Maehr & Midgley, 1996).

We look forward to further refinements in goal theory and to other theories that not only will help us to understand the relation between the learning environment and patterns of adaptive and maladaptive learning, but also will provide educators with helpful and meaningful ways to enhance motivation and learning.

REFERENCES

Ames, C. (1987). The enhancement of student motivation. In *Advances in motivation and achievement: Enhancing motivation* (Vol. 5, pp. 123–148). Greenwich, CT: JAI.

Ames, C. (1990, April). *Achievement goals and classroom structure: Developing a learning orientation.* Paper presented at the annual meeting of the American Educational Research Association, Boston.

Ames, C. (1992). Achievement goals and the classroom motivational climate. In D. H. Schunk & J. L. Meece (Eds.), *Student perceptions in the classroom* (pp. 327–348). Hillsdale, NJ: Lawrence Erlbaum Associates.

Carnegie Task Force on the Education of Young Adolescents (1989). *Turning points: Preparing American youth for the 21st century.* New York: Carnegie Corporation.

Dweck, C. S., & Leggett, E. L. (1988). A social-cognitive approach to motivation and personality. *Psychological Review, 95,* 256–273.

Elliot, A. J. (1997). Integrating the "classic" and the "contemporary" approaches to achievement motivation: A hierarchical model of approach and avoidance achievement motivation. In M. L. Maehr & P. R. Pintrich (Eds.), *Advances in motivation and achievement* (Vol. 10, pp. 143–179). Greenwich, CT: JAI.

Entwisle, D. R. (1990). Schools and the adolescents. In S. Feldman & G. R. Elliott (Eds.), *At the threshold* (pp. 197–224). Cambridge, MA: Harvard University Press.

Heyman, G. D., & Dweck, C. S. (1992). Achievement goals and intrinsic motivation: Their relation and their role in adaptive motivation. *Motivation and Emotion, 16,* 231–247.

Maehr, M. L. (1989). Thoughts about motivation. In C. Ames & R. Ames (Eds.), *Research on motivation in education: Vol. 3. Goals and cognitions.* New York: Academic Press.

Maehr, M. L., & Midgley, C. (1996). *Transforming school cultures.* Boulder, CO: Westview Press.

Nicholls, J. G. (1989). *The competitive ethos and democratic education.* Cambridge, MA: Harvard University Press.

Pintrich, P. R. (2000). Multiple goals, multiple pathways: The role of goal orientation in learning and achievement. *Journal of Educational Psychology, 92,* 544–555.

Weiner, B. (1990). History of motivational research in education. *Journal of Educational Psychology, 82,* 616–622.

1

Methods for Studying Goals, Goal Structures, and Patterns of Adaptive Learning

Eric M. Anderman
University of Kentucky

Carol Midgley
University of Michigan

The Patterns of Adaptive Learning Study is a large-scale, longitudinal study using goal orientation theory as the framework for examining the emotional, social, and academic well-being of young adolescents. This chapter provides information about the methods used in the study. Whereas additional detail about the methods used for specific studies is provided in subsequent chapters, this chapter is designed to give a comprehensive overview. In addition, we briefly compare our measurement of goals and goal structures on surveys to those used by others using survey methods.

The Patterns of Adaptive Learning Study included a large survey component, as well as classroom observations and interviews with students and parents. We begin with an overview of the research design; the characteristics of the sample; and the recruitment of the districts, schools, principals, teachers, and students. We then describe the survey component, including the collection of data from students, teachers, principals, and school records. We follow that with information about the development of measures; the coding, processing, and preliminary analysis of the data; and the validation of the scales assessing personal goals and perceptions of the goal structure in the classroom. Because

chapter 9 (this volume) provides extensive information about the methods used in the observation component, we do not provide additional information here. Similarly, chapters 6 and 7 (this volume) provide information about the methods used in two studies that included interviews with students, so only a brief overview is included in this chapter.

RESEARCH DESIGN

The research design reflects our special interest in examining the relation between students' personal goals and perceptions of the goal structure in the learning environment from the last year of elementary school through the first year of high school. We were particularly interested in changes associated with the transition to middle school and the transition to high school. Our original plan was to examine both within-year and across-year changes, collecting data from students in the late fall and early spring each year. We were able to do this in the fifth grade in elementary school (1994–1995) and in the sixth grade in middle school (1995–1996). However, we became aware during the second year in the middle schools (seventh grade) that both the students and teachers were finding that scheduling two waves of data collection each year was burdensome. Thus we modified the design and thereafter collected data from students only in the spring of the seventh-, eighth-, and ninth-grade years (1997, 1998, and 1999). In the eighth-grade year (1998), we collected data from a subsample of students in three of the middle schools in the fall (see Table 1.1 for a description of the waves and years that surveys were given to students, teachers, and principals).

RECRUITMENT OF DISTRICTS AND SCHOOLS

Because the nature of the study required many visits to schools to collect survey data, conduct observations, interview participants, and gather information from student records, we first identified districts that were within a 2-hour drive from the University of Michigan. From that pool of potential districts, we identified those that included some racial and economic diversity. This was important for several reasons. As noted recently, educational psychology as a field has been particularly negligent in terms of addressing socioeconomic issues and including socioeconomic variables (Murdock, 2000). In addition, studies using a goal theory framework have been criticized for not including African American participants (Graham, 1994). Finally, because we were interested in examining the effects of the transition to middle and high school, we selected districts in which students made those transitions in the sixth grade (middle school) and ninth grade (high school), because this is the most common pattern. We then contacted the district superintendents in the pool of po-

TABLE 1.1

The Patterns of Adaptive Learning Study: Waves and Years

Fall 1994	Student Survey, Wave 1	Fifth Grade, Elementary
Spring 1995	Student Survey, Wave 2	Fifth Grade, Elementary
Fall 1994	Teacher Survey Individual, Wave 1	Fifth Grade, Elementary
Spring 1995	Teacher Survey Individual, Wave 2	Fifth Grade, Elementary
1994–1995	Teacher Survey General, Year 1	All Elementary Teachers
1994–1995	Principal Survey, Year 1	All Elementary Principals
Fall 1995	Student Survey, Wave 3	Sixth Grade, Middle School
Spring 1996	Student Survey, Wave 4	Sixth Grade, Middle School
Fall 1995	Teacher Individual Survey, Wave 3	Sixth Grade, Middle School Math Teachers
Spring 1996	Teacher Survey Individual, Wave 4	Sixth Grade, Middle School Math Teachers
1995–1996	Teacher Survey General, Year 2	All Middle School Teachers
1995–1996	Principal Survey, Year 2	All Middle School Principals
Spring 1997	Student Survey, Wave 5	Seventh Grade, Middle School
1996–1997	Teacher Survey General Year 3	Seventh Grade, Middle School Math Teachers
Fall 1997	Student Survey, Wave 6	Eighth Grade, Middle School (subsample)
Spring 1998	Student Survey, Wave 7	Eighth Grade, Middle School
1997–1998	Teacher Survey General, Year 4	Eighth Grade, Middle School Math Teachers
Spring 1998	Student Survey, Wave 8	Ninth Grade, High School
1998–1999	Teacher Survey General, Year 5	All High School Teachers
1998–1999	Principal Survey	All High School Principals

tential districts, briefly describing the goals of the study, our commitment to providing them with helpful information, and our record regarding the conduct of high-quality research. In some of the districts the superintendent indicated that they either were heavily involved with other research projects, or were un-

dergoing a particularly difficult situation, such as a potential teacher strike. Most of the superintendents agreed to look over a brief written description of the project that clearly stated what their commitment would be, and what they would gain from participation. Packets with this information were sent to the superintendents, and in follow-up phone calls, four districts were selected that met the criteria listed previously. In one district we were required to submit a proposal to a research review committee. This was a lengthy process, but the proposal was approved. After districts agreed to participate, a graduate student was appointed to serve as a liaison between the research team and the district (with a different graduate student assigned to each district).

All of the districts were located in southeastern Michigan. Some of the districts were quite close to the university, whereas others were located at greater distances. Three of the districts could best be described as working class, whereas the other one was predominantly middle class. In three of the four districts, over 50% of the students were African American. Those three districts had the largest numbers of classrooms in the study, as compared with the remaining district, which was over 90% Euro-American. The districts varied in size, from the smallest district, which contained 3 elementary schools, 1 middle school, and 1 high school, to the largest district, which contained 24 elementary schools, 4 middle schools, and 2 high schools. (See Table 1.2 for a description of the four participating districts.)

The superintendents helped us make arrangements to meet with the principals and fifth-grade teachers in the elementary schools. We described the study to them and answered questions. With only a few exceptions, all elementary schools and fifth-grade teachers agreed to participate. In the largest district, the Director of Evaluation, Testing, and Research selected a sample of schools that reflected diversity in student achievement and ethnicity, and school size. We also met with middle school administrators to discuss the study, because their support would be important during the second year. We did not meet with representatives from the high schools, because the original grant that funded the study covered only the elementary and middle school years. We later received funding to follow the sample into the high schools. In all, 21 elementary schools, 10 middle schools, and 5 high schools participated in the study.

RECRUITMENT OF THE STUDENT SAMPLE

Recruitment of a representative student sample was a high priority. In each district the graduate student research assistant (liaison) worked to develop a positive rapport with the participating fifth-grade teachers. The research assistant consulted with each teacher regarding his or her preferences for the distribution and collection of permission forms. The research assistants were present in the classrooms when permission forms were distributed in order to encour-

TABLE 1.2

The Patterns of Adaptive Learning Study: Description of Districts

District	Number of Schools in the District	Number of Participating Schools	SES	Ethnicity
District 1	3 elementary 1 middle 1 high school	3 elementary 1 middle school	Working class	Over 90% Euro-American
District 2	6 elementary 2 middle 1 high school	5 elementary 2 middle 1 high school	Working class	About 60% Euro-American, 35% African American
District 3	10 elementary 3 middle 2 high schools	6 elementary 3 middle 2 high schools	Middle class	About 60% African American 35% Euro-American
District 4	24 elementary 4 middle 2 high schools	7 elementary 4 middle 2 high schools	Working class	About 55% African American, 30% Euro-American 15% Hispanic

Note. One elementary school in District 2 declined to participate in the study; in District 3, we limited participation to six of the elementary schools; in District 4, a sample of seven elementary schools was selected for us.

age students to return them to school. In some cases the assistants visited a classroom several times to help with recruitment. Pencils with a University of Michigan logo were given to students who returned their permission forms. Students received the pencils for returning the forms regardless of whether they had or had not received parental permission to participate.

Permission forms were given to 1,091 students; 899 were given permission by parents to participate, 83 were not granted permission, and 109 students failed to return their permission forms. The final participation rate was 82%. When the first wave of surveys was administered, 856 students completed the surveys, because some students had moved and others were absent over an extended period of time. Because there had been an economic downturn in some of the districts, we realized that families might be more mobile than would be the case in better economic times. Consequently, we recruited more students than we originally had proposed, anticipating greater than expected attrition in the sample.

Relocating the Participating Students in Middle School

Students moved from 21 elementary schools to 10 middle schools. The relocation of students after they had made the transition from elementary to middle school was a complex process because the students in some elementary

schools were assigned to several different middle schools. Early in the fall of 1995, we contacted middle school teachers and principals. In collaboration with them, we were able to determine in which middle schools our participants were enrolled, and arranged for them to complete surveys. The third wave of surveys was administered during November and early December of 1995, and the fourth wave of surveys was administered during the spring of 1996. Attrition was as expected in three of the four districts, but was somewhat higher in one of the districts. Administrators in that district told us that they always experienced a significant loss of students after the fifth grade because some parents chose to send their children to private and parochial schools at that juncture.

As mentioned earlier, the original proposal for funding included examining the transition from elementary to middle school. When our proposal to obtain funding to continue following students through middle school and into high school was approved, we contacted all districts to determine if they were willing to extend the study. One of the districts declined. The superintendent had resigned, and the new superintendent was reluctant to do anything that would put further pressure on teachers and parents. We sent letters to the parents of all participating students in the other three districts indicating that the study was to be extended and asked them to contact us by mail or phone if they did not want their child to continue. None of the parents withdrew their children from the study.

Supplementing the Student Sample

After the first four waves of data were collected during the fifth- and sixth-grade years, we decided to supplement the original sample with students from one of the participating middle schools. This school was selected because attrition from that school had been high, and also because the staff at the school had been very supportive of the study. All of the 99 seventh-grade students in that school who were not already in the study were given permission forms; 82 of the students received permission to participate. In addition, when the students were in the eighth grade, we supplemented the sample in another middle school. The parents of 172 eighth-grade students in that school who were not participating in the study were mailed a permission form and a letter describing the study; 104 permission forms were returned, with 92 students receiving permission.

Relocating the Participating Students in High School

After the eighth grade, students moved from nine middle schools (the district that decided not to continue with the study after the sixth-grade year had only

one middle school) to five high schools. We contacted the principals of each of the five high schools, and explained the history of the research project. All of the high schools provided us with lists of the ninth-grade students. We were able to relocate 572 of the students participating in our study. Some students had moved and others had transferred to private schools, or had been assigned to "alternative" schools. Students in one district who had been assigned to alternative schools also took some classes in the two mainstream high schools. In that case, they continued to participate in the study.

RECRUITMENT OF THE TEACHER SAMPLE

All teachers in the 36 schools (21 elementary, 10 middle, and 5 high schools) were asked to participate by completing a general survey (Teacher Survey General—TSG). Elementary teachers filled out this survey Year 1 (return rate of 70%), middle school teachers filled it out Year 2 (return rate of 74%), and high school teachers filled it out Year 5 (return rate of 93%). In addition, during the seventh- and eighth-grade years, participating students' mathematics teachers completed TSGs. Over 90% of the math teachers completed the surveys.

Fifth-grade elementary school teachers and sixth-grade mathematics teachers were also asked to complete a one-page survey (Teacher Survey Individual—TSI) for each participating student in their classes both in the fall and in the spring. Most of the teachers completed these surveys. Although this was not a particularly difficult task for elementary teachers who had perhaps 25 participating students in their self-contained classrooms, it was burdensome for sixth-grade middle school mathematics teachers who taught as many as five sections of math. As a result, TSI data were not collected at the remaining waves of the study. (See Table 1.1 for a description of when the two types of surveys were given to teachers.) More in-depth descriptions of the nature of these surveys is provided later in this chapter.

PRINCIPAL SAMPLE

A survey was administered to principals of all participating schools. This survey asked principals about demographic characteristics of their schools, and also about policies and practices in the school that would convey an emphasis on mastery and/or performance goals. We received a survey from all 36 principals, although in a couple of cases the assistant principals filled out the survey. We did not consider this to be a problem, given the nature of the questions on the survey. (See Table 1.1 for a description of when the surveys were given to principals.)

PROCEDURES

Administration of Student Surveys

Surveys were administered to fifth-grade students in their classrooms. Teachers were asked to remain in the classroom. In most cases, teachers filled out their own surveys while the research assistants were administering surveys to the students. In the middle and high schools, surveys were often administered in special rooms, such as the media center or the cafeteria. In that case, we tried to keep the groups to 40 or fewer students, and asked a school administrator to be present.

Research assistants described the purpose of the study to students, assured them that all information would be completely confidential, told them it was not a test and there were no right or wrong answers, and explained how to use a 5-point Likert-type scale. The first item on the survey was a sample item. Questions were solicited and students were told that they could ask additional questions at any time during survey administration. Students were also told that they could skip questions that they did not want to answer or that were unclear. Students had very few questions and there was little missing data. In the elementary and middle schools, all questions were read aloud by research assistants while students followed along and answered. When students were absent during survey administration, make-up sessions were scheduled.

Administration of Teacher and Principal Surveys

At the elementary level, surveys were given to teachers so they could fill them out while research assistants were administering surveys to students. A brief reminder about the purpose of the survey was included in a cover letter. Teachers were assured that we were not evaluating them, that there were no "right" answers, and that all information would be confidential. If teachers were not able to complete the survey at that time, they were given a prestamped mailer so that they could return it directly to the project office. At the middle and high school levels, surveys were usually put in teachers' mailboxes with a cover letter and a prestamped mailer. Many follow-up letters and phone calls were necessary in order to obtain surveys from a representative sample of teachers. As teachers became more aware of the value of the study to their districts, it became easier to retrieve the surveys. Principals were contacted individually by project staff to describe the survey, to assure them that we were not evaluating or comparing districts, and to urge them to return the survey to us as soon as possible. Principal surveys were delivered to the schools with a cover

letter and a prestamped mailer. In some schools, many contacts were made before principal surveys were retrieved.

Collection of Record Data

Data were collected from students' school records at the end of each academic year. Information about students' gender, ethnicity, and free/reduced-fee lunch status was collected at the end of the first year. Students' grades in the core subjects were collected every year. In addition, at various points in time, scores on standardized achievement tests, number of absences, information about suspensions, and special education status were recorded. Although free/reduced-fee lunch status is not the best indicator of socioeconomic status, we were not able to get information about family income. School districts followed state guidelines in determining eligibility for the lunch program based on family size and income, but eligibility criteria varied somewhat among the districts. Because we recognized the limitations of lunch status as a measure of income or socioeconomic status (SES; Entwistle & Astone, 1994; Hauser, 1994), we also asked students, on one survey, about their parents' occupations and highest levels of education. For both variables, parental occupation and education, considerable data were missing. Many students told the survey administrators they did not know this information or did not want to provide it. The correlations between reports of mother's or father's level of education and lunch status were low. However, the correlations between reports of father's occupation and lunch status ($r = .40$) and mother's occupation and lunch status ($r = .50$) were moderate and provided some support for the use of lunch status as a proxy measure of SES.

MEASURES

One of the major contributions by our research group has been the development of survey measures. Although we began to develop measures before the Patterns of Adaptive Learning Study began, scales were refined during the course of the study and new scales were added. This process continues with our involvement in a new study (J. Turner & C. Midgley, *Avoidance Beliefs and Behaviors Before and After the Transition to Middle-Level Schools: Classroom Influences*) funded by the Spencer Foundation. Detailed information about the Patterns of Adaptive Learning Scales (PALS) and their psychometric properties has been assembled in a manual (Midgley et al., 2000). The PALS manual can be downloaded from our Web site: http://www.umich.edu/~pals/.

PALS includes scales used on student surveys and on the general teacher survey (TSG), but not the scales used on the teacher survey of individual students (TSI) or the principal survey. Information about the principal survey is included in chapter 8 (this volume). Student scales included in PALS assess personal achievement goals (mastery, performance-approach, and performance-avoid); perceptions of the goal structure in the classroom (mastery, performance-approach, and performance-avoid); achievement-related beliefs, attitudes, and strategies; and perceptions of parents and home life. At the elementary level, because most students were in self-contained classrooms with one teacher, we phrased items in terms of the class or schoolwork in general. At the middle and high school level, because students typically learned different subjects in different classrooms, items were adapted to measure subject-specific (e.g., math) goals and perceptions. Teacher scales included in PALS assess perceptions of the goal structure in the school, goal-related approaches to instruction, and personal teaching efficacy. We use 5-point Likert-type scales. Items on the student scales are anchored at 1 = "Not at all true," 3 = "Somewhat true," and 5 = "Very true." Items on the teacher scales are anchored at 1 = "Strongly disagree," 3 = "Somewhat agree," and 5 = "Strongly agree." In constructing a survey, we mix items from various scales whenever possible, rather than presenting them as a set. We do not recommend using these scales with students who are in third grade or lower.

DATA MANAGEMENT AND ANALYSIS

Coding and Entry of Data into Computer Files

As a first step, standardized instructions were developed for the coding of each type of survey. Research assistants then coded surveys. Assistants checked for any missing information (such as teacher name, class period, or school) and also for ambiguous markings. For example, the coding instructions indicated that if students circled both a 4 and 5 on a scale, the assistant was to circle the 4, as the more conservative answer. All surveys were independently checked by a second research assistant. Data were then entered into computer files by a local data entry firm. They were instructed to verify data entry, which meant that all data were entered twice and then checked for inconsistencies and corrected. In some cases, shorter surveys were entered into computer files by research assistants and verified by another assistant.

Processing of Data

Standardized instructions were developed for the statistical processing of data sets. Instructions included how to create SPSS dictionary files, identify and cor-

rect wild codes, and merge data sets. In addition, these instructions included lists of abbreviations, file names, and variable numbers to be used in processing the data. Variable names were chosen in a logical manner, so that they related in meaningful waves to the constructs and to the various waves of data.

All processing of data was done with the SPSS statistical package, although some of the subsequent analyses were conducted using other statistical software, including LISREL and HLM. For the initial processing of the data with SPSS, Macintosh computers were used. First, raw data files were converted from ASCII files into SPSS system files. After system files were created, they were checked for wild codes (e.g., an entry of a "6" when the only possible responses were 1 through 5). When wild codes were found, we went back to the original surveys, determined what the correct code should be, and corrected the file.

Initial Analyses

Frequency distributions were examined for all responses on all surveys. Exploratory factor analyses were run, and scales were constructed. It should be pointed out that exploratory factor analysis was undertaken at every wave for every data source. Items that needed to be reverse-coded for scale construction were appropriately reversed. Scales were created using the mean of responses to items on a scale. Cronbach alpha was used to assess the internal consistency of scales. Descriptive statistics, including means, standard deviations, and skew, were generated for each scale from each source at each wave. As we collected additional data, confirmatory factor analyses were conducted on some of the scales using LISREL VIII. Correlations among scales were examined both within waves and across waves.

Correlations Among the Personal Goal Scales.
In studies conducted by Nicholls and his colleagues, scales assessing personal task (mastery) and ego (performance) goals were correlated, but at levels low enough to prompt the statement that they were "more or less orthogonal." In a study that included all three personal goal scales, we found that mastery goals were unrelated to performance-approach ($r = .04$) and performance-avoid goals ($r = .01$), but performance-approach and performance-avoid goals were highly positively correlated ($r = .56$) (Middleton & Midgley, 1997).

The personal goal scales exhibited moderate stability over time, with stability within an academic year somewhat higher than stability across years (when students moved to a new learning context), as would be expected. For example, the correlations within the eighth-grade year (Waves 6 and 7) were .60 for mastery goals, .61 for performance-approach goals, and .54 for performance-avoid goals. The correlations across the eighth- and ninth-grade years (Waves 7 and 8) were .55 for mastery goals, .58 for performance-approach goals, and .39 for performance-avoid goals.

Validation of the Personal Goal Scales

Extensive evidence of the validity of the scales used in the Patterns of Adaptive Learning Study to assess personal goals (mastery, performance-approach, performance-avoid) is presented in Midgley et al. (1998). A very brief summary of that evidence is presented here. To assess discriminant validity, confirmatory factor analysis (using LISREL VIII; Joreskog & Sorbom, 1993) was conducted to determine if the three goal scales could be differentiated from each other. In evaluating the fit of the model, we used multiple indices of fit. All indices indicated a good fit for the proposed structure of the scales. We next tested this model for White and African American students and for girls and boys. The scales operated similarly for boys and girls, and for White and African American students.

During the first wave of survey administration, we included scales developed by Nicholls and his colleagues to assess task (mastery) and ego (performance) goals (Nicholls, 1989) on half of the surveys. The correlations between Nicholls' scales and our scales were positive and significant ($r = .63$ for ego-orientation and performance-approach goals; $r = .67$ for task and mastery goals), providing evidence of convergent validity.

Construct validity was determined by examining the relation between each of the three personal goal scales and academic efficacy, reported use of adaptive and maladaptive learning strategies, and affect at school. The personal goal scales related in consistent and expected ways to these constructs. Further evidence of construct validity is provided in studies that compare elementary and middle school students. These studies are described in chapter 5. A description of policies and practices in elementary and middle schools provides support for the theoretical prediction that middle schools emphasize mastery goals less and performance goals more than do elementary schools (Midgley, 1993). In an earlier cross-sectional study with a different sample, we found that middle school students were more oriented to performance goals and less oriented to mastery goals than were upper elementary school students (Midgley, E. M. Anderman, & Hicks, 1995). In a longitudinal study (E. M. Anderman & Midgley, 1997), we found that students were less oriented to mastery goals in sixth grade in middle school than in fifth grade in elementary school. However, there was no change in performance goals. A study comparing elementary, middle, and high school teachers was conducted in conjunction with the Patterns of Adaptive Learning Study (see chap. 8, this volume). Elementary teachers perceived a greater emphasis on mastery goals and less of an emphasis on performance goals in the school, and reported using mastery approaches to instruction more and performance approaches less than did middle or high school teachers. Middle school teachers perceived a greater emphasis on mas-

tery goals and reported using mastery approaches to instruction more than did high school teachers. It should be pointed out, however, that a study examining changes in students' perceptions of the goal structure from Waves 7 to 8 (eighth grade in middle school to ninth grade in high school) failed to find patterns of change that would be consistent with the teacher data (see chap. 5, this volume). However, the teacher data included all high school teachers and the student data included only the perceptions of ninth-grade high school students.

Validation of the Scales Assessing Perceptions of the Goal Structure

As part of the Patterns of Adaptive Learning Study, we have conducted a number of studies that included students' perceptions of the mastery and performance-approach goal structure in the classroom (e.g., L. H. Anderman, 1999; L. H. Anderman & E. M. Anderman, 1999; Kaplan & Midgley, 1999; Midgley & Urdan, 2001; Ryan, Gheen, & Midgley, 1998; Ryan & Patrick, 2001; Urdan, Midgley, & E. Anderman, 1998). These studies provide evidence of the validity of those two scales. Further evidence of the validity of the scales is provided in a study by Patrick, L. H. Anderman, Ryan, Edelin, and Midgley (2001) that used observation data to interpret different patterns of perceived goal structures (described in chap. 9, this volume).

Only recently (Wave 8, Grade 9) did we develop a scale assessing student perceptions of the performance-avoid goal structure in the classroom (Middleton, Gheen, Midgley, Hruda, & E. Anderman, 2000). Following exploratory factor analysis, confirmatory factor analysis was conducted for the three classroom goal structure scales. A three-factor model was confirmed with an adequate fit for the model, as suggested by a goodness of fit index of .94 and an adjusted goodness of fit index of .91.

DIFFERENCES AMONG RESEARCHERS IN THE MEASUREMENT OF PERSONAL GOALS AND GOAL STRUCTURES ON SURVEYS

In this section we compare our approach to the measurement of personal goals and goal structures on surveys with approaches used by other researchers using survey methods. We do this not to try to prove that one approach is better than another, but rather to point out that approaches to measurement have differed somewhat. Earlier scales (e.g., Ames & Archer, 1988) included items assessing personal goals ("I work hard to learn") and perceptions of the goal structure in the classroom ("Students are given a chance to correct mistakes") on the same scale. We assess personal achievement goals separately from perceptions of the goal structure in the learning environment, and find that they factor separately.

The Measurement of Students' Personal Goals on Surveys

Scales developed by Nicholls and his colleagues to assess personal goals have been used in a number of studies (Nicholls, 1989). Items ask students when they feel successful and separate scales assess "task" goals ("I feel successful when I learn something new") and "ego" goals ("I feel successful if I show people I'm smart") (e.g., Nolen, 1988; Nolen & Haladyna, 1990a, 1990b). In some studies the phrasing of the items was changed, with task goals assessed by items such as "I wanted to learn as much as possible," and ego goals assessed by items such as "I wanted others to think I was smart" (e.g., Meece, Blumenfeld, & Hoyle, 1988; Schunk, 1996). In addition, in some studies items assessing the goal of social approval (e.g., "It was important to me that the teacher thought I did a good job") were combined with items assessing ego goals ("I wanted others to think I was smart") to form a scale assessing "ego/social" goals (e.g., Meece et al., 1988; Nicholls, Patashnick, & Nolen, 1985; Thorkildsen, 1988). Nicholls later regretted this decision, stating that "On reflection, these social orientation items are more ambiguous than desirable. The nature of social orientations is a topic in its own right and we deal with it poorly in that study" (Nicholls, Cheung, Lauer, & Patashnick, 1989, p. 70).

Rather than assessing mastery and performance goals independently, Dweck (e.g., 1999) made the case for using items that "pit" mastery goals against performance goals by asking which is more important to students (looking smart vs. attempting challenging tasks). For example, "Although I hate to admit it, I sometimes would rather do well in a class than learn a lot" and "It's much more important for me to learn things in my classes than it is to get the best grades." Dweck indicated that these survey items are suitable for students age 12 and older.

Similar to other researchers, we began by measuring mastery goals ("An important reason I do my class work is because I like to learn new things") and performance-approach goals ("Doing better than other students is important to me"). We did not develop a scale assessing performance-avoid goals ("It's important to me that I don't look stupid in class") until the students in the Patterns of Adaptive Learning Study were in the sixth grade. At that point in time, Elliot and Harackiewicz (1996) pointed out that theorists have traditionally described motivation in terms of both approach and avoidance tendencies (e.g., Atkinson & Feather, 1966; McClelland, 1951). Individuals may be motivated by the desire to attain success or to avoid failure. For some, the goal of avoiding looking stupid or avoiding negative judgments from others may be salient. However, until recently the goal to avoid the demonstration of lack of ability has not played a major role in studies using survey methods. In their early work, Nicholls and his colleagues (e.g., Nicholls et

al., 1989) developed a two-item scale to assess the goal of avoiding looking stupid or dumb, which they labeled "avoid inferiority." However, factor analysis indicated that these items loaded with the items assessing the goal to demonstrate superiority, an approach goal. Accordingly, they combined items from the two scales and labeled it "ego-orientation." In subsequent studies, the items assessing "avoid inferiority" were dropped from the ego orientation scale.

In a study by Elliot and Church (1997) using a sample of undergraduates, six items were used to assess performance-avoid goals. Many of the items assessed worries, fears, and concerns (e.g., "I worry about the possibility of getting a bad grade in this class" and "I often think to myself, 'What if I do badly in this class?'"), which are correlates of goals. In a sample of sixth- and eighth-grade students in Norway, Skaalvik (1997) developed two scales to assess ego goals, which he called "self-enhancing" and "self-defeating" and which are analogous to the approach and avoidance components of performance goals. To assess the avoidance component, he included items such as "When I am working on the blackboard, I am concerned about what my classmates think about me" and "When I give a wrong answer in class, I am most concerned about what my classmates think about me." Although other researchers have included scales in their studies assessing the goal to avoid work ("I feel most successful when I get out of work") (e.g., Nicholls et al., 1985), this goal is conceptually different from the goal to avoid the demonstration of lack of ability.

Recently we refined our personal goal scales in conjunction with a new study. We eliminated items that assessed intrinsic value, and removed references to specific behaviors. We undertook these changes in order to focus more directly on goals as orienting frameworks within which students function rather than specific behaviors or interests that students exhibit. Because the revised scales are relatively new, we included both the original scales and the revised scales in PALS: 2000 (available on our Web site). Samples of items assessing mastery, performance-approach, and performance-avoid goals include "One of my goals is to master a lot of new skills this year," "One of my goals is to show others that I'm good at my class work," and "One of my goals in class is to avoid looking like I have troubles doing the work," respectively. To assess the discriminant validity of the revised personal goal scales, we conducted confirmatory factor analysis on the 14 personal goal orientation items to examine the factor structure of the three sets of items (mastery, performance-approach, and performance-avoid). LISREL VIII (Joreskog & Sorbom, 1993) confirmed the expected model. Goodness of fit indices suggested that the model fits the data well (GFI = 0.97, AGFI = 0.95). Specifically, personal mastery, performance-approach, and performance-avoid goals loaded on different latent factors.

The Measurement of Students' Perception of the Goal Structure in the Learning Environment on Surveys

Ames has taken the lead in pointing to the association between the classroom goal structure and students' motivation and approach to learning (e.g., Ames, 1992a, 1992b). As mentioned earlier, Ames and Archer (1988) developed scales to assess the saliency of mastery and performance goals in the classroom. Each item begins with the stem "in this class," with some items asking about the teacher ("In this class, the teacher makes sure I understand the work"), some items asking about the class as whole ("In this class, students feel bad when they do not do as well as others"), and some items asking about the student ("I work hard to learn").

Nolen and Haladyna (1990a) asked high school students about their teachers' emphasis on mastery ("The teacher wants us to understand why things happen") and independent thinking ("The teacher wants us to think for ourselves"). Scales assessing students' perceptions of their teachers' emphasis on performance goals were not included in this study. Our group has also developed scales to assess students' perceptions of their teachers' goals and used them in the Patterns of Adaptive Learning Study. Items include "My teacher wants us to understand our work, not just memorize it" (mastery) and "My teacher points out those students who get good grades as an example to all of us" (performance-approach).

In a new study we not only assessed student perceptions of their teachers' goals, but have included scales assessing students' perceptions of the goal structure in the classroom (we do not intend to use them in the same study). Sample items include "In our class, really understanding the material is the main goal" (mastery) and "In our class, getting right answers is very important" (performance). We also developed a scale assessing the emphasis in the classroom on avoiding the demonstration of lack of ability ("In our class, it's important that you don't make mistakes in front of everyone"). As was done with the revised personal goals, to validate the classroom goal structure scales we conducted confirmatory factor analysis on the mastery goal structure, performance-approach goal structure, and performance-avoid goal structure items. Once again, LISREL VIII (Joreskog & Sorbom, 1993) confirmed that the items loaded on different latent factors (GFI = 0.96, AGFI = 0.94).

Because responses to survey items that ask students about the goals emphasized in the classroom are aggregated to form scales, it is difficult to determine which aspects of the classroom are most important in communicating the perceived goal structure (Urdan, 1997). Studies that combine observational data and survey data (see chap. 9, this volume) are providing important information, as well as studies in which an intervention takes place to change the sa-

liency of goals in the learning environment (Ames, 1990; E. M. Anderman, Maehr, & Midgley, 1999; Maehr & Midgley, 1996).

THE INTERVIEW COMPONENT

Three interview studies were conducted. In all cases, permission was required from parents in order for their children to participate. Participants were told that they could refrain from answering any question at any time. Interviews were audio taped and then transcribed. A study conducted by Kimberley Edelin Freeman, based on interviews with African American sixth-grade students from one of the participating middle schools, is described in detail in chapter 6 (this volume), including the methods that were used. Another study based on interviews with 49 seventh-grade middle school students was conducted by Revathy Kumar and is also described in chapter 6 (this volume). Additional information about the methods used is not included here. In addition, interviews were conducted with low-income, African American parents and their children in one of the participating school districts. The interviews were conducted during the summer prior to entry into the sixth grade, and early in the fall of the sixth-grade year. This study did not use goal orientation theory as the guiding framework. Rather, the purpose was to investigate the role of students, teachers, schools, and families in facilitating academic achievement during the transition from elementary to middle school. Readers interested in these studies are directed to Gutman and Midgley (2000) and Gutman and McLoyd (2000). Follow-up interviews were conducted when the students were in high school and the data are currently being analyzed.

EXPERIMENTAL METHODS

We would like to acknowledge the very important role that experimental methods have played in the development of goal theory. The Patterns of Adaptive Learning Study did not include experimental methods, but our thinking has been affected in profound ways by those studies. The various methodologies that have been used have different strengths and weaknesses, and we see them as complementing each other in ways that enhance our understanding of goals and goal structures.

TRIANGULATION

Although the primary method of data collection in the Patterns of Adaptive Learning Study was through the use of surveys, the data from observations and

interviews made it possible for us to combine these different sources of data. In particular, as described in chapter 9 (this volume), the combination of survey and observation data has allowed us to gain a deeper understanding of the processes in classrooms that are related to students' personal goals and their perceptions of social and academic dimensions of the learning environment. Studies that combine methods are expensive and demanding, but we believe are particularly important as goal theory matures.

REFERENCES

Ames, C. (1990, April). *Achievement goals and classroom structure: Developing a learning orientation.* Paper presented at the annual meeting of the American Educational Research Association, Boston.

Ames, C. (1992a). Achievement goals and the classroom motivation climate. In D. Schunk & J. Meece (Eds.), *Students' perceptions in the classroom: Causes and consequences* (pp. 327–348). Hillsdale, NJ: Lawrence Erlbaum Associates.

Ames, C. (1992b). Classrooms: Goals, structures, and student motivation. *Journal of Educational Psychology, 84,* 261–271.

Ames, C., & Archer, J. (1988). Achievement goals in the classroom: Students' learning strategies and motivation processes. *Journal of Educational Psychology, 80,* 260–270.

Anderman, E. M., Maehr, M. L., & Midgley, C. (1999). Declining motivation after the transition to middle school: Schools can make a difference. *Journal of Research and Development in Education. 32,* 131–147.

Anderman, E. M., & Midgley, C. (1997). Changes in achievement goal orientations, perceived academic competence, and grades across the transition to middle level schools. *Contemporary Educational Psychology, 22,* 269–298.

Anderman, L. H. (1999). Classroom goal orientation, school belonging and social goals as predictors of students' positive and negative affect following the transition to middle school. *Journal of Research and Development in Education, 32,* 90–103.

Anderman, L. H., & Anderman, E. M. (1999). Social predictors of changes in students' achievement goal orientations. *Contemporary Educational Psychology, 25,* 21–37.

Atkinson, J. W., & Feather, N. T. (1966). *A theory of achievement motivation.* New York: Wiley.

Dweck, C. S. (1999). *Self-theories: Their role in motivation, personality, and development.* Philadelphia: Psychology Press.

Elliot, A. J., & Church, M. A. (1997). A hierarchical model of approach and avoidance achievement motivation. *Journal of Personality and Social Psychology, 72,* 218–232.

Elliot, A. J., & Harackiewicz, J. M. (1996). Approach and avoidance achievement goals and intrinsic motivation: A matutinal analysis. *Journal of Personality and Social Psychology, 70,* 461–475.

Entwistle, D. R., & Astone, N. M. (1994). Some practical guidelines for measuring youth's race/ethnicity and socioeconomic status. *Child Development, 65,* 1521–1540.

Graham, S. (1994). Motivation in African Americans. *Review of Educational Research, 64,* 55–117.

Gutman, L. M., and McLoyd, V. C. (2000). Parents' management of their children's education within the home, at school, and in the community: An examination of high-risk African American families. *Urban Review, 32,* 1–24.

Gutman, L. M., & Midgley, C. (2000). The role of protective factors in supporting the academic achievement of poor African American students during the middle school transition. *Journal of Youth and Adolescence, 29,* 223–248.

Hauser, R. M. (1994). Measuring socioeconomic status in studies of child development. *Child Development, 65,* 1541–1545.

Joreskog, K., & Sorbom, D. (1993). *LISREL VIII.* Chicago: Scientific Software.

Kaplan, A., & Midgley, C. (1999). The relationship between perceptions of the classroom goal structure and early adolescents' affect in school: The mediating role of coping strategies. *Learning and Individual Differences, 11,* 187–212.

Maehr, M. L., & Midgley, C. (1996). *Transforming school cultures.* Boulder, CO: Westview Press.

McClelland, D. C., Atkinson, J. W., Clark, R. A., & Lowell, E. L. (1953). *The achievement motive.* New York: Appleton-Century-Crofts.

Meece, J. L., Blumenfeld, P. C., & Hoyle, R. H. (1988). Students' goal orientation and cognitive engagement in classroom activities. *Journal of Educational Psychology, 80,* 514–523.

Middleton, M. J., Gheen, M., Midgley, C., Hruda, L., & Anderman, E. (2000, August). *Approach and avoid goal structures: Relating classroom and personal goal orientations.* Paper presented at the annual meeting of the American Psychological Association, Washington, DC.

Middleton, M., & Midgley, C. (1997). Avoiding the demonstration of lack of ability: An under explored aspect of goal theory. *Journal of Educational Psychology, 89,* 710–718.

Midgley, C. (1993). Motivation and middle level schools. In P. Pintrich & M. L. Maehr, (Eds.), *Advances in motivation and achievement: Vol. 8. Motivation in the adolescent years* (pp. 219–276). Greenwich, CT: JAI.

Midgley, C., Anderman, E. M., & Hicks, L. (1995). Differences between elementary and middle school teachers and students: A goal theory approach. *Journal of Early Adolescence, 15,* 90–113.

Midgley, C., Kaplan, A., Middleton, M., Maehr, M. L., Urdan, T., Anderman, L. H., Anderman, E., & Roeser, R. (1998). The development and validation of scales assessing students' achievement goal orientations. *Contemporary Educational Psychology, 23,* 113–131.

Midgley, C., Maehr, M. L., Hruda, L. Z., Anderman, E., Anderman, L., Freeman, K. E., Gheen, M., Kaplan, A., Kumar, R., Middleton, M. J., Nelson, J., Roeser, R., & Urdan, T. (2000). *Manual for the Patterns of Adaptive Learning Scales.* Ann Arbor: University of Michigan.

Midgley, C., & Urdan, T. (2001). Academic self-handicapping and performance goals: A further examination. *Contemporary Educational Psychology, 26,* 61–75.

Murdock, T. (2000). Incorporating economic context into educational psychology: Methodological and conceptual challenges. *Educational Psychologist, 35,* 113–124.

Nicholls, J. G. (1989). *The competitive ethos and democratic education.* Cambridge, MA: Harvard University Press.

Nicholls, J. G., Cheung, P. C., Lauer, J., & Patashnick, M. (1989). Individual differences in academic motivation: Perceived ability, goals, beliefs, and values. *Learning and Individual Differences, 1,* 63–84.

Nicholls, J. G., Patashnick, M., & Nolen, S. B. (1985). Adolescents' theories of education. *Journal of Educational Psychology, 77,* 683–692.

Nolen, S. B. (1988). Reasons for studying motivational orientations and study strategies. *Cognition and Instruction, 5,* 269–287.

Nolen, S. B., & Haladyna, T. M. (1990a). Motivation and studying in high school science. *Journal of Research in Science Teaching, 27,* 115–126.

Nolen, S. B., & Haladyna, T. M. (1990b). Personal and environmental influences on students' beliefs about effective study strategies. *Contemporary Educational Psychology, 15,* 116–130.

Patrick, H., Anderman, L. H., Ryan, A. M., Edelin, K., & Midgley, C. (2001). Teachers' communication of goal orientations in four fifth-grade classrooms. *Elementary School Journal, 102,* 35–58.

Ryan, A. M., Gheen, M. H., & Midgley, C. (1998). Why do some students avoid asking for help? An examination of the interplay among students' academic efficacy, teachers' social-emotional role, and the classroom goal structure. *Journal of Educational Psychology, 90,* 528–535.

Ryan, A. M., & Patrick, H. (2001). The classroom social environment and changes in adolescents' motivation and engagement during middle school. *American Educational Research Journal, 38,* 437–460.

Schunk, D. H. (1996). Goal and self-evaluative influences during children's cognitive skill learning. *American Educational Research Journal, 33,* 359–382.

Skaalvik, E. M. (1997). Self-enhancing and self-defeating ego orientation: Relations with task and avoidance orientation, achievement, self-perceptions, and anxiety. *Journal of Educational Psychology, 89,* 71–81.

Thorkildsen, T. A. (1988). Theories of education among academically able adolescents. *Contemporary Educational Psychology, 13,* 323–330.

Urdan, T. (1997). Achievement goal theory: Past results, future directions. In P. Pintrich & M. Maehr (Eds.), *Advances in motivation and achievement* (pp. 99–142). Greenwich, CT: JAI.

Urdan, T., Midgley, C., & Anderman, E. (1998). The role of classroom goal structure in students' use of self-handicapping strategies. *American Educational Research Journal, 35,* 101–122.

2

Achievement Goals and Goal Structures

Avi Kaplan
Ben Gurion University of the Negev, Israel

Michael J. Middleton
George Mason University

Tim Urdan
Santa Clara University

Carol Midgley
University of Michigan

In this chapter, we describe the theoretical framework that has guided the research we have conducted in conjunction with the Patterns of Adaptive Learning Study—achievement goal theory. This theory provides a comprehensive conceptualization of the relations between learning environments and students' motivation, emotional well-being, and performance. We review results of studies conducted by us and by others who have examined these relations. We also discuss recent theoretical developments that have challenged some of the assumptions that have guided this research and examine the implications of these developments for future research as well as for teacher practice and school reform.

ACHIEVEMENT GOAL THEORY: DEFINING GOALS AND GOAL STRUCTURES

Defining Achievement Goals

Achievement goal theory emerged during the late 1970s and early 1980s as several researchers investigating motivation in competence-relevant settings had somewhat similar insights concerning the roots of differences in students' patterns of learning (e.g., Ames, 1984, Dweck, 1986; Maehr, 1984; Nicholls, 1984). These researchers were interested not only in differences in the direction and strength of students' engagement in learning, but also in the quality of their engagement. Although students may appear to be working diligently on a task, the quality of their investment may be quite different. For example, one student could be using deep learning strategies, interpreting difficulty as a challenge, and experiencing positive affect toward the task; whereas another student could be trying to memorize the information, feeling frustrated when difficulty arises, and wishing that he or she could be doing something else. The researchers attributed these differences in the quality of engagement to different motivational orientations. Conducting research aimed at understanding the development of children's conception of ability (Nicholls, 1984), the different responses of children with similar ability to difficulty and failure (Dweck & Leggett, 1988), the effect of different reward structures on students' academic engagement (Ames, 1984), and the different meaning of achievement among students of different cultures (Maehr & Nicholls, 1980), these researchers reached a similar conclusion. They proposed that it is the *meaning* or *purpose* for engaging in academic behavior, as construed by students, that affects their motivation (Maehr, 1984; Molden & Dweck, 2000; Nicholls, 1989). This purpose—the "achievement goal"—is concerned with *why* a student engages in achievement-related behavior (E. M. Anderman & Maehr, 1994; Dweck, 1992). Thus, the achievement goal is defined in broader terms than the specific aims that students may have, and is thought of as a comprehensive psychological "program" with "cognitive, affective, and behavioral consequences" (Elliott & Dweck, 1988, p. 11) that involves "ways of thinking about oneself, one's task, and task outcomes" (Ames, 1992b, p. 262).

It is important to note that achievement goals include both a situational component and a more enduring personal component. Laboratory manipulations reveal that situational demands can orient students toward different achievement goals (e.g., Elliot & Harackiewicz, 1996; Elliott & Dweck, 1988). However, survey research suggests that there are also individual differences in the goal orientations that students hold, and that these goal orientations are somewhat stable over time (Meece, Blumenfeld, & Hoyle, 1988; Wolters, Yu,

& Pintrich, 1996) and across academic (Pintrich & De Groot, 1990) and activity domains (Duda & Nicholls, 1992). It appears that individuals may differ in their goal orientations but are capable of pursuing similar goals in a particular achievement situation in response to the goals emphasized in those situations. In this chapter, we describe both the goal orientations of individuals and the goal emphases in the learning environment. We call the former *personal* goals and the latter *goal structures*.

Types of Personal Achievement Goals

Researchers have concluded that the purposes for engaging in achievement behavior can be meaningfully categorized into groups or types (e.g., Maehr, 1984). Whereas several types of purposes or achievement goals have been mentioned in the literature (e.g., Maehr & Braskamp, 1986; Urdan & Maehr, 1995), during the last two decades research has focused in particular on two types of goals. One type is labeled a *mastery goal*, *learning goal*, or *task goal*. The other type is labeled a *performance goal*, *ego goal*, or *ability goal*. Although researchers view these achievement goals slightly differently, for the most part there is considerable overlap among these different conceptions (Ames, 1992b; Ames & Archer, 1987; Heyman & Dweck, 1992). At a general level, a mastery goal can be thought of as engaging in achievement behavior with the purpose of *developing one's competence* (cf. White, 1959), and a performance goal can be thought of as engaging in achievement behavior with the purpose of *demonstrating one's competence or avoiding the demonstration of lack of competence* (see also Dweck, 1986). More specifically, a mastery goal refers to a focus on the task at hand, and to motivational orientations such as wanting to learn and understand the material, wanting to master the skills required for doing the task, or wanting to improve over past performance on similar tasks. A performance goal refers to a focus on the self, and more specifically on one's ability, and to motivational orientations such as wanting to achieve with little effort and demonstrating that one is able or avoiding demonstrating lack of ability (Ames, 1992b). Because performance goals reflect a concern with appearing able, and because students often develop their judgments about their own ability by comparing themselves to others, a performance goal orientation often involves a strong social comparison element. In these cases, the goal of appearing able includes the goal of appearing more able than others or not appearing less able than others (Nicholls, 1989).

During the two decades after achievement goal theory was introduced, research was conducted that conceptualized a performance goal orientation as a unitary conception "in which individuals seek to maintain positive judgments of their ability *and* avoid negative judgments" (Elliott & Dweck, 1988, p. 5, emphasis added). This combined motivational orientation was treated as an

"approach" form of motivation (Nicholls, Cheung, Lauer, & Patashnick, 1989). Elliot and his colleagues (Elliot, 1997, 1999; Elliot & Church, 1997) suggested that researchers should distinguish between performance-approach goals—an orientation toward the demonstration of high ability—and performance-avoid goals—an orientation toward *avoiding* the demonstration of low ability. In addition, it appears that students may pursue more than one type of achievement goal at a time, a point we return to later in the chapter.

Goal Structures

Personal goals represent the goals that individuals pursue in general or in specific achievement situations. As experimental, survey, and observational research have all demonstrated, there are also goal-related messages that are made salient in the achievement setting (i.e., the laboratory, classrooms, schools) that are related to, and most likely influence, the personal goals that individuals pursue in those settings. We refer to these environmental goal emphases as goal structures, and we have attempted to measure goal structures at both the classroom and school levels.

Building on the work of Ames and her colleagues (Ames, 1990, 1992a, 1992b; Ames & Archer, 1988), as well as our own previous research (e.g., Roeser, Midgley, & Urdan, 1996), we conceptualized goal structures in terms of the various classroom- and school-level policies and practices that make mastery or performance goals salient, as well as the explicit goal-related messages teachers communicate to their students. At the classroom level, for example, teachers may post a list on the wall that rank-orders the reading level of each student in the class or students' performance on the last exam. Similarly, teachers may display only the "best" work on the classroom walls, or give high-achieving students special privileges in the classroom. Additionally teachers may tell students that getting right answers or good grades is the main goal in class. Such practices and messages make salient the differences between students in ability and performance and may create the perception that doing better than others and getting right answers is important, thereby conveying a performance goal structure. Alternatively, teachers may emphasize the importance of learning and intellectual development by recognizing students for effort and improvement or by encouraging students to delve more deeply into topics that they find interesting. Additionally, they may convey to students that trying hard and understanding the material is the main goal in the classroom, thereby conveying a mastery goal structure. Similar processes create mastery and performance goal structures at the school level.

We have used a variety of methods to assess goal structures. Students have been asked (via surveys) about their teacher's emphasis on mastery goals (e.g., "My teacher thinks mistakes are okay as long as we are learning") and perfor-

mance goals (e.g., "My teacher points out those students who get good grades as an example to all of us"). More recently, we have also asked students about the emphasis in their classrooms on mastery goals (e.g., "In our class, how much you improve is really important") and performance goals (e.g., "In our class, there is a lot of competition among students for good grades"). In addition, teachers themselves were asked about goal-related approaches to instruction that could reflect an emphasis on mastery goals (e.g., "I make a special effort to recognize students' individual progress, even if they are below grade level") and performance goals (e.g., "I help students understand how their performance compares to others"). Studies that have combined these two sources of information have found positive correlations between students' and teachers' reports of the classroom goal structures, but have also revealed that these two data sources explain independent portions of the variance in some student outcomes (e.g., Urdan, Midgley, & E. Anderman, 1998). We have also conducted classroom observations in conjunction with student survey data to identify the goal-related messages and practices that are salient in the classroom (e.g., Patrick, L. H. Anderman, Ryan, Edelin, & Midgley, 2001; see also chap. 9, this volume).

It is important to note that, despite the multiple methods with which we have measured school and classroom goal structures, we consider goal structures to be primarily a subjective construction. The power of environmental goal messages to influence the personal goals that students adopt and, by extension, their motivation and performance, probably depends more on how students *perceive* the various policies and practices in the school or classroom than on the objective reality of the policies or practices themselves (Ames, 1992b; Urdan, Kneisel, & Mason, 1999). For example, two students in the same classroom may notice the rank-ordered list of test scores posted on the classroom wall. Although such a list makes ability differences among students salient, the degree of saliency may vary from student to student. Moreover, it will not necessarily lead both of these students to adopt a personal performance goal orientation in the classroom. One may perceive the list posted on the wall as an indication that relative standing is an important and valued feature of that classroom and strive to do better than other students on the next test (a performance goal orientation). The other student may not focus on the relative ability information on the list, noticing instead how her own test score provides information about how much she learned and how much she improved or failed to improve. We believe that, in general, goal structures encourage the adoption of similar personal goal orientations among students, but we recognize that students vary in their interpretation of the goal messages present in the learning environment. The need to understand the sources of these differences represents an interesting area for future research and a topic that we return to later in this chapter. In addition, as is true for personal goals, students may perceive

multiple goal structures. That is, classrooms do not necessarily emphasize one goal structure or the other; they may emphasize both, one more than the other, or neither.

CORRELATES AND CONSEQUENCES OF PERSONAL GOALS AND GOAL STRUCTURES

Research on achievement goals and goal structures has revealed a wide variety of cognitive, motivational, affective, and behavioral variables that are correlated with, and perhaps caused by, different personal goals and environmental goal structures. In this section, we briefly review some of this research, paying particular attention to the work done in conjunction with the Patterns of Adaptive Learning Study.

Correlates and Consequences of Personal Achievement Goals

Research has established that mastery goals are consistently associated with adaptive patterns of learning (see Urdan, 1997, for a review). Converging evidence from studies using methods such as surveys, interviews, and experiments, suggests that when students report that they do their schoolwork with the purpose of learning, understanding, and improving, they are also likely to report adaptive cognitive, behavioral, and emotional outcomes. For example, mastery goals have been found to be associated with feeling academically efficacious, preferring challenging tasks, and persisting in the face of difficulties. Also, mastery goals have been found to be associated with the use of effective cognitive and metacognitive strategies; the attribution of success to effort, interest, and strategy use; positive attitudes toward school and schoolwork; and even with positive general well-being (see Ames, 1992b; Urdan, 1997, for recent reviews).

Results of studies concerning performance goals have not been as consistent (Elliot, 1999; Midgley, Kaplan, & Middleton, 2001; Urdan, 1997). A number of studies have suggested that when performance goals are salient, students are likely to report a maladaptive pattern of outcomes such as experiencing negative affect in response to difficulty and challenge, using "low-level" learning strategies, and attributing failure to low ability (see Ames, 1992b; Dweck & Leggett, 1988, for reviews). Other studies, however, have found no relation between performance goals and negative outcomes, and some have found positive relations between performance goals and outcomes such as academic efficacy, grades, and test scores (for reviews see Elliot, 1999; Midgley et al., 2001; Urdan, 1997). Furthermore, whereas some studies have supported the predic-

tion that perceived ability would moderate the relations between performance goals and outcomes (Dweck & Leggett, 1988), others have not (e.g., Kaplan & Midgley, 1997; Miller, Behrens, Greene, & Newman, 1993). Despite the inconsistencies in research findings, performance goals have generally been thought of as a less desirable motivational orientation than mastery goals (Ames, 1992b; Dweck & Leggett, 1988; Midgley et al., 2001; Nicholls, 1989), and recommendations for school reform have focused on enhancing students' mastery goals (Ames, 1990; Fuchs et al., 1997; Maehr & Midgley, 1996).

There are a variety of factors that may explain why the correlates and consequences associated with performance goals are not as clear-cut as those associated with mastery goals. Some of these factors include the way that performance goals have been defined and measured, the role of perceived ability and/or different cultural processes in explaining the differential effects of performance goals, and the moderating effect of pursuing mastery goals while simultaneously pursuing performance goals. Each of these factors is considered in turn.

The Approach–Avoidance Distinction.   Recent research suggests that the inconsistency in findings concerning performance goals may be the result of the failure to distinguish between the approach and avoidance components of performance goals. Performance-approach goals represent a concern with appearing able and outperforming others, whereas performance-avoid goals represent a concern with avoiding appearing unable, or less able than others. Findings from research conducted thus far seem to be consistent in suggesting that performance-avoid goals are associated with a negative pattern of outcomes. Students who were oriented to avoiding the demonstration of low ability were also likely to feel anxious, have a low sense of academic efficacy, avoid seeking help in the classroom, engage in academic self-handicapping, and have lower grades (Elliot & Church, 1997; Middleton & Midgley, 1997; Midgley & Urdan, 2001; Skaalvik, 1997; see also chap. 3, this volume). Performance-approach goals not only have emerged as more positive than performance-avoid goals, but when they are included with performance-avoid goals in analyses, they look more "positive" than in previous studies where performance-avoid goals were not included. In many cases they emerge as unrelated to negative outcomes. Middleton and Midgley found that performance-approach goals were unrelated to academic efficacy, self-regulation, and the avoidance of help seeking when both components of performance goals were included in the same model. However, they still emerged as positive predictors of test anxiety. Midgley and Urdan found that academic self-handicapping was positively correlated with both performance-approach and performance-avoid goals, but the relationship with performance-avoid goals was stronger. Additionally, in regression analyses, performance-avoid goals positively predicted handicapping, whereas performance-approach goals did not. In a study including both self-defeating and

self-enhancing ego orientations (Skaalvik, 1997), the approach (self-enhancing) dimension of performance goals was associated positively with grades, academic self-concept, academic efficacy, and intrinsic motivation, and was unrelated to anxiety. Additional studies including both components of performance goals with a variety of student outcomes will help us to understand the effects of performance-approach goals.

We recently considered this issue in considerable detail (Midgley et al., 2001). Using the results of research conducted by ourselves and others, we argued that the potential benefits of a performance-approach goal orientation may depend on a number of factors, including the age of the students, whether students are in a highly competitive context, and the types of skills that are valued in that context (e.g., complex cognitive processes or more shallow processing strategies). Performance-approach goals, like all goal orientations, are part of a more general system of beliefs concerning the purpose of schooling and the meaning of achievement. A performance-approach goal orientation is part of a world view in which success is defined as demonstrating high ability. Such a belief may put performance-approach-oriented students at risk for adopting attitudes and behaviors that, although contributing to their goals of demonstrating high ability, may be maladaptive when circumstances change and the possibility of demonstrating high ability becomes uncertain. In such circumstances, the concern with appearing able may direct students' attention to the possibility of demonstrating low ability and may cause them to adopt a performance-avoid goal orientation. Indeed, we have found that for some students, a performance-approach goal orientation in sixth grade predicted a performance-avoid goal orientation in seventh grade (Middleton, Kaplan, & Midgley, 2001).

Just as there is a distinction between the approach and avoidance dimensions of performance goals, Elliot (1999) and Pintrich (2000b) recently suggested that this distinction might also apply to mastery goals. Elliot suggested, for example, that mastery-avoid goals should be conceptualized as a motivational orientation in which the person is trying to avoid failure that is defined in mastery goal terms: the loss or the stagnation of skills and competence. Mastery-avoid goals could include fearing that one is going to forget what one has learned or miss an opportunity to master a task. Elliot argued that such a motivational orientation could be common among the elderly who feel that their abilities and skills are slowly deteriorating. Mastery-avoid goals may also be adopted by students who realize that they may not be able to master the task or learn the material in the time that is allotted for the task. At present, there is too little research on mastery-avoid goals to suggest whether this motivational orientation is associated with positive or negative outcomes. It may be, as both Elliot and Pintrich suggested, that these goals will be associated with positive outcomes such as persistence as well as with negative outcomes such as frus-

tration and loss of interest. It is also not clear whether this class of achievement goals would prove useful to educators in conceptualizing student motivation. Perhaps these goals are not so prevalent among students as they are among the elderly. Hopefully, future research will shed light on these issues.

Perceived Ability.   Another factor that may be related to an inconsistent pattern of associations between performance goals and outcomes is the possible moderating role of students' perceived ability. From the earliest conceptions of achievement goals, there has been a strong presumption that mastery and performance goals are related to beliefs about the nature of ability and intelligence. Dweck and her colleagues have shown that a mastery goal orientation is generally associated with the belief that intelligence and ability are malleable qualities that can be enhanced with effort, which Dweck has called an *incremental* view of intelligence (Dweck, 1999; Dweck & Leggett, 1988). Similarly, they have demonstrated that a performance goal orientation is often associated with a belief that intelligence and ability are fixed qualities that are difficult to change (an *entity* view of intelligence). Therefore, when performance goal oriented, students are concerned with demonstrating that they possess more of this quality (intelligence/ability) than others do or that they are not less intelligent or able than others. In addition, Nicholls and his colleagues argued that a mastery goal orientation corresponds with an *undifferentiated* conception of ability whereas a performance goal orientation is related to a *differentiated* conception of ability. An undifferentiated conception of ability includes the belief that ability and effort are positively related and that increased effort results in increased ability (Nicholls, 1984, 1990). In contrast, a differentiated conception includes the view that ability and effort are inversely related such that greater effort implies lower ability.

Because mastery and performance goal orientations are associated with different beliefs about intelligence and ability, it is logical to assume that these different types of goals would also be associated with students' perceptions about their own ability levels (i.e., perceived ability). Specifically, when mastery goal oriented, students should believe that they can increase their ability with effort, a belief that would exist regardless of whether students have high or low perceptions of their own ability. Thus, a mastery goal orientation should have the same positive influence on effort, motivation, and performance regardless of students' perceived ability. In contrast, perceived ability should moderate the relation between performance goals and motivation, effort, and performance.

Dweck in particular has noted that the influence of goals on subsequent behavior depends on the level of an individual's perceived ability (e.g., Dweck, 1986; Dweck & Leggett, 1988). For example, in an experimental study in which goals were manipulated, Elliott and Dweck (1988) found that individu-

als in the mastery goal condition displayed an adaptive pattern regardless of the level of their perceived skill at performing the task. However, the pattern exhibited by individuals in the performance goal condition depended on their perceptions of their skill. Individuals under the performance goal condition who assessed their skill as high exhibited adaptive patterns, whereas those who assessed their skill as low exhibited maladaptive patterns. Thus, perceived skill at performing the task moderated the relationship between performance goals and behavior.

Although there has been some support for the hypothesis that perceived ability moderates the relationship between performance goals and motivational and performance outcomes (Dweck & Leggett, 1988), other researchers have not found a moderating effect of perceived ability (e.g., Kaplan & Midgley, 1997; Miller et al., 1993). Whereas it seems reasonable to expect that perceived ability may influence whether a performance goal orientation is expressed in approach or avoidance terms, and thereby influence the pattern of motivation and behavior associated with performance goals among students of different levels of perceived ability, further research is needed to determine whether, and under what conditions, perceived ability moderates the relationship between both performance and mastery goals and patterns of learning.

Ethnic and Cultural Differences.   Most research investigating mastery and performance achievement goals has been conducted with White, middle-class North American students. However, in recent years, researchers have also been interested in the usefulness of achievement goal theory for conceptualizing achievement motivation among students of different ethnicities and cultures. A few studies have been conducted with participants from minority groups in the United States (e.g., Kaplan & Maehr, 1999; Midgley, Arunkumar, & Urdan, 1996; see also chap. 7, this volume), and with English-speaking populations from other countries (e.g., Archer, 1994; D. M. McInerney, 1995). In addition, surveys, interviews, and experimental manipulations have been translated into other languages such as Hebrew, Arabic, French, Norwegian, Japanese, and Chinese, to test the generalizability of the theory in non-English-speaking populations.

Although the effects of pursuing mastery goals are expected to be similar across ethnic and cultural groups, there is reason to suspect that the consequences of a performance goal orientation may differ. Performance goals contain at least two elements that can reasonably be expected to differ between cultures and perhaps between ethnic groups. First, performance goals involve an element of self-consciousness, or a concern with how one appears to others. Because there is evidence that self-perceptions differ across cultural and ethnic groups, it is possible that the effect of performance goals on motivation and performance may also differ between groups (e.g., Markus & Kitayama, 1991). Mastery goals, which are generally considered to involve a greater con-

cern with the task itself than with self-perceptions, may not be affected by differences in self-definition across culture. Second, performance goals include a competitive element in which a concern with doing better, or not doing worse, than others is salient. It is likely that some cultural and ethnic groups value competition and outperforming others more than others do, thereby suggesting differences in the effects of performance goals across cultures and ethnicities.

Research examining differences in self-definitions suggests that people differ in the degree to which they hold an individualistic or collectivist sense of self (Markus & Kitayama, 1991; Triandis, 1989). An individualistic sense of self involves viewing the self as distinct from others, placing an emphasis on individuation and separation from others, as well as striving for personal accomplishment that distinguishes the individual from others. The collectivist definition of self involves a strong sense that one is defined as a member of a larger in-group. With this sense of self, behavior is motivated by a desire to maintain one's membership in the group and achievement is defined as that which brings recognition, honor, or benefit to the in-group. Because different definitions of self produce such different goals and definitions of success (i.e., as distinguishing oneself from others vs. striving for group solidarity and recognition), it is likely that performance goals may operate differently for students with different definitions of self.

Some have argued that these differences in the definition of self can be found between different ethnic and cultural groups within the United States (Landrine, 1992; Triandis, Leung, Villareal, & Clack, 1985). Research conducted by Fuligni and his colleagues supports these assertions. They have found that among students from Latino/Hispanic and Asian cultures, there is a greater sense of family obligation, which may have roots in a collectivist sense of self (Fuligni & Tseng, 1999; Fuligni, Tseng, & Lam, 1999). It has been suggested that students from Latin American and Asian backgrounds, due to the collectivist orientation of their cultures, may prefer collaborative classroom activities and dislike the competition inherent in American classrooms (E. E. Garcia, 1992; Vasquez, 1990). It is important to note that there is wide variation within a specific population or cultural/ethnic group. One potential source of within-group variation is the degree to which members of the group have assimilated into mainstream American culture. The connection to traditional cultural values, such as a collectivist sense of self or a sense of obligation to the family, may gradually weaken the longer it has been since the family immigrated to the United States (Fuligni & Tseng, 1999).

Additional research by Steele and his colleagues suggests that when self-perceptions are made a salient feature of the achievement situation (as when performance goals are emphasized), gender and ethnic stereotypes can affect motivation and performance. For example, Steele and his colleagues (Steele, 1997; Steele & Aronson, 1995) have found that many African American stu-

dents experience "stereotype threat" in academic achievement situations. Stereotype threat involves the fear and anxiety produced when people feel that they are in danger of fulfilling a negative stereotype about their group, such as when African American students are concerned about performing badly on an academic task. This threat produces anxiety and, over time, may lead to a devaluing of academic achievement. Interestingly, this effect emerges when students are placed in situations where social comparison information is available and, presumably, a performance goal orientation is adopted.

In our own research, we have found limited evidence of ethnic differences in the associations between performance goals and motivational or behavioral outcomes. In one study we found that among a sample of eighth-grade students, performance goals were positively related to the use of self-handicapping strategies among African American students but not among Euro-American students (Midgley et al., 1996). Similarly, there is some indication that the relations among achievement goals and self-processes may differ between Euro-American and African American students (Kaplan & Maehr, 1999). In other studies, however, we failed to find ethnic differences either in the mean levels of mastery and performance goals or in the associations between performance goals and outcomes. A summary of the results from the Patterns of Adaptive Learning Study regarding ethnic differences is presented in chapter 7, this volume.

Clearly more research is needed to determine whether mastery and performance goals have the same meaning and operate the same among students of different groups. There has been very little research offering an in-depth analysis of achievement goals processes in one ethnic minority or cultural group (see the qualitative study by Edelin and her colleagues described in chap. 7, this volume, as an exception). The few findings of differences suggest that such research is needed. In addition to the studies conducted by us, other researchers have found that different cultural groups may have different dispositions toward certain achievement goals (e.g., D. M. McInerney, Roche, V. McInerney, & Marsh, 1997), and that, in some cases, achievement goals may be related to outcomes in somewhat different ways (D. M. McInerney, Hinkley, Dowson, & Van Etten, 1998). Even this research, however, points to the strong similarities in the structure of achievement goals and their relations with outcomes among students of different cultures. Future research should use diverse research methods, particularly methods that are sensitive to differences in meaning of concepts, to investigate the nature of goals in different ethnic groups and cultures.

Multiple Goals.   Another factor that may partially explain inconsistent effects of performance goals is that students may pursue these goals while simultaneously pursuing mastery goals. Research examining mastery and performance goals has often contrasted the effects of these two goal orientations

without exploring how these two goals may combine to influence motivation and performance. In many studies there has been no correlation or only a weak positive correlation between mastery and performance goals (Midgley et al., 1998; Nicholls et al., 1989). This suggests that students may hold mastery and performance goals simultaneously and to varying degrees (Meece & Holt, 1993). This has been supported by qualitative studies in which students expressed multiple purposes or goals for engaging in schoolwork (e.g., Dowson & D. M. McInerney, 1997; Lee & C. W. Anderson, 1993; Levy, Kaplan, & Patrick, 2000). If the consequences of a performance goal orientation differ depending on the simultaneous level of mastery goal orientation, then studies that consider the effects of performance goals without taking into account the level of mastery goals may yield inconsistent results.

Research that has examined the effects of different profiles of mastery and performance goals provides evidence that holding low mastery and low performance goals simultaneously is almost always associated with a negative pattern of cognition, emotion, and behavior. Holding low mastery and high performance goals has also been shown to be associated with a negative pattern of outcomes, although not as negative as that associated with the low-mastery and low-performance profile. Studies contrasting the effects of a high-mastery/low-performance goal profile with a high-mastery/high-performance goal profile have produced mixed results. In most studies, both of these profiles manifested a relatively positive pattern of outcomes. However, in some studies, the high-mastery/low-performance goal profile was found to be more adaptive than the high-mastery/high-performance goal profile (e.g., Kaplan & Bos, 1995; Meece & Holt, 1993; Pintrich & T. Garcia, 1991). In other studies, there was little evidence of differences between the two profiles (e.g., Pintrich, 2000a; Urdan, 1996). In still other studies, the high-mastery/high-performance goal profile was more adaptive than the high-mastery/low-performance goal profile (e.g., Bouffard, Boisvert, Vezeau, & Larouche, 1995; Bouffard, Vezeau, & Bordeleau, 1998).

Some researchers have suggested that holding both high mastery and high performance goals could be more adaptive than having only high mastery goals, as students can more easily adjust to the demands of different tasks and situations (e.g., Harackiewicz, Barron, & Elliot, 1998; Pintrich & T. Garcia, 1991; Wentzel, 1992). It may be, for example, that students who have both mastery and performance goals in their repertoire are able to adjust their personal definitions of success—for example, from normative based to self-referenced—in accordance with their evaluation of the demands of the task and their potential to succeed in the situation. In this way, students may be able to motivate themselves to succeed in diverse achievement contexts and avoid some of the negative consequences of performance goals. The mixed results of examinations of multiple goals profiles suggests that we still do not know what combination of goals is most adaptive, or whether the most beneficial multiple

goals profile may depend on characteristics such as the students' age, gender, or achievement level or on characteristics of the achievement context and task (e.g., Bouffard et al., 1998; Harackiewicz et al., 1998; Midgley et al., 2001; Pintrich, 2000a). At present, however, it is clear that much more research is needed on the issue of multiple goals.

Correlates and Consequences of Environmental Goal Structures

Achievement goals have been found to meaningfully characterize the motivational orientations of students, and explain significant differences in students' patterns of learning. However, as the usefulness of a motivational theory to education is measured by its ability to inform practice, it may be that the most important contribution of achievement goal theory to the field of education has been its application to the study of learning environments. The investigation of the relations between different features of learning environments and student outcomes has a long history (e.g., Moos, 1979; Walberg & G. Anderson, 1968). In this section, we describe research examining the correlates and consequences of students' perceptions of the classroom- and school-level goal structures.

Perceiving an Emphasis on Mastery and Performance Goals in the Classroom.   For the most part, studies investigating the relations between the environmental emphasis on achievement goals and student outcomes have found that a classroom or school mastery goal structure was associated with positive outcomes, whereas a performance goal structure was associated with negative outcomes (see Kaplan & Maehr, 2001, for a review). This research suggests that when students perceive that their classrooms or schools emphasize understanding, improvement, and mastery of knowledge and skills, they are more likely to use effective learning strategies (Ames & Archer, 1988; Kaplan & Midgley, 1999; Ryan, Gheen, & Midgley, 1998; Urdan et al., 1998) and feel better about themselves and about being in school (Kaplan & Maehr, 1999; Roeser et al., 1996) than when they perceive that what is emphasized in the classroom or school is normative comparison of student ability.

A number of studies conducted with the data from the Patterns of Adaptive Learning Study examined the correlates and consequences of classroom-level goal structures. These studies have generally supported earlier research revealing a more positive pattern of motivational, affective, and performance outcomes associated with students' perceptions of a mastery goal structure than with a perceived performance goal structure. Research from the study has extended previous findings in a number of ways by using longitudinal data, a variety of data sources, and more advanced statistical methods than were previously available.

Three studies from the Patterns of Adaptive Learning Study looked at the change in students' perceptions of the classroom goal structure as they moved from elementary school to middle school to determine how these changes were related to students' cognition, emotion, and behavior. One study found that changes in the perceived mastery goal structure were more strongly related to changes in cognition, affect, and performance than were changes in the perceived performance goal structure both across the transition to middle school (fifth to sixth grade) and during middle school (sixth to seventh grade) (Urdan, Midgley, & Hruda, 2000). The most negative pattern of change was associated with a perceived decrease in the mastery goal structure. Students who experienced less emphasis on mastery goals as they moved from one learning environment to another also experienced a decrease in academic efficacy, felt less positively about school, and had lower grades. Students who experienced an increased emphasis on mastery goals did not exhibit these negative patterns of change, and on some outcomes they exhibited positive change. Another longitudinal study found that changes in the perceived classroom goal structure across the transition from elementary to middle school were related to changes in positive and negative affect (L. H. Anderman, 1999). A greater emphasis on performance goals in the new classroom than in the previous classroom was associated with increased negative affect, whereas a greater emphasis on mastery goals in the new classroom was associated with increased positive affect. The third longitudinal study of classroom goal structures stemming from the Patterns of Adaptive Learning Study revealed that over time, a perceived classroom mastery goal structure was related to positive coping with failure and in turn to positive affect, whereas a perceived performance goal structure was related to projective and denial coping and, in turn, to negative affect (Kaplan & Midgley, 1999).

A number of studies have taken advantage of hierarchical linear modeling (HLM) to examine whether classroom goal structures were predictive of variation in several constructs across classrooms. For example, we found that fifth graders' use of self-handicapping strategies varied significantly across different classrooms and that students were more likely to use self-handicapping strategies if they were in classrooms that they perceived to have a greater emphasis on performance goals. Students were also more likely to use these strategies in classrooms in which their teachers reported using performance-oriented approaches to instruction (Urdan et al., 1998). In another HLM study, Gheen and Midgley (1999) found that student reports of wanting to avoid novel approaches to their academic work were negatively related to a perceived emphasis on mastery goals in the classroom and positively related to a perceived performance goal structure. Moreover, the association between self-efficacy and novelty avoidance was weaker in classrooms where teachers reported encouraging students to engage in social comparison for the sake of gaining information about what they had misunderstood in the lesson or assignment. This association was

stronger in classes where teachers reported encouraging students to use social comparison to gauge their standing in the class relative to others. In other words, when teachers encouraged students to be concerned about appearing more or less able than other students, students who were lower in academic efficacy were more likely to avoid the kinds of novel activities that lead to learning. But in those classrooms where teachers encouraged students to learn from their mistakes by comparing their work with their classmates, this association between self-efficacy and novelty avoidance was reduced.

In a study conducted in conjunction with the Patterns of Adaptive Learning Study that combined survey data with classroom observations, Patrick and her colleagues identified four classrooms that differed in the patterns of mastery and performance goal structures perceived by students (Patrick et al., 2001; see also chap. 9, this volume). Using survey data, they identified one classroom in which students perceived a high emphasis on both mastery and performance goals, one classroom in which students perceived a high emphasis on mastery goals and a low emphasis on performance goals, one classroom in which students perceived a low emphasis on mastery goals and a high emphasis on performance goals, and one classroom in which students perceived a low emphasis on both goals. Classroom observations in each of these classrooms revealed that the teachers in the low-mastery classrooms believed in a transmission model of teaching and learning whereas teachers in the two high-mastery classrooms spoke about learning as an active and personally constructed process. Instructional practices in each type of classroom matched these belief statements, with teachers in the low-mastery classrooms emphasizing the importance of getting the correct answer and teachers in the high-mastery classrooms focusing more on the process of learning and understanding than on the correctness of answers. Patrick and her colleagues also found that teachers in the high-mastery classrooms were more enthusiastic about academics and more likely to demonstrate and encourage mutual respect between students and teachers than were teachers in the low-mastery classrooms.

Overall, research from the Patterns of Adaptive Learning Study has extended the existing research on the consequences and correlates of classroom goal structures considerably. We have broadened the range of variables examined in relation to classroom goal structures to include self-handicapping (Midgley & Urdan, 2001; Urdan et al., 1998), avoidance of help seeking (Ryan et al., 1998), avoidance of novelty (Gheen & Midgley, 1999), positive and negative affect (L. H. Anderman, 1999; Kaplan & Midgley, 1999; Urdan et al., 1999), and positive and negative forms of coping (Kaplan & Midgley, 1999). These advances, when combined with the multiple methods used to study classroom goal structures, make the area of classroom goal structures one of the most important contributions made by the Patterns of Adaptive Learning Study to research on achievement goals.

Research on School-Level Goal Structures. In addition to our work examining classroom goal structures, we have also conducted a limited number of studies examining how perceived mastery and performance goal structures at the school level are associated with students' motivational and behavioral outcomes. In an earlier study, Roeser et al. (1996) found, for example, that a perceived mastery goal structure at the school level was related to middle school students' personal mastery goals, which in turn were related to students' sense of belonging in school. A perceived performance goal structure at the school level was related to students' personal performance goals, which, in turn, were related to academic self-consciousness, that is, being afraid to make mistakes publicly and feeling nervous about performing in front of others.

In another study, we found direct relations between the goal structure in the environment and outcomes, in addition to those that were mediated by students' personal achievement goals (Kaplan & Maehr, 1999). Kaplan and Maehr found that in addition to mediated relations through students' personal achievement goals, the school's mastery and performance goal structure had direct relations to students' sense of well-being in school and to their reports of engaging in disruptive behavior. These findings suggest that regardless of their personal achievement goals, students engage more adaptively and feel better in schools where they believe that the emphasis is on self-improvement and on learning than in schools where the emphasis is on social comparison of ability.

Summary. Our research on the correlates and consequences of school and classroom goal structures suggests that there are important differences between classrooms and schools in the types of goals that are emphasized and perceived by teachers and students. It also appears that these environmental goal structures are associated with a variety of motivational, affective, and behavioral outcomes including students' personal goals, avoidance behaviors, and the social dimensions of the classroom experience. These results are compelling and suggest the importance of future research in this area. However, there are still a number of methodological and empirical questions and challenges that remain. We turn our attention to this and other issues in the next section of the chapter.

Implications and Future Directions

The research on personal goal orientations and environmental goal structures that has been generated by the Patterns of Adaptive Learning Study has implications for both research and practice.

Implications for Research on Personal Achievement Goals. The research conducted on achievement goals in this project has improved our understanding of the relations among mastery, performance-approach, and per-

formance-avoid goals, as well as between these goals and a variety of cognitive, affective, and behavioral outcomes. In addition to the knowledge gained, the power of this research may lie in the implications of this research for future research in this area.

One important lesson is that there is much to be learned from longitudinal studies of the effects of achievement goals. Specifically, the results of the study by Middleton et al. (2001) suggest that the long-term effects of a performance-approach goal orientation may be best understood in the context of changes in achievement, feelings of efficacy, and contextual goal structures over time. Another longitudinal study revealed that achievement goals, coping strategies, and affect in school are intertwined in a complex reciprocal way over time (Kaplan & Midgley, 1999). To understand this complexity, longitudinal research is needed.

Of course, the recommendation that goals be examined longitudinally suggests that goals are more than simply a situation-specific cognitive state. Rather, it implies that achievement goals are somewhat stable and can influence, and be influenced by contextual, cognitive, and affective variables over time (e.g., L. Anderman & E. M. Anderman, 1999). There is also evidence from our research and others that the specific goals pursued in any given achievement situation are influenced by the demands of the achievement situation. More research is needed to investigate the complex interaction of personal goal orientations and the more volatile, situationally influenced goals pursued in a specific situation.

Another implication of our research is that goals are associated with social and emotional variables, in addition to more academic outcomes such as grades and scores, self-efficacy, and cognitive strategy use. For example, we have found an association between the school goal structure, personal goals, and outcomes such as emotional tone and impulse control (e.g., Kaplan & Maehr, 1999). Similarly, we have found that achievement goals and goal structures are related to a variety of social aspects of classroom life, including various types of social goals (e.g., status, responsibility), social interaction among students, and the facilitation of respect among members of the classroom (Anderman & Anderman, 1999; see also chap. 4, this volume). These results suggest that the correlates and consequences of various goal pursuits may extend beyond the realm of traditionally examined academic variables to include the emotional well-being of students and social aspects of classroom life that may be very important in determining the quality of school experiences for adolescents.

Finally, the division of performance goals into approach and avoidance components has important implications for future research in this area. Whereas others have brought this distinction to the fore (see Elliot & Harackiewicz, 1996), the work on this project has contributed to the understanding of the different effects of performance-approach and performance-avoid goals. Specifically, we

have found that there is a clearly negative pattern of associations between performance-avoid goals and a variety of outcomes including negative affect, lower achievement, and the use of self-handicapping strategies. The correlates of performance-approach goals are less clear. As one of our studies suggests, a general concern with whether one appears able relative to others (i.e., a performance goal orientation) may have consequences that extend beyond the approach–avoidance distinction (Middleton et al., 2001). Our results suggest that the benefits of performance-approach goals may be fragile over time. With a change in context or an academic setback, performance-approach goals may shift to a performance-avoid goal orientation. This is an issue that deserves further attention.

Implications for Research on Achievement Goal Structures. The results of our research on achievement goal structures, both in conjunction with the Patterns of Adaptive Learning Study and in earlier research, suggest that an emphasis on mastery goals in the learning environment has a number of direct and indirect benefits for students whereas an emphasis on performance goals can be problematic. Although these trends persisted whether we used student reports, teacher reports, or classroom observations as our data source, there are a number of questions regarding research on goal structures that remain.

One question is whether our various attempts to measure school and classroom goal structures have successfully captured these constructs. Is it valid to rely on student reports of environmental goal structures? On the one hand, the influence of such goal structures on students' motivational and performance outcomes cannot be separated from their subjective interpretations of these goal structures. If students believe that there is an emphasis on competition and demonstrating ability, these beliefs should affect their own motivation and behavior even if impartial observers perceive no such emphasis on performance goals. On the other hand, if the effect of perceived goal structures is entirely subjective, there is little to be gained by trying to actually alter the goal structures in schools and classrooms. The results of our studies suggest that students do differ in their perceptions of school and classroom goal structures, but that these perceptions are moderately related to teacher reports of their mastery- and performance-goal-oriented practices and to our observations of the activities in some of these classrooms. Nonetheless, it is likely that students' perceptions of environmental goal structures are partially influenced by students' existing goal orientations (e.g., Roeser et al., 1996). Future research needs to do more to identify the processes through which students attend to and interpret the goal-related messages in their classrooms and schools (Urdan et al., 1999).

Another implication of our research is that there is a need to understand and measure the performance-avoid dimension of classrooms and schools. The division of personal performance goals into approach and avoidance dimensions has

proven extremely valuable. Does a similar distinction exist at the classroom and school goal structure levels? It may be that the approach and avoidance distinction is made at the student level rather than at the classroom level. It may be that in the classroom, social comparison information is made salient and students respond to this information by developing either personal performance-approach or performance-avoid goals. Which orientation they adopt may depend on factors such as their perceived ability, their achievement level, their existing goal orientation, or even their gender or cultural background.

We have attempted to develop separate scales to assess perceptions of classroom performance-approach and performance-avoid goal structures. Our initial findings suggest that students do indeed distinguish between an emphasis on performance-approach goals and an emphasis on performance-avoid goals in the learning environment (Kaplan, Gheen, & Midgley, in press; Middleton, Gheen, Hruda, & Midgley, 2000). In these studies, students' perceptions of mastery and performance-approach classroom goal structures varied between classrooms, but students' perceptions of the classroom performance-avoid goal structure did not. Thus, students in different classrooms were more likely to disagree about the emphasis on mastery and performance-approach than about the emphasis on performance-avoid goals. It could also be that classrooms in this sample did not vary with regard to their emphasis on performance-avoid goals. This research is also beginning to examine the relation between approach and avoidance goal structures and adaptive and maladaptive outcomes.

In a recent study, Church, Elliot, and Gable (2001) found that personal performance-approach goals were associated with college students' perceived emphasis on evaluation in the course, personal performance-avoid goals were associated with a perceived emphasis on evaluation and that the evaluation was harsh, and personal mastery goals were associated with a perceived emphasis on the facilitation of interest and negatively associated with a perceived emphasis on evaluation or that evaluation was harsh. Other researchers are beginning to build on this research to further explicate not only the relation between students' perceptions of goal-related aspects of the learning environment and their personal goals, but also the relation between teacher discourse and observed instruction and students' perceptions of the goal structure in the classroom (e.g., Turner, Meyer, Midgley, & Patrick, 2001; Turner, Midgley et al., 2002). No research, thus far, has examined the effects of students' perceptions of mastery-approach and mastery-avoidance goal structures, although some experimental work on eliciting these different goals is underway (A. J. Elliot, personal communication, April 2000). Furthermore, similar to the different personal achievement goals that can be held simultaneously by students, learning environments can, and probably often do, emphasize more than one achievement goal. Very little research has looked at the consequences for students of perceiving an emphasis on multiple goals in the learning environment. Turner

and her colleagues (Turner, Meyer, Midgley, & Patrick, 2001) have recently compared teacher discourse in two classrooms perceived by students to be high in both mastery and performance-approach goals, and have suggested that the relation between this high/high pattern and students' negative affect and use of avoidance strategies may depend on the level of affective support that teachers communicate in the classroom. A study by Middleton and his colleagues (Middleton, Kaplan, Midgley, & E. Anderman, 2001) suggests that the outcomes associated with different patterns of perceived multiple-goal structures may be similar to that of multiple personal achievement goals. A perceived goal structure that included an emphasis on mastery goals was associated with lower levels of disruptive behavior and lower reports of cheating regardless of whether the emphasis on performance-approach goals was high or low. When the emphasis in the goal structure was high on performance-approach goals and low on mastery goals, disruptive behavior and cheating were higher. Of course, these are initial results with a limited set of outcomes. Future research should evaluate these interactions in much more depth.

Implications for Practice.   In addition to the implications of these studies for research, there are a number of implications for practice. Clearly, both this research and the research of others suggest that there are benefits associated with pursuing mastery goals and problems associated with a performance-avoid goal orientation, at least for some outcomes. But does this research suggest that goal structures are impervious to changes in the classroom or school? If not, can we recommend that educators alter their practices to create mastery goal structures while reducing the emphasis on performance goals? Is the evidence compelling enough to recommend that teachers discourage their students from adopting performance-approach goals? And what are the implications of these recommendations in the current climate of high-stakes testing?

These are important questions that require more thought. We discuss these issues here, albeit briefly. First, there is compelling evidence from experimental manipulations in the lab, survey research conducted in schools, field-based observations, and school and classroom interventions to suggest that students' achievement goal orientations, motivational beliefs, affect, and performance are at least partially determined by the goal-related messages present in the achievement or learning context. Although students in any given classroom will vary in their perceptions of the classroom goal structures, there is little doubt that teachers' approaches to instruction, classroom and school policies, and even student norms can and do influence the personal goals that students pursue in the classroom. Given this, what can educators do to create an optimal motivational environment for their students?

We believe that in thinking about motivating students, educators should first and foremost think about what they want to promote in their schools: Do they

want to promote high scores on tests or in-depth learning? Do they want to encourage memorization and test-taking skills or the comprehension and synthesis of knowledge? Do they want to promote competition among students or collaboration and the sharing of knowledge? This is a decision that educators will need to make for themselves.

Students' achievement goals are important for understanding their behavior and emotions in school. However, these understandings by themselves should not guide practice but should always be considered as tools for promoting the educational goals that are deemed desirable. We believe there is growing evidence that encouraging students to focus on understanding the material, mastering new concepts and skills, and developing and improving their competency (i.e., mastery goals) will encourage students to engage in schoolwork in ways that are conducive to learning and well-being. Therefore, we believe there is reason to recommend that educators seek ways to create mastery goal structures in their classrooms and schools. But what about the influence of performance goal structures? Is there sufficient evidence to suggest that educators take steps to reduce or eliminate performance goal structures? Or does the research suggest that in certain circumstances performance goals may be beneficial for students (Harackiewicz et al., 1998)?

Indeed, it may be that promoting performance-approach goals would contribute to students' interest and achievement. It may also be the case that facilitating a motivational orientation that combines performance-approach goals and mastery goals would alleviate some of the less desirable characteristics associated with performance goals. However, educators should also consider whether encouraging performance goals will inevitably lead to some maladaptive outcomes, at least for those students most disaffected from learning and schooling (see chap. 6, this volume). Interviews with young adolescents conducted as part of the Patterns of Adaptive Learning Study indicate that disaffected students frequently mention their negative reaction to an emphasis on the demonstration of ability in the classroom, and particularly the comparison of one student's ability to another's (see chap. 6, this volume).

We know of only one study that has found that performance goals are facilitative for these students. Barron and Harackiewicz (1999) conducted a study in which university students were taught new methods for solving mathematical problems. They created a multiple-goal condition in which both mastery and performance goals were assigned and compared the multiple-goal condition to a mastery-goal-only condition and a performance-goal-only condition. On measures of intrinsic motivation, the effects of assigned goals were moderated by achievement orientation. When students were low in achievement orientation, the mastery goal condition promoted the highest levels of interest in the mathematics activity. In contrast, when participants were high in achievement orientation, the performance goal condition promoted the highest

level of interest. The multiple-goal condition led to moderate levels of interest for students both high and low in achievement motivation. They concluded: "Although the multiple goal condition did not promote the highest levels of interest, it appeared to at least offer some buffer to low achievers when assigned a performance goal ... " (p. 247).

If educators decide that they do want to change the goal structures in their classrooms and schools, can goal theorists provide support and guidance if it is solicited? We do not believe that achievement goal theory will or should result in a list of specific practices that all schools should enact in order to become mastery oriented. When we are invited to talk with teachers about our research, we tell them that we do not come with a package or a program. We believe that a change in thinking about the purpose and meaning of schooling is a prerequisite to long-term change in policies and practices. We also recognize that schools serve constituencies with different philosophies and opinions about teaching and learning.

But that does not mean that achievement goal theory research cannot be used to inform teaching. As we mentioned earlier, a strength of achievement goal theory is its attention to the meanings that are conveyed by the context, and there is a growing body of research that points to aspects of the learning environment that convey emphases on mastery and performance goals (e.g., Meece, 1991; Patrick et al., 2001; Turner, Meyer et al., 2001; see also chap. 9, this volume). In addition, collaborations between theorists and practitioners have been very helpful in understanding both the kinds of changes that can be made in schools that are supported by achievement goal research, and the real-world issues practitioners face as they make these changes (e.g., Ames, 1990; Maehr & Midgley, 1996).

About a decade ago, Carole Ames worked with a group of elementary school teachers to develop specific strategies that are conceptually consistent with a mastery orientation. The assumption underlying this intervention was that a mastery goal orientation is not dependent on a singular set of strategies or a particular instructional method; instead it involves a constellation of strategies that are conceptually related to a common achievement goal. Ames' intervention focused on six dimensions of the learning environment (academic tasks, opportunities for student choice and authority, recognition systems, grouping practices, evaluation methods, and time use). Specific strategies within each dimension that were conceptually consistent with a mastery orientation were created and implemented by the teachers. Strategies were assembled in a large notebook and included, for example, sample report cards that emphasized individual progress and improvement, ideas such as "Teacher of the Day" or "Adopt-A-Class" to give students a sense of responsibility and opportunities for leadership, suggestions for using cooperative learning in various subject matter areas, and examples of contracts to encourage students to set their own goals and monitor their own progress. This program had a positive

impact on the students in the participating classrooms. At the end of 1 year, at-risk students in the classrooms in which the strategies were introduced reported that their classrooms were more mastery oriented than did at-risk children in control classrooms. In addition, students in these classrooms showed a stronger preference for challenging work, had more positive attitudes toward math and school, had higher self-concepts of ability, were more intrinsically motivated, and used more effective learning strategies than did peers in control classrooms (Ames, 1990).

Our approach to school reform, using achievement goal theory as the framework, builds on the Ames intervention. Like Ames, we believe that an emphasis on mastery goals is conveyed through the totality of the learning environment. In our collaboration with teachers, we identified a broad range of school-level policies, practices, and procedures that define learning and thus influence students' motivational orientations (Maehr & Midgley, 1996).

Table 2.1 presents a list of strategies that a coalition of researchers and middle school teachers devised with the aim of fostering an emphasis on mastery goals and de-emphasizing performance goals. It is important to note that the various elements that comprise this list are not independent, although they are presented separately. For example, the use of time affects the nature of tasks; the type of grouping that is used (ability grouping, cooperative learning, grouping by interest) influences the approach to assessment and evaluation. It should also be noted that many of these elements, although guided by policies at the school level (such as a policy on homogeneous ability grouping), are put into operation at the classroom level. We worked with teachers to examine and change a wide range of policies and practices in a way that would move toward an emphasis on task mastery, problem solving, effort, challenge, and academic progress and away from an emphasis on competition, relative ability, and comparative performance. It has now been 6 years since this collaborative school-change effort ended, but the schools have continued to make changes in line with the principles of achievement goal theory and have described to us the positive effects on their students.

Where Is Theory and Research in Achievement Goal Theory Heading?

Theoretical developments and research based on achievement goal theory have been proliferating during the last few years. On the theoretical front, there are many developments that arguably can be categorized into two complementary trends. The first includes those developments that look deeper into achievement goals as theoretical concepts or empirical constructs and attempt to dissect them to more distinct orientations that have significantly dif-

TABLE 2.1

Examples of Mastery-Focused Practices Used in the Coalition

Target Area	Issues	Instructional Practices
Task	What is the student asked to do in school?	Team teaching in the sixth and seventh grades. Though team teaching in and of itself is not necessarily a task-focused practice, it served as an enabling mechanism to allow teachers to collaborate and change the nature of academic tasks.
		Some use of interdisciplinary units.
		Administrators gave priority to programs, activities, in-services, and training to aid teachers in providing meaningful, challenging academic tasks to students.
Authority	What kinds of choices are given? How is student sense of responsibility enhanced?	Faculty discussed and implemented new opportunities for students to make choices about course materials (e.g., what books to read in English).
		Upon transition into the seventh grade, students could choose whether or not they wanted to be in a "small house" or traditional environment.
Recognition	What outcomes and behaviors are especially attended to? What reward and recognition policies are followed?	The emphasis on recognizing students for effort and improvement increased.
		Faculty developed "principles of recognition" for the school, which emphasized individual growth and development, rather than grades and competition.
		School "bumper stickers" changed from "Proud Parent of a Beta Middle School Honor Student" to "Proud Parent of a Beta Middle School Student."
Grouping	Is ability grouping an implicit or explicit policy? Is learning viewed as an individual and/or social constructive process?	Ability grouping was eliminated in the sixth grade.
		Ability grouping was eliminated in the seventh grade in all subjects except mathematics.

continued on next page

TABLE 2.1 *(continued)*

Examples of Mastery-Focused Practices Used in the Coalition

Target Area	Issues	Instructional Practices
		A "small house" was established at the sixth-grade level and a smaller experimental "small house" was established for the seventh graders, where students experienced team-teaching and some interdisciplinary units without ability grouping. Two teachers experimented with self-contained classrooms, which emphasized task-focused practices. The small house and self-contained classrooms served as enabling mechanisms.
Evaluation	What do assessment and "grading" procedures imply about school objectives?	The use of portfolios was discussed. Teachers expressed a desire to learn how to use portfolios for assessment to emphasize improvement.
Time	Is the 40- to 50-minute instructional period "sacred"? What flexibility is there for accommodating the need for larger blocks of time?	The number of bells between classes was reduced.
		Some block scheduling was implemented as teachers began to collaborate.
		Common planning time was initiated for small-house teachers and sixth-grade teachers working in teams.

Note. From E. Anderman, M. Maehr, and C. Midgley (1999). Copyright © 1999 by *Journal of Research and Development in Education*. Adapted by permission.

ferent associations with outcomes. This trend is marked most significantly by the distinction between the approach and avoidance components of performance goals (Elliot, 1997, 1999). It continues with recent suggestions for further distinctions. For example, Elliot and McGregor (2000) and Urdan (2000) suggested that a distinction could be made in performance-approach goals between an orientation that focuses on the "evaluative" component of these goals and an orientation that focuses on the "demonstrative" component. As these scholars argued, whereas an orientation that focuses on the evaluative component may be associated, at times, with negative patterns of learning, a focus on the demonstrative component may not show these negative associations and could be found to be an adaptive motivational orientation. In the case of mastery goals, Middleton (2001) suggested that a distinction can be made between the "thoughtful" component—that is, an orientation in which the student focuses on thinking and understanding—and

the "enjoyment" component—an orientation in which the student focuses on enjoying the activity for its own sake. Whereas both orientations are hypothesized to be associated with positive outcomes, it seems likely that the former would be associated more strongly with cognitive processes, whereas the latter would be associated more strongly with affective processes. Elliot (1999) also suggested that a distinction can be made between different components of mastery goals. He noted that mastery-oriented students may be oriented toward task-based or past-referential standards for competence evaluation. Being oriented to task-based standards is likely to lead the student to define success as doing well on the task. Being oriented to the past-referential standards is likely to lead the student to define success as making progress and improving over past performance.

The second trend includes those developments that look at the larger psychological processes within which achievement goals operate, and that involve a search for more general, parsimonious frameworks that would integrate achievement goal theory with other literatures. This trend can be seen in the work that attempts to generalize from the research on achievement goals to underlying motives (Elliot, 1997; Elliot & Church, 1997), to social cognition (e.g., Dweck, Chiu, & Hong, 1995a), to self- and identity processes (Kaplan & Flum, 2001; Maehr & Kaplan, 2000), and to general meaning-construction processes (Kaplan & Maehr, 2001; Molden & Dweck, 2000). Dweck (1999) and her colleagues (Dweck, Chiu, & Hong, 1995b), for example, have been developing a framework that relates achievement goals and a multitude of other processes such as interpersonal perception and judgment and social coping to people's theories concerning self-attributes such as intelligence, morality, and personality traits and whether these are fixed or malleable. Maehr and Kaplan (2000; Kaplan & Maehr, 2001) have been developing a framework that relates achievement goals and other types of social behaviors such as aggressive behavior and intergroup relations to self-processes such as self-awareness, self-development, and self-enhancement.

Conclusion

Currently, achievement goal theory is considered to be an influential framework for conceptualizing student motivation (Elliot, 1999; Pintrich, 1994) and it is being established as a dominant motivation theory in other fields as well (Button, Mathieu, & Zajac, 1996). Its strength is in its appeal to those who are interested in individual differences as well as to those who focus on socio-contextual influences and its explanatory power that provides a framework for interventions. Yet, as a theory it is still but a tool that, in the hands of psychologists and educators, serves to establish and sometimes reproduce so-

cial structures and world views. As such, it should always be evaluated in light of the social and ethical goals that are desirable and the visions of school and of society that are espoused.

REFERENCES

Ames, C. (1984). Competitive, cooperative, and individualistic goal structures: A cognitive-motivational analysis. In C. Ames & R. Ames (Eds.), *Research on motivation in education* (Vol. 1, pp. 177–207). New York: Academic Press.

Ames, C. (1990, April). *The relationship of achievement goals to student motivation in classroom settings.* Paper presented at the annual meeting of the American Educational Research Association, Boston.

Ames, C. (1992a). Achievement goals and the classroom motivational climate. In D. Schunk & J. Meece (Eds.), *Student perceptions in the classroom* (pp. 327–348). Hillsdale, NJ: Lawrence Erlbaum Associates.

Ames, C. (1992b). Classrooms: Goals, structures, and student motivation. *Journal of Educational Psychology, 84,* 261–271.

Ames, C., & Archer, J. (1987). Mothers' beliefs about the role of ability and effort in school learning. *Journal of Educational Psychology, 79,* 409–414.

Ames, C., & Archer, J. (1988). Achievement goals in the classroom: Student learning strategies and motivation processes, *Journal of Educational Psychology, 80,* 260–267.

Anderman, E. M., & Maehr, M. L. (1994). Motivation and schooling in the middle grades. *Review of Educational Research, 64,* 287–309.

Anderman, E., Maehr, M. L., & Midgley, C. (1999). Declining motivation after the transition to middle school: Schools can make a difference. *Journal of Research and Development in Education, 32,* 131–147.

Anderman, L. H. (1999). Classroom goal orientation, school belonging, and social goals as predictors of students' positive and negative affect following the transition to middle school. *Journal of Research and Development in Education, 32,* 89–103.

Anderman, L., & Anderman, E. M. (1999). Social predictors of changes in students' achievement goal orientations. *Contemporary Educational Psychology, 25,* 21–37.

Archer, J. (1994). Achievement goals as a measure of motivation in university students. *Contemporary Educational Psychology, 19,* 430–446.

Barron, K. E., & Harackiewicz, J. M. (1999). Achievement goals and optimal motivation: A multiple goals approach. In C. Sansone & J. Harackiewicz (Eds.), *Intrinsic and extrinsic motivation: The search for optimal motivation and performance* (pp. 229–254). San Diego: Academic Press.

Bouffard, T., Boisvert, J., Vezeau, C., & Larouche, C. (1995). The impact of goal orientation on self-regulation and performance among college students. *British Journal of Educational Psychology, 65,* 317–329.

Bouffard, T., Vezeau, C., & Bordeleau, L. (1998). A developmental study of the relation between combined learning and performance goals and students' self-regulated learning. *British Journal of Educational Psychology, 68,* 309–319.

Button, S. B., Mathieu, J. E., & Zajac, D. M. (1996). Goal orientation in organizational research: A conceptual and empirical foundation. *Organizational Behavior and Human Decision Processes, 67,* 26–48.

Church, M. A., Elliot, A. J., & Gable, S. (2001). Perceptions of classroom context, achievement goals, and achievement outcomes. *Journal of Educational Psychology, 93,* 43–54.

Dowson, M., & McInerney, D. M. (1997, March). *Psychological parameters of students' social and academic goals: A qualitative investigation.* Paper presented at the annual meeting of the American Educational Research Association, Chicago.

Duda, J. L., & Nicholls, J. G. (1992). Dimensions of achievement motivation in schoolwork and sport. *Journal of Educational Psychology, 84,* 290–299.

Dweck, C. S. (1986). Motivational processes affecting learning. *American Psychologist, 41,* 1040–1048.

Dweck, C. S. (1992). The study of goals in psychology. *Psychological Science, 3,* 165–167.

Dweck, C. S. (1999). *Self-theories: Their role in motivation, personality, and development.* Philadelphia, PA: Psychology Press.

Dweck, C. S., Chiu, C., & Hong, Y. (1995a). Implicit theories: Elaboration and extension of the model. *Psychological Inquiry, 6,* 322–333.

Dweck, C. S., Chiu, C., & Hong, Y. (1995b). Implicit theories and their role in judgments and reactions: A world from two perspectives. *Psychological Inquiry, 6,* 267–285.

Dweck, C. S., & Leggett, E. L. (1988). A social-cognitive approach to motivation and personality. *Psychological Review, 95,* 256–273.

Elliot, A. J. (1997). Integrating the "classic" and "contemporary" approaches to achievement motivation: A hierarchical model of approach and avoidance achievement motivation. In M. L. Maehr & P. R. Pintrich (Eds.), *Advances in motivation and achievement* (Vol. 10, pp. 143–179). Greenwich, CT: JAI.

Elliot, A. J. (1999). Approach and avoidance motivation and achievement goals. *Educational Psychologist, 34,* 169–189.

Elliot, A. J., & Church, M. A. (1997). A hierarchical model of approach and avoidance achievement motivation. *Journal of Personality and Social Psychology, 72,* 218–232.

Elliot, A. J., & Harackiewicz, J. M. (1996). Approach and avoidance achievement goals and intrinsic motivation: A mediational analysis. *Journal of Personality and Social Psychology, 70,* 461–475.

Elliot, A. J., & McGregor, H. A. (2000, April). *Approach and avoidance goals and autonomous-controlled regulation: Empirical and conceptual relations.* Paper presented at the annual meeting of the American Educational Research Association, New Orleans.

Elliott, E. S., & Dweck, C. S. (1988). Goals: An approach to motivation and achievement. *Journal of Personality and Social Psychology, 54,* 5–12.

Fuchs, L. S., Fuchs, D., Karns, K., Hamlett, C. L., Katzaroff, M., & Dutka, S. (1997). Effects of task-focused goals on low-achieving students with and without learning disabilities. *American Educational Research Journal, 34,* 513–543.

Fuligni, A. J., & Tseng, V. (1999). Family obligation and the academic motivation of adolescents from immigrant and American-born families. In T. Urdan (Ed.), *Advances in motivation and achievement* (Vol. 11, pp. 159–183). Greenwich, CT: JAI.

Fuligni, A. J., Tseng, V., & Lam, M. (1999). Attitudes toward family obligations among American adolescents with Asian, Latin American, and European Backgrounds. *Child Development, 70,* 1030–1044.

Garcia, E. E. (1992). "Hispanic" children: Theoretical, empirical, and related policy issues. *Educational Psychology Review, 4,* 69–94.

Gheen, M., & Midgley, C. (1999, April). *"I'd rather not do it the hard way": Student and classroom correlates of eighth graders' avoidance of academic challenge.* Paper presented at the meeting of the American Educational Research Association, Montreal.

Harackiewicz, J. M., Barron, K. E., & Elliot, A. J. (1998). Rethinking achievement goals: When are they adaptive for college students and why? *Educational Psychologist, 33,* 1–21.

Heyman, G. D., & Dweck, C. S. (1992). Achievement goals and intrinsic motivation: Their relation and their role in adaptive motivation. *Motivation and Emotion, 16,* 231–247.

Kaplan, A., & Bos, N. (1995, April). *Patterns of achievement goals and psychological well-being in young adolescents.* Poster session presented at the annual meeting of the American Educational Research Association, San Francisco.

Kaplan, A., & Flum, H. (2001). *Not on competence alone: Mastery goals and self-processes.* Manuscript in preparation.

Kaplan, A., Gheen, M., & Midgley, C. (in press). The classroom goal structure and student disruptive behavior. *British Journal of Educational Psychology.*

Kaplan, A., & Maehr, M. L. (1999). Achievement goals and student well-being. *Contemporary Educational Psychology, 24,* 330–358.

Kaplan, A., & Maehr, M. L. (2001). *The contributions and prospects of a goal orientation theory perspective on achievement motivation.* Manuscript submitted for publication.

Kaplan, A., & Midgley, C. (1997). The effect of achievement goals: Does level of perceived academic competence make a difference? *Contemporary Educational Psychology, 22,* 415–435.

Kaplan, A., & Midgley, C. (1999). The relationship between perceptions of the classroom goal structure and early adolescents' affect in school: The mediating role of coping strategies. *Learning and Individual Differences, 11,* 187–212.

Landrine, H. (1992). Clinical implications of cultural differences: The referential versus the indexical self. *Clinical Psychology Review, 12,* 401–415.

Lee, O., & Anderson, C. W. (1993). Task engagement and conceptual change in middle school science classrooms. *American Educational Research Journal, 30,* 585–610.

Levy, I., Kaplan, A., & Patrick, H. (2000, April). *Achievement goals, intergroup processes, and attitudes towards collaboration.* Poster session presented at the annual meeting of the American Educational Research Association, New Orleans.

Maehr, M. L. (1984). Meaning and motivation: Toward a theory of personal investment. In C. Ames & R. Ames (Eds.), *Research on motivation in education* (Vol. 1, pp. 115–144). New York: Academic Press.

Maehr, M. L., & Braskamp, L. A. (1986). *The motivation factor: A theory of personal investment.* Lexington, MA: Lexington.

Maehr, M. L., & Kaplan, A. (2000, April). *It might be all about self: Self-consciousness as an organizing scheme for integrating understandings from self-determination theory and achievement goal theory.* Paper presented at the annual meeting of the American Educational Research Association, New Orleans.

Maehr, M. L., & Midgley, C. (1996). *Transforming school cultures.* Boulder, CO: Westview Press.

Maehr, M. L., & Nicholls, J. G. (1980). Culture and achievement motivation: A second look. In N. Warren (Ed.), *Studies on cross-cultural psychology* (Vol. 2, pp. 221–267). New York: Academic Press.

Markus, H. R., & Kitayama, S. (1991). Culture and the self: Implications for cognition, emotion, and motivation. *Psychological Review, 98,* 224–253.

McInerney, D. M. (1995). Goal theory and indigenous minority school motivation: Relevance and application. In M. L. Maehr & P. R. Pintrich (Eds.), *Advances in motivation and achievement* (Vol. 10, pp. 153–181). Greenwich, CT: JAI.

McInerney, D. M., Hinkley, J., Dowson, M., & Van Etten, S. (1998). Aboriginal, Anglo, and immigrant Australian students' motivational beliefs about personal academic success: Are there cultural differences? *Journal of Educational Psychology, 90,* 621–629.

McInerney, D. M., Roche, L. A., McInerney, V., & Marsh, H. W. (1997). Cultural perspectives on school motivation: The relevance and application of goal theory. *American Educational Research Journal, 34,* 207–236.

Meece, J. L. (1991). The classroom context and students' motivational goals. In M. L. Maehr & P. R. Pintrich (Eds.), *Advances in motivation and achievement* (Vol. 7, pp. 261–285). Greenwich, CT: JAI.

Meece, J. L., Blumenfeld, P. C., & Hoyle, R. H. (1988). Students' goal orientations and cognitive engagement in classroom activities. *Journal of Educational Psychology, 80,* 514–523.

Meece, J. L., & Holt, K. (1993). A pattern analysis of students' achievement goals. *Journal of Educational Psychology, 85,* 582–590.

Middleton, M. (2001). *Mastery goals: A focus on developing interest or engagement?* Manuscript in preparation.

Middleton, M., Gheen, L., Hruda, L., & Midgley, C. (2000, August). *Classroom predictors of students' personal goals.* Paper presented at the annual meeting of the American Psychological Society, Boston.

Middleton, M. J., Kaplan, A., & Midgley, C. (2001). *The relations among middle school students' achievement goals in math over time.* Manuscript submitted for publication.

Middleton, M., Kaplan, A., Midgley, C., & Anderman, E. (2001). *Classroom goal structure: Perceiving an emphasis on multiple goals.* Manuscript in preparation.

Middleton, M., & Midgley, C. (1997). Avoiding the demonstration of lack of ability: An under-explored aspect of goal theory. *Journal of Educational Psychology, 89,* 710–718.

Midgley, C., Arunkumar, R., & Urdan, T. (1996). "If I don't do well tomorrow, there's a reason": Predictors of adolescents' use of academic self-handicapping strategies. *Journal of Educational Psychology, 88,* 423–434.

Midgley, C., Kaplan, A., & Middleton, M. J. (2001). Performance-approach goals: Good for what, for whom, under what circumstances, and at what cost? *Journal of Educational Psychology, 93,* 77–86.

Midgley, C., Kaplan, A., Middleton, M., Maehr, M. L., Urdan, T., Hicks Anderman, L., Anderman, E., & Roeser, R. (1998). The development and validation of scales assessing students' achievement goal orientations. *Contemporary Educational Psychology, 23,* 113–131.

Midgley, C., & Urdan, T. (2001). Academic self-handicapping and achievement goals: A further examination. *Contemporary Educational Psychology, 26,* 61–75.

Miller, R. B., Behrens, J. T., Greene, B. A., & Newman, D. (1993). Goals and perceived ability: Impact on student valuing, self-regulation, and persistence. *Contemporary Educational Psychology, 18,* 2–14.

Molden, D. C., & Dweck, C. S. (2000). Meaning and motivation. In C. Sansone & J. Harackiewicz (Eds.), *Intrinsic and extrinsic motivation: The search for optimal motivation and performance* (pp. 131–159). New York: Academic Press.

Moos, R. G. (1979). *Evaluating educational environments.* San Francisco: Jossey-Bass.

Nicholls, J. G. (1984). Achievement motivation: Conceptions of ability, subjective experience, task choice, and performance. *Psychological Review, 91,* 328–346.

Nicholls, J. G. (1989). *The competitive ethos and democratic education.* Cambridge, MA: Harvard University Press.

Nicholls, J. G. (1990). What is ability and why are we mindful of it? A developmental perspective. In R. Sternberg & J. Kolligian (Eds.), *Competence considered* (pp. 11–40). New Haven, CT: Yale University Press.

Nicholls, J. G., Cheung, P. C., Lauer, J., & Patashnick, M. (1989). Individual differences in academic motivation: Perceived ability, goals, beliefs, and values. *Learning and Individual Differences, 1,* 63–84.

Patrick, H., Anderman, L. H., Ryan, A. M., Edelin, K., & Midgley, C. (2001). Teachers' communication of goal orientations in four fifth-grade classrooms. *Elementary School Journal, 102,* 35–58.

Pintrich, P. R. (1994). Continuities and discontinuities: Future directions for research in educational psychology. *Educational Psychologist, 29,* 137–148.

Pintrich, P. R. (2000a). Multiple goals, multiple pathways: The role of goal orientation in learning and achievement. *Journal of Educational Psychology, 92,* 544–555.

Pintrich, P. R. (2000b). The role of goal orientation in self-regulated learning. In M. Boekarts, P. Pintrich, & M. Zeidner (Eds.), *Handbook of self-regulation: Theory, research and applications* (pp. 452–502). San Diego: Academic Press.

Pintrich, P. R., & De Groot, E. V. (1990). Motivational and self-regulated learning components of classroom academic performance. *Journal of Educational Psychology, 82,* 33–40.

Pintrich, P. R., & Garcia, T. (1991). Student goal orientation and self-regulation in the college classroom. In M. L. Maehr & P. R. Pintrich (Eds.), *Advances in motivation and achievement* (Vol. 7, pp. 371–402). Greenwich, CT: JAI.

Roeser, R. W., Midgley, C., & Urdan, T. C. (1996). Perceptions of the school psychological environment and early adolescents' psychological and behavioral functioning in school: The mediating role of goals and belonging. *Journal of Educational Psychology, 88,* 408–422.

Ryan, A. M., Gheen, M. H., & Midgley, C. (1998). Why do some students avoid asking for help? An examination of the interplay among students' academic efficacy, teachers' social-emotional role, and the classroom goal structure. *Journal of Educational Psychology, 90,* 1–8.

Skaalvik, E. M. (1997). Self-enhancing and self-defeating ego orientation: Relations with task and avoidance orientation, achievement, self-perceptions, and anxiety. *Journal of Educational Psychology, 89,* 71–81.

Steele, C. M. (1997). A threat in the air: How stereotypes shape the intellectual identities and performance of women and African Americans. *American Psychologist, 52,* 613–629.

Steele, C. M., & Aronson, J. (1995). Stereotype threat and the intellectual test performance of African Americans. *Journal of Personality and Social Psychology, 69,* 797–811.

Triandis, H. C. (1989). The self and social behavior in differing cultural contexts. *Psychological Review, 96,* 506–520.

Triandis, H. C., Leung, K., Villareal, M. J., & Clack, F. L. (1985). Allometric versus idiocentric tendencies: Convergent and discriminant validation. *Journal of Research in Personality, 19,* 395–415.

Turner, J. C., Meyer, D. K., Midgley, C., & Patrick, H. (2001). Teacher discourse and students' affect and achievement-related behaviors in two high mastery/high performance classrooms. Invited paper for a special issue on motivation for the *Elementary School Journal.*

Turner, J. C., Midgley, C., Meyer, D., Gheen, M., Anderman, E., Kang, Y., & Patrick, H. (2002). The classroom environment and students' reports of avoidance behaviors in mathematics: A multi-method study. *Journal of Education Psychology, 94.*

Urdan, T. (1996, April). *Examining students' multiple goals profiles.* Poster presented at the annual meeting of the American Educational Research Association, New York.

Urdan, T. (1997). Achievement goal theory: Past results, future directions. In P. R. Pintrich and M. L. Maehr (Eds.), *Advances in motivation and achievement* (Vol. 10, pp. 99–142). Greenwich, CT: JAI.

Urdan, T. (2000, April). *The intersection of self-determination and achievement goal theories: Do we need to have goals?* Paper presented at the annual meeting of the American Educational Research Association, New Orleans.

Urdan, T., Kneisel, L., & Mason, G. (1999). Interpreting messages about motivation in the classroom: Examining the effects of achievement goal structures. In T. Urdan (Ed.), *Advances in motivation and achievement* (Vol. 11, pp. 123–158). Greenwich, CT: JAI.

Urdan, T. C., & Maehr, M. L. (1995). Beyond a two-goal theory of motivation and achievement: A case for social goals. *Review of Educational Research, 65,* 213–243.

Urdan, T., Midgley, C., & Anderman, E. (1998). The role of classroom goal structure in students' use of self-handicapping strategies. *American Educational Research Journal, 35,* 101–122.

Urdan, T., Midgley, C., & Hruda, L. (2000). *Changes in the perceived classroom goal structure and patterns of adaptive learning during early adolescence.* Manuscript submitted for publication.

Vasquez, J. A. (1990). Teaching to the distinctive traits of minority students. *The Clearing House, 63,* 299–304.

Walberg, H., & Anderson, G. (1968). Classroom climate and individual learning. *Journal of Educational Psychology, 59,* 414–419.

Wentzel, K. R. (1992). Motivation and achievement in adolescence: A multiple goals perspective. In D. H. Schunk & J. Meece (Eds.), *Student perceptions in the classroom* (pp. 287–306). Hillsdale, NJ: Lawrence Erlbaum Associates.

White, R. W. (1959). Motivation re-considered: The concept of competence. *Psychological Review, 66,* 279–333.

Wolters, C. A., Yu, S. L., & Pintrich, P. R. (1996). The relation between goal orientation and students' motivational beliefs and self-regulated learning. *Learning and Individual Differences, 8,* 211–238.

3

Goals, Goal Structures, and Avoidance Behaviors

Tim Urdan
Santa Clara University

Allison M. Ryan
University of Illinois

Eric M. Anderman
University of Kentucky

Margaret H. Gheen
University of Michigan

OVERVIEW

Most research and discussion regarding motivation and motivated behavior in learning contexts such as classrooms and schools focuses on *approach* tendencies. Researchers, teachers, and parents are often concerned with encouraging students to more fully engage in academic work, to take academic risks, and to put more effort into their schoolwork. In other words, the concern is with helping students move *toward* engagement in the academic endeavor, hence the term approach tendencies or approach motivation. The flip side of the approach coin is *avoidance* tendencies, motivation, and behavior. Although approach tendencies have received the lion's share of the attention in motivation research, there is also a history of research and theory on avoidance motivation and has recently received more attention. In this chapter, we describe research, particularly the research we have conducted in conjunction with the Patterns of

Adaptive Learning Study, examining four different avoidance behaviors: self-handicapping, avoidance of help seeking, avoidance of challenge and novelty, and cheating.

All of these avoidance behaviors reflect motivation to move away from, or avoid, some perceived threat in the learning context. In some cases, failure is the perceived threat. For example, a student may worry that if she attempts a novel task, she will fail at it. Similarly, when taking a test a student may feel ill prepared and decide to cheat to avoid failing the exam. To fully understand avoidance behavior, however, it is not enough simply to realize that many students want to avoid failing. It is also important to understand *why* students try to avoid failure in school. One reason that students are concerned with not failing is because they want to avoid being perceived as academically unable, or as unintelligent. Self-handicapping and avoidance of help seeking are two behaviors that clearly represent a desire to avoid appearing unable to teachers, peers, parents, and perhaps one's self.

Avoidance behaviors are problematic because they often undermine student learning and performance in school. Learning and growth occur when students are willing to attempt moderately challenging tasks, even though they may initially fail at them. Similarly, learning is augmented by seeking and gaining the assistance of teachers and more knowledgeable peers when one needs help. Sometimes, as is the case with self-handicapping, students actually undermine their own performance by not trying, or by procrastinating, so that they can have a ready excuse other than lack of ability when and if they fail. These various strategies for avoiding failure or avoiding the appearance of academic inability are very distressing to educators and parents because they actually inhibit learning. There are few things more frustrating to teachers than being confronted with a student who actively and purposefully avoids learning opportunities. Increasingly, we are finding evidence that engaging in these frustrating avoidance behaviors may actually be encouraged by the motivational climate in the learning context.

In the remainder of this chapter, we provide some historical background regarding the study of avoidance motivation and then review the research generated from our longitudinal study regarding the correlates and consequences of these four avoidance behaviors. We focus particularly on the relations among personal achievement goals, classroom and school goal structures, and avoidance behaviors.

A BRIEF HISTORY OF AVOIDANCE
MOTIVES AND BEHAVIORS

References to avoidance motives can be found in early conceptualizations of achievement motivation, including those of Lewin and his colleagues (Lewin,

Dembo, Festinger, & Sears, 1944) and of Murray (1938). In these early models of motivation, the avoidance motive was posited to represent a desire, or a need, to avoid failure. Atkinson (1957) and McClelland (1951) also included the motive to avoid failure in their motivation models. Atkinson, in particular, described the specific role of the motive to avoid failure (M_{af}) in individuals' resultant tendencies, or achievement motivation. Specifically, he argued that the motive to avoid failure was a dispositional characteristic predisposing individuals to feel shame upon failure. When combined with the incentive value of avoiding failure and the perceived probability of failing, the motive to avoid failure would lead to avoidance behaviors or *tendencies* (i.e., T_{af}) that would inhibit achievement motivation. Atkinson also argued that avoidance tendencies were independent of approach tendencies, and that an individual's motivated behavior would be avoidance behavior if the avoidance tendency were stronger than the approach tendency for that particular achievement situation (for a good summary of this theory, see Elliot, 1997). A dispositional tendency toward avoiding failure, combined with a strong desire not to fail and a high perceived likelihood of failure should produce avoidance behaviors, according to Atkinson.

These early models of motivation generally defined avoidance motivation in stable, trait like ways. In the Atkinson model, for example, M_{af} was defined as the dispositional capacity to experience shame upon failure, and was a necessary component of avoidance behavior (T_{af}). In subsequent theories of motivation, there has been a greater emphasis on cognitive explanations for avoidance behaviors. For example, attribution theory (Weiner, 1985) posits that when students attribute their failure on an academic task to stable causes (particularly internal, stable causes, such as a lack of ability), they are more likely to avoid engaging in similar tasks in the future. Similarly, some motivation researchers have argued that avoidance motives and behaviors are at least partly attributable to the way that individuals conceive of intelligence. For example, Covington and his colleagues (Covington, 1992; Covington & Omelich, 1984) argued that a fundamental concern of people is to maintain their feelings of self-worth. Intelligence and, by extension, academic ability are core elements of people's self-perceptions. Therefore, when students perceive that they may fail at an academic activity, they also perceive a threat to their self-worth, because such a failure will expose their lack of intelligence or ability. This is particularly true when students try hard and still fail because in these instances lack of effort is not a possible explanation for their poor performance. For many students, then, effort and ability are perceived as inversely related. Avoidance behaviors (such as withdrawal of effort) will be likely to occur when students fear that trying hard and failing will be indicative of low ability, and threaten their self-worth.

Elements of self-worth theory and attribution theory have been adopted by goal theorists to explain avoidance motives and behaviors. Dweck and her col-

leagues (Dweck, 1986; Dweck & Leggett, 1988; Elliott & Dweck, 1988) argued that some students adopt a "helpless" pattern of attributions to explain their failure at a task. This helpless pattern includes making stable, internal attributions for failure, such as a lack of ability. Dweck further argued that one source of this helpless attributional pattern was a belief that intelligence was a fixed entity that could not be changed. Those students who failed at the task and believed that their failure was caused by their lack of ability were more likely to avoid engaging in similar tasks if they also believed that intelligence was a fixed entity. This is logical. Why should students try again if they believe their failure on the last task was caused by a lack of ability and they believe they cannot change how much ability they have? Nicholls (1990; Nicholls & Miller, 1984) found that in early childhood, children generally believe that intelligence can be increased through effort. However, in late childhood children begin to believe that intelligence and effort are inversely related, leading to ego-protective avoidance behaviors (like effort withdrawal) when they fear that failure on a task is indicative of intelligence or ability.

Recent Approaches to the Examination of Avoidance Goals

Although goal theorists such as Nicholls and Dweck clearly argued that there are avoidance goals distinct from approach goals, until recently avoidance goals have not received much attention. Most empirical examinations of goals from 1980 to 1995 focused on the distinction between mastery goals and performance goals, both conceptualized as approach motives (Elliot, 1997). Mastery goals represent a concern with *developing* competence through learning, mastering tasks and information, and improving knowledge and skills. Performance goals have generally been described as a concern with *demonstrating* competence by outperforming peers, finishing work quickly, and earning public recognition for academic achievement. Both of these goal orientations are thought to represent approach forms of motivation because both goals can be attained by successfully engaging in some achievement-related activity. One can neither develop nor demonstrate competence by avoiding the achievement activity. In much of the goal theory research conducted in the 1980s and early 1990s, using both experimental and survey designs, the goals of developing and demonstrating competence were measured or manipulated. But during the last 5 years, a concerted effort has begun to also examine students' concerns with *avoiding* the demonstration of inability. We call this a *performance-avoidance* goal orientation and distinguish it from the more commonly examined *performance-approach* goal (see chap. 1, this volume). There has also been some recent theorizing about mastery-avoidance goals (Pintrich, 2000). There is little empirical research on mastery-avoidance goals at this

point, so in this chapter we limit our consideration of avoidance goals to performance-avoidance goals.

Although there are examples of avoidance goals in the literature before 1995 (e.g., Nicholls' "work avoidance" goals discussed in Nicholls, Patashnick, & Nolen, 1985), these goals either were not competence based or were not included very often in goal theory research. In 1996, however, Elliot and Harackiewicz published an article in which they described the experimental manipulation of mastery, performance-approach, and performance-avoidance goals, finding that participants in the performance-approach and performance-avoidance goal conditions differed in their levels of intrinsic motivation and task absorption. Specifically, students in the performance-approach condition did not differ from students in the mastery condition, but both of these groups were higher than students in the performance-avoidance condition on intrinsic motivation and task absorption measures. In subsequent research by Elliot and his colleagues (Elliot, 1997; Elliot & Church, 1997) and others (Middleton & Midgley, 1997; Skaalvik, 1997), a pattern has emerged indicating that whereas performance-avoidance goals are associated with negative educational and motivational outcomes (e.g., low achievement, low perceptions of ability, greater avoidance behavior), a more complex set of positive and negative correlates of performance-approach goals has emerged (Midgley, Kaplan, & Middleton, 2001; Urdan, 1997).

The recent research that has separated the approach and avoidance dimensions of performance goals has greatly enhanced our understanding of the relations among students' motivational orientations and their performance, behavior, and cognitions in school. In the following section of this chapter, we describe our own research using achievement goal theory as the framework for examining four different avoidance behaviors that students sometimes use in school. We begin by defining the four behaviors and preferences (self-handicapping, avoidance of help seeking, preference for avoiding novelty, and cheating) and then summarize the relations among these behaviors, students' personal achievement goals, and goals emphasized in students' learning environments (goal structures).

OUR RESEARCH EXAMINING AVOIDANCE BEHAVIORS AND PREFERENCES

Defining Avoidance Behaviors and Preferences

Self-handicapping, avoidance of help seeking, avoidance of novelty, and cheating all share two characteristics. First, they are united by their common avoidance component in that each represents movement away from, rather than toward, activity that will produce learning, achievement, and competence. Second, each represents an action, or the inclination to act, that is intentional

and goal directed. To achieve the goal of avoiding failure, shame, and the appearance of inability, the student must purposefully engage in a behavior (e.g., cheat) or purposefully not engage in a behavior (e.g., avoid seeking help). It is important to note that for the purposes of this chapter, behaviors such as failing to seek help when it is needed or failing to study for an upcoming exam or preferring not to do a math problem in a novel way (assumed to be related to behavior), that is, purposeful *inaction*, are all considered avoidance behaviors because they are all examples of inaction for the purpose of achieving the goal of avoiding appearing academically unable. We now define each of these behaviors in turn.

Self-Handicapping. Berglas and Jones (1978), commonly regarded as the modern pioneers of self-handicapping research, defined it as "any action or choice of performance setting that enhances the opportunity to externalize (or excuse) failure, thus enabling the individual to avoid or discount negative implications of [poor] performance" (p. 202). This definition implies that handicapping is an active process; individuals must actually do something. It also implies that the purpose of the action is to create some explanation for a potential poor performance that is external to the individual. As the name implies, self-handicapping generally involves engaging in some action that may inhibit performance (e.g., not studying for an exam). One potential by-product of such an action is that, if one somehow succeeds despite the handicap, there may be some augmenting of self-esteem. Garcia (1995) noted that self-handicapping is a self-regulatory strategy designed to regulate one's affective response to poor performance. Covington (1992) made a similar suggestion, arguing that handicapping is a strategy students use to maintain self-worth by avoiding looking stupid when they perform poorly in school.

A wide variety of behaviors and feelings have been listed as possible self-handicaps, including test anxiety, social anxiety, procrastination, lack of effort or practice, illness, shyness, excuses, moodiness, drug or alcohol use, lack of sleep, and over involvement with friends or activities (see Higgins, Snyder, & Berglas, 1990, for a table summarizing those studies). Although self-handicapping is closely related to attributions, there are important distinctions. Because self-handicapping is a proactive attempt to manipulate others' perceptions of the causes of performance outcomes, it provides the *basis* for an attribution; it is not the attribution itself. For example, saying that you did not do well because you were tired is an attribution; whereas deliberately staying up late in order to use lack of sleep as an excuse in case you should do poorly is a self-handicapping strategy. Students may make attributions that are private and not meant to influence others' judgments of their ability in any way. Studies in which researchers ask students if they would attribute success or failure to different outcomes based on whether they were explaining the results to adults or peers (e.g., Juvonen &

Murdock, 1993) have more in common with handicapping studies. They are similar because both represent attempts to influence others' perceptions regarding the causes of poor performance. They differ in that handicapping involves a behavior, aimed at avoiding the appearance of incompetence that *precedes* performance and can undermine performance.

We have developed a six-item, paper-and-pencil measure of self-handicapping (see Appendix). One sample item from this scale is "Some students purposely don't try hard in school so that if they don't do well, they can say it's because they didn't try. How true is this for you?" This item includes the behavior (effort withdrawal), the reason (to use effort withdrawal as an excuse), and the a priori timing of the strategy (reduced effort *before* low academic achievement). It is not an excuse made up after low achievement occurs. All of the items in the self-handicapping scale have these same features. This is important because it is these three elements (the behavior, the reason for the behavior, and the timing of the behavior) that distinguish self-handicapping behavior from other types of behaviors (e.g., simply making excuses for low performance, reducing effort due to boredom or fatigue, etc.).

Clearly, self-handicapping represents a form of avoidance behavior in that it often involves a reduction of effort and an undermining of performance. Just as the expectancy-value models of Atkinson and his colleagues suggested that approach tendencies would decrease as expectancy for success decreased, researchers have established that self-handicapping behaviors are elicited when expectancies for success are low. Although self-handicapping involves avoidance behaviors and low expectancies for success, it should be noted that there appears to be a distinct approach element to self-handicapping as well. Attempts to manipulate attributions regarding the causes of high or low performance on a task require some personal investment in the task. If students do not care about, or identify with, their performance on a test, there is no need to self-handicap. Indeed, research has shown that people are more likely to self-handicap when they consider the task important and relevant, such as one that is diagnostic of intelligence or academic ability (Shepperd & Arkin, 1989).

Avoidance of Help Seeking. At some time during their educational careers, all students are confronted with situations when they need help in the classroom. Whether they are unsure about procedural issues (e.g., how to complete an assignment) or confused about the material (e.g., their answer differs from the teacher's answer to a math problem), when students become aware that they need help, they must decide whether to actually seek help. Considerable research has identified this stage as a critical juncture in the overall help-seeking process. Dillon (1988) wrote "95 percent of the questions that we have in mind to ask we never go on to utter ... we may think the better of it and follow one of the numerous other paths available. These include keeping quiet and giving off that we

know and understand" (p. 20). It is this juncture in the help-seeking process that our research has focused on: the decision to avoid asking for help when students know they need help. For example, a student might skip a problem altogether or put down any answer rather than ask for help.

We are interested in this decision to avoid help seeking because when students do not garner help when it is needed, they put themselves at a disadvantage for learning and performance. Help seeking is an important self-regulatory strategy that contributes to student learning (Karabenick & Sharma, 1994; Newman, 1994; Zimmerman & Martinez-Pons, 1988). Inevitably, students will encounter ambiguity or difficulty in their schoolwork and need assistance. In such a situation, it is adaptive for students to use others as a resource to secure the necessary help and continue the learning process (McCaslin & Good, 1996).

Our survey items for measuring avoidance of help seeking were developed by Ryan (Ryan & Pintrich, 1997) and are included in the Appendix. A sample item is "I don't ask questions in math class, even when I don't understand the lesson." All of the items refer to instances when a student (a) has identified that she needs help and (b) chooses not to seek it. Thus, all help-seeking items are worded in the conditional sense (e.g., "If I need help with my math work" or "when I don't understand the lesson") to control for students' need for help (Arbreton, 1993; Karabenick & Knapp, 1991; Newman, 1991).

Avoidance of Novelty and Challenge.   Why do some students avoid novel and challenging work? This question has important implications for educational practice and learning. Constructivist theories of education such as those proposed by Vygotsky (1978) argue that learning is optimal when individuals engage in tasks lying just beyond their present capabilities. The importance of challenge also is noted in theories of optimal motivation, wherein students achieve "flow" in their work when the challenges of the task, students' efficacy, and students' skill are in balance (e.g., Csikszentmihaly, 1982). Others note that challenging tasks provide important information about improvement and therefore are integral for maintaining self-efficacy (Bandura, 1986) and intrinsic motivation (Deci, 1975). Although teachers are often encouraged to create academic work that is moderately challenging for all students, they often find that students actively resist engaging in such activities because there is a real possibility that they may fail. Not all students seek out challenging and novel work when such academic opportunities present themselves, and others may outright avoid it (Brophy, 1998; Covington, 1992; Meyer, Turner, & Spencer, 1997). Students may avoid challenging work to protect themselves from shame by increasing the probability of good performance, although poor performance after an easy task is particularly threatening (Atkinson & Raynor, 1974; Kuhl, 1978).

Clifford (1984) distinguished among several related features of challenge seeking. Three subscales of the School Failure Tolerance measure assessed

students' preference for difficult tasks (e.g., "I like to try difficult assignments even if I get some wrong"), affect after failure (e.g., "I feel terrible when I make a mistake in school"), and flexible use of strategies when making mistakes (e.g., "When I make mistakes in my schoolwork I just keep trying and trying"). Meyer and her colleagues (1997) used Clifford's measure in their study of fifth- and sixth-grade students. They found that compared to challenge seekers, challenge avoiders reported higher negative affect after failure, were more performance oriented, and had lower self-efficacy.

Research suggests that avoidance of challenge may be related to motives and goals in somewhat complex ways. Elliott and Dweck (1988), in an experimental study, found that when children were oriented toward mastery goals they were more likely to choose tasks described as challenging and offering opportunities to learn, regardless of their level of perceived ability. But when students were oriented toward performance goals, they chose challenging tasks that served to enhance others' high opinions of their abilities only if they perceived their ability to be high. Children who perceived their ability to be low and were oriented toward performance goals, in contrast, tended to choose tasks described as easy but that would avoid unfavorable judgments of their ability. Some students may feel they are in a double-bind, preferring easy work that does not threaten their self-worth, yet taking on difficult tasks in order to demonstrate their competence or superiority (Brophy, 1998; Covington & Omelich, 1979). Elliot and Church (1997) found that performance-approach goals were positively associated with measures of both challenge-avoidance (fear of failure) and challenge-seeking motives (achievement motivation). Avoidance of challenge, then, appears to be positively associated with performance-avoidance goals and negatively related with mastery goals, but may have a more complex relationship with performance-approach goals.

In our work, we have assessed avoidance of novelty and challenge through students' self-reports. As the items in the Appendix indicate, we have measured students' preferences for avoiding novelty and challenge rather than reports of their actual avoidance behaviors. Indeed, the items assess preference for avoiding novelty more than preference for avoiding challenge, but we see these constructs as conceptually similar. Example items include "I would prefer doing math problems the usual way, rather than try something different" and "I would choose math problems I knew I could do, rather than those that might be a challenge."

Cheating.   Cheating is such a widespread and embedded part of the academic experience that it may need no definition: Everyone knows what cheating is. But in the context of this chapter, there are two questions that must be addressed regarding the definition of cheating: Is cheating an avoidance behavior? And how have we measured it?

Cheating is related to avoidance behaviors such as self-handicapping, avoiding academic novelty and challenge, and avoiding help seeking in several ways; however, there also are important differences that distinguish cheating as a somewhat different type of behavior. The main similarity is that both avoidance behaviors and cheating can be used by students when they are not performing well academically or fear that they may not perform well. If avoidance behaviors are driven by avoidance motives such as fear of failure and wanting to avoid the feelings of shame that accompany failure, then cheating is certainly an avoidance behavior if done for these reasons. There are a number of methods that students can choose to avoid appearing academically unable, and cheating is one of them.

It is important to note that cheating behavior also differs from other avoidance behaviors in some important ways. Anderman, Griesinger, and Westerfield (1998) argued that cheating differs from self-handicapping in that self-handicapping strategies can be used to *explain* one's poor academic performance, whereas by cheating, students actually can unfairly *improve* academic performance. Whereas self-handicapping and avoidance of help seeking actually undermine academic achievement, cheating is designed to raise students' achievement levels, if not their actual mastery of the material. Another distinction between cheating and other avoidance behaviors is that the motives that direct cheating behavior are not always avoidance motives. Students may cheat because they want to get good grades for the sake of gaining acceptance to a prestigious college. In such instances, students are concerned with gaining some desired outcome rather than with avoiding failure and embarrassment.

We have measured cheating behaviors and attitudes students have about cheating using the items in the Appendix. Items such as "I cheat on my math work" refer to students' actual behaviors, whereas "Is it okay to cheat on math work?" are indicative of students' acceptance of cheating behavior.

ANTECEDENTS, CONSEQUENCES, AND CORRELATES OF AVOIDANCE BEHAVIORS

Over the past several years members of our research team have conducted a number of studies examining these four avoidance behaviors. In this section of the chapter, we review this research focusing particularly on three areas: (a) the relations between personal goal orientations and avoidance behaviors, (b) the relations between goals emphasized in the learning environment (i.e., classroom- and school-level goal structures) and avoidance behaviors, and (c) additional correlates of avoidance behaviors. Although a number of scholars have examined these issues, in this chapter we limit our review primarily to our own research. A summary of the results of our studies is presented in Table 3.1.

TABLE 3.1

Summary of Results for Analyses Examining Avoidance Behaviors

Behavior	Reference	Results
Self-handicapping	1. Midgley & Urdan, 1995	1. Self-handicapping was negatively related to academic achievement (grade point average—GPA), positively related to extrinsic goals, and to associating with friends who did not value academic achievement. Not related to mastery or performance goals or school goal structures.
	2. Midgley, Arunkumar, & Urdan, 1996	2. Self-handicapping was positively related to performance-approach goals for African American but not for Euro-American students. GPA was negatively related to handicapping. Neither self-esteem nor mastery goals predicted self-handicapping.
	3. Urdan, Midgley & Anderman 1998 (Wave 2a)	3. Self-handicapping was higher among boys low-achievers and students with lower perceived academic competence. Students' perceptions of the classroom performance goal structure and teachers' reports of using instructional practices that reflected performance goals both positively predicted students' self-handicapping.
	4. Midgley & Urdan 2001 (Wave 6a)	4. Self-handicapping was predicted by personal performance-avoidance but not performance-approach goals. Classroom performance goal structure also predicted self-handicapping. Both personal mastery goals and classroom mastery goal structures were negatively related to self-handicapping. Students high in performance-avoidance goal orientation handicapped more than those low in performance-avoidance goals regardless of level of mastery goals. When low in performance-avoidance goals, students high in mastery goal orientation handicapped less than those low in mastery goals.
Avoidance of help seeking	5. Ryan & Pintrich, 1997.	5. Avoidance of help seeking negatively related to academic self-efficacy, academic achievement, and mastery goals and positively related to performance-approach goals.
	6. Ryan, Hicks, & Midgley, 1997 (Wave 1a)	6. Avoidance of help seeking negatively related to academic self-efficacy, academic achievement, and mastery goals and positively related to performance-approach goals, particularly among students with lower GPAs. It is positively related to having a social status goal orientation and negatively related to social intimacy goals.

continued on next page

TABLE 3.1 *(continued)*

Summary of Results for Analyses Examining Avoidance Behaviors

Behavior	Reference	Results
	7. Ryan, Gheen, & Midgley, 1998 (Wave 5[a])	7. Classrooms differed significantly in students' reports of avoidance of help seeking. Perceived mastery classroom goal structure associated with less avoidance of help seeking. The relationship between students' academic self-efficacy and avoidance of help seeking was weaker in classrooms where teachers were perceived to be concerned with students' social and emotional needs.
	8. Middleton & Midgley, 1999 (Wave 7[a])	8. Avoidance of help seeking was negatively related to personal mastery goals and positively related to personal performance-approach goals.
Avoidance of challenge	1. Gheen & Midgley, 1999 (Wave 7[a])	9. Avoidance of challenge was negatively related to students' academic self-efficacy, but this relationship was stronger in classrooms where teachers reported making relative ability information salient and weaker in classrooms where teachers encouraged students to discuss ways to improve their work (informative social comparison). Perceived classroom mastery goal structure was negatively related to avoidance of challenge but perceived classroom performance goal structure was positively related to avoidance of challenge.
	2. Middleton & Midgley, 1999 (Wave 7[a])	10. Avoidance of challenge was negatively related to personal mastery goals and positively related to personal performance-approach goals.
Cheating	3. Anderman, Griesenger, & Westerfield, 1998	11. Self-reported cheating levels were higher among students who perceived their schools emphasized performance goals and their classrooms emphasized extrinsic goals. Students were more likely to believe that cheating was acceptable if they were extrinsically oriented and perceived their classroom to be extrinsically oriented. Cheating behaviors and attitudes were positively related to self-handicapping.

[a]Denotes studies in which participants were part of our Patterns of Adaptive Learning Longitudinal Research Project (described in chap. 1, this volume). Wave 1 = fall of fifth grade, Wave 2 = spring of fifth grade, Wave 3 = fall of sixth grade, Wave 4 = spring of sixth grade, Wave 5 = fall of seventh grade (a smaller subsample participated at this wave), Wave 6 = spring of seventh grade, Wave 7 = spring of eighth grade, and Wave 8 = spring of ninth grade.

Avoidance Behaviors and Personal Goal Orientations

To distinguish students' individual goal pursuits from the goals that are emphasized and made salient in the learning environment, we have adopted the terms
personal goals or *personal goal orientations* to refer to the former and *goal
structures* to refer to the latter. Our examinations of the associations between
personal goals and avoidance behaviors have focused primarily on mastery
and performance-approach goals. In some of our studies, however, we have
also examined extrinsic goals (Anderman et al., 1998; Ryan & Pintrich, 1997)
and performance-avoidance goals (Middleton & Midgley, 1997; Midgley &
Urdan, 2001).

As expected, across avoidance behaviors, personal mastery goal orientations
have either been unrelated or negatively related to avoidance behaviors. Midgley
and Urdan (2001) found that personal mastery goals were negatively related to
self-handicapping among a sample of seventh grade students. Similarly, Ryan and
her colleagues found a negative relationship between personal mastery goals and
avoidance of help seeking, indicating that students are less likely to avoid seeking
the help they need when they are higher in their personal mastery goal orientation
(Ryan & Pintrich, 1997; Ryan, Hicks, & Midgley, 1997). Although the research
examining the relations among mastery goals and avoidance of help seeking has
consistently revealed a negative relationship between these constructs in our research as well as others (e.g., Butler & Neuman, 1995; Newman, 1991, 1994), evidence of this negative relationship is not as consistent for the other avoidance
behaviors we have examined. Midgley and Urdan found that mastery goals were
negatively related to self-handicapping in their most recent study, but they found
no relation between these variables in their three studies of self-handicapping conducted previously. Similarly, we have not found a significant relationship between
personal mastery goals and cheating (Aderman et al., 1998). This is somewhat
puzzling given that mastery goals represent a desire for learning, improvement,
and mastery of the material. Such a goal orientation should lead students to avoid
behaviors that undermine learning (i.e., handicapping) and to disdain cheating, but
such relations have often not been found in our data.

Because avoidance behaviors reflect an underlying fear of failure and concern with appearing unintelligent or academically unable, they should perhaps
be more strongly associated with performance goals than with mastery goals.
In our research, we have found that all of the avoidance behaviors except for
cheating are, in fact, associated positively with performance goals. However,
because we did not separate performance goals into approach and avoidance
dimensions until recently, several of our studies included only the performance-approach goal dimension and therefore produced somewhat inconsistent results. As with the results involving personal mastery goals, our studies

involving avoidance of help seeking have consistently demonstrated a relationship between personal performance-approach goals and avoidance of help seeking. Students with a performance-approach goal orientation are concerned about how others will evaluate them because external evaluation will determine how they compare to others. This goal orientation increases the threat to competency associated with help seeking and increases the avoidance of help seeking (Butler & Neuman, 1995; Newman 1991, 1994; Ryan et al., 1997; Ryan & Pintrich, 1997). Interestingly, Ryan et al. found that the relation between adolescents' performance-approach goal orientation and their help-seeking behavior was strongest among low-achieving students. Thus, when students adopt a goal to outperform others but receive information that they are not achieving that goal, they are particularly vulnerable to negative perceptions about help seeking and more likely to avoid it. These findings, which support the results of an experimental study by Butler and Neuman, are troubling but provide insight into which students in the classroom do not seek help when they need it. Because lower achieving students feel more threatened and report more avoidance of help seeking when needed than do higher achieving students, it appears that the very students who need help the most seek it the least, and a performance goal orientation exacerbates the situation.

Midgley and Urdan (1995, 2001) found a null relationship between performance-approach goals and the use of handicapping strategies, but did find a positive relationship between self-handicapping and performance-avoidance goals in the more recent study. In a study of eighth-grade students, we found a positive relationship between performance-approach goals and self-handicapping for African American students but a null relationship for Euro-American students (Midgley, Arunkumar, & Urdan, 1996). Middleton and Midgley (1999) found that performance-approach goals were positively related to avoidance of novelty and challenge. In a separate study, Middleton and Midgley (1997) also found that performance-avoidance goals were more strongly related to avoidance of help seeking than were performance-approach goals.

Taken together, these results suggest three important points regarding the association between avoidance behaviors and preferences, and the most commonly examined personal goal orientations. First, it appears that personal performance goals are more strongly related to avoidance behaviors and preferences than are mastery goals. This is particularly true for self-handicapping, cheating, and avoidance of novelty and challenge. Second, avoidance behaviors and preferences may be more strongly and consistently associated with performance-avoidance goals than with performance-approach goals, although our research suggests that both types of performance goals are associated with avoidance behaviors and preferences. As Elliot and his colleagues have noted, both performance-approach and performance-avoidance goals are associated with fear of failure (Elliot, 1997; Elliot & Church, 1997). Because avoidance be-

haviors and preferences are also rooted in fear and shame associated with academic failure, we would expect these behaviors and preferences to be related to both the approach and avoidance dimensions of performance goals. Third, the association between performance-approach goals and avoidance behaviors appears to be particularly complex. Our results indicate that such variables as achievement level, perceived competence, and ethnicity moderate the relation between performance-approach goals and avoidance behaviors and preferences.

Extrinsic goals are another type of goal that we have included in some of our research on avoidance behaviors. Extrinsic goals represent students' concerns with obtaining some sort of reward for their academic efforts (such as a high grade) or avoiding some unpleasant consequence of poor achievement (such as getting in trouble with the teacher). Midgley and Urdan (1995) found that extrinsic goals were positively related to self-handicapping among eighth-grade students. Similarly, Anderman and his colleagues (1998) found that students higher in their endorsement of extrinsic goals were more likely to believe that cheating was acceptable. Ryan and Pintrich (1997) found that students who endorsed extrinsic goals were more likely to worry that the teacher would think they lacked ability if they asked for help and accordingly were more likely to report that they avoided help seeking. As students' perceptions of competence decreased, the endorsement of extrinsic goals was associated with higher levels of worry about what the teacher would think if they asked for help. Thus, students who did their math work to stay out of trouble or receive rewards and believed they were not particularly competent at their math were particularly vulnerable to worries about others' reactions if they asked for help.

Avoidance Behaviors and Contextual Goal Structures

In the learning environments of classrooms and schools, students are exposed to and perceive various messages about the purposes of achievement. For example, students can perceive that in their classroom or school, there is an emphasis on learning, understanding, and improvement (a mastery goal structure). Similarly, they can perceive messages that suggest that getting the highest grades on the test and outperforming their classmates are valued most in the classroom or school (a performance goal structure). Sometimes, these perceptions are influenced by teacher practices that emphasize a mastery or performance goal structure, such as when teachers post only the work of the highest achieving students in the class (performance-goal-oriented instructional practices). In our research we have examined how students' avoidance behaviors are related to the goal structures in classrooms and schools. In addition to mastery and performance goal structures and instructional practices, we have explored the relations among some of these avoidance behaviors and ex-

trinsic classroom goal structures as well as the social environment of the classroom.

Because avoidance behaviors represent a concern with avoiding failure and/or appearing academically unable, we would expect a performance goal structure to be more strongly related to avoidance behaviors than would a mastery goal structure. Moreover, we would expect the relationship between avoidance behaviors and contextual goal structures to be positive for performance goal structures and negative or null for mastery goal structures. For the most part, our results have confirmed these expectations. For example, our studies of self-handicapping have revealed that the perceived school performance goal structure is weakly, positively related to self-handicapping among a sample of middle school students (Midgley & Urdan, 1995) and that the perceived classroom performance goal structure is a positive predictor of self-handicapping among a sample of fifth grade students (Urdan, Midgley, & Anderman, 1998) and the same sample 2 years later when they were in seventh grade (Midgley & Urdan, 2001). In addition, teachers' reports of their performance-goal-oriented approaches to instruction also positively predicted self-handicapping (Urdan et al., 1998). Although mastery goal structures were also included in these analyses, they emerged as a significant, negative predictor of handicapping in only our most recent study (Midgley & Urdan, 2001). There was no relationship between mastery goal structures and self-handicapping in the other studies.

Ryan, Gheen, and Midgley (1998) used multilevel analyses to investigate how the classroom goal structure related to avoidance of help seeking. They examined differential patterns of help avoidance across 63 seventh-grade math classrooms. First, students' reported levels of avoidance of help seeking did vary across classrooms. Thus, some classrooms were characterized by higher levels of help avoidance than others. They then explored whether this variability in levels of help avoidance could be explained by the classroom goal structure. Students' perceptions of a mastery classroom goal structure were associated with a lower level of help avoidance whereas their perceptions of a performance classroom goal structure were associated with a higher level of help avoidance. In classrooms where students perceived that the focus was on understanding, mastery, and the intrinsic value of learning, compared to classrooms where the focus was on competition and proving one's ability, students were less likely to avoid seeking help with their work when they needed it.

Gheen and Midgley (1999) examined the relations among classroom goal structures and the avoidance of novelty and challenge. As with the examinations of self-handicapping and avoidance of help seeking, they examined students' perceptions of the classroom mastery and performance goal structures. In addition, they examined two separate dimensions of teachers' performance goal practices. Teachers may indicate that students should share work in order to "see who got the right answer" or to "get hints for when you have difficulty."

The former represents social comparison for *relative ability* purposes, and the latter presents social comparison as a way of *acquiring information* about the task. Among a sample of 325 eighth-grade math students and 10 math teachers in 24 classrooms, they examined whether student reports of avoiding challenging and novel academic tasks were related to students' perceptions of the classroom goal structure (mastery and performance) and teachers' reports of their encouragement of social comparison (for relative ability or task-information purposes).

They found that students' perceptions of the goal structure related to avoidance of novelty and challenge. When students perceived that their classrooms emphasized mastery goals, they reported lower levels of avoidance, but when they perceived their classrooms emphasized performance goals, they were more likely to say they preferred to avoid novel and challenging work. Furthermore, Gheen and Midgley (1999) examined how teachers' reports of social comparison practices related to avoiding novelty and challenge. They found that teachers' reports of informative social comparison practices related to slightly higher levels of avoidance. However, these practices weakened the association between self-efficacy and avoiding novelty and challenge. In classrooms where teachers were high in their use of interstudent discussion about how to improve one's own work, low- and high-efficacy students were on a more equal footing when it came to avoiding novelty challenge. However, in classrooms where teachers reported using high levels of relative ability social comparison practices, low self-efficacy students' avoidance was higher than that of high self-efficacy students'.

In their study of cheating behaviors and attitudes among early adolescent students, Anderman and his colleagues (1998) included measures of the perceived goal structures at the school and classroom levels. They found that higher incidences of self-reported cheating were related to perceiving middle schools as emphasizing performance goals and perceiving their classrooms as being extrinsically oriented. They also found that perceptions of an extrinsically oriented classroom environment were related to the belief that cheating is acceptable. Overall, results of this study suggest that cheating is more likely to occur and to be viewed as acceptable when students perceived an emphasis on extrinsic outcomes. Actual cheating behaviors may be more likely to occur when schools are perceived as emphasizing performance goals.

Avoidance Behaviors and Additional Related Variables

Our research examining avoidance behaviors has included a variety of variables in addition to goals and goal structures. In a number of our studies, for example, we have found that avoidance behaviors are associated with low academic achievement and low perceptions of ability (e.g., Midgley &

Urdan, 1995; Ryan & Pintrich, 1997; Ryan et al., 1997; Urdan et al., 1998). In some of these studies, the relationship between academic self-efficacy (or perceived competence) and the avoidance behavior was mediated by contextual factors, such as whether the teacher encouraged students to seek relative ability or task-relevant information (e.g., Gheen & Midgley, 1999) and whether teachers were perceived to be concerned with students' emotional and social well-being (Ryan et al., 1998; see also chap. 4, this volume). The social component of avoidance of help seeking was also demonstrated by Ryan and her colleagues (1997). They found that students concerned with gaining social status were more likely to avoid seeking help whereas those concerned with developing intimate social relationships were less likely to avoid seeking help. In some studies, demographic variables were found related to the avoidance behavior, but such findings were not consistent. For example, Urdan and his colleagues (1998) found that boys reported engaging in handicapping more than did girls, but significant gender differences were not found in our other studies of handicapping. Similarly, race and achievement level were found to moderate the relations between personal performance goals and avoidance behaviors in some studies (e.g., Midgley et al., 1996; Ryan et al., 1998), but not others. More research is needed to understand these complex relationships, including the processes through which goals and goal structures influence avoidance behaviors and how these processes may differ depending on the characteristics of the students.

IMPLICATIONS FOR PRACTICE

When discussing the issue of student motivation with teachers, we have often heard teachers describe the frustration they feel when working with students who engage in one or more of these avoidance behaviors. There is little that is more frustrating to teachers than when students perform beneath their capabilities. This frustration stems from two sources. First, teachers are aware that when students self-handicap, cheat, fail to seek help when they need it, and avoid the types of challenging and novel academic tasks that produce real learning, they are undermining their own learning and development. Over time, such behavior can produce a self-perpetuating cycle of academic failure and increased avoidance (Zuckerman, Kieffer, & Knee, 1998). Second, teachers are often unsure of what they can or should do to reduce their students' reliance on avoidance behaviors. In this section of the chapter, we present some suggestions, based on our research results, for reducing students' engagement in avoidance behaviors in the classroom.

Collectively, the results of our studies suggest that avoidance behavior is more common in schools and classrooms that emphasize performance goals, primarily by making ability differences between students and competition sa-

lient features of the learning environment. These results are intuitive. When students find themselves in learning environments that promote social comparison and make ability differences between students salient, it makes sense that they will be concerned with looking able compared to others. For those students who fear or expect that they may not compare favorably with their classmates, the adoption of strategies to avoid such negative social comparisons is to be expected. For educators interested in reducing avoidance behavior, then, a logical starting point may be to reduce the emphasis on performance goals and social comparison information in the classroom.

But how can this be done? As many teachers have told us, students (particularly adolescents) are naturally curious about how they compare to their peers and will engage in social comparison activities on their own. Although this is true and, arguably, an important way of discovering one's strengths and weaknesses in various domains, the goal of teachers should be to reduce the *emphasis* on performance goals in the classroom, not to eliminate all social comparison behavior among students. One way that teachers can do this is to reduce the amount of relative ability information that they provide to students. For example, when teachers publicly rank-order students (e.g., by posting an ordered list of students' test scores on the board or announcing what "place" each student occupies in the race to read the most books), they send the message to students that where they stand relative to other students is more important than the quality of their work or how much they have learned and improved over time. Similarly, when teachers offer rewards or special privileges to only the highest achievers in the class (e.g., allowing students with the top three scores on the history test to skip the next homework or only letting the "A" students hand out papers), they send the message that there is an ability hierarchy in the class and those with the most ability are the most valued. At the school level, the posting of the "All A" honor roll, typically filled with mostly the same names semester after semester, suggests to students that higher achievers get the rewards, regardless of the degree of effort or improvement necessary for those high grades.

Although such blatant relative-ability practices can be found in schools and classrooms, it may be the subtler practices that encourage avoidance behaviors most. One such practice is giving all of the students in the class the same academic tasks to complete. When all students are given the same tasks, it is easy for them to see who finishes first, who gets the most answers correct, and who the slowest and least proficient workers are. The best alternative to giving all students the same work is not, in our opinion, dividing the class into three or four easily identifiable ability groups. Rather, one alternative for minimizing the salience of relative ability and, by extension, avoidance behaviors, is to incorporate individualized instruction and tasks in the classroom. Although teacher-led whole-class instruction can be an important and effective tool for explaining concepts and modeling appropriate behaviors, it does not necessar-

ily follow that all students in the class should work on the same academic tasks at the same time. There are many ways to develop competence in a given domain or topic, and students may benefit from a choice of tasks. Such a choice may also limit the availability of social comparison information. Of course, individualized instruction also generally involves a greater commitment of time and effort by teachers.

A final suggestion for minimizing performance goals in the learning environment is to reduce the emphasis on correct answers and to increase the emphasis on the *process* of developing the answers, or products, of the academic task. When students are encouraged to believe that each academic problem has a single correct answer, and that reaching this correct answer is of paramount importance, they associate correct answers with intelligence and academic ability. Moreover, they come to believe that those students who come up with the most correct answers, and are the quickest to do so, are the most intelligent. When some students begin to expect that they will not produce the most correct answers or be the fastest to find the correct answer, they may take steps to protect their image and self-worth by engaging in avoidance behaviors. But when teachers encourage students to pay attention to *how* they develop their solutions to problems, there is a greater opportunity for students with a variety of valid methods and approaches to become engaged in the endeavor. There is also some evidence that they will learn more (Stigler, Gallimore, & Hiebert, 2000).

It is important to note that teachers can promote social comparison among students without necessarily encouraging the type of relative ability comparisons that lead to avoidance behavior. As Gheen and Midgley (1999) found, the negative relationship between students' self-efficacy and avoidance of novelty was exacerbated in classrooms in which teachers encouraged students to compare their work in order to determine *who did better* (relative ability social comparison). In contrast, the negative relationship between self-efficacy and avoidance of novelty was weaker in classrooms in which teachers reported they encouraged their students to engage in informational social comparison. However, even informational social comparison appears to pose a risk of increasing students' avoidance of novelty. Nonetheless, students' perceptions of an emphasis on mastery goals appears to be the most important factor for reducing avoidance of novelty for all students. This result suggests that encouraging students to simply compare the final results of their academic endeavors (e.g., their grades or test scores) may lead to greater avoidance behavior among students who are unsure of their competency if it directs them to attend to relative performance. In contrast, when teachers encourage students to compare their work to their classmates' in order to get ideas, to inform their own progress, to collaborate for joint improvement, and to gain information regarding whether they are on the "right track," students at all levels of efficacy may ex-

perience the benefits if they perceive that their teachers are committed to mastery goals in the classroom.

Although the results of our analyses involving mastery goal structures were less consistent than those involving performance goal structures, they also have implications for practice. In several of our studies, we found that when students perceived a greater emphasis on mastery goals in their classrooms, they were less likely to engage in avoidance behavior (Gheen & Midgley, 1999; Midgley & Urdan, 2001; Ryan et al., 1998). These results suggest that teachers may discourage avoidance behavior among their students when they encourage students to focus on mastering the material, improvement, and understanding the relevance of classroom work in their lives. Although it makes sense that students should be less concerned with protecting their image in classrooms that emphasize understanding of the material and personal, individual standards of achievement, our results suggest that de-emphasizing performance goals may be more important than increasing the emphasis on mastery goals in the classroom when trying to reduce avoidance behaviors among students. Even in classrooms that contain some of the curricular elements of a mastery goal structure, such as the constructivist principle of assigning open-ended, inquiry-based projects and tasks, students may avoid novelty and challenge if they believe that, ultimately, what matters is how their performance compares to their peers.

Our results also indicate that both cheating behavior and acceptance of cheating are higher in classrooms that emphasize extrinsic reasons for engaging in academic tasks. This suggests that teachers who are concerned about cheating may want to de-emphasize extrinsic rewards as reasons for academic achievement. In the cheating study by Anderman and his colleagues (1998), results indicated that both cheating and the belief in the acceptability of cheating were greater when students felt that they could get out of doing assignments or homework as a "reward" for doing well in class. Although it is tempting and efficient for teachers to reward students by allowing them to skip assignments, such incentives are associated with cheating. In addition, students may come to expect and depend on such incentives, which ultimately may undermine their intrinsic motivation (Lepper, Greene, & Nisbett, 1973).

FUTURE DIRECTIONS AND FUTURE RESEARCH

Although avoidance motives and behaviors have been part of the motivational literature for over half a century, they have only recently begun to receive sustained attention in goal theory research. Because of this, there is currently much more that we do not know about these behaviors than we know. There is a virtually limitless array of directions and research questions that future re-

search on avoidance behaviors may take. In this concluding section of the chapter, we examine just a few of the issues that future research may fruitfully examine, including the definition of avoidance behaviors, the relations among performance-approach and performance-avoidance goals and avoidance behaviors, and the processes through which classroom goal structures eventuate in avoidance behaviors among students.

Definition

In this chapter, we began by presenting four specific examples of avoidance behaviors (self-handicapping, avoidance of help seeking, avoidance of novelty challenge, and cheating) that may be driven by a motive to avoid failure or to avoid appearing unintelligent or academically unable. These examples, however, do not allow us to determine whether avoidance behaviors are, by definition, any behaviors driven by avoidance motives or if they are only behaviors that cause students to actually avoid engaging in tasks that promote genuine learning. If it is the former, then there are a variety of behaviors, encouraged by avoidance motives, that would actually be considered *approach* behaviors. For example, students who are afraid of failing an upcoming test, and risking appearing unable, may actually decide to study for the test to ward off failure. It is not uncommon to hear world-class athletes explain that their exhaustive preparation activities were undertaken to assuage their fear of failing before a national or international television audience. If we use the latter definition of avoidance behaviors, then it is possible that avoidance behaviors may sometimes be guided by approach motives. For example, students may cheat to gain entrance into a college, not to avoid looking stupid. In this example, the motivation is to demonstrate competence to others (i.e., the admissions board). Future work in this area needs to pay careful attention to how avoidance behaviors are defined, paying particular attention to the distinction between the motivational source of the behavior and the direction of subsequent action either toward or away from engagement in the task.

The Relations Among Performance
Goals and Avoidance Behaviors

In our research, we have generally found a positive relationship between personal performance-approach goals and avoidance behaviors (Middleton & Midgley, 1999; Midgley et al., 1996; Ryan et al., 1997; Ryan & Pintrich, 1997). However, in some studies, we found no relationship between performance goals and the avoidance behavior being examined (Midgley & Urdan, 1995, 2001). In other studies the relationship between performance-approach goals and the avoidance behavior was moderated by a third variable, such as the ethnicity of the student (Midgley et al., 1996) or their achievement level (Ryan et

al., 1997). Future research examining avoidance behaviors should perhaps try to better understand how these behaviors are related to performance goals. We offer some specific suggestions next.

First, with the recent development of reliable scales to measure the separate approach and avoidance dimensions of performance goals, it is now possible to examine more precisely how these two types of performance goals are associated with avoidance behaviors. In a study of self-handicapping behavior, we found that when both performance-approach and performance-avoidance goals were included in a regression model, only the performance-avoidance goal orientation emerged as significant predictor of self-handicapping (Midgley & Urdan, 2001). Similarly, Middleton and Midgley (1997) found that performance-avoid goals predicted the avoidance of help seeking, with both components of performance goals in the model. Because self-handicapping and the avoidance of help seeking are avoidance behaviors, we were not surprised that these results emerged. These results helped us to understand the ambiguous results we had found in earlier studies regarding the relationship between performance-approach goals and handicapping. Future studies examining the relations among these two types of performance goals and other avoidance behaviors should help us gain a better understanding of the antecedents of those avoidance behaviors as well.

It would also be interesting to use performance goals to gain a better understanding of the motive–behavior cycle over time. We have some evidence that it may be the avoidance dimension of performance goals that is most strongly associated with avoidance behaviors. We also have some evidence that performance-approach goal orientations can be transformed into performance-avoid goal orientations over time, particularly among students with high self-efficacy beliefs (Middleton, Kaplan, & Midgley, 1999). Research aimed at understanding the role of avoidance behaviors in this goal orientation change may prove useful. When students shift their concern from trying to appear more able than their peers (performance-approach goals) to trying to avoid looking less able than peers, do they also experience a simultaneous increase in their avoidance behaviors? Do some avoidance behaviors emerge before others, as students become performance-avoidance goal oriented? And, because most avoidance behaviors actually undermine performance, might students who engage in such behaviors actually be more likely to shift from a performance-approach to a performance-avoidance goal orientation over time?

How Achievement Goal Structures Are Translated Into Avoidance Behaviors by Students

Perhaps the most important results from our research, from a practical standpoint, are those indicating a link between goal structures in the learning envi-

ronment and avoidance behaviors among students. Some of this research suggests that students' perceptions of the classroom performance and social environment moderate the relation of self-efficacy and avoidance behaviors (Gheen & Midgley, 1999; Ryan et al., 1998). Research examining variables other than avoidance behaviors has also revealed that students differ in their perceptions of classroom goal structures and the effects of these structures on assorted motivational and performance variables (Urdan & Giancarlo, 2000; Urdan, Kniesel, & Mason, 1999). To fully understand how the goal structures in the achievement context influence students' use of avoidance behaviors, both directly and through interactions with other variables, we may need to develop a better understanding of the process through which students interpret goal structures and translate them into avoidance behaviors.

One variable that may explain the goal structure–avoidance behavior connection is perceived ability. When in a classroom that makes ability differences between students salient, students who perceive themselves to be high in ability may have higher expectations of doing well and appearing able compared to their classmates. Such expectations would not likely produce avoidance behavior among these students. Students with low perceptions of ability, in contrast, should be more likely to view a classroom performance goal structure as a threat to their image (i.e., an environment with opportunities to fail and get embarrassed), leading to greater avoidance behavior. In addition to differences by perceived ability, the relationship between a performance goal structure and avoidance behaviors may differ by the developmental level of the student. Younger students are less likely than older students to attribute poor academic performance to stable intellectual deficits and therefore may be less aware than adolescent and adults students that a performance goal structure creates increased opportunities for embarrassing social comparisons, thereby weakening or severing the link between the goal structure and avoidance behaviors. An exploration of the potential moderating effects of perceived ability, developmental level, and other variables can help researchers better understand the process through which environmental goal stresses become avoidance behaviors.

CONCLUSION

The recent research examining avoidance behaviors conducted by our research team and other scholars has helped bring to light a particularly vexing motivational problem. When students self-handicap, avoid seeking help when they need it, shy away from novel and challenging academic work, and cheat they are not only robbing themselves of opportunities to learn; they are also telling us that they are trying to avoid failure and embarrassment. Unfortunately, the strategies these students have adopted to avoid failure and embarrassment are likely to undermine performance and promote embarrassment in the future,

creating a vicious cycle of failure and avoidance behavior. We are only beginning to understand the personal and contextual factors that are associated with these avoidance behaviors. With additional research and the increased understanding of these behaviors that this research will bring, scholars can hopefully help educators develop methods for reducing students' reliance on these avoidance behaviors.

REFERENCES

Anderman, E. M., Griesinger, T., & Westerfield, G. (1998). Motivation and cheating during early adolescence. *Journal of Educational Psychology, 90,* 84–93.

Arbreton, A. (1993). *When getting help is helpful: Developmental, cognitive, and motivational influences on students' academic help seeking.* Unpublished doctoral dissertation, University of Michigan, Ann Arbor.

Atkinson, J. W. (1957). Motivational determinants of risk taking behavior. *Psychological Review, 64,* 359–372.

Atkinson, J. W., & Raynor, J. O. (1974). *Motivation and achievement.* New York: Wiley.

Bandura, A. (1986). *Social foundations of thought and action.* Englewood Cliffs, NJ: Prentice-Hall.

Berglas, S., & Jones, E. E. (1978). Drug choice as a self-handicapping strategy in response to noncontingent success. *Journal of Personality and Social Psychology, 36,* 405–417.

Brophy, J. (1998). *Motivating students to learn.* Boston: McGraw-Hill.

Butler, R., & Neuman, O. (1995). Effects of task and ego achievement goals on help-seeking behaviors and attitudes. *Journal of Educational Psychology, 87,* 261–267.

Clifford, M. M. (1984). Thoughts on a theory of constructive failure. *Educational Psychologist, 19,* 108–120.

Covington, M. V. (1992). *Making the grade: A self-worth perspective on motivation and school reform.* New York: Cambridge University Press.

Covington, M. V., & Omelich, C. L. (1979). Effort: The double-edged sword in school achievement. *Journal of Educational Psychology, 71,* 169–182.

Covington, M. V., & Omelich, C. L. (1984). Task-oriented versus competitive learning structures: Motivational and performance consequences. *Journal of Educational Psychology, 76,* 1038–1050.

Csikszentmihaly, M. (1982). Toward a psychology of optimal experience. In L. Wheeler (Ed.), *Review of personality and social psychology* (Vol. 3, pp. 13–36). Beverly Hills, CA: Sage.

Deci, E. L. (1975). *Intrinsic motivation.* New York: Plenum.

Dillon, J. T. (1988). *Questioning and teaching: A manual of practice.* New York: Teachers College Press.

Dweck, C. S. (1986). Motivational processes affecting learning. *American Psychologist, 41,* 1040–1048.

Dweck, C. S., & Leggett, E. L. (1988). A social-cognitive approach to motivation and personality, *Psychological Review, 95,* 256–273.

Elliot, A. J. (1997). Integrating the "classic" and the "contemporary" approaches to achievement motivation: A hierarchical model of approach and avoidance achievement motivation. In M. L. Maehr & P. R. Pintrich (Eds.), *Advances in motivation and achievement* (Vol. 10, pp. 143–179). Greenwich, CT: JAI.

Elliot, A. J., & Church, M. A. (1997). A hierarchical model of approach and avoidance motivation. *Journal of Personality and Social Psychology, 72,* 218–232.

Elliot, A. J., & Harackiewicz, J. M. (1996). Approach and avoidance goals and intrinsic motivation: A mediational analysis. *Journal of Personality and Social Psychology, 70,* 461–475.

Elliott, E. S., & Dweck, C. S. (1988). Goals: An approach to motivation and achievement. *Journal of Personality and Social Psychology, 54,* 5–12.

Garcia, T. (1995). The role of motivational strategies in self-regulated learning. *New Directions for Teaching and Learning, 63,* 29–42.

Gheen, M., & Midgley, C. (1999, April). *"I'd rather not do it the hard way": Student and classroom correlates of eighth graders' avoidance of academic challenge.* Paper presented at the meeting of the American Educational Research Association, Montreal.

Higgins, R. L., Snyder, C. R., & Berglas, S. (1990). *Self-handicapping: The paradox that isn't.* New York: Plenum.

Juvonen, J., & Murdock, T. (1993). How to promote social approval: Effects of audience and achievement outcome on publicly communicated attributions. *Journal of Educational Psychology, 85,* 365–376.

Karabenick, S. A., & Knapp, J. R. (1991). Relationship of academic help-seeking to the use of learning strategies and other achievement behavior in college students. *Journal of Educational Psychology, 83,* 221–230.

Karabenick, S. A., & Sharma, R. (1994). Seeking academic assistance as a strategic learning resource. In P. R. Pintrich, D. R. Brown, & C. E. Weinstein (Eds.), *Student motivation, cognition, and learning: Essays in honor of Wilbert J. McKeachie* (pp. 189–211). Hillsdale, NJ: Lawrence Erlbaum Associates.

Kuhl, J. (1978). Standard setting and risk performance: An elaboration of the theory of achievement motivation and an empirical test. *Psychological Review, 85,* 239–248.

Lepper, M. R., Greene, D., & Nisbett, R. E. (1973). Undermining children's intrinsic interest with extrinsic rewards: A test of the "overjustification" hypothesis. *Journal of Personality and Social Psychology, 28,* 129–137.

Lewin, K., Dembo, T., Festinger, L., & Sears, P. (1944). Level of aspiration. In J. Hunt (Ed.), *Personality and the behavioral disorders* (Vol. 1, pp. 333–378). New York: Ronald.

McCaslin, M., & Good, T. L. (1996). The informal curriculum. In D. Berliner & R. Calfee (Eds.), *Handbook of educational psychology* (pp. 622–670). New York: Macmillan.

McClelland, D. C. (1951). *Personality.* New York: Dryden Press.

Meyer, D. K., Turner, J. C., & Spencer, C. A. (1997). Challenge in a mathematics classroom: Students' motivation and strategies in project-based learning. *Elementary School Journal, 97,* 501–521.

Middleton, M., Kaplan, A., & Midgley, C. (1999). *The relations among middle school students' achievement goals in math over time.* Unpublished manuscript, University of Michigan, Ann Arbor.

Middleton, M., & Midgley, C. (1997). Avoiding the demonstration of the lack of ability: An under-explored aspect of goal theory. *Journal of Educational Psychology, 89,* 710–718.

Middleton, M., & Midgley, C. (1999, August). *Beyond motivation: Middle school students' perception of press for understanding.* Paper presented at the meeting of the American Psychological Association, Boston.

Midgley, C., Arunkumar, R., & Urdan, T. (1996). "If I don't do well tomorrow, there's a reason": Predictors of adolescents' use of self-handicapping strategies. *Journal of Educational Psychology, 88,* 423–434.

Midgley, C., Kaplan, A., & Middleton, M. (2001). Performance goals: Good for what, for whom, under what circumstances, and at what cost? *Journal of Educational Psychology, 93,* 77–86.

Midgley, C., & Urdan, T. (1995). Predictors of middle school students' use of self-handicapping strategies. *Journal of Early Adolescence, 15,* 389–411.

Midgley, C., & Urdan, T. (2001). Academic self-handicapping and achievement goals: A further examination. *Contemporary Educational Psychology, 26,* 61–75,

Murray, H. A. (1938). *Explorations in personality.* New York: Oxford University Press.

Newman, R. S. (1991). Goals and self-regulated learning: What motivates children to seek academic help? In M. L. Maehr & P. R. Pintrich (Eds.), *Advances in motivation and achievement: Vol. 7. Goals and self-regulatory processes* (pp. 151–183). Greenwich, CT: JAI.

Newman, R. S. (1994). Adaptive help-seeking: A strategy of self-regulated learning. In D. Schunk & B. Zimmerman (Eds.), *Self-regulation of learning and performance: Issues and educational applications* (pp. 283–301). Hillsdale, NJ: Lawrence Erlbaum Associates.

Nicholls, J. G. (1990). What is ability and why are we mindful of it? A developmental perspective. In R. Sternberg & J. Kolligian (Eds.), *Competence considered* (pp. 11–40). New Haven, CT: Yale University Press.

Nicholls, J. G., & Miller, A. T. (1984). Reasoning about the ability of self and others: A developmental study. *Child Development, 55,* 1990–1999.

Nicholls, J. G., Patashnick, M., & Nolen, S. B. (1985). Adolescents' theories of education. *Journal of Educational Psychology, 77,* 683–692.

Pintrich, P. R. (2000). An achievement goal theory perspective on issues in motivation terminology, theory, and research. *Contemporary Educational Psychology, 25,* 92–104.

Ryan, A. M., Gheen, M., & Midgley, C. (1998). Why do some students avoid asking for help? An examination of the interplay among students' academic efficacy, teacher's social-emotional role and classroom goal structure. *Journal of Educational Psychology, 90,* 528–535.

Ryan, A. M., Hicks, L. & Midgley, C. (1997). Social goals, academic goals, and avoiding seeking help in the classroom. *Journal of Early Adolescence, 17,* 152–171.

Ryan, A. M., & Pintrich, P. R. (1997). Should I ask for help?: The role of motivation and attitude in adolescents' help seeking in math class. *Journal of Educational Psychology, 89,* 329–341.

Shepperd, J. A., & Arkin, R. M. (1989). Determinants of self-handicapping: Task importance and the effects of preexisting handicaps on self-generated handicaps. *Personality and Social Psychology Bulletin, 15,* 101–112.

Skaalvik, E. M. (1997). Self-enhancing and self-defeating ego orientation: Relations with task and avoidance orientation, achievement, self-perceptions, and anxiety. *Journal of Educational Psychology, 89,* 71–81.

Stigler, J. W., Gallimore, R., & Hiebert, J. (2000). Using video surveys to compare classrooms and teaching across cultures: Examples and lessons from TIMSS video studies. *Educational Psychologist, 35,* 87–100.

Urdan, T. (1997). Achievement goal theory: Past results, future directions. In P. R. Pintrich & M. L. Maehr (Eds.), *Advances in motivation and achievement* (Vol. 10, pp. 99–142). Greenwich, CT: JAI.

Urdan, T. C., & Giancarlo, C. (2000, April). *A fresh look at the relationship between classroom goal structures and student motivation.* Poster session presented at the meetings of the American Educational Research Association, New Orleans.

Urdan, T., Kneisel, L., & Mason, V. (1999). The effect of particular instructional practices on student motivation: An exploration of teachers' and students' perceptions. In T. Urdan (Ed.), *Advances in motivation and achievement: Vol. 11. Motivation in context* (pp. 123–158). Stamford, CT: JAI.

Urdan, T., Midgley, C., & Anderman, E. (1998). The role of classroom goal structure in students' use of self-handicapping strategies. *American Educational Research Journal, 35,* 101–122.

Vygotsky, L. S. (1978). *Mind in society: The development of higher psychological processes.* Cambridge, MA: Harvard University Press.

Weiner, B. (1985). An attributional theory of motivation and emotion. *Psychological Review, 92,* 548–573.

Zimmerman, B. J., & Martinez-Pons, M. (1988). Construct validation of a strategy model of student self-regulated learning. *Journal of Educational Psychology, 80,* 284–290.

Zuckerman, M., Kieffer, S. C., & Knee, C. R. (1998). Consequences of self-handicapping: Effects on coping, academic performance, and adjustment. *Journal of Personality and Social Psychology, 74,* 1619–1628.

APPENDIX

SURVEY ITEMS FROM THE PATTERNS OF ADAPTIVE LEARNING SURVEY USED TO MEASURE AVOIDANCE BEHAVIORS

Self-Handicapping

1. Some students put off doing their schoolwork until the last minute so that if they don't do well on their work they can say that is the reason. How true is this of you?

2. Some students let their friends keep them from paying attention in class or from doing their homework. Then if they don't do as well as they had hoped, they can say friends kept them from working. How true is this of you?

3. Some students purposely don't try hard in school so that if they don't do well, they can say it is because they didn't try. How true is this of you?

4. Some students purposely get involved in lots of activities. Then if they don't do as well on their schoolwork as they hoped, they can say it is because they are involved with other things. How true is this of you?

5. Some students fool around the night before a test so that if they don't do well they can say that is the reason. How true is this of you?

6. Some students look for reasons to keep them from studying (not feeling well, having to help their parents, taking care of a brother or sister, etc.). Then if they don't do well on their schoolwork, they can say this is the reason. How true is this of you?

Avoidance of Help Seeking

1. When I don't understand my math work, I often guess instead of asking someone for help.
2. I don't ask questions in math class, even when I don't understand the lesson.
3. When I don't understand my math work, I often put down any answer rather than ask for help.
4. I usually don't ask for help with my math work, even if the work is too hard to do on my own.
5. If my math work is too hard for me, I just don't do it rather than ask for help.

Avoidance of Novelty and Challenge

1. I would prefer doing math problems the usual way, rather than try something different.
2. I would choose math problems I knew I could do, rather than those that might be a challenge.
3. I would prefer to do math problems that are familiar to me, rather than those I would have to learn how to do.
4. I would prefer to do math problems that are not very different from what I am used to doing.
5. I would prefer doing math problems that don't make me think too hard.

Cheating Behaviors

1. When I don't understand my math work, I get the answers from my friends.
2. I use cheat-sheets when I take math tests.
3. I copy answers from other students on math tests.
4. I cheat on my math work.
5. I copy answers from other students when I do my math work.

Cheating Beliefs

1. How serious do you think it is if somebody cheats on math work? (reversed)
2. If you were sure you wouldn't get caught, would you cheat on your math work?
3. Is it okay to cheat on math work?

4

Social Motivation and the Classroom Social Environment

Helen Patrick
Purdue University

Lynley H. Anderman
University of Kentucky

Allison M. Ryan
University of Illinois

Hannah has many friends in her class, so although she feels unprepared for next week's history test she knows that Karen and Nicole will study with her during lunch and explain things she doesn't understand. Feeling equally unprepared, Lauren also has many friends with whom she could do homework and study. However she doesn't, because she thinks that looking interested in schoolwork will make her look "dorky" to her friends and they would probably tease her. None of the other kids that Lauren hangs out with do well in history, so it doesn't matter to her if she doesn't either. Ronnie doesn't understand why the Pilgrims left England in the 1600s, which he thinks will be on the test, but he doesn't want to ask the teacher because he thinks she is mean and will probably get impatient with him. Ronnie doesn't have any friends in his class, but he thinks about asking Kyle, who does well in history. Last time he asked Kyle something, though, Kyle answered as if the question was really easy and then told him to stop bugging him, leaving Ronnie feeling upset. Ronnie spends so much time thinking about the other kids not seeming to like him, and his not liking school, that he doesn't hear the teacher announcing a homework assignment.

Social relationships constitute a significant and salient feature of the school context for students. Daily, students' social experiences, as well as their expec-

tations and concerns about possible social encounters affect the way they engage in school activities. The strong associations between the academic and the social dimensions of school are reflected in researchers' arguments that these dimensions are almost inextricable; that "cognitive processes and social relations are so intricately interwoven in learning at school that it is difficult to separate them" (Perret-Clermont, Perret, & Bell, 1991, p. 58). It follows, then, that in order to understand students' motivation and performance in school we must consider social factors.

Indeed, there is evidence that children's and adolescents' social relationships are associated with their success at school. Students with positive social skills, who relate well to classmates, and who are accepted by their classmates tend to report liking school as well as being engaged in and doing well at school (e.g., Berndt, 1999; Patrick, 1997; Wentzel, 1991b). Conversely, students with unsatisfactory peer relationships and low levels of peer acceptance tend to have achievement and adjustment difficulties at school, and are at high risk for dropping out (e.g., Hymel, Comfort, Schonert-Reichl, & McDougall, 1996; Parker & Asher, 1987).

A number of reasons have been posited for the link between students' social relationships and their academic engagement and success. Wanting to, and knowing how to, relate positively to classmates and teachers provides an array of resources for instrumental help and for socioemotional encouragement and support. Task-related anxiety, which undermines efficient task-related cognitive engagement (Boekarts, 1993), may be decreased by positive interactions or even knowledge that such interactions are possible. Furthermore, when adolescents feel comfortable socially they may be less self-conscious about their academic performance or concerned about exhibiting bravado. Such self-consciousness and concern with appearances may lead to anxiety or avoidant strategies and detract from enjoyment and learning. Positive relationships also enable students to work productively while experiencing less conflict. For example, when friends work together on problem-solving tasks they stay more focused on the task at hand, communicate well with each other, and generate an affective climate conducive to exploration and problem solving more than when nonfriends work together (Hartup, 1996; Jehn & Shah, 1997).

To begin this chapter we discuss the importance of social relationships during adolescence, and their implications for adolescents' motivation and engagement at school. Next, we consider a range of social beliefs that adolescents hold about themselves and being at school, and how these beliefs are associated with achievement goal orientations and other indices of academic motivation and engagement. We focus first on adolescents' personal beliefs about themselves relating to others at school, including their social goals and social efficacy. We then consider adolescents' appraisals of their comfort within the school environment, focusing on teacher support and feelings of belonging.

Third, we address dimensions of the classroom social environment, in particular, students' perceptions that the teacher promotes mutual respect and promotes interaction among students. Furthermore, we discuss evidence that associations between the classroom social environment and adolescents' motivation and engagement may be associated with gender and race. Finally, we speculate on directions for future research regarding social processes and current views of teaching and learning.

THE IMPORTANCE OF SOCIAL RELATIONSHIPS DURING ADOLESCENCE

The Patterns of Adaptive Learning Study followed students throughout early and middle adolescence. The nature of social relationships undergoes significant change during this time, and many of these changes have implications for students' motivation for, and engagement in, school. Therefore, in order to contextualize our research developmentally, we begin by discussing the importance of social relationships during the early and middle adolescent period.

Although peer relationships are likely to be important to motivation and engagement for students of all ages, they may be particularly important for young adolescent students. Peer relationships take on special significance, compared to earlier periods of development (Furman & Buhrmester, 1992; Hartup, 1993; Savin-Williams & Berndt, 1990). As children develop into adolescents, they spend an increasing amount of time with peers compared to being with family members or on their own (Csikszentmihalyi & Larson, 1984). Peer relationships during this age are widely viewed as more intense, close, and influential than during childhood (Berndt, 1982). Interactions become more reflective, intimate, and self-disclosing (Berndt, 1982; Buhrmester & Furman, 1987). These changes are facilitated by adolescents' cognitive development, which enables them to reflect on abstract dimensions (e.g., values, friendship, identity; Keating, 1990).

In addition to changes at the dyadic level, changes at the larger peer group level surface during early adolescence. Distinct peer groups, with different identifying characteristics, reputations, and status hierarchies, emerge and become increasingly salient and important to adolescents (B. B. Brown, 1990). Associated with this emergence of cliques and crowds is concern about how one is viewed by others. Adolescents' ability to reflect on how they are seen by others and the associated consideration of the "imaginary audience," made possible by cognitive development, may give rise to greater self-consciousness and concern about social image (Elkind, 1967; Keating, 1990).

Adolescents' relationships with adults change relative to the preadolescent period. After elementary school adolescents typically interact with a considerably greater number of teachers and other school personnel (Feldlaufer, Midgley, & Eccles, 1988). Furthermore, nonparental adults, such as teachers,

become especially important role models and sources of support during adolescence (Midgley, Feldlaufer, & Eccles, 1989). For example, longitudinal research has shown teacher support to be related more strongly to junior high school students' motivational beliefs than to elementary school students' motivation (Midgley et al., 1989).

The changes in adolescents' social relationships have implications for their motivation and engagement at school. Adolescents' developing perceptions of themselves—who they are, what they are good and not good at, and what they want to invest time and energy in, are influenced by their interactions with others. The intimate disclosures and honest feedback exchanged with peers can affect self-perceptions, values, and aspirations, including interest in academics. The increasing intimacy and time spent with peers also provides greater opportunities for social comparison than previously.

The developments in adolescents' social perceptions and relationships have implications for creating developmentally appropriate learning environments. Meeting adolescents' developmental needs involves addressing the changes in social perceptions, concerns, and relationships, mentioned previously. These include adolescents' increased need for positive and supportive relationships with both peers and nonparental adults, and increased self-consciousness and sensitivity regarding social comparison (Eccles & Midgley, 1989; Midgley & Feldlaufer, 1987).

PERSONAL SOCIAL GOALS AND EFFICACY

Dweck (1996) noted that motivation constructs, and patterns among them, are similar for both the social and academic domains. In conceptualizing adolescents' social motivation we chose to use personal goals and self-efficacy—the same motivational constructs that were guiding the research of the larger project. Therefore, we considered social goals that students may pursue, and that may affect their motivation and engagement for academics. We believed, too, that in order to engage adaptively at school, students need to feel confident relating socially to others. Therefore we also considered students' perceptions of their social efficacy.

Social Goals

Young adolescents' objectives and intentions for interactions with others, or their social goals, are related to their social behavior (e.g., Chung & Asher, 1996). However, social goals are also associated with different patterns of academically related beliefs and behaviors. There are a number of different social goals that students pursue in academic contexts, such as social approval, eq-

uity, or prosocial goals (Ford, 1992; Urdan & Maehr, 1995). Our research has focused on three different social goals: social responsibility, social intimacy or relationship, and social status goals (see L. Anderman, 1999b, for more extensive theoretical discussion).

Responsibility Goals.   A social responsibility goal involves students' desire and willingness to meet the formal social demands and role expectations of the classroom (Wentzel, 1991a, 1991c). As such, responsibility goals can be thought of as a student's expressed goal of being a "good citizen" in the social context of the classroom, including his or her willingness to adhere to class rules, to follow directions, and to behave in ways that are not distracting to others.

Consonant with research that has found girls, as compared to boys, to be more compliant and exhibit fewer conduct problems in the classroom (e.g., Eisenberg, Martin, & Fabes, 1996), we have found consistently that early adolescent girls, on average, endorse responsibility goals to a greater extent than do boys (L. H. Anderman & E. M. Anderman, 1999; Hicks, Murphy, & Patrick, 1995; Patrick, Hicks, & Ryan, 1997). Furthermore, students' endorsement of social responsibility goals is associated with important school-related outcomes. Wentzel (1989, 1993) demonstrated that students who report pursuing higher levels of responsibility goals tend to receive higher grades in school, although the mechanisms underlying this association have not been well documented. Our research has attempted to uncover potential explanations for that relation by examining aspects of students' academic motivation and school-related affect.

Patrick, Hicks, and Ryan (1997) reasoned that students who strive to comply with the social norms of their classroom may also feel more able to meet the academic demands of that setting. That is, when students understand and are willing to meet the social expectations of a given class, they may feel more confident with respect to learning and understanding their schoolwork in that class. Using data from fifth-grade classes, in which all students were taught in self-contained classrooms, we found that students' social responsibility goals were related positively to their academic efficacy. Indeed, the strength of this association was stronger than that for students' prior achievement, a well-established influence on students' efficacy (e.g., Schunk, 1983).

In addition to academic efficacy, social responsibility goals are related to changes in students' personal achievement goal orientations (L. H. Anderman & E. M. Anderman, 1999). In this study, we examined students' personal mastery and performance (approach) goal orientations before and after the transition from elementary to middle school. Using hierarchical analyses, we accounted first for the effects of students' prior achievement and perceptions of the goal structure in their new, sixth-grade classes. We then assessed the extent to which students' sense of school belonging and social goals added additional,

unique explanatory power to the prediction of changes in personal achievement goal orientations from fifth to sixth grade. In terms of social responsibility goals, we found a positive association with changes in personal mastery goals but no effect for changes in performance goals. That is, students who endorsed higher levels of responsibility goals in sixth grade were more likely to report an increase from fifth to sixth grade in engaging in schoolwork to increase understanding and competence (mastery goals). Given that a mastery orientation is linked theoretically and empirically to the use of adaptive learning strategies (e.g., Nolen, 1988; Pintrich & De Groot, 1990), these findings provide one explanation for the previously reported association between responsibility goals and grades.

Finally, students' endorsement of social responsibility goals is associated with their affect in school (L. Anderman, 1999a). Students who reported high levels of pursuing responsibility goals in sixth grade also reported an increase from fifth grade in positive school-related affect, including feelings of contentment, happiness, and excitement in school. Furthermore, this association was found after students' prior academic achievement was taken into account. Interesting to note, responsibility goals were unrelated to changes in negative school-related affect (including anger, frustration, and anxiety). Thus, it seems clear that students' ability and willingness to accept and conform to the social expectations of class membership are associated with adaptive motivational and affective outcomes which, in turn, are theorized to increase learning and achievement. To date, however, a full model of the mechanisms that underlie all of these associations has not been developed.

Intimacy or Relationship Goals.   In contrast to being oriented to the adult social norms and requirements of school, a goal for intimacy or social relationships involves wanting to form and maintain close friendships with peers in school. Again, there are consistent gender differences in endorsement of intimacy goals, with girls expressing greater endorsement than do boys (L. H. Anderman & E. M. Anderman, 1999; Patrick, Hicks, & Ryan, 1997). This finding is consistent with Eccles' research (e.g., 1985; Eccles & Harold, 1992) which found that adolescent girls, more than boys, tend to value social relationships.

In the previously described studies of the transition to middle school, students' endorsement of intimacy goals was associated with increases in both personal performance (approach) goals (L. H. Anderman & E. M. Anderman, 1999) and positive school-related affect (L. Anderman, 1999a). These findings are not unexpected in that students who endorse intimacy goals are more likely to seek out companionship and support from others in school. In contrast, students who do not report wanting to form friendships with students in their peer group following the transition may be expected to report lower levels of contentment and excitement in school. In terms of students' increased perfor-

mance goal orientation, it may be that students who are focused on their social relationships with peers may also be more likely to look to their peers as a comparison group against which to judge their own academic success and progress. That is, they may adopt an increased orientation toward performing well in relation to other students.

Students' intimacy goals may also have a positive influence on their use of adaptive learning strategies in class, particularly in situations where students are required to work cooperatively. Ryan, Hicks, and Midgley (1997) examined fifth grade students' self-reported avoidance of seeking help with academic work in the classroom. In this study, we reasoned that students who endorse intimacy goals may view seeking help from a peer as a legitimate opportunity for peer interaction in the classroom and thus may be less likely to avoid seeking help when they need it. This hypothesis received modest support, when students' academic goal orientations, gender, and prior achievement were taken into account.

Status Goals. A social status goal also involves an orientation to peers, but is focused on students' desire for social visibility and prestige within the larger peer group rather than with forming dyadic friendships. That is, whereas intimacy goals refer to students' goals of forming positive relationships with peers in school, status goals refer to the goal of gaining affiliation with "the popular group" at school. The emergence of various hierarchically arranged social groups (or crowds), and the social dominance of the popular group in early adolescence have been documented in several ethnographic studies (e.g., B. B. Brown & Lohr, 1987; Eder, 1985; Kinney, 1993). B. B. Brown (1990) defined crowds as "reputation-based collectives of similarly stereotyped individuals" (p. 177) and suggested that crowd membership is based not only on students' social skills or desires but also on their status among others. Thus, the goal to be affiliated with the popular group reflects a desire to be judged as visible and powerful within the larger peer group. Whereas social responsibility goals represent an acceptance of the formal social norms and expectations of classroom life, social status goals represent an acceptance of the informal social norms of the peer group. Students who endorse status goals are demonstrating their recognition of the hierarchical organization of adolescent social groups, as well as their willingness to participate in that hierarchy.

We have found consistent gender differences in early adolescents' status goals. Boys indicate on average a greater focus on social status than do girls (L. Anderman, 1999a; Ryan et al., 1997). There are at least two potential explanations for this finding. First, given that some researchers (e.g., Roeser, Midgley, & Urdan, 1996) have found that boys tend to report a greater performance goal orientation in academic situations than do girls, it may be that boys are more concerned with their "public image" and comparison to peers in both social

and academic domains. Second, it is well established that boys' and girls' peer friendships develop differently and can be characterized by different shared activities (e.g., Buhrmester & Furman, 1987; Maccoby, 1990). Boys' friendships are described typically as involving larger groups of peers than are girls', and as revolving around shared activities such as team sports (Berndt, 1982). It may be that this combining of competitive activities with interpersonal relationships heightens boys' awareness of group visibility and status issues. The development of boys' and girls' social status goals and their importance for academic engagement and learning merits further research.

Students' endorsement of social status goals has emerged as a significant predictor of school-related motivation, affect, and strategy use in our research. In terms of achievement goal orientations, students' social status goals in sixth grade were associated with an increase in personal performance approach goals, from fifth to sixth grades (L. H. Anderman & E. M. Anderman, 1999). As discussed earlier, one reason for this association may be that students who endorse social status goals may be more likely than others to look to the peer group for evidence of their own academic success and achievement. This may be particularly true for social status goals that tap explicitly into students' view of their social network as hierarchical. That is, students who construct their social world in terms of social comparison and ranking of individuals may also be more likely to approach academic pursuits with a similar orientation.

In the previously discussed study of students' help seeking in class (Ryan et al., 1997), social status goals were associated with both students' self-reported avoidance of seeking help when it is needed, and their perception that seeking help in class is threatening to their self-worth. That is, students who reported wanting to achieve social status at school were more likely to report that seeking help with academic tasks may incur negative reactions or judgments from others. Interesting to note, students' intimacy goals were not associated with such a perceived threat. That is, when students are focused on forming positive relationships with peers, as opposed to maintaining their social standing, help seeking is not perceived as a threat to self-worth.

Finally, in terms of students' affective reaction to school, social status goals interacted with their perceptions of a mastery goal structure in their classes, to predict change in negative affect in school (L. Anderman, 1999a). Students reported a decrease in anger, frustration, and anxiety between fifth and sixth grades if they perceived that their sixth grade classroom emphasized mastery goals. The strength of this decrease, however, varied depending on students' endorsement of social status goals, such that students who were higher in status goals reported the greatest decrease. Thus, the students who were least likely to report a decrease in negative affect were those who perceived little emphasis on personal improvement and learning in their classes, and who also reported low interest in gaining social status with their peers. This combination suggests a degree of

alienation from two major foci of school life that, understandably, could be reflected in a negative affective reaction to school. Such findings reinforce the importance of examining social and academic motivational variables simultaneously, to understand students' experiences of schooling.

Social Efficacy

In addition to desiring different types of social interactions and relationships, students need confidence in their own ability to interact effectively with others in order to realize their goals. This confidence, or social efficacy, is related also to adolescents' beliefs about school and academics. In our research we focused on two qualitatively different types of relationships in the classroom—those with classroom peers and those with the teacher. Peer relationships have been termed horizontal, in that they tend to be characterized by reciprocity, egalitarian expectations, and a similar degree of social power (Hartup, 1989). Adolescents' relationships with their teachers, however, are vertical, in that they involve unequal power, status, and knowledge (Hartup, 1989). Accordingly, students need different knowledge and behaviors (e.g., knowing and following different social norms and rules) for each type of relationship.

Efficacy With Peers.   The measure of social efficacy we developed addressed adolescents' confidence in negotiating social tasks with classmates, such as explaining their views, initiating social interactions, and working out social problems. Researchers have identified these tasks as being especially difficult, and as differentiating between less and more socially skilled children (Coie & Kupersmidt, 1983; Dodge, 1983).

Adolescents' confidence to interact effectively with classmates during classroom activities is important for a range of academic beliefs and behaviors. Believing that one can relate well to peers may boost confidence in learning and being successful at academic tasks, even if interaction is not integral to the task. Peers serve as potential sources of instrumental help with schoolwork, and students may find it beneficial to seek clarification of instructions, help with specific tasks, or general reassurance that what they are doing is correct. Consistent with this view, we have found social efficacy to be associated uniquely with academic efficacy, even after demographic characteristics and prior achievement were accounted for (Patrick, Hicks, & Ryan, 1997). Furthermore, consistent with the previously discussed research indicating that social relationships appear to promote more effective task engagement, social efficacy with peers is associated positively with students' self-regulated learning (Ryan & Patrick, 2001).

Social efficacy relating to peers is associated also with changes in adolescents' school-related affect. We found that students' perceptions that they

could interact successfully with classmates contributed significantly to increased positive affect, decreased negative affect, and decreased feelings of depression after moving from elementary to middle school (Patrick, Edelin, Hicks, Middleton, & Midgley, 1997). These effects are consistent with Berndt and Mekos' (1995) finding that peer relationships become extremely salient to early adolescents, both in an anticipatory manner when they are about to make the transition to junior high school and just after making the transition.

Efficacy With the Teacher.   Our measure of efficacy relating to the teacher paralleled that developed with respect to peers. As expected, correlations between peer and teacher efficacy were only moderate, supporting arguments that they are different types of relationships (Hartup, 1989). Our research has indicated that, although they comprise distinct factors, social efficacy relating to the teacher is correlated strongly with social responsibility goals (Patrick, Hicks, & Ryan, 1997). This indicates that adolescents who are willing to conform to the authority structure at school also believe they can negotiate the necessary social norms and interactions with authority figures.

Confidence in one's ability to relate effectively to the teacher is associated also with motivation for, and engagement in, academics. Social efficacy with the teacher is related to academic efficacy (Patrick, Hicks, & Ryan, 1997), arguably because a belief that one knows how to communicate effectively with the teacher inspires confidence in receiving maximum support and assistance when necessary, thus facilitating learning and achievement. Feeling confident relating to the teacher is associated also with students' self-regulated learning, and associated negatively with disruptive behavior in that teacher's class (Ryan & Patrick, 2001).

In addition to academic beliefs and behaviors, efficacy relating to teachers is associated with changes in adolescents' affect from elementary to middle school. We found that students' perceptions that they could interact successfully with their teachers contributed significantly to increased positive school-related affect, decreased negative affect, and decreased feelings of anger (Patrick, Edelin et al., 1997).

PERCEPTIONS OF TEACHER SUPPORT
AND SCHOOL BELONGING

In addition to social goals and efficacy perceptions at the personal level, students' perceptions of the fit between themselves and the school environment are important for adaptive motivation and engagement. Two aspects of fit, or socio emotional comfort, are perceptions of support from the teacher and feelings of belonging at school.

Teacher Support

Teacher support has been defined slightly differently by various researchers (e.g., Fraser & Fisher,1982; Goodenow, 1993a; Midgley et al., 1989; Skinner & Belmont, 1993) but it generally involves characteristics such as caring, friendliness, understanding, dedication, and dependability. Thus, teacher support refers to the extent to which students believe that teachers value and establish personal relationships with them.

Teacher support is important for students' achievement motivation. Perceptions of support arguably foster feelings of confidence and self-worth, allay anxiety, encourage persistence in times of difficulty, and sustain the necessary motivation to use effortful, adaptive learning and metacognitive strategies. Indeed, researchers have found positive associations between teacher support and adaptive motivational patterns. For example, when students view their teacher as supportive they report higher levels of interest, valuing, and enjoyment in their schoolwork (Fraser & Fisher, 1982; Midgley et al., 1989), and greater expectancies for success (Goodenow, 1993a).

We were interested in extending this research, and investigated effects of teacher support on students' academic and social engagement at school (Ryan & Patrick, 2001). Specifically, we focused on changes in students' reports of self-regulated learning and disruptive behavior from seventh to eighth grade. We argued that perceptions of teacher supportiveness and confidence that help will be available if needed would decrease students' anxiety about task engagement. Such anxiety undermines self-regulated learning (Pintrich & De Groot, 1990). We expected, therefore, that teacher support would be related positively to students' self-regulated learning and negatively to off-task and disruptive behavior. As hypothesized, we found that when students perceived that their eighth grade teacher valued and cared about them, their self-regulated learning increased and disruptive behavior decreased relative to seventh grade, even after accounting for demographic factors and prior achievement.

School Belonging

School belonging refers to a sense of relatedness and psychological membership in a supportive community, in addition to a sense of identification with that community. A sense of belonging at school is related to greater adjustment, including expectations for success and intrinsic value for school, participation in school activities, and achievement (Finn, 1989; Goodenow, 1993b). Furthermore, students' sense of school community predicts their liking of school (Battistich, Solomon, Kim, Watson, & Schaps, 1995).

Adding to this research, we have found that a sense of belonging at school is associated with changes in students' achievement goal orientations and school-related affect as they make the transition from elementary to middle school. Students' sense of belonging, reported at the beginning of sixth grade, was associated with both an increase in their personal mastery goal orientation and a decrease in their performance goal orientation, relative to their fifth-grade goal orientations (L. H. Anderman & E. M. Anderman, 1999). Furthermore, school belonging demonstrated a significant, unique effect on goal orientations, even when students' perceptions of the goal structures of their sixth grade classes were taken into account. Whereas previous research had reported a link between school belonging and general achievement motivation (Goodenow, 1992), this study provided evidence that the sense that one is respected and feels "a part of" one's school is associated with a mastery goal orientation specifically. This suggests that students who experience a relatively smooth transition into their new middle school and come to feel comfortable quickly in their new social environment are more likely than their peers to approach academic tasks for the purposes of personal understanding and increased competence. In contrast, students who do not feel accepted and that they can "be themselves" in their new school, are more likely to approach tasks as opportunities to demonstrate ability and compete with others.

Students' sense of school belonging in sixth grade was also an important predictor of both increased positive affect and decreased negative affect in school, across the transition (L. Anderman, 1999a). Students who felt that they were a part of their new school felt more happy and enthusiastic, and less angry, frustrated, and bored than they did in fifth grade. Although not surprising, these findings have important implications for educational practice. Serious educational outcomes such as dropping out of school are preceded by a chain of negative experiences, often spanning several years (Finn, 1989). It may well be that the lack of a sense of belonging in the early months of middle school sets the tone for negative affect that contributes to later truancy and withdrawal from school for some students.

PERCEPTIONS OF THE CLASSROOM SOCIAL ENVIRONMENT

In addition to students' perceptions of themselves and their relationships at school, we are interested in students' perceptions of their classroom environment and how teachers contribute to creating classroom environments that elicit and sustain adaptive patterns of motivation and engagement. Goal orientation theory gives the classroom context a primary role in the explanation of students' motivation and achievement (Ames, 1992; Maehr & Midgley, 1996). Although understudied, an important dimension of the classroom context is

the social environment. Teachers contribute to constructing the classroom social environment in many ways: by creating norms and rules for student social behavior in the classroom, by giving explicit messages and rules regarding students' interactions with their classmates, by assigning students to groups, by the types of academic tasks they assign (e.g., if they encourage or dissuade cooperation and sharing of expertise), by the types of participation structures they establish, and by how they recognize and evaluate students (see Patrick, L. Anderman, Ryan, Edelin, & Midgley, 2001, for case studies).

As a way of addressing the classroom social environment, we have investigated different types of messages that teachers send about relationships and interactions among students (Ryan & Patrick, 2001). Specifically, we have considered three different dimensions that characterize teachers' communication with students about their relationships with peers around academic tasks: (a) other students are valuable resources with whom you work to increase learning *(promoting interaction);* (b) other students are to be shown respect and support *(promoting mutual respect);* and (c) other students are markers of your relative ability, with whom you are compared and compete *(promoting performance goals).* We included this latter classroom dimension because it is social in nature; that is, an emphasis on competition and relative ability inevitably involves other students. However, because the classroom performance goal structure is addressed elsewhere in this book (see chap. 2, this volume), we discuss only the first two dimensions in this chapter.

Promoting Interaction

Social constructivist theories of learning assume that children learn from hearing others' thoughts and ideas, and from articulating their own emerging understandings (e.g., Vygotsky, 1978). This interaction may encompass the sharing of ideas and approaches during whole-class lessons, working together in small-group activities, or informal help seeking and help giving during individual seatwork. Whatever form it takes, however, interaction among students is a critical component of student-centered instructional approaches. When students are encouraged to interact and exchange ideas with each other they have opportunities to justify, evaluate, and refine their own position and to gain exposure to other possibilities (Good, Mulryan, & McCaslin, 1992; Webb & Palincsar, 1996). Interaction among classmates helps also to develop perspective-taking ability. Students can see that there are often multiple ways to construe, approach, and solve problems, and that others' perspectives on issues are often different but equally legitimate. Promoting interaction among students in the classroom may be especially beneficial for adolescents' motivation and engagement, because of their increased capacity for considering others' perspectives, generating alternative options, being reflective, and evaluating alternatives

(Keating, 1990). Encouraging student–student interaction is also a way for teachers to promote positive social development at a time when middle school structures typically make it difficult for adolescents to establish meaningful relationships with peers (Eccles et al., 1993; Hicks, 1997). Despite theoretical arguments about the benefits of promoting student interaction, teachers vary in the extent to which they encourage, or even allow, students to interact with one another during classroom activities (e.g., Patrick et al., 2001).

We investigated whether students' perceptions that their eighth grade math teacher promoted interaction contributed to changes in their efficacy for mathematics between seventh and eighth grades (Ryan & Patrick, 2001). We argued that students should feel more efficacious about their ability to learn and complete activities successfully when interaction among students is promoted, because they have a greater array of resources on which to draw than if they were only working individually. The interest generated from interacting with peers is likely to support students' willingness to engage in and persist with those tasks, even when the tasks themselves are seen to be uninteresting or difficult. However, contrary to our expectation, there was no unique effect of promoting interaction on changes in students' academic efficacy, once prior achievement and efficacy, and demographic factors were taken into account. Although only conjecture, a reason that promoting interaction may not have been a significant factor in this study is that the math curricula used by the schools did not explicitly encourage and utilize extensive student interactions.

One reason that teachers may feel wary about promoting interaction among students during class activities is a concern that encouraging interaction may make it easier for students to become off-task and disruptive. Conversely, though, legitimizing opportunities for students to talk with one another and meet social needs may be associated with decreased disruptive behavior in the classroom. Interestingly, we found that promoting interaction in the classroom was not related to changes in disruptive behavior between seventh and eighth grades, indicating that students do not typically become more disruptive when they are encouraged to talk with one other during lessons.

Promoting Mutual Respect

A focus on mutual respect in the classroom should help create an environment where students communicate positively with one another, are not afraid to share their thoughts and ideas even when tentative, and are not fearful of ridicule when experiencing difficulty. Such environments are most conducive to student exploration, problem solving, and cognitive risk-taking processes that are integral to both motivation and self-regulated learning. When students are anxious or worried about making mistakes they are less likely to engage in their academic work in an effortful and strategic manner (Turner, Thorpe, &

Meyer, 1998). Resource allocation theory suggests this may be due to negative affect increasing task-irrelevant thoughts that overload working memory, thereby reducing the available cognitive capacity (Ellis & Ashbrook, 1987). A climate of respect is important for learning at any age. However, because early adolescence is typically a time of increased self-consciousness and sensitivity (Elkind, 1967; Harter, 1990) promoting a feeling of mutual respect in the classroom may be especially beneficial to adolescents' adaptive motivational beliefs and engagement.

Teachers vary in the values that they communicate to students about relating to and respecting peers. An observational study of 19 classrooms found considerable variability in the nature of interactions among students and between the teacher and students (Anderson, Stevens, Prawat, & Nickerson, 1988). Whereas some classrooms were characterized by positive and comfortable relationships and frequent prosocial and cooperative interactions, other classrooms had an unpleasant affective tone and frequent negative student interactions such as bickering, criticism, and insults.

We investigated whether students' perceptions that their eighth-grade math teacher promoted mutual respect in the classroom supported their academic efficacy and self-regulated learning, as suggested by related research (Ryan & Patrick, 2001). Indeed, as hypothesized, students' efficacy for learning math increased significantly, relative to their efficacy in seventh grade, when they perceived they were in a classroom in which the math teacher promoted mutual respect. This indicates that being in an environment in which students' ideas and efforts are respected, with minimal threat of being laughed at or ridiculed, boosts students' confidence that they can learn their work successfully. Additionally, promoting mutual respect in the classroom was related to increased self-regulated learning from seventh to eighth grade. This indicates that when students believe they will not be embarrassed or teased if they have difficulty, they devote more cognitive resources to engaging with the tasks in hand.

We have argued to this point that aspects of the classroom social environment are important for all students' motivation and engagement. Although we believe that is so, there is some evidence that dimensions of the social environment may be especially important for girls, and for students of color. We address this research next.

Associations Between Gender and the Classroom Social Environment

There is some evidence that boys and girls typically experience their school contexts differently from one another (Eisenberg et al., 1996). They tend to be treated differently by their teachers. For example, boys tend to receive more teacher comments about management and procedures, and more indiscrimi-

nate criticism than do girls. Boys' negative feedback tends to be focused more on conduct and less on ability and the intellectual adequacy of their work than the negative feedback girls receive (Eisenberg et al., 1996). These differential gender-based experiences may contribute to boys and girls perceiving their classroom social environment differently from one other. For example, because boys tend to be criticized for misbehavior more often, girls, more than boys in the same class, may perceive that their teacher promotes interaction in the classroom. Indeed, we found that girls, on average, did report that their teacher promoted interaction among students more than did boys (Ryan & Patrick, 1999).

Some researchers have suggested that attention to social factors within classes, particularly in the areas of math and science, may enhance girls' motivation, engagement, and learning. This includes incorporating the use of instructional practices that foster interaction among students, small-group work, and collaborative activities, because such practices are believed to match girls' preferences for learning (American Association of University Women, 1999; Eccles, 1997; Eccles, Wigfield, & Schiefele, 1998). There is a need, however, for researchers to address such suggestions.

Related to this general issue of "girl-friendly classrooms" (Eccles et al., 1998) is consideration of whether some aspects of the social environment affect the motivation or engagement of one gender to a greater extent than the other gender (i.e., an interaction effect). For example, following from the argument that girls tend to prefer interaction and collaboration during learning activities, a classroom where the math teacher is perceived as encouraging interaction among peers during class work may be especially positive for girls' motivation. Indeed, Middleton and Midgley (1999) found that girls in math classes where the teacher was perceived to promote high levels of interaction tended to report greater self-efficacy for learning math relative to the whole sample of girls. However an interactive environment seemed less positive for the boys, who tended to report lower self-efficacy relative to the full sample of boys. That is, an interactive environment in math class appears to be related to reducing the typical gender gap in efficacy (Wigfield, Eccles, MacIver, Reuman, & Midgley, 1991), albeit at the expense of boys' typically higher sense of efficacy.

Related to the positive effect of an interaction-promoting environment for girls' motivation, we have found teacher support to be associated more positively with girls' efficacy relating to their math teacher than with boys' efficacy (Ryan & Patrick, 1999). Taken with Goodenow's (1993a) finding that teacher support was related more strongly to academic motivation for girls than for boys, it appears that viewing their teacher as supportive is especially important for girls, at least in mathematics.

Associations Between Race and Ethnicity
and the Classroom Social Environment

Researchers have suggested that students of color may experience a cultural mismatch between the interactional styles that they prefer and engage in within families and peer groups and those found within classrooms (Losey, 1995; Phelan, Davidson, & Yu, 1998). For example, many of these students' cultures value cooperation, collaboration, and interdependence, whereas schools tend to value independence and competitiveness more highly. Classrooms in which the norms, expectations, and student experiences are congruent and compatible with those in their home and community are believed to generate greater interest and participation of students of color (Phelan et al., 1998).

Classroom instructional approaches that include promoting student interaction, collaborative small-group work, and interdependence have been argued to be particularly beneficial for students of color (Gay, 1997; Ladson-Billings, 1995; Losey, 1995). For example, Ladson-Billings identified social features in the classroom that were incorporated by teachers who were especially effective with African American students. These include connectedness, reciprocity, mutuality, collaborative learning, and a noncompetitive focus. These aspects are also congruent with features of classrooms in which Mexican-American students are most successful (Losey, 1995). In such classrooms, teachers employ practices that involve open and warm communication between teacher and students (e.g., communicating through journal writing), class discussion, collaborative learning, student-initiated questions, elaborating on ideas, voicing opinions, respect and equal status for English and Spanish, and responsiveness to students' interests and experiences. Phelan and her colleagues (1998) also noted that instructional approaches that include oral participation, auditory activities, and group displays of knowledge where the teacher does not dominate the classroom interaction are particularly adaptive for Hispanic and Asian students.

Arguments that teachers' use of certain instructional practices is particularly adaptive for African American or Hispanic students imply possible differential effects of the social environment by race or ethnicity. The practices and classroom features just discussed parallel closely the constructs of teacher support and dimensions of the classroom social environment of interest to us. Accordingly, we investigated whether teacher support, promoting student interaction, and promoting mutual respect in the classroom are especially important for African American students' motivation and engagement (Ryan & Patrick, 1999). That is, we examined whether race moderates the relation between perceptions of the classroom social environment and adolescents' motivation and engagement. We found that race moderated the association between

the promotion of student interaction during math class and change in students' disruptive behavior in class—an indication of their interest and engagement. Specifically, when African American students perceived their eighth-grade teacher as promoting interaction during math class they reported less disruptive behavior relative to seventh grade, whereas promoting interaction was unrelated to changes in Euro-American students' disruptive behavior. These findings support the premise (e.g., Ladson-Billings, 1995) that having opportunities to interact with others is important for African American students' engagement in academics.

We also investigated possible interactions between race and gender with respect to students' motivation and engagement. There was a significant interaction between race and gender for students' social efficacy relating to the teacher. Race was a factor for boys', but not for girls', confidence relating to their teacher. Specifically, being an African American boy was related to lower efficacy for relating positively to the teacher in eighth grade. Furthermore, there was a significant interaction between race and gender on changes in social efficacy from seventh to eighth grade. Being an African American boy was related to decreased efficacy for relating effectively to the eighth-grade teacher. Furthermore, African American boys' efficacy for relating to their teacher declined more than that of any other group from seventh to eighth grade. Given that positive teacher relationships are important for school adjustment (Harter, 1996; Ryan, Stiller, & Lynch, 1994), this finding indicates that this may be a particularly vulnerable time for African American boys. Future research examining if African American boys' perceptions of their relationships with teachers continue to decline appears to be important, because this may be an important precursor of academic problems for some male African American students.

THE IMPORTANCE OF SOCIAL DIMENSIONS WITHIN SOCIAL CONSTRUCTIVIST-BASED INSTRUCTION

The students who participated in the Patterns of Adaptive Learning Study experienced relatively traditional instructional activities and formats. Increasingly, however, schools are using new and innovative curricula that are grounded in social-constructivist theories of learning and development. The tasks and instructional approaches associated with these reforms differ from traditional approaches to teaching and learning in significant ways. Therefore it seems likely that the social environment of those classes differs significantly from that of classes that use more traditional approaches. Furthermore, there may be differences in patterns of social interactions and perceptions associated with different types of instruction. Our research on social factors associated with students' motivation and engagement, and aspects of the classroom social environment,

relates predominantly to math classes that use traditional instruction. It is important, however, for researchers to examine how students' motivation and engagement can be promoted best within classrooms that use innovative instructional approaches (Blumenfeld, Marx, Patrick, Krajcik, & Soloway, 1997).

Social-constructivist-based instruction typically is centered on students' construction of personal understanding in the context of addressing real-world problems and issues. These problems, by their realistic nature, are typically complex, ill defined, and generative, in that they often lead to asking further questions. Important characteristics of this mode of instruction include authentic tasks and tool use, emphasizing student interaction and collaboration, and creating artifacts (J. S. Brown, Collins, & Duguid, 1989; Newman, Griffin, & Cole, 1989). Tasks, too, tend to be more complex, lengthier, and less neatly specified than those used with traditional instructional approaches (Blumenfeld et al., 1991).

Aspects of the classroom social environment may be especially crucial for students' adaptive motivation and engagement during social-constructivist-based instruction. It would be particularly important, presumably, for teachers using such curricula and approaches to actively promote interaction among students. However there has been little research about how to best establish student interactions to facilitate learning within these innovative curricula (Blumenfeld et al., 1997). Having all students interact and share their suggestions and hypotheses publicly may require a strong emphasis in the learning environment on mutual respect and an absence of overt ability or performance comparisons. Related to that, support from teachers may also be particularly important for students engaging cognitively in innovative tasks. Interacting and collaborating with peers in activities and projects over time demands greater interpersonal skills on the part of students than is the case with traditional individual tasks. Interactions and social support may serve important motivational functions in supporting persistence and allaying frustration during complex and challenging long-term projects. Accordingly, successful engagement in these types of learning activities may depend on students interacting effectively with peers to a greater degree than is common with traditional, individual classroom tasks.

In summary, because the social environment plays a crucial role in affording opportunities for learning, there is a need to investigate how social relationships and social aspects of classrooms can support or undermine students' motivation and engagement. This includes expanding our understanding of how the teacher can help to create a social climate in which students' motivation, engagement, and understanding can flourish.

REFERENCES

American Association of University Women. (1999). *Gender gaps: Where schools still fail our children.* New York: Marlowe & Company.

Ames, C. (1992). Classrooms: Goals, structures, and student motivation. *Journal of Educational Psychology, 84,* 261–271.

Anderman, L. (1999a). Classroom goal orientation, school belonging, and social goals as predictors of students' positive and negative affect following the transition to middle school. *Journal of Research and Development in Education, 32,* 89–103.

Anderman, L. (1999b). Expanding the discussion of social perceptions and academic outcomes: Mechanisms and contextual influences. In T. C. Urdan (Ed.), *Advances in motivation and achievement* (Vol. 11, pp. 303–336). Greenwich, CT: JAI.

Anderman, L. H., & Anderman, E. M. (1999). Social predictors of changes in students' achievement goal orientations. *Contemporary Educational Psychology, 25,* 21–37.

Anderson, L. M., Stevens, D. D., Prawat, R. S., Nickerson, J. (1988). Classroom task environments and students' task-related beliefs. *The Elementary School Journal, 88,* 281–295.

Battistich, V., Solomon, D., Kim, D., Watson, M., & Schaps, E. (1995). Schools as communities, poverty levels of student populations, and students' attitudes, motives, and performance: A multi-level analysis. *American Educational Research Journal, 32,* 627–658.

Berndt, T. J. (1982). The features and effects of friendship in early adolescence. *Child Development, 53,* 1447–1460.

Berndt, T. J. (1999). Friends' influence on students' adjustment to school. *Educational Psychologist, 34,* 15–28.

Berndt, T. J., & Mekos, D. (1995). Adolescents' perceptions of the stressful and desirable aspects of the transition to junior high school. *Journal of Research on Adolescence, 5,* 123–142.

Blumenfeld, P. C., Marx, R. W., Patrick, H., Krajcik, J. S., & Soloway, E. (1997). Teaching for understanding. In B. J. Biddle, T. L. Good, & I. F. Goodson (Eds.), *International handbook of teachers and teaching* (pp. 819–878). Dordrecht, Netherlands: Kluwer Academic Press.

Blumenfeld, P. C., Soloway, E., Marx, R. W., Krajcik, J. S., Guzdial, M., & Palincsar, A. (1991). Motivating project-based learning: Sustaining the doing, supporting the learning. *Educational Psychologist, 26,* 369–398.

Boekarts, M. (1993). Being concerned with well being and with learning. *Educational Psychologist, 28,* 149–167.

Brown, B. B. (1990). Peer groups and peer cultures. In S. S. Feldman & G. R. Elliott (Eds.), *At the threshold: The developing adolescent* (pp. 171–196). Cambridge, MA: Harvard University Press.

Brown, B. B., & Lohr, M. (1987). Peer group affiliation and adolescent self-esteem: An integration of ego-identity and symbolic interaction theories. *Journal of Personality and Social Psychology, 52,* 47–55.

Brown, J. S., Collins, A., & Duguid, P. (1989). Situated cognition and the culture of learning. *Educational Researcher, 18,* 32–42.

Buhrmester, D., & Furman, W. (1987). The development of companionship and intimacy. *Child Development, 58,* 1101–1113.

Chung, T., & Asher, S. R. (1996). Children's goals and strategies in peer conflict situations. *Merrill–Palmer Quarterly, 42,* 125–147.

Coie, J. D., & Kupersmidt, J. B. (1983). A behavioral analysis of emerging social status in boys' groups. *Child Development, 54,* 1400–1416.

Csikszentmihalyi, M., & Larson, R. (1984). *Being adolescent.* New York: Basic Books.

Dodge, K. A. (1983). Behavioral antecedents of peer social status. *Child Development, 54,* 1386–1399.

Dweck, C. S. (1996). Social motivation: Goals and social-cognitive processes. A comment. In J. Juvonen & K. R. Wentzel (Eds.), *Social motivation: Understanding children's school adjustment* (pp. 181–195). Cambridge, England: Cambridge University Press.

Eccles, J. (1985). Why doesn't Jane run? Sex differences in educational and occupational patterns. In F. D. Horowitz & M. O'Brien (Eds.), *The gifted and talented: A developmental perspective* (pp. 251–295). Washington, DC: American Psychological Association.

Eccles, J. (1997). User-friendly science and mathematics: Can it interest girls and minorities in breaking through the middle school wall? In D. Johnson (Ed.), *Minorities and girls in school: Effects on achievement and performance* (pp. 65–104). Thousand Oaks, CA: Sage.

Eccles, J., & Harold, R. D. (1992). Gender differences in educational and occupational patterns among the gifted. In N. Colangelo, S. G. Assouline, & D. L. Ambroson (Eds.), *Talent development: Proceedings from the 1991 Henry B. and Jocelyn Wallace National Research Symposium on Talent Development* (pp. 3–29). Unionville, NY: Trillium Press.

Eccles, J. S., & Midgley, C. (1989). Stage-environment fit: Developmentally appropriate classrooms for young adolescents. In C. Ames & R. Ames (Eds.), *Research on motivation in education* (Vol. 3, pp. 139–186). New York: Academic Press.

Eccles, J., Midgley, C., Wigfield, A., Buchanan, C. M., Reuman, D., Flanagan, C., & MacIver, D. (1993). Development during adolescence: The impact of stage-environment fit on young adolescents' experience in schools and families. *American Psychologist, 48,* 90–101.

Eccles, J. S., Wigfield, A., & Schiefele, U. (1998). Motivation to succeed. In W. Damon & N. Eisenberg (Eds.), *The handbook of child psychology: Vol. 3. Social, emotional, and personality development* (5th ed., pp. 1017–1095). New York: Wiley.

Eder, D. (1985). The cycle of popularity: Interpersonal relations among female adolescents. *Sociology of Education, 58,* 154–165.

Eisenberg, N., Martin, C. L., & Fabes, R. A. (1996). Gender development and gender effects. In D. C. Berliner & R. C. Calfee (Eds.), *Handbook of educational psychology* (pp.358–398). New York: Macmillan.

Elkind, D. (1967). Egocentrism in adolescence, *Child Development, 38,* 1025–1034.

Ellis, H. C., & Ashbrook, P. W. (1987). Resource allocation model of the effects of depressed mood states. In K. Fielder & J. Forgas (Eds.), *Affect, cognition, and social behavior* (pp. 25–43). Toronto: Hogrefe.

Feldlaufer, H., Midgley, C., & Eccles, J. S. (1988). Student, teacher, and observer perceptions of the classroom environment before and after the transition to junior high school. *Journal of Early Adolescence, 8,* 133–156.

Finn, J. (1989). Withdrawing from school. *Review of Educational Research, 59,* 117–142.

Ford, M. (1992). *Motivating humans: Goals, emotions, and personal agency.* Newbury Park, CA: Sage.

Fraser, B. J. & Fisher, D. L. (1982). Predicting student outcomes from their perceptions of classroom psycho social environment. *American Educational Research Journal, 19,* 498–518.

Furman, W., & Buhrmester, D. (1992). Age and sex differences in perceptions of networks of personal relationships. *Child Development, 63,* 103–115.

Gay, G. (1997). Educational equality for students of color. In J. A. Banks & C. A. M. Banks (Eds.), *Multicultural education: Issues and perspectives* (pp. 195–228). Boston: Allyn & Bacon.

Good, T., Mulryan, C., & McCaslin, M. (1992). Grouping for instruction in mathematics: A call for programmatic research on small-group processes. In D. A. Grouws (Ed.), *Handbook of research on mathematics teaching and learning* (pp. 165–196). New York: Macmillan.

Goodenow, C. (1992). Strengthening the links between educational psychology and the study of social contexts. *Educational Psychologist, 27,* 177–196.

Goodenow, C. (1993a). Classroom belonging among early adolescent students: Relationships to motivation and achievement. *Journal of Early Adolescence, 13,* 21–43.

Goodenow, C. (1993b). The psychological sense of school membership among adolescents: Scale development and educational correlates. *Psychology in the Schools, 30,* 79–90.

Harter, S. (1990). Self and identity development. In S. S. Feldman & G.R. Elliot (Eds.), *At the threshold: The developing adolescent* (pp. 352–387). Cambridge, MA: Harvard University Press.

Harter, S. (1996). Teacher and classmate influences on scholastic motivation, self-esteem, and level of voice in adolescents. In J. Juvonen & K. R. Wentzel (Eds.), *Social motivation: Understanding children's school adjustment* (pp. 11–42). Cambridge, England: Cambridge University Press.

Hartup, W. W. (1989). Social relationships and their developmental significance. *American Psychologist, 44,* 120–126.

Hartup, W. W. (1993). Adolescents and their friends. In B. Laursen (Ed.), *Close friendships in adolescence* (pp. 3–22). San Francisco: Jossey-Bass.

Hartup, W. W. (1996). The company they keep: Friendships and their developmental significance. *Child Development, 67,* 1–13.

Hicks, L. (1997). How do academic motivation and peer relationships mix in an adolescent's world? *Middle School Journal, 28,* 18–22.

Hicks, L., Murphy, A. M., & Patrick, H. (1995, March). *Social goals and achievement goals in early adolescence.* Poster session presented at the biennial meeting of the Society for Research in Child Development, Indianapolis, IN.

Hymel, S., Comfort, C., Schonert-Reichl, K., & McDougall, P. (1996). Academic failure and school dropout: The influence of peers. In J. Juvonen & K. R. Wentzel (Eds.), *Social motivation: Understanding children's school adjustment* (pp. 313–345). New York: Cambridge University Press.

Jehn, K. A., & Shah, P. P. (1997). Interpersonal relationships and task performance: An examination of mediating processes in friendship and acquaintance groups. *Journal of Personality and Social Psychology, 72,* 775–790.

Keating, D. P. (1990). Adolescent thinking. In S. S. Feldman & G. R. Elliot (Eds.), *At the threshold: The developing adolescent* (pp. 54–89). Cambridge, MA: Harvard University Press.

Kinney, D. A. (1993). From "nerds" to "normals": Adolescent identity recovery within a changing social system. *Sociology of Education, 66,* 21–40.

Ladson-Billings, G. (1995). Toward a theory of culturally relevant pedagogy. *American Educational Research Journal, 32,* 465–491.

Losey, K. M. (1995). Mexican American students and classroom interaction: An overview and critique. *Review of Educational Research, 65,* 283–318.

Maccoby, E. E. (1990). Gender and relationships: A developmental account. *American Psychologist, 45,* 513–520.

Maehr, M. L., & Midgley, C. (1996). *Transforming school cultures.* Boulder, CO: Westview Press.

Middleton, M. J., & Midgley, C. (1999, April). *Classroom effects on the gender gap in middle school students' math self-efficacy.* Poster session presented at the annual meeting of the American Educational Research Association, Montreal.

Midgley, C., & Feldlaufer, H. (1987). Students' and teachers' decision-making fit before and after the transition to junior high school. *Journal of Early Adolescence, 7*, 225–241.

Midgley, C., Feldlaufer, H., & Eccles, J. S. (1989). Student/teacher relations and attitudes toward mathematics before and after the transition to junior high school. *Child Development, 60*, 981–992.

Newman, D., Griffin, P., & Cole, M. (1989). *The construction zone: Working for cognitive change in school.* Cambridge, England: Cambridge University Press.

Nolen, S. B. (1988). Reasons for studying: Motivational orientations and study strategies. *Cognition and Instruction, 5*, 269–287.

Parker, J. G., & Asher, S. R. (1987). Peer relations and later personal adjustment: Are low-accepted children at risk? *Psychological Bulletin, 102*, 357–389.

Patrick, H. (1997). Social self-regulation: Exploring the relations between children's social relationships, academic self-regulation, and school performance. *Educational Psychologist, 32*, 209–220.

Patrick, H., Anderman, L. H., Ryan, A. M., Edelin, K., & Midgley, C. (2001). Teachers' communication of goal orientations in four fifth-grade classrooms. *Elementary School Journal, 102*, 35–58.

Patrick, H., Edelin, K., Hicks, L., Middleton, M., & Midgley, C. (1997, March). *Social influences of students' emotional adjustment: Different effects for African-American and European-American students.* Paper presented at the annual meeting of the American Educational Research Association, Chicago.

Patrick, H., Hicks, L., & Ryan, A. M. (1997). Relations of perceived social efficacy and social goal pursuit to self-efficacy for academic work. *Journal of Early Adolescence, 17*, 109–128.

Perret-Clermont, A. N., Perret, J., & Bell, N. (1991). The social construction of meaning and cognitive activity in elementary school children. In L. B. Resnick, J. M. Levine, & S. D. Teasley (Eds.), *Perspectives on socially shared cognition* (pp. 41–62). Washington, DC: American Psychological Association.

Phelan, P., Davidson, A. L., & Yu, H. C. (1998). *Adolescents' worlds: Negotiating family, peers, and school.* New York: Teachers College Press.

Pintrich, P. R., & De Groot, E. V. (1990). Motivational and self-regulated learning components of classroom academic performance. *Journal of Educational Psychology, 82*, 33–40.

Roeser, R., Midgley, C., & Urdan, T. C. (1996). Perception of the school psychological environment and early adolescents' psychological and behavioral functioning in school: The mediating role of goals and belonging. *Journal of Educational Psychology, 88*, 408–422.

Ryan, A. M., Hicks, L., & Midgley, C. (1997). Social goals, academic goals, and avoiding seeking help in the classroom. *The Journal of Early Adolescence, 17*, 152–171.

Ryan, A. M., & Patrick, H. (1999, April). *The classroom social environment and adolescents' motivation and engagement at school.* Poster session presented at the annual meeting of the American Educational Research Association, Montreal.

Ryan, A. M., & Patrick, H. (2001). The classroom social environment and changes in adolescents' motivation and engagement during middle school. *American Educational Research Journal, 38*, 437–460.

Ryan, R. M., Stiller, J. D., & Lynch, J. H. (1994). Representations of relationships to teachers, parents, and friends as predictors of academic motivation and self-esteem. *Journal of Early Adolescence, 14*, 226–249.

Savin-Williams, R. C., & Berndt, T. J. (1990). Friendship and peer relations. In S. S. Feldman & G. R. Elliott (Eds.), *At the threshold: The developing adolescent* (pp. 277–307). Cambridge, MA: Harvard University Press.

Schunk, D. (1983). Ability versus effort attributional feedback: Differential effects on self-efficacy and achievement. *Journal of Educational Psychology, 75,* 848–856.

Skinner, E. A., & Belmont, M. J. (1993). Motivation in the classroom: Reciprocal effects of teacher behavior and student engagement across the school year. *Journal of Educational Psychology, 85,* 571–581.

Turner, J. C., Thorpe, P. K., & Meyer, D. K. (1998). Students' reports of motivation and negative affect: A theoretical and empirical analysis. *Journal of Educational Psychology, 90,* 758–771.

Urdan, T. C., & Maehr, M. L. (1995). Beyond a two-goal theory of motivation and achievement: A case for social goals. *Review of Educational Research, 65,* 213–243.

Vygotsky, L. S. (1978). *Mind in society: The development of higher psychological processes.* Cambridge, MA: Harvard University Press.

Webb, N. M., & Palincsar, A. S. (1996). Group processes in the classroom. In D. C. Berliner & R. C. Calfee (Eds.), *Handbook of educational psychology* (pp. 841–873). New York: Simon & Schuster.

Wentzel, K. R. (1989). Adolescent classroom goals, standards for performance, and academic achievement: An interactionist perspective. *Journal of Educational Psychology, 81,* 131–142.

Wentzel, K. R. (1991a). Classroom competence may require more than intellectual ability: Reply to Jussim (1991). *Journal of Educational Psychology, 83,* 156–158.

Wentzel, K. R. (1991b). Relations between social competence and academic achievement in early adolescence. *Child Development, 62,* 1066–1078.

Wentzel, K. R. (1991c). Social competence at school: Relation between social responsibility and academic achievement. *Review of Educational Research, 61,* 1–24.

Wentzel, K. R. (1993). Motivation and achievement in early adolescence: The role of multiple classroom goals. *Journal of Early Adolescence, 13,* 4–10.

Wigfield, A., Eccles, J., MacIver, D., Reuman, D., & Midgley, C. (1991). Transitions during early adolescence: Changes in children's domain-specific self-perceptions and general self-esteem across the transition to junior high school. *Developmental Psychology, 27,* 552–565.

5

Stage–Environment Fit Revisited: A Goal Theory Approach to Examining School Transitions

Carol Midgley
University of Michigan

Michael J. Middleton
University of New Hampshire

Margaret H. Gheen
University of Michigan

Revathy Kumar
University of Toledo

For more than a decade, members of our research team have been conducting studies aimed at understanding the effect on students of the transition from elementary to middle-level schools. Certainly one of the reasons we have pursued this issue has been our interest in young adolescents and middle-level schools, and in middle school reform. However, there is another reason our research has focused on school transitions. Educational research has suffered from a lack of variation across classrooms and schools (Lipsitz, 1977; McPartland & Karweit, 1979; Sarason & Klaber, 1985). That is, many classrooms and schools do not differ markedly from one another, and thus research comparing students across classrooms or schools, or following students from one classroom or school to an-

other, has often produced disappointing results. In contrast, transitions from one school level to another provide an opportunity to look at the effects of normative change. We know that middle-level schools differ in specific ways from elementary schools. Using theory, we can make predictions regarding how those differences will be related to changes in students' perceptions, beliefs, and behaviors, and to differences between elementary and middle school teachers, thereby testing the theory.

In this chapter we first describe the thesis we articulated almost two decades ago, based on a review of the literature and on our own studies, that there is a lack of *stage–environment fit* between many young adolescents and the learning environment they experience when they move to middle-level schools. We discuss the various assumptions that are inherent in stage–environment fit and whether and how studies examining school transitions inform these assumptions. Our initial study of the transition to middle-level schools (Eccles, Midgley, Wigfield, Buchanan, Reuman, Feldlaufer, & MacIver, 1993) used expectancy–value theory as the motivational framework. In subsequent studies, including the Patterns of Adaptive Learning Study, we used goal theory to examine and interpret differences in the learning environment and changes in students' patterns of learning across school transitions. Our studies using goal theory have included the transition from elementary schools to "traditional" middle schools, as well as from elementary schools to middle schools incorporating at least some of the reforms that have been recommended in the past decade (e.g., Carnegie Task Force, 1989). Studies examining changes within the middle school years and during the transition to high school are also described. We conclude by considering the implications of these findings for students, teachers, and school reform at both the middle and high school levels.

STAGE–ENVIRONMENT FIT[1]

Stage–environment fit is based on the assumption that if changes in needs are aligned with changes in opportunities at a certain stage of life, positive outcomes will result. The concept of stage–environment fit has been applied in particular to early adolescents and middle-level schools. In a review article (Eccles & Midgley, 1989), we summarized evidence of deterioration in beliefs about the self, motivation, and performance during early adolescence, and in particular after the transition to middle-level schools. We then reviewed the literature to determine if there was evidence of developmental changes in young adolescents' needs and in the opportunities afforded by the learning environment during the transition to middle-level schools, expecting to find that needs

---

[1]Some of the sections in this chapter were adapted from papers and chapters published previously, including Eccles and Midgley (1989), Midgley (1993), and Midgley and Edelin (1998).

changed and opportunities did not. That is not what we found. We found that the learning environment did change, but in a way that would predict lower motivation to achieve at any stage of life, but especially in conjunction with the changes associated with early adolescence and with puberty. We challenged the long-held view that the deterioration in motivation and performance at this stage of life was the inevitable result of changes associated with puberty, and emphasized the importance of considering the nature of the transition, as well as the timing.

We began by viewing these findings from the perspective of person–environment fit theory. This theory states that an individual's behavior is jointly determined by characteristics of the person and properties of the immediate environment (e.g., Lewin, 1935). When the needs or goals of the individual are congruent with the opportunities afforded by the environment, then favorable motivational, affective, and behavioral outcomes should result. When they are not congruent, then unfavorable outcomes should result. Lewin expressed this in terms of the formula: $B = f(P, E)$, or Behavior is a function of the Person and the Environment. No judgment was made as to whether the needs expressed by the individual were "good" or "bad" or "age-appropriate." Subsequently, Hunt (1975) accused educational psychologists of having an "excessively restrictive definition of person/environment fit" (p. 209). He extended the initial conceptualization by adding a developmental perspective, saying that change in behavior is an interactive function of the person's developmental stage and the experienced environment. He suggested that growth or the lack of it was the dependent variable. "Growth" was defined in terms of developmental needs. Thus Hunt added two important assumptions to the original conceptualization of person–environment fit: first, that it was important to consider developmental change, and second, that a judgment should be made regarding whether the change enhanced or arrested growth:

> Person characteristics, therefore, need not only be potentially compatible with current environmental effects but should also index variations in developmental change. Maintaining a developmental perspective becomes very important in implementing person–environment matching because a teacher should not only take account of a student's contemporaneous needs by providing whatever structure he currently requires, but also view his present need for structure on a developmental continuum along which growth toward independence and less need for structure is the long-term objective. (Hunt, 1975, p. 221)

Note that in this quote needs are defined in terms of what students "require" for growth, not solely in terms of their personal needs and characteristics.

Building on Hunt's (1975) thesis, we suggested that the developmental characteristics of early adolescents and the opportunities afforded in the middle school environment could be viewed in terms of "stage–environment fit." It

was our belief that changes in characteristics or needs of students at this stage of life should be considered in relation to differences in the experienced environment before and after the transition. We acknowledged that when there is a fit between the needs of students in general at this stage of life and the opportunities afforded by the learning environment, there will still be individual students who experience a discrepancy between their needs and opportunities. For example, students on average may increase in their desire for autonomy and decision making during early adolescence (e.g., Midgley & Feldlaufer, 1987), but some students may actually desire less autonomy as they mature. As articulated by Hunt, changes in the learning environment should reflect the need for young adolescents to take greater responsibility and to participate more in decision making as they grow toward adulthood. As is the case with Hunt, we make certain assumptions, based on theory, about the kind of learning environment that is growth enhancing at this stage of life:

> As children move through early adolescence, they are becoming more knowledgeable and skillful and are developing cognitively. They are able to use critical thinking to explore open-ended questions or moral dilemmas rather than dealing primarily with rote, right answer, memorization. They develop a more differentiated ability concept, moving from equating ability and effort to perceiving ability or intellectual capacity as relatively stable (Nicholls, 1986). They typically express a desire for more control over their lives (Lee, 1979). At the same time many children are experiencing the changes associated with puberty. They become self-focused and concerned about themselves in comparison to others (Elkind & Bowen, 1979; Simmons, Rosenberg, & Rosenberg, 1973). Relationships with friends and extra parental adults become especially important (Miller, 1974). Does it make sense to put these developing children in a classroom environment that is less demanding cognitively, that promotes ability evaluation and social comparison, that decreases opportunities for student self-management and choice, and that is more formal and impersonal? We suggest that there is a developmental mismatch resulting from changes in the classroom environment that are at odds with physiological, psychological, and cognitive changes in the young adolescent. (Eccles & Midgley, 1989, p. 174)

In the next section we first describe research we conducted two decades ago on the transition to junior high school, including a study that provided an explicit test of stage/environment fit. Second, we provide an overview of studies that we have conducted examining differences in the learning environment before and after the transition from elementary to middle school, during the middle school years, and during the transition from middle to high school. We consider whether those changes can be considered growth enhancing or growth arresting for students at this stage of life. Third, we provide an overview of our studies that have examined the link between perceived change in the learning environment during the transition to both middle and high school and change in students' patterns of learning (cognition, affect, behavior). Finally, we take a somewhat different ap-

proach and consider whether there is evidence that younger adolescents (early middle school) are more sensitive to both the positive and negative effects of the learning environment than are older adolescents (early high school), and consider whether there is evidence that stage–environment fit is a particularly relevant concept for younger adolescents.

SCHOOL TRANSITIONS AND STAGE–ENVIRONMENT FIT

After writing our review article (Eccles & Midgley, 1989), we conducted a large-scale study following over 2,000 students as they moved from the last year of elementary school (fall and spring of their sixth-grade year) to the first year of junior high school (fall and spring of their seventh-grade year). We found evidence that changes in students' expectancies and values in mathematics were related to differences in the classroom environment before and after the transition (MacIver & Reuman, 1988; Midgley, Eccles, & Feldlaufer, 1991; Midgley, Feldlaufer, & Eccles, 1989a, 1989b). Most students moved to a less facilitative learning environment in math after the transition (e.g., experienced a less positive student–teacher relationship, had teachers with a lower sense of efficacy, had fewer opportunities for decision making) and suffered declines in their perceptions of their performance and potential in mathematics, and in their valuing of math. Those students who experienced the opposite pattern showed either no change or positive changes in their math-related expectancies and values. The expectancies and values of lower achieving students were particularly sensitive to both negative and positive changes in the learning environment during the transition. We concluded that although the timing of the transition to middle-level schools may render early adolescents particularly vulnerable, these studies showed that they were vulnerable to both negative and positive influences.

Stage–Environment Fit: An Explicit Test

In conjunction with the larger study described previously, we conducted an explicit test of stage–environment fit in one domain: needs and opportunities for decision making in the classrooms (MacIver & Reuman, 1988; Midgley & Feldlaufer, 1987). An explicit test of stage–environment fit would include an assessment of change in needs by students at a particular stage of life (such as an increase in the desire for student self-management and choice), an assessment of change in opportunities (such as a decrease in opportunities for student self-management and choice), and an examination of the effects on students of various patterns of change in needs and opportunities. On surveys given during the sixth grade in elementary school and a year later during the seventh grade in junior high school, both students and their teachers were asked about the deci-

sions students were able to make during math instruction, and also about those they *should* be able to make. On average, students expressed a desire for more decision-making opportunities after the transition than before (increase in needs) and reported that they received fewer opportunities after the transition than before. Their junior high school teachers believed that students should have fewer decision-making opportunities than did their sixth-grade elementary school teachers. Looking at the motivational consequences, students who reported a greater discrepancy between their needs and opportunities for decision making after the transition than before, showed the largest decline in their intrinsic interest in math as they moved from the sixth to seventh grade.

DIFFERENCES IN THE LEARNING ENVIRONMENT ACROSS SCHOOL TRANSITIONS

We now move to studies that have examined three of the mismatches described by Eccles and Midgley (1989) in the earlier quotation: (a) the decline in the emphasis on critical thinking, (b) the increase in the emphasis on relative ability and social comparison, and (c) the deterioration in the student–teacher relationship. We conceptualize the first two in terms of achievement goal theory. That is, the emphasis on relative ability is conceptualized as a performance goal and the emphasis on critical thinking is conceptualized as a mastery goal (see chap. 2, this volume). We acknowledge that our assessment of mastery goals in the learning environment has focused more on the emphasis on learning, understanding, improvement, and effort, and less on the nature of academic tasks. We agree with Blumenfeld (1992) that the variety, diversity, challenge, control, and meaningfulness of academic tasks influence student perceptions of the classroom goal orientation, and that the key dimensions may be meaningfulness and value. We hope that future research on the classroom goal structure will focus more on the nature of academic tasks. However, for the purposes of this chapter, we believe that the emphasis on learning and understanding is somewhat analogous to the emphasis on critical thinking as articulated by Eccles and Midgley (1989). The affective, "social" dimension of the learning environment (the aforementioned Item c) is not integral to achievement goal theory, although there are those who believe it is an important component of a mastery goal structure (e.g., Meece, 1991; Patrick, Anderman, Ryan, Edelin, & Midgley, 2001; Turner, Meyer, Midgley, & Patrick, 2001; Turner, Midgley et al., in press).

We focus in particular on whether the learning environment changes in a way that theory and research would characterize as growth enhancing or growth arresting. We do this in conjunction with evidence from our studies and other studies and even "common wisdom" that suggests a change in early ado-

lescents' needs, but in this section we do not provide explicit evidence of a link between changes in needs, changes in the environment, and changes in patterns of learning. In the studies cited in the following sections, unlike the study of decision-making fit just described, changes in the needs and characteristics of students are not assessed directly.

Differences in the Relationship Dimension in Elementary and Middle-Level Schools

We begin this section by talking generally about differences between elementary and middle schools that might contribute to a negative change in the quality of relationships when students make the transition to middle-level schools. Then we describe recommendations that have been made, and in some cases implemented, to address this problem. We also cite studies we have conducted that have examined changes in the relationship dimension during the transition to traditional middle schools and also during the transition to middle schools in which reforms aimed at improving interpersonal relationships have been undertaken.

Elementary schools are frequently referred to as "neighborhood" schools. Students spend most of the school day with one teacher and one set of peers, some of whom are friends from the neighborhood. In most cases, middle schools[2] are larger than elementary schools and students from several elementary feeder schools attend one middle school. Thus it is not surprising that a number of studies have provided evidence of a decline in the quality of interpersonal relationships after the transition (e.g., Berndt & Hawkins, 1993; Estrada, 1993; Hirsch & Rapkin, 1987; Lynch & Cicchetti, 1997; Seidman, Allen, Aber, Mitchell, & Feinman, 1994). In the study we conducted in the early 1980s, both students and classroom observers perceived deterioration in the student–teacher relationship after the transition to junior high school (Feldlaufer, Midgley, & Eccles, 1988).

As a result of research such as this and the growing dissatisfaction of parents, teachers, and students, a number of recommendations were made to improve the quality of relationships in middle-level schools. Some of these recommendations focused on "preparing" students for the new environment, assuming that if students had a better understanding of what was ahead, they would be better able to adjust (Bruene, 1985; Combs, 1993). Others focused on helping students during the first few months in middle school by, for example, providing "buddies" (Ferguson & Bulach, 1994) or special programs for stu-

---

[2]We use the term *middle schools* henceforth, but acknowledge that there are many different terms used to describe middle-level schools, including *intermediate schools*, *junior high schools*, and *middle schools*.

dents, particularly those who were thought to be "at risk" for difficulties associated with the transition (Alspaugh, 1998; Felner, Gintner, & Primavera, 1982). Thus the emphasis was on changing the student to fit the school, rather than changing the school to fit the student. Although these programs did show positive effects at least in the short run, they were not aimed at changing the learning environment in middle-level schools.

In contrast, the Carnegie Task Force on the Education of Young Adolescents (1989), in their widely read document *Turning Points*, recommended that "the enormous middle school be restructured in a more human scale. The student should, upon entering middle grade school, join a small community in which people—students and adults—get to know each other well to create a climate for intellectual development" (p. 37). The California State Department of Education (Superintendent's Middle Grade Task Force, 1987) stated that "large schools need to be divided into smaller, more easily managed units. Whether called 'house,' 'school-within-a-school,' or some other term, the primary purpose is to allow a sense of closeness to develop between students and staff which enhances the development of intellectual growth, academic achievement, and emotional and social maturity" (p. 101). Almost all middle school reform documents proposed some form of team teaching and recommended the establishment of advisor–advisee programs linking each student with a staff member for special guidance and support.

Many middle school educators took these recommendations seriously, and relationships in those schools improved. In 1987 the Lilly Endowment initiated the Middle Grades Improvement Program (MGIP) by targeting grants to middle schools in 16 urban school districts in Indiana. Each of the middle schools crafted their own improvement plans, following guidelines developed by Lilly. In a recent report, they wrote: "Even the most jaded of observers agree that there is little question that many of the MGIP schools 'feel' better: they are, for the most part, friendlier, warmer, more relaxed, and more respectful. In the best of them there is an energetic calm, more collegiality, and more focused attachments between adults and children" (Lipsitz, 1997, p. 555). Our research conducted in conjunction with the Patterns of Adaptive Learning Study in schools initiating some reforms confirms this change in the relationship dimension. Overall, students no longer reported a deterioration in the quality of student–teacher relationships (Midgley et al., 1998), and remarkably, their sense of school belonging increased after the transition to middle school (Kumar & Midgley, 2001). Before we looked at the data, we had reason to believe that these results might emerge. As part of a qualitative interview study (see chap. 7, this volume), Kimberley Edelin Freeman spent 2 or 3 days a week over a period of several months in one of the middle schools participating in our study. She reported that students seemed to feel reasonably good about their relationships with others in school and generally were positive about their

current and future circumstances. She was surprised and pleased. However, she expressed serious concern about the lack of emphasis on learning, understanding, and challenge in the school. She expressed concern that some middle schools might be providing a friendlier, more emotionally supportive environment for young adolescents but might not be strengthening the academic aspect of caring—that is, helping students really learn and understand. This leads us to the second mismatch described by Eccles and Midgley (1989): young adolescents' growing cognitive sophistication and the decline in the emphasis on critical thinking. Here we turn to goal theory to provide the framework within which to interpret the findings.

Differences Between Elementary and Middle-Level Schools in the Goal Structure

We have used goal theory to guide our recent studies of the transition to middle and high school. Theorists have described two achievement goals in particular: the goal to develop ability (a mastery goal) and the goal to demonstrate ability or to avoid the demonstration of lack of ability (a performance goal) (see chap. 2, this volume). There has been remarkable consistency, over a host of studies, regarding the relation between mastery goals and adaptive patterns of learning (for reviews see Ames, 1992; Dweck & Leggett, 1988; Pintrich & Schunk, 1996; Urdan, 1997). The research on performance goals has been less consistent (Midgley, Kaplan, & Middleton, 2001).

In a cross-sectional study (Midgley, E. Anderman, & Hicks, 1995), middle school teachers and students perceived that the school learning environment was more focused on performance goals and less focused on mastery goals than did elementary teachers and students. Elementary teachers also reported using practices that emphasized mastery goals, and endorsed mastery goals for their students more than did middle school teachers. In a longitudinal study (E. Anderman & Midgley, 1997), students perceived a greater emphasis on performance goals after the transition to middle school than before. These studies were conducted in the early 1990s in schools that had not implemented middle school reforms.

As part of the Patterns of Adaptive Learning Study, we conducted similar studies in the mid-1990s in four school districts in which some middle school reforms had been adopted. In a longitudinal study following students from fifth grade in elementary school to sixth grade in middle school, students no longer perceived an increase in the emphasis on performance goals after the transition (Midgley et al., 1998). Many of the reforms being implemented by these middle schools were aimed at reducing the saliency of ability differences among students. For example, all students were required to take a core of common subjects and the use of homogeneous ability grouping was reduced. Some of these

schools also eliminated programs to reward students for high grades. It appears that these changes may have had an influence on students' perceptions of the emphasis on performance goals in middle schools. In contrast, as in earlier studies, students still perceived a decrease in the emphasis on understanding, effort, mastery, and improvement (mastery goal structure) when they moved to middle-level schools (Midgley & Edelin, 1998; Midgley et al., 1998). Less is known about how to create mastery goals in schools than how to affect the saliency of performance goals (e.g., Bergin, 1995). There is considerable rhetoric in the middle school reform documents about emphasizing "real understanding" and "challenging students to think deeply" but few guidelines regarding what teachers should do in the classroom. Additionally, assigned textbooks, the press to "cover" the curriculum, and high-stakes testing may limit teachers' ability to provide meaningful and valuable academic tasks to students.

In Eccles and Midgley (1989), we suggested that a decline in academic challenge at a time when students were developing cognitively was an example of a lack of stage–environment fit. In contrast to Eccles and Midgley, others claimed that early adolescence was a time of little brain growth and that students at this age needed a "psycho social moratorium." Epstein (1978) claimed that during early adolescence the brain undergoes a plateau in growth and students have difficulty initiating new cognitive skills. As interpreted by Toepfer and Marani (1980), "Epstein's research suggests that inappropriate expectations for cognitive learning during the period of plateau in brain growth (ages twelve to fourteen) could result in difficulties for students" (p. 175). They went on to say that these data "suggest that there is a need to study the degree to which existing programs in the middle grades may be over-challenging students during the plateau in brain growth at ages twelve to fourteen. It is possible that this over-challenging occurs because schools are providing learning inputs for which the children have not yet developed receptors" (p. 276).

We think it important to state that the claim that the brain does not grow during early adolescence has now been refuted. In a recent study, researchers at the University of California at Los Angeles, the National Institutes of Health, and McGill University found that even in the midteens, the amount of gray matter in the brain can double (Thompson et al., 2000). One of the researchers told the *Washington Post*: "The teenage years are a kind of critical time to optimize the brain." This research provides support for the thesis articulated by Eccles and Midgley (1989), that young adolescents are developing cognitively and that the lack of challenge in middle schools, and the emphasis on the completion of work sheets and the memorization of facts are at odds with their needs and potential for learning. We do not know if the work of Epstein and others in the 1970s and 1980s influenced educators' thinking about the appropriate learning environment for young adolescents, but we are pleased to see that this research

has been refuted and that the ability of young adolescents to profit from complex learning is now acknowledged.

DIFFERENCES ACROSS THE MIDDLE SCHOOL GRADES IN THE GOAL STRUCTURE

In conjunction with the Patterns of Adaptive Learning Study, we also assessed changes in students' perceptions of the goal structure across the middle school years (Grades 6, 7, and 8 in this study). Although *Turning Points* (Carnegie Task Force, 1989) recommended systemic reforms at all grade levels within middle schools, many of the reforms that were implemented focused on the first year of middle school. Conversations with middle school teachers and reports from school administrators indicated to us that reforms did focus primarily on the sixth-grade level. Note that in Fig. 5.1, which is based on reports from the middle school principals in the Patterns of Adaptive Learning Study, keeping the same group of students together across at least three subject matter areas was reported in the sixth grade by 60% of the schools, and was reported in the seventh and eighth grade by only 10% of the schools. Assignment to math classes based on ability was reported at the sixth-grade level in 50% of the middle schools, but was reported at the seventh-grade level in 70% of the schools and at the eighth-grade level in 80% of the schools. Although this is only limited evidence that reforms have focused in particular on the first year of middle

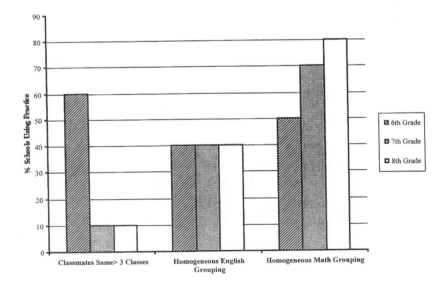

FIG. 5.1.   Principals' report of middle school practices. From Roeser, Midgley, and Wood (1995).

school, it does point to the need to examine more than the years before and after the transition from elementary to middle school. If this pattern of change within the middle school years is prevalent, we might expect that the quality of relationships would show a negative change from sixth to seventh grade, and perceptions of an emphasis on performance goals would increase across the middle school years. We did indeed find a significant drop in students' perceptions of the quality of their relationships with their teachers from sixth to seventh grade. Contrary to expectations, reports from students indicated that, on average, the perceived emphasis on performance goals declined across the middle school years. In addition, we did not find evidence of a further decline in students' perceptions of a mastery goal emphasis (Midgley et al., 2000). Qualitative studies, including both classroom observations and interviews with students, might shed some light on these unexpected findings.

DIFFERENCES BETWEEN MIDDLE AND HIGH SCHOOLS IN THE GOAL STRUCTURE

In a review of the literature on the effects of the high school learning environment on adolescents' beliefs and behaviors, we found little discussion of the developmental stage of these students, though high school students are continuing to develop cognitively, physically, and socially. Studies of the high school transition have tended to focus more on changes in school performance, participation in extracurricular activities, disciplinary incidents, and absenteeism than on self-perceptions, motivation, or learning strategies. For example, the transition to high school has been associated with a drop in grades (Barone, Aguirre-Deandreis, & Trickett, 1991; Blyth, Simmons, & Carlton-Ford, 1983; Owings & Peng, 1992), an increase in disciplinary problems (Weldy, 1990) and the dropout rate (Owings & Peng, 1992), and poorer attendance (Barone et al., 1991). As with the transition from middle to high school, many of the recommendations regarding the high school transition have focused on helping students adjust (e.g., DaGiau, 1997; Marshall, 1992) rather than on creating a more facilitative learning environment.

In the Patterns of Adaptive Learning Study, we also examined changes in the relationship dimension and in the goal structure during the transition to high school (eighth grade and the following year in ninth grade; e.g., Gheen, Hruda, Middleton, & Midgley, 2000). While the study was taking place, we visited the high schools to explain the study, to give surveys, to collect information from school records, and to provide feedback to principals and teachers. We noticed many differences between the high schools and the middle schools, even within the same district. The high schools were larger and more bureaucratic than were the middle schools, with departments and department chairs assuming special importance. There was no evidence of interdisciplinary

teaming in the high schools, with most students moving from class to class approximately every 40 minutes with a changing peer group. Counselors tended to deal with behavior problems or to dispense information about college applications and job opportunities rather than to serve as "advisors." Classes homogeneous in ability, including remedial and advanced placement courses, were more prevalent in the high schools than in the middle schools. Honor rolls and honor assemblies were pervasive in the high schools. It should also be noted that the high schools tended to have more resources than the middle schools, such as video and computer equipment, technically sophisticated media centers, well-equipped science laboratories, and better sports facilities.

Very few studies have compared either the quality of relationships or the nature of the goal structure in middle and high schools; therefore our hypotheses were based on what we have observed and what others have written about differences between middle and high schools. With the increase in the number of teachers and students, and the decline in the incidence of teaming in high schools as compared to middle schools, we suggested that the quality of the student–teacher relationship might also decline. We also suggested that the emphasis on performance goals might increase after the transition to high school, as students are assigned to advanced placement and remedial classes, and as testing and the recognition of relative ability become widespread. Note that in Fig. 5.2, the percentage of high schools using performance-focused practices (as reported by the principals of those schools) was higher than the percentage of middle schools on a range of practices including the distribution of bumper stickers to parents of high-achieving students, programs to reward students for high grades, and the incidence of gifted and talented programs. The only practices on which the percentage of middle and high schools was similar was the use of public honor rolls and academic recognition assemblies, in that all schools at both the middle and high school levels reported these practices. On the other hand, we suggested that the emphasis on mastery goals might also be greater in high school, with more complex and challenging courses and with the expectation that students do more than memorize facts and perform on tests.

In the Patterns of Adaptive Learning Study, we examined data from middle and high school teachers, and from students before and after the transition to high school. In a study assessing differences in elementary, middle, and high school teachers' perceptions of the school goal structure and their use of mastery and performance approaches to instruction in the classroom, high school teachers reported using mastery approaches in their classrooms less than did middle school teachers, and perceived less of an emphasis on mastery goals in their schools (Marachi, Gheen, & Midgley, 2001). There were no differences in middle and high school teachers' reports of using performance approaches to instruction in the classroom or in their perceptions of the emphasis on per-

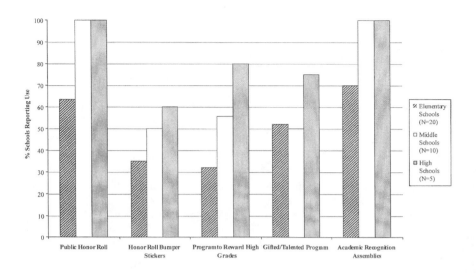

FIG. 5.2.   Principals' reports of performance-focused practices by school level. From
Roeser, Midgley, and Wood (1995). Unpublished manuscript. Adapted by permission.

formance goals in the school. However, both middle and high school teachers
reported using performance-focused approaches to instruction more than did
elementary teachers, and perceived a greater emphasis on performance goals
in the school than did elementary teachers. These patterns are shown in Figs.
5.3 and 5.4.

There is little evidence, however, that the differences in the goal structure at
the middle and high school levels, as reported by teachers, were perceived by
students as they moved from eighth to ninth grade (Gheen et al., 2000; Midgley
et al., 2000). Students, on average, reported no change in the emphasis on mastery goals and a decrease in the emphasis on performance goals during the transition to high school (see Fig. 5.5). It should be kept in mind, however, that
student perceptions were at the ninth-grade level in high school and both principals and teachers were reporting on the school as a whole, which included the
9th, 10th, 11th, and 12th grades. Principals told us, for example, that homogeneous ability grouping in math at the 9th and 10th grades was practiced in 50%
of the high schools, whereas it was practiced in 75% of the schools at the 11th
and 12th grade levels. Unlike the middle schools, where there were no differences in the use of homogeneous ability grouping in English across Grades 6,
7, and 8, at the high school level the incidence of homogeneous ability grouping in English was exactly the same as in math, with the incidence higher at the

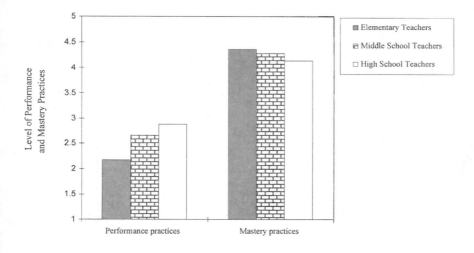

FIG. 5.3.   Elementary, middle, and high school teachers' reports of own performance and mastery approaches in the classroom.

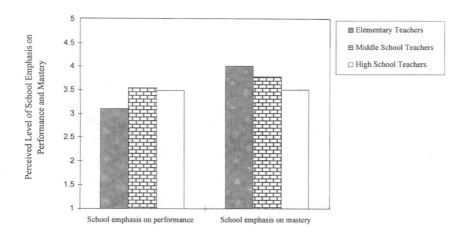

FIG. 5.4.   Elementary, middle, and high school teachers' perceptions of the school's emphasis on performance and mastery.

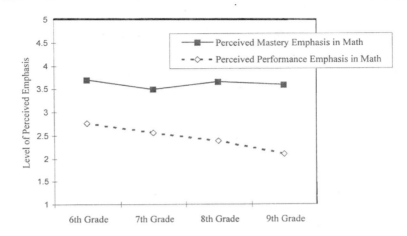

FIG. 5.5.   Change in students' perceptions of the emphasis on mastery and performance in math class from sixth to ninth grade.

upper grade levels than at the lower grade levels. We acknowledge that these practices form only one small part of what it means to emphasize performance goals, but at least there is a hint here that the upper grades in high school may be different in this respect than in the lower grades. We also found no evidence of a change in the perceived student–teacher relationship when students moved to the larger high school environment (Midgley et al., 2000).

Not surprisingly, we also found little evidence of changes in students' patterns of learning across the transition from eighth grade in elementary school to ninth grade in middle school. For example, there was no mean change in students' sense of academic efficacy, their reports of self-regulated learning, their avoidance of novel approaches to academic work, or their use of self-handicapping (Gheen et al., 2000). There was however, a significant drop in their grade point average (GPA).

We have described our studies comparing differences in the quality of relationships, and in the nature of the goal structure across the transition to middle school, during the middle school years, and across the transition from middle to high school. In some of these studies, changes in students' patterns of learning were also assessed. But assessing parallel change does not mean that they are linked. That is, this cannot be seen as direct evidence that changes in perceptions of the student–teacher relationship or the goal structure were linked to changes in students' patterns of learning. Studies linking changes in perceptions of the goal structure and students' patterns of learning are considered next.

THE ASSOCIATION BETWEEN CHANGES
IN RELATIONSHIPS AND IN THE GOAL STRUCTURE
AND STUDENTS' PATTERNS OF LEARNING

In our studies examining the transition to middle school, the results indicated that perceiving an emphasis on mastery goals in middle school was associated with positive changes in students from fifth to sixth grade, whereas perceiving an emphasis on performance goals in middle school was associated with negative changes from fifth to sixth grade. For example, L. H. Anderman (1999) found that perceiving an emphasis on mastery goals in middle school predicted positive affect in sixth grade, controlling for positive affect in fifth grade. She also found that perceiving an emphasis on performance goals in middle school was associated with negative affect in sixth grade, controlling for negative affect in fifth grade. Urdan and Midgley (2000) looked at the effect on students of perceiving an increase, no change, or a decrease in the mastery and performance goal structure during the transition to middle school and also from sixth to seventh grade within the middle school. Changes in the mastery goal structure were more strongly related (in the expected direction) to changes in self-regulation, self-efficacy, positive and negative affect in school, and grades than were changes in the performance goal structure both across the transition and during middle school. The most negative pattern of change was associated with a perceived decrease in the mastery goal structure.

In our examination of the transition to high school, we found further evidence that students' reports of the emphasis on mastery and/or performance goals were related to changes in their academic beliefs and behaviors. For example, students who reported a low emphasis on mastery goals in the eighth grade in middle school and a high emphasis on mastery goals in the ninth grade in high school, based on median splits, also reported that they felt more efficacious and that they used academic self-regulatory strategies more than they did the previous year. When students reported a low emphasis on demonstrating ability (performance goal structure) in the eighth grade and a high emphasis on performance goals in the ninth grade, they also reported an increase in their use of maladaptive strategies such as preferring to avoid novel approaches to academic tasks and withdrawing effort to protect self-worth (Gheen et al., 2000; see Figs. 5.6 and 5.7 for the findings regarding changes in the perceived emphasis on performance goals). We also found that students who perceived a less positive student-teacher relationship in the eighth grade and a more positive student-teacher relationship in the ninth grade showed an increase in self-regulated learning and a decrease in self-handicapping and the avoidance of help seeking (see Figs. 5.8, 5.9, and 5.10). Thus although there is little evidence of mean change in either the learning environment or in patterns of learning when students move to high school, individual students' perceptions of changes in

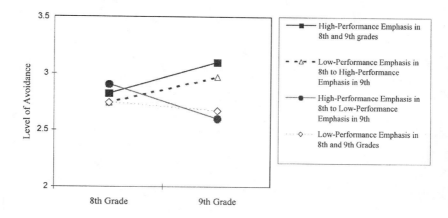

FIG. 5.6.   Change in preference to avoid novelty for students perceiving a high or low emphasis on performance in eighth-grade math classes and perceiving a high or low emphasis on performance in ninth-grade math classes.

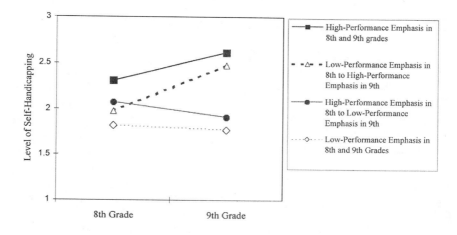

FIG. 5.7.   Change in self-handicapping for students perceiving a high or low emphasis on performance in eighth-grade math classes and perceiving a high or low emphasis on performance in ninth-grade math classes.

the learning environment and changes in their beliefs and behaviors provide evidence of the importance of students' perceptions of the student–teacher relationship and the goal structure in the classroom.

THE SPECIAL VULNERABILITY OF EARLY ADOLESCENTS

Are young adolescents particularly susceptible to both the positive and negative aspects of the learning environment, because puberty makes them particularly "vulnerable"? This goes beyond the supposition that changing opportunities in the learning environment should be congruent with the changing needs of students at any stage of life, to suggest that young adolescents may be particularly vulnerable. Note that Eccles and Midgley (1989) suggested that "changes in the academic environment that children experience when they move to junior high school would predict lower motivation to achieve and more negative self-perceptions at any age, but we believe that these changes are particularly detrimental for this age group" (p. 173). Maehr (1991), however, found that the goal emphases that characterized the "psychological environment" of the school had a stronger relation to students' motivation at successive grade levels (4th, 6th,

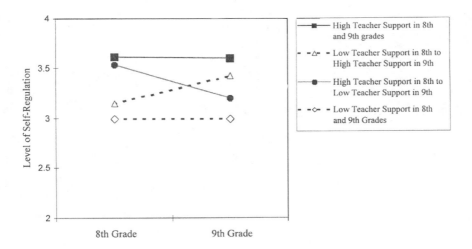

FIG. 5.8.   Change in self-regulation for students perceiving high or low teacher support in eighth-grade math classes and perceiving high or low teacher support in ninth-grade math classes.

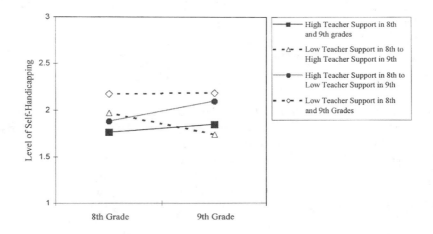

FIG. 5.9.   Change in self-handicapping for students perceiving high or low teacher support in eighth-grade math classes and perceiving high or low teacher support in ninth-grade math classes.

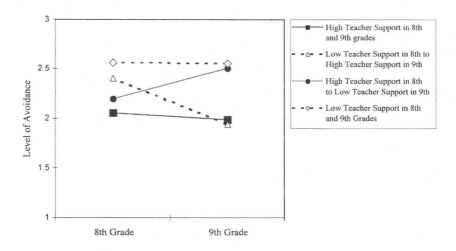

FIG. 5.10.   Change in avoiding help seeking for students perceiving high or low teacher support in eighth-grade math classes and perceiving high or low teacher support in ninth-grade math classes.

8th, 10th grades), with the strongest effect at the 10th-grade level. His study suggested that older adolescents, rather then younger adolescents, may be particularly sensitive to the nature of the goal structure in the learning environment.

As we wrote this chapter, we wondered if there was evidence from the Patterns of Adaptive Learning Study that the classroom goal structure was related more strongly to academic self-efficacy, use of avoidance strategies, and reports of disruptive behavior for younger adolescents than for older adolescents. We selected these variables because they were included on surveys when students were both younger and older, because they were specific to math (we wanted to focus on one subject domain), and because they represented both positive and negative outcomes. With data collected in the spring of each year from fifth to eighth grade, we ran regression analyses controlling for gender, grades in mathematics the previous year, and free-lunch status to determine the power of the perceived mastery and performance goal structure in predicting each outcome. We then divided the unstandardized regression coefficient by the standard deviation of the outcome to calculate effect sizes. Effect sizes indicate the amount of gain in score per standard deviation unit in the outcome measures. Generally, an effect size of 0 to .1 is considered minimal, .1 to .2 is considered small, .2 to .4 is considered moderate, and above .4 is considered strong.

On two of the four variables (self-handicapping and academic self-efficacy) the effect sizes appeared to be similar for younger and older adolescents. The effect size for the negative relation between perceiving an emphasis on mastery goals and reported engagement in disruptive behavior was stronger at the ninth-grade level than at the lower grade levels, supporting the findings of Maehr (1991). Although these results must be considered preliminary and exploratory, this finding should be pursued in other longitudinal studies. Because disruptive behavior has been reported to be particularly problematic at the high school level, this finding suggests that an emphasis on mastery goals may be particularly important for ninth-grade students, and that movement into a learning environment that is less focused on learning and understanding may represent a lack of stage–environment fit for high school students, at least in terms of their engagement in disruptive behavior. The only evidence of a stronger effect of the goal structure on younger adolescents than on older adolescents was for avoiding seeking help in the classroom. For example, the effect size for the negative relation between a perceived emphasis on mastery goals and avoiding seeking help was .24 at the sixth-grade level and .15 at the ninth-grade level. The effect size for the positive relation between a perceived emphasis on performance goals and avoiding seeking help was .29 at the sixth-grade level and .18 at the ninth-grade level. Certainly these limited findings cannot be used to suggest that young adolescents are particularly vulnerable to both the positive and negative effects of the learning environment as suggested by Eccles and Midgley (1989). It may be, however, that if students

had been followed to 11th and 12th grade, or other outcome variables were considered, there would be evidence in support of that claim. That remains for a future study.

ETHNICITY, SCHOOL TRANSITIONS, AND STAGE–ENVIRONMENT FIT

The study of the transition to middle-level schools conducted by Eccles, Midgley, and their colleagues almost 20 years ago was based on a largely White, middle-class sample of students (Eccles et al., 1993). As discussed earlier, this study pointed to aspects of the learning environment that represented a fit, or a lack of fit, with the needs of students at that stage of life. Whether the same kind of environment fits the needs of minority students and poor students has not received the same level of scrutiny. As noted by Williamson and Johnston (1999), two activists in the middle school movement:

> Relying strictly upon generalized descriptions of student developmental characteristics for school reform and program innovation virtually assures that equally compelling contextual issues will be ignored. In recent decades, the social and economic conditions in which our students live threaten to overwhelm both the occurrence and timing of developmental tasks. At a minimum, these conditions determine in very profound ways how the developmental tasks will be played out in the lives of individual students. (p. 14)

The few transition studies that have been conducted using racially mixed samples have, for the most part, failed to uncover different patterns based on race. Hirsch and Rapkin (1987) found that both Black and White students perceived a decline in the quality of school life after the transition to middle school. Seidman and his colleagues conducted a study with a sample of Black, White, and Latino students in impoverished urban schools and found a decline in self-esteem, class preparation, and grades after the transition (Seidman et al., 1994). They suggested that these youth may be especially vulnerable because the stress associated with living in poor urban communities may add to the stress associated with making the transition, however comparisons between the racial groups or with other groups were not included. Simmons, Black, and Zhou (1991) found a greater drop in GPA for Black than for White students after the transition to junior high school. Although the grades of both groups of students declined after the transition, the grades of Black students "plummeted."

In the Patterns of Adaptive Learning Study, no evidence has been found of especially negative changes for Black early adolescents, as compared to White early adolescents, during the transition to middle school (see chap. 7, this vol-

ume). For example, on measures of self-esteem, self-efficacy, and GPA, Black and White students did not differ in their patterns of change across the transition. Indeed, feelings of self-deprecation decreased significantly across the transition for Black students but not for White students (Arunkumar, Midgley, & Urdan, 1999). In another transition study conducted with data from the Patterns of Adaptive Learning Study, the effects of race, neighborhood quality, and the classroom mastery goal structure on changes in self-esteem and GPA were examined (Edelin & Midgley, 2001). Both neighborhood quality and the mastery goal structure were related to changes in self-esteem and GPA after the transition, but race did not emerge as a significant predictor.

Although not discussed in this chapter, some studies conducted in conjunction with the Patterns of Adaptive Learning Study have included extrinsic goals, as well as mastery and performance goals. The exploratory analysis presented in chapter 7 (this volume), using data from the Patterns of Adaptive Learning Study, suggests that an emphasis on extrinsic goals may be a better fit for Black students at this stage of life than for White students. We suggested in that chapter that the facilitative effect of extrinsic goals for Black students may represent a "realistic" need to get passing grades, to be promoted to the next grade, to graduate, and to find a job in a society that has not always supported these goals for poor and minority students. At the same time, we cited many studies that show a negative effect of extrinsic goals on students and questioned whether these goals are indeed the "best" goals for Black students. In any event, these results need to be replicated and expanded upon before they can be seen as evidence of a different pattern of fit for Black and White students.

Steele and his colleagues (Steele, 1997; Steele & Aronson, 1995) have proposed that achievement-oriented African American students may be particularly vulnerable to the negative effects of an emphasis on relative ability. This would suggest that a performance goal structure would be a particularly poor fit for Black early adolescents. In support of this thesis, in an earlier study we found that an orientation to performance goals was associated with self-handicapping (purposefully withdrawing effort to protect self-worth) for Black middle school students but not for White students (Midgley, Arunkumar, & Urdan, 1996). However, in the exploratory analysis reported in chapter 7 (this volume), there was essentially no evidence of a differential effect of performance goals on Black and White students.

In 1975 Massey, Scott, and Dornbusch published the results of a study that assessed high school students' perceptions of themselves and their academic environments. Their study provides insights into two issues: first, the emphasis on relationships and the de-emphasis on academic challenge for Black students, and second, the discrepancy between the attitudes and performance of Black students (e.g., Mickelson, 1990). Regarding the relationship dimension, Black students perceived that their teachers were warmer and friendlier than

did White, Hispanic, or Asian students, even though most of the teachers were White. Black students also received the greatest amount of praise. Regarding the academic dimension, Black students were doing the least amount of schoolwork and often received assignments that were not sufficiently challenging. The authors concluded that although teachers were not overtly racist or hostile toward Black students, they were doing great damage by "… expressing warmth toward black students, but … not accompanying their friendliness with challenging academic standards" (p. 10). In the interview study reported in chapter 7 (this volume), Black students provided little evidence of an emphasis on mastery goals in their classrooms.

In a large-scale study of schools representing a broad range of socioeconomic levels, the relation between students' sense of school community and their academic and social attitudes, motives, and performance was examined (e.g., Battistich, Solomon, Kim, Watson, & Schaps, 1995). Sense of school community was positively associated with most of the measures of academic attitudes and motives. However, sense of school community had only a small and generally nonsignificant relationship with the measures of students' academic performance. The strongest positive effects of school community occurred among schools with the most disadvantaged student populations. They concluded that "a caring, supportive, and responsive community would be particularly important in schools with poor student populations" (p. 649). We would go further and say that this study and the studies cited earlier support our belief that it is the combination of positive relationships and an emphasis on learning, understanding, and excellence (mastery goals) that may be the most positive combination, particularly for poor and minority students (Midgley & Edelin, 1998). This hypothesis should be explored in future studies.

REVISITING STAGE–ENVIRONMENT FIT

Having revisited stage–environment fit, we summarize our current thinking. We believe that stage–environment fit provides an informed and useful way to think about the characteristics and needs of learners at a certain stage of life and the opportunities afforded them in the learning environment. In line with Hunt's (1975) suggestion, we believe that stage–environment fit is best examined in terms of a developmental perspective. We suggest that understanding stage–environment fit is enhanced by looking at change, and going back to our initial supposition, it is best tested by looking at a time when change in both the person and the environment is expected. The need for longitudinal studies is often expressed and may be especially true in the case of stage–environment fit. As articulated by Hunt (1975), "longitudinal evidence to evaluate an interactive developmental theory is not easy to come by since, ideally, it requires not only periodic mea-

sures obtained from the same students, but also some indication of the environment they have experienced in the intervening time period" (p. 223).

We believe that stage–environment fit may be particularly appropriate in conceptualizing early adolescents and middle-level schools. However, we also believe that it is applicable to any stage of life. The needs and characteristics of older adolescents may require a somewhat different kind of a learning environment in order to provide an optimal fit. The needs of middle-aged learners may differ somewhat from those of younger learners, and the needs of learners in their 70s and 80s may differ from learners at other stages of life. However, we know much less about the changing needs of learners as they move though adolescence and adulthood than we know about learners who move from childhood to early adolescence. We thought it was interesting that in a recent issue of the newsletter published by the Society for Research on Adolescence, Shelton (2001) called for an awareness of college students' developmental status to help teachers select information and examples that connect to their experiences.

Acknowledging that needs may differ at various stages of life, we also believe that the tenets of achievement goal theory are applicable at any stage of life. That is, we believe that an emphasis on mastery goals is facilitative at any stage of life, and an emphasis on performance goals is less facilitative, though much more research is needed to support or refute this assumption. There is some evidence that performance goals are less debilitating for older students than for younger students, and indeed may be facilitative for older students if mastery goals are also salient (see Midgley et al., 2001, for a discussion of these issues). Results from our examination of the transition to high school (Gheen et al., 2000) indicate that for some outcomes, performance goals are less "harmful" for older than younger students, but neither are they beneficial. Unfortunately, studies examining age differences are often confounded by concurrent changes in the learning context. Harackiewicz, Elliot, and their colleagues have written about the facilitative nature of performance goals among college students in large-enrollment lecture classes graded on the curve (e.g., Harackiewicz, Barron, & Elliot, 1998). They said, "in this performance-oriented setting, students who adopt performance goals might actually be striving to attain good grades in a manner that is consistent with the classroom context, and a performance goal orientation might prove more adaptive than in other educational contexts" (p. 15). It is possible that performance goals are "adaptive" in these environments—that is, they lead to higher grades—because the tasks in these classes (e.g., demonstrating the memorization of facts on multiple-choice tests) typically do not require complex thinking.

In the case of middle schools, adding theory to the need for developmental responsiveness provides a much stronger argument in support of middle school reform. We believe that the cognitive development that characterizes students at this stage of life does enhance their ability to profit from environments that

encourage thoughtfulness, understanding, and the probing of complex issues and problems (a mastery-focused environment), and makes them more sensitive to the negative aspects of an emphasis on relative ability and social comparison (a more performance-focused environment). Those differences distinguish early adolescents from younger children. Is there evidence that further cognitive development in older adolescents and adults affects their reaction to the goal structure in the learning environment in ways that differ from early adolescents and that their needs are thus different? This is a question that merits further attention.

We also believe that characteristics of the person, regardless of stage of life, make some students particularly sensitive to positive and negative changes in the learning environment. For example, Midgley and her colleagues (1989a, 1989b) found that lower achieving students were particularly vulnerable to both the positive and negative effects of changes in the learning environment during the transition to middle school. As described in chap. 6 (this volume), we believe, and there is evidence that, students who are disaffected from learning and schooling may be particularly sensitive to the nature of the goal structure in the learning environment.

We find it very interesting, because we have used goal theory to examine stage–environment fit, that Hunt (1975) said that one does not ask, "Which instructional approach is better?" but also asks "for whom?" and "for what purpose?" (p. 218). Although Hunt's work predated goal theory, the question of purpose is central to goal theory. Similarly, Williamson and Johnston (1999) suggested that "in the absence of a clear sense of purpose and vision, parents see the middle school curriculum as mundane" (p. 10). They call upon advocates of middle school education to "grapple with important issues of purpose and function rather than rely on organizational or structural changes" (p. 11). We suggest that goal theory would provide an organizing framework within which to grapple with issues of purpose and function.

Finally, Hunt (1975) pointed to the importance of the practical implications of person–environment interaction "so that the conceptions can be enriched by application" (p. 281). We have taken that route by working with teachers to translate stage–environment fit and goal theory into specific recommendations for middle school reform, and collaborating with both elementary and middle schools to test the relevancy of these ideas for the real world of students, teachers, and schools (e.g., Maehr & Midgley, 1996; Midgley, 1993; Midgley & Maehr, 1999).

IMPLICATIONS FOR TEACHERS AND SCHOOLS

We have written extensively about the implications of goal theory for learning and schooling, and in particular the implications for schools serving young ad-

olescents (e.g., E. Anderman & Maehr, 1994; E. Anderman, Maehr, & Midgley, 1999, Maehr & Midgley, 1996; Midgley, 1993; Midgley & Edelin, 1998; Midgley & Urdan, 1992; Urdan, Midgley, & Wood, 1995). We do not repeat that here. Our writings are based on both the empirical studies we have conducted and our experiences collaborating for 3 years with principals and teachers in a local elementary school and middle school to move toward an emphasis on mastery goals and away from an emphasis on performance goals (Maehr & Midgley, 1996). We learned from our experiences in schools that changing the goal structure involves a change in thinking about the purpose of schooling. There needs to be time for teachers to read, talk, debate, and reflect (Urdan et al., 1995). But we all know that teachers in this country are not given time to do this kind of thinking and reflecting. We also know that teachers and principals need to work within the constraints imposed on them at the state level, the district level, and by the parents of the students in their schools. When we speak at schools, we emphasize that we do not have a recipe for change, or a program that we are trying to sell. We talk about a change in thinking about the purposes of learning, and the messages that schools and teachers convey to students about these purposes through policies and practices. We conclude this chapter by including two tables that were generated by the teachers with whom we collaborated. Table 5.1 includes suggestions from teachers regarding how to move toward a mastery-focused middle school environment. Table 5.2 includes a list of principles that were put together by the elementary teachers to guide the recognition of students. We hope these tables illustrate that the goal structure is expressed through a constellation of policies and practices that convey to students the purpose of achieving in school.

TABLE 5.1

Strategies to Move Toward a Mastery-Focused Middle School Environment

	Move Away From	*Move Toward*
Grouping	Grouping by ability	Grouping by topic, interest, student choice
		Frequent reformation of groups
Competition/ Cooperation	Competition between students	Cooperative learning
	Contests with limited winners	
Assessment	Using test data as a basis for comparison	Using test data for diagnosis
	Overuse of standardized tests	Alternatives to tests such as portfolios

continued on next page

TABLE 5.1 *(continued)*

Strategies to Move Toward a Mastery-Focused Middle School Environment

	Move Away From	*Move Toward*
Grading	Normative grading	Grading for progress, improvement
	Public display of grades	Involving students in determining their grades
Recognition/ Rewards/ Incentives	Recognition for relative performance	Recognition of progress, improvement
	Honor rolls for high grades	An emphasis on learning for its own sake
	Overuse of praise, especially for the completion of short, easy tasks	
Student Input	Decisions made exclusively by administrators and teachers	Opportunities for choice, electives
		Student decision-making, self-scheduling, self-regulation
Approaches to the Curriculum	Departmentalized approach to curriculum	Thematic approaches/ interdisciplinary focus
		Viewing mistakes as a part of learning
		Allowing students to redo work
		Encouraging students to take academic risks
Academic Tasks	Rote learning and memorization	Providing challenging, complex work to students
	Overuse of work sheets and textbooks	Giving homework that is enriching, challenging
	Decontextualized facts	Encouraging problem solving, comprehension
Remediation	Pull-out programs	Cross-age tutoring, peer tutoring
	Retention	Enrichment

Note. These strategies serve as examples. Strategies will depend on the characteristics of the school, the identified needs, and the preferences of the school staff. Strategies such as cross-age grouping, block scheduling, small house, and team teaching, although not listed here, are recommended as enabling mechanisms.

TABLE 5.2

Principles of Recognition

1. Recognize individual student effort, accomplishment, and improvement.
2. Give all students opportunities to be recognized.
3. Give recognition privately whenever possible.
4. Avoid using "most" or "best" for recognizing or rewarding—as in "best project" or "most improved." These words usually convey comparisons with others.
5. Avoid recognizing on the basis of absence of mistakes. For example, avoid giving awards for students who get "fewer than five words wrong on a spelling test."
6. Avoid using the same criteria for all students. For example, avoid giving an award to "all students who get an A on the science test," or "all students who do four out of five projects."
7. Recognize students for taking on challenging work or for stretching their own abilities (even if they make mistakes). This gives a powerful message about what is valued in the classroom.
8. Recognize students for coming up with different and unusual ways to solve a problem or a novel way to approach a task. Again, you are telling students what you value.
9. Try to involve students in the recognition process. What is of value to them? How much effort do they feel they put in? Where do they feel they need improvement? When do they feel successful? How do they know when they have reached their goals?
10. It's OK to recognize students in various domains (behavior, athletics, attendance, etc.), but every student should have the opportunity to be recognized academically.
11. Try to recognize the quality of students' work rather than the quantity. For example, recognizing students for reading a lot of books could encourage them to read easy books.
12. Avoid recognizing grades and test scores. This takes the emphasis away from learning and problem solving.
13. Recognition must be real. Do not recognize students for accomplishing something they have not really accomplished, for improving if they have not improved, or for trying hard if that is not the case. The important factor is letting students know that they have the opportunity to be recognized in these areas.

Writing this chapter has helped us to understand how much we know and how much we do not know about stage–environment fit. This is certainly a topic that will need to be revisited again as further research is conducted, assumptions are examined, and issues are debated.

REFERENCES

Alspaugh, J. W. (1998). Achievement loss associated with the transition to middle school and high school. *Journal of Educational Research, 92,* 20–25.

Ames, C. (1992). Classrooms: Goals, structures, and student motivation. *Journal of Educational Psychology, 84,* 261–271.

Anderman, E. M., & Maehr, M. L. (1994). Motivation and schooling in the middle grades. *Review of Educational Research, 64,* 287–309.

Anderman, E., Maehr, M. L., & Midgley, C. (1999). Declining motivation after the transition to middle school: Schools can make a difference. *Journal of Research and Development in Education, 32,* 131–147.

Anderman, E., & Midgley, C. (1997). Changes in personal achievement goals and the perceived classroom goal structures across the transition to middle level schools. *Contemporary Educational Psychology, 22,* 269–298.

Anderman, L. H. (1999). Classroom goal orientation, school belonging, and social goals as predictors of students' positive and negative affect following the transition to middle school. *Journal of Research and Development in Education, 32,* 90–103.

Arunkumar, R., Midgley, C., & Urdan, T. (1999). Perceiving high or low home-school dissonance: Longitudinal effects on adolescent emotional and academic well-being. *Journal of Research on Adolescence, 9,* 441–466.

Barone, C., Aguierre-Deandreis, A. I., & Trickett, E. J. (1991). Means–end problem-solving skills, life stress, and social support as mediators of adjustment in the normative transition into high school. *American Journal of Community Psychology, 19,* 207–255.

Battistich, V., Solomon, D., Kim, D. L., Watson, M., & Schaps, E. (1995). Schools as communities, poverty levels of student populations, and students' attitudes, motives, and performance: A multilevel analysis. *American Educational Research Journal, 32,* 627–658.

Bergin, D. (1995). Effects of mastery versus competitive motivation situation on learning. *Journal of Experimental Education, 63,* 303–314.

Berndt, T. J., & Hawkins, J. A. (1993). *Stability and change in friendship after the transition to junior high school.* Unpublished manuscript, Purdue University, West Lafayette, IN.

Blumenfeld, P. C. (1992). Classroom learning and motivation: Clarifying and expanding goal theory. *Journal of Educational Psychology, 84,* 272–281.

Blyth, D. A., Simmons, R. G., & Carlton-Ford, S. (1983). The adjustment of early adolescents to school transitions. *Journal of Early Adolescence, 3,* 105–120.

Bruene, L. (1985, April). *Training students in thinking skills for solving social problems: A strategy for helping students cope constructively with school stressors.* Paper presented at the annual meeting of the American Educational Research Association, Chicago.

Carnegie Task Force on the Education of Young Adolescents. (1989). *Turning points: Preparing American youth for the 21st century.* New York: Carnegie Corporation.

Combs, H. J. (1993). A middle school transition program: Addressing the social side of schooling. *ERS Spectrum, 11,* 12–21.

DaGiau, B. J. (1997). *A program of counseling and guidance to facilitate the transition from middle school to high school* (ERIC Document Reproduction Service No. ED413562).

Dweck, C. S., & Leggett, E. L. (1988). A social-cognitive approach to motivation and personality. *Psychological Review, 95,* 256–273.

Eccles, J. S., & Midgley, C. (1989). Stage/environment fit: Developmentally appropriate classrooms for early adolescents. In R. E. Ames & C. Ames (Eds.), *Research on motivation in education* (Vol. 3, pp. 139–186). New York: Academic Press.

Eccles, J. S., Midgley, C., Wigfield, A., Buchanan, C. M., Reuman, D., Flanagan, C., & MacIver, D. (1993). Development during adolescence: The impact of stage/environment fit on young adolescents' experiences in schools and families. *American Psychologist, 48,* 90–101.

Edelin, K., & Midgley, C. (2001). *Changes in psychological well-being, motivation, and academic performance during early adolescence: The role of race, neighborhood quality, and the middle school transition.* Manuscript in preparation.

Elkind, D., & Bowen, R. (1979). Imaginary audience behavior in children and adolescents. *Developmental Psychology, 15,* 38–44.

Epstein, H. T. (1978). Growth spurs during brain development: Implications for educational policy. In J. S. Chall & A. F. Mirsky (Eds.), *Education and the brain: Seventy-seventh yearbook of the National Society for the Study of Education, Part II* (pp. 343–370). Chicago: University of Chicago Press.

Estrada, P. (1993, April). *Changes in teacher support during the transition to middle school and its relation with educational functioning in peer urban youth.* Paper presented at the meeting of the American Educational Research Association, Atlanta.

Feldlaufer, H., Midgley, C., & Eccles, J. S. (1988). Student, teacher, and observer perceptions of the classroom environment before and after the transition to junior high school. *Journal of Early Adolescence, 8,* 133–156.

Felner, R. D., Gintner, M., & Primavera, J. (1982). Primary prevention during school transitions: Social support and environmental structure. *American Journal of Community Psychology, 10,* 277–290.

Ferguson, J., & Bulach, C. (1994). *The effect of the shadow transition program on the social adjustment of Whitewater middle school students.* Fayette County, GA: Fayette County Public Schools. (ERIC Document Reproduction Service No. ED380878).

Gheen, M. H., Hruda, L. Z., Middleton, M. J., & Midgley, C. (2000). *Using goal orientation theory to examine the transition from middle to high school.* Paper presented at the annual meeting of the American Educational Research Association, New Orleans.

Harackiewicz, J. M., Barron, K. E., & Elliot, A. J. (1998). Rethinking achievement goals: When are they adaptive for college students and why? *Educational Psychologist, 33,* 1–21.

Hirsch, B. J., & Rapkin, B. D. (1987). The transition to junior high school: A longitudinal study of self-esteem, psychological symptomatology, school life, and social support. *Child Development, 58,* 1235–1243.

Hunt, D. E. (1975). Person-environment interaction: A challenge found wanting before it was tried. *Review of Educational Research, 45,* 209–230.

Kumar, R., & Midgley, C. (2001). *The interplay of individual and contextual factors in change in dissonance between home and school across the transition from elementary to middle school.* Manuscript submitted for publication.

Lee, P. (1979). *A developmental study of children's prerogatives and constraints in several domains of school experience.* Report to the National Institute of Education, Washington, DC.

Lewin, K. (1935). *A dynamic theory of personality.* New York: McGraw-Hill.

Lipsitz, J. (1977). *Growing up forgotten: A review of research and programs concerning early adolescence.* Lexington, MA: Lexington.

Lipsitz, J. (1997). Middle Grades Improvement Program. *Phi Delta Kappan, 78,* 555.

Lynch, M., & Cicchetti, M. (1997). Children's relationships with adults and peers: An examination of elementary and junior high school students. *Journal of School Psychology, 35,* 81–99.

MacIver, D., & Reuman, D. A. (1988, April). *Decision-making in the classroom and early adolescents' valuing of mathematics.* Paper presented at the annual meeting of the American Educational Research Association, New Orleans.

Maehr, M. L. (1991). The "psychological environment" of the school: A focus for school leadership. In *School leadership* (Vol. 2, pp. 51–81). Greenwich, CT: JAI.

Maehr, M. L., & Midgley, C. (1996). *Transforming school cultures*. Boulder, CO: Westview Press.

Marachi, R., Gheen, M., & Midgley, C. (2001). *An examination of elementary, middle, and high school teachers' beliefs and behaviors using a goal theory framework*. Manuscript submitted for publication.

Marshall, D. (1992). Making a smooth move to high school. *Middle School Journal, 24,* 26–29.

Massey, G. C., Scott, M. V., & Dornbusch, S. M. (1975). Racism without racists: Institutional racism in urban schools. *The Black Scholar, 7,* 10–19.

McPartland, J. M., & Karweit, N. (1979). Research on educational effects. In H. J. Walberg (Ed.), *Educational environments and effects: Evaluation, policy, and productivity* (pp. 371–385). Berkeley, CA: McCutchan.

Meece, J. L. (1991). The classroom context and students' motivational goals. In M. L. Maehr & P. R. Pintrich (Eds.), *Advances in motivation and achievement: Vol. 7. Goals and self-regulatory processes* (pp. 261–286). Greenwich, CT: JAI.

Mickelson, R. (1990). The attitude–achievement paradox among black adolescents. *Sociology of Education, 63,* 44–61.

Midgley, C. (1993). Motivation and middle level schools. In P. Pintrich & M. L. Maehr (Eds.), *Advances in motivation and achievement: Vol. 8. Motivation in the adolescent years* (pp. 219–276). Greenwich, CT: JAI.

Midgley, C., Anderman, E., & Hicks, L. (1995). Differences between elementary and middle school teachers and students: A goal theory approach. *Journal of Early Adolescence, 15,* 90–113.

Midgley, C., Arunkumar, R., & Urdan, T. (1996). "If I don't do well tomorrow there's a reason": Predictors of adolescents' use of academic self-handicapping strategies. *Journal of Educational Psychology, 88,* 423–434.

Midgley, C., Eccles, J. S., & Feldlaufer, H. (1991). Classroom environment and the transition to junior high school. In B. J. Fraser & H. J. Walberg (Eds.), *Educational environments: Evaluation, antecedents and consequences* (pp. 113–139). New York: Pergamon.

Midgley, C., & Edelin, K. (1998). Middle school reform and early adolescent well-being: The good news and the bad. *Educational Psychologist, 33,* 195–206.

Midgley, C., & Feldlaufer, H. (1987). Students' and teachers' decision-making fit before and after the transition to junior high school. *Journal of Early Adolescence, 7,* 225–241.

Midgley, C., Feldlaufer, H., & Eccles, J. S. (1989a). Change in teacher efficacy and student self- and task-related beliefs in mathematics during the transition to junior high school. *Journal of Educational Psychology, 81,* 247–258.

Midgley, C., Feldlaufer, H., & Eccles, J. S. (1989b). Student–teacher relations and attitudes toward mathematics before and after the transition to junior high school. *Child Development, 60,* 375–395.

Midgley, C., Kaplan, A., & Middleton, M. J. (2001). Performance-approach goals: Good for what, for whom, under what circumstances, and at what cost? *Journal of Educational Psychology, 93,* 77–86.

Midgley, C., & Maehr, M. L. (1999). Using motivational theory to guide school reform. In A. J. Reynolds, H. J. Walberg, & R. P. Weissberg (Eds.), *Promoting positive outcomes: Issues in children's and families' lives* (pp. 129–159). Washington, DC: Child Welfare League of America.

Midgley, C., Maehr, M. L., Gheen, M., Hruda, L., Marachi, R., Middleton, M., & Nelson, J. (2000). *The transition to high school study: Report to participating schools and districts*. Ann Arbor: University of Michigan.

Midgley, C., Maehr, M. L., Gheen, M., Hruda, L., Middleton, M., & Nelson, J. (1998). *The Michigan middle school study: Report to participating schools and districts.* Ann Arbor: University of Michigan.

Midgley, C., & Urdan, T. (1992). The transition to middle level schools: Making it a good experience for all students. *Middle School Journal, 24,* 5–14.

Miller, D. (1974). *Adolescence: Psychology, psychopathology and psychotherapy.* New York: Aronson.

Nicholls, J. G. (1986, April). *Adolescents' conceptions of ability and intelligence.* Paper presented at the annual meeting of the American Educational Research Association, San Francisco.

Owings, J., & Peng, S. (1992). *Transitions experienced by 1988 eighth graders.* Washington, DC: National Center for Education Statistics.

Patrick, H., Anderman, L. H., Ryan, A. M., Edelin, K., & Midgley, C. (2001). Teachers' communication of goal orientations in four fifth-grade classrooms. *Elementary School Journal, 102,* 35–58.

Pintrich, P. R., & Schunk, D. H. (1996). *Motivation in education: Theory, research, and application.* Englewood Cliffs, NJ: Prentice-Hall.

Roeser, R., Midgley, C., & Wood, S. (1995). *Personal achievement goals and classroom goal structures in middle level schools: Principal, teacher, and student perspectives.* Unpublished manuscript.

Sarason, S. E., & Klaber, M. (1985). The school as a social situation. *Annual Review of Psychology, 36,* 115–140.

Seidman, E., Allen, L., Aber, J. L., Mitchell, C., & Feinman, J. (1994). The impact of school transitions in early adolescence on the self-system and perceived social context of poor urban youth. *Child Development, 65,* 507–522.

Shelton, L. G. (2001). Developmentally responsive pedagogy, *Newsletter of the Society for Research on Adolescence, Spring,* 4, 8.

Simmons, R. G., Black, A., & Zhou, Y. (1991). African-American versus White children and transition into junior high school. *American Journal of Education, 99,* 481–520.

Simmons, R. G., Rosenberg, F., & Rosenberg, M. (1973). Disturbance in the self-image at adolescence. *American Sociological Review, 38,* 553–568.

Steele, C. M. (1997). A threat in the air: How stereotypes shape intellectual identity and performance. *American Psychologist, 52,* 613–629.

Steele, C. M., & Aronson, J. (1995). Stereotype threat and the intellectual test performance of African Americans. *Journal of Personality and Social Psychology, 69,* 797–811.

Superintendent's Middle Grade Task Force. (1987). *Caught in the middle: Educational reform for young adolescents in California public schools.* Sacramento, CA: State Department of Education.

Thompson, P. M., Giedd, J. N., Woods, R. P., MacDonald, D., Evans, A. C., & Toga, A. W. (2000). Growth patterns in the developing brain detected by using continuum mechanical tensor maps. *Nature, 404*(6774), 190–193.

Toepfer, C. F., & Marani, J. V. (1980). School-based research. In M. Johnson (Ed.), *Toward adolescence: Seventy-ninth yearbook of the National Society for the Study of Education* (pp. 169–281). Chicago: University of Chicago Press.

Turner, J. C., Midgley, C., Meyer, D. K., Gheen, M., Anderman, E., Kang, Y., & Patrick, H. (in press). The classroom environment and students' reports of avoidance behaviors in mathematics: A multi-method study, *Journal of Educational Psychology.*

Urdan, T. (1997). Achievement goal theory: Past results, future directions. In M. L. Maehr & P. R. Pintrich (Eds.), *Advances in motivation and achievement* (Vol. 10, pp. 99–141). Greenwich, CT: JAI.

Urdan, T., & Midgley, C. (2000, May). *Developmental changes in the relations among goal structures, motivational beliefs, affect, and performance.* Paper presented the 7th Workshop on Achievement and Task Motivation, Leuven, Belgium.

Urdan, T., Midgley, C., & Wood, S. (1995). Special issues in reforming middle level schools. *Journal of Early Adolescence, 15,* 9–37.

Weldy, G. R. (Ed.). (1990). *Stronger school transitions improve student achievement: A final report on a three-year demonstration project "Strengthening school transitions for students K–13."* Reston, VA: National Association of Secondary School Principals.

Williamson, R., & Johnston, J. H. (1999). Challenging orthodoxy: An emerging agenda for middle level reform. *Middle School Journal, 30,* 10–17.

6

Goal Structures in the Learning Environment and Students' Disaffection From Learning and Schooling

Revathy Kumar
University of Toledo

Margaret H. Gheen
The University of Michigan

Avi Kaplan
Ben Gurion University of the Negev, Israel

Students who are disengaged from learning and schooling are a primary concern of researchers, educators, parents, and the nation at large. Unfortunately, some students do not like school, do not feel like a valued member of the school community, are skeptical about the value of schooling for their future lives, feel a disjunction between their lives at home and at school, and engage in disruptive behavior. In and of itself, this is disheartening. But the long-term implications of these indicators of disaffection are profound. These signs of disaffection are often the early signs of impending school failure, school dropout, and risky behaviors (Comer, 1987; Finn, 1989; Ianni, 1989; Steinberg, Blinde, & Chan, 1984). Research on school failure and dropout indicates that they are not discrete events in students' lives. Rather they are processes, often with a host of experiences and indicators foreshadowing them, and often with long-term consequences that extend beyond the event itself (Kerckhoff & Bell,

143

1997–1998). Negative experiences that lead to dropping out of high school can start much earlier in elementary and middle schools (Krohn, Lizotte, & Perez, 1997). Furthermore, these processes of disengagement need not lead to dropping out or failure per se—students may remain in school long enough to graduate, but they may be "virtual dropouts," disengaged from the academic and social experiences of school, with long-term negative implications.

Not surprisingly, considerable research has been devoted to studying the causes and consequences of student disaffection from learning and schooling. Many journal articles and books have been written on the subject, offering various reasons for students' disengagement and suggestions for keeping students connected to school. Some of the reasons focus on the larger society and issues such as poverty, access to health care, and availability of resources in the community. Others focus on the family, including the quality of parenting and the involvement of parents in their children's schools. Others point to "deficits" in the child that are associated with the tendency to disengage from school (see Dryfoos, 1990, for a consideration of these various antecedents). Some suggest that peers have a very important influence on students' academic engagement or disengagement (Berndt & Keefe, 1995). We agree that the factors just mentioned can and do contribute to student disaffection, and that some students are more at risk for disaffection than are others. However, we also believe that the nature of the learning environment can play an important role in exacerbating vulnerability or promoting resilience in students who are at risk for disaffection. In this chapter we focus on the relation between the learning environment in classrooms and schools, and students' disaffection from learning and schooling. We focus in particular on how the achievement goals that teachers convey and students perceive in classrooms and schools are related to indicators of students' disaffection. We conclude by making specific recommendations for changing the learning environment in order to reduce students' vulnerability to disaffection.

THE LEARNING ENVIRONMENT AND STUDENT DISAFFECTION FROM SCHOOL AND SCHOOLING

Recognition that classrooms and schools play a role in students' engagement in learning and schooling has led to numerous recommendations for reducing student disaffection (e.g., Dryfoos, 1990, 1994). In 1999, President Clinton announced the Safe Schools/Healthy Students Initiative:

> Activities that may be funded as part of this Initiative include, but are not limited to, truancy prevention, after school activities, teen courts, alternative education, purchasing security equipment and services, mentoring, programs such as conflict resolution, life skills, school-based anti-drug curricula, nursing home visitation, family strengthening and staff professional development. These activities are designed to promote healthy development, enhance resilience, and build on personal

strengths. Additional funds will also be available for hiring law enforcement officers to work in schools as part of this Initiative. http://www.samhsa.gov/news/news.html

These programs are certainly important. However, many seem to focus on treating specific problems and not on reducing students' negative affect toward school, feelings of alienation, or estrangement from the school community.

Other programs have focused more specifically on enhancing students' feelings of belonging in classrooms and schools, promoting positive relations between students and teachers, and involving parents in the life of the school (e.g., Comer, 1988; O'Donnell, Hawkins, Catalano, & Abbott, 1995). For example, there is evidence that programs such as cooperative learning, when implemented properly, promote positive feelings among students so that those who might otherwise be seen as "different" or "deficient" are perceived as contributing members of the classroom (Slavin, 1983). Forming teacher teams at the middle school level has been suggested as a way to enhance student–teacher relations and reduce student disaffection by enabling teachers to interact with fewer students for a longer period of time each day (Carnegie Task Force, 1989). Developing programs that are aimed at making all parents feel respected and welcomed at school has proven successful in some cases, and may help both students and parents feel connected with school (Harley & Lustbader, 1997; Haynes, Comer, & Hamilton-Lee, 1988). However, as Wang and Walberg (1987) noted, few reforms have succeeded in effectively sustaining students' engagement in the learning process beyond the short term.

Though many school reform programs take into account important aspects of students' emotions and behavior, many of them touch only indirectly on what we see as a core determinant of students' experiences: *the purpose of being in school*. We argue that this purpose is a primary motive that affects students' cognition, affect, and behavior. Different purposes or motives are associated with adaptive and maladaptive patterns of learning, including indicators of disaffection from school. We further argue that the learning environment in classrooms and schools plays an important role in sending messages to students about the purpose of learning and thus affects students' own purposes for learning and levels of engagement or disengagement in school. We suggest that what is missing in many reform programs is a focus on, and a commitment to, creating environments that promote learning, understanding, intellectual development, and individual growth as the fundamental purpose of schooling. This focus is the foundation of our conceptualization of achievement goal theory (Maehr & Midgley, 1996; see also chap. 2, this volume)—the theory that has guided our thinking and research on students' disaffection from school and schooling.

In this chapter, we explain the relevance of achievement goal theory to research on students' disaffection from school. We review studies, including those that have been conducted in conjunction with the Patterns of Adaptive

Learning Study, that point to the relation between different types of learning environments and indicators of student disaffection from school. In particular, we describe the research that links the goal structure in the learning environment—that is, the emphasis on different purposes for being in school and for doing schoolwork—and positive or negative affect toward school, the coping strategies students use when facing difficulties in school, their sense of belonging in school, and their tendency to engage in disruptive behavior in the classroom. We then present evidence that students who experience a discord between their lives at home and at school ("home–school dissonance") are at risk for disaffection, and that the goal structure in the learning environment can exacerbate or ameliorate that risk. Home–school dissonance concerns the difficulty or ease with which individuals negotiate the boundaries between different contexts in their lives. For adolescents, the two main contexts are home and school. In some cases these two contexts overlap so much that the boundaries become blurred, and adolescents are easily able to integrate their roles across the two contexts. In other cases, adolescents may experience considerable discrepancy between these contexts, leading to feelings of dissonance. We present findings from both quantitative and qualitative studies that explored ways in which the emphasis in the learning environment on different achievement goals might be related to home–school dissonance. We conclude by briefly highlighting guidelines for creating learning environments that may decrease students' dislike of school, disaffection from learning, and disengagement from the learning process.

ACHIEVEMENT GOAL THEORY AND DISAFFECTION FROM LEARNING AND SCHOOLING

What is the purpose of school? Why am I here? As novices to the educational system, young students and new teachers often respond: To learn! To understand! To improve! To help children grow and develop! To instill in children the love of learning! But over time, students and teachers appear to "burn out," and these goals lose their vigor (LeCompte & Dworkin, 1991). Students and teachers alike can lose their initial enthusiasm, and find themselves asking more cynically "Why *am* I here, anyway?" Concurrently, as students move through school, many grow more alienated and feel more negatively about school, engage in more disruptive behavior, and increasingly sense that school has little relevance for their future lives (Biafora et al., 1993; Ogbu, 1987). What is it that accounts for this shift?

In an attempt to understand the reasons for students' disaffection, researchers in motivation have turned to theories that highlight the importance of students' academic efficacy (Zimmerman, Bandura, & Martinez-Pons, 1992), their valuing of academic tasks and subject matters (Wigfield & Eccles, 1994),

and their opportunities for self-determination (Deci, Vallerand, Pelletier, & R. M. Ryan, 1991). Although these motivational approaches do provide insights into students' disengagement from school, they do not always provide a coherent theoretical framework or point to specific programs or reforms that are consistent with the theory and that can be implemented in schools. We believe that achievement goal theory, which in the past two decades has emerged as a preeminent approach to the study of student motivation (Elliot, 1999; Midgley, Kaplan, & Middleton, 2001; Pintrich, 1994; Weiner, 1990), provides a comprehensive perspective on students' disaffection from school and leads to specific recommendations for changing the learning environment so that the likelihood of disaffection is reduced. Achievement goal theory focuses on the same questions those students and teachers may be asking themselves: Why am I here? What is my purpose? How can I be successful? For this reason, this theory offers a powerful framework for understanding student disaffection from learning and schooling.

Two distinct purposes or achievement goals have received the most attention: mastery goals and performance goals (see chap. 2, this volume, for a comprehensive overview of goal theory). Mastery goals focus on the development of competence through learning, understanding, and improvement. Performance goals focus on the demonstration of competence or avoiding the demonstration of incompetence, which in school is often done by outperforming others or succeeding with little effort (e.g., Ames, 1992b; E. M. Anderman & Maehr, 1994; Dweck & Leggett, 1988; Nicholls, 1984). In some classrooms, the instructional approaches teachers use and the messages they convey emphasize the importance of learning, understanding, and improving—a mastery goal structure—whereas in other classrooms they emphasize the importance of doing well on tests, demonstrating ability, and competing favorable with other students—a performance goal structure. In many educational environments, both goals may be conveyed, though one goal may be emphasized more than another (e.g., Middleton, Kaplan, Midgley, & E. Anderman, 2001).

Schools differ in the extent to which they emphasize mastery and/or performance goals (E. M. Anderman & Maehr, 1994; Kaplan & Maehr, 1997; Maehr & Midgley, 1991). School policies, teachers' practices, and the achievement orientation adopted by peers can emphasize to students either that the purpose of being in school and doing schoolwork is learning, mastering knowledge and skills, and improving, or that the purpose is demonstrating one's ability and comparing favorably with others in the class. The structures that comprise the learning environment in schools, such as the type of tasks that are assigned, the recognition and evaluation systems, the grouping practices, and the norms of social interaction among classroom members, embody the schools' achievement goal structure (Ames, 1992b; Kaplan & Maehr, 1999b). When teachers emphasize that mistakes are a necessary part of learning, encourage students to

take on challenging tasks on which they are likely to encounter difficulty and learn by overcoming it, recognize students for investing effort, and evaluate students on the basis of their progress, they convey the message that the purpose of doing schoolwork is learning and developing knowledge and competence. When teachers emphasize the importance of doing better than other students, recognize those whose work is error-free, compare students on the basis of their performance, and praise students who succeed with little effort, they send the message that the purpose of doing schoolwork is demonstrating high ability.

THE GOAL STRUCTURE AND STUDENTS' VULNERABILITY TO DISAFFECTION

One of the main distinctions between mastery and performance goals is a focus on the task versus a focus on the self. Although we use the term *mastery* in this chapter, there are other researchers who use the term *task* or *task mastery* to describe an orientation to learning and understanding (e.g., Meece & Miller, 1999). The kinds of questions posed within a mastery goal structure include: Are students challenged by the task, do students find the task engaging, is student work improving, do students understand the concepts, have students mastered the task? In contrast, the kinds of questions posed within a performance goal structure include: Do students get high grades, do students make mistakes, do students make the honor roll, who is smart and who is not so smart? The nature of the task is not an issue here; rather, the focus is on student performance, particularly relative to others.

The risk and resilience literature suggests that students who are at risk for cutting classes, disruptive behavior, and dropping out often have a history of low grades. It seems intuitive that in a learning environment that emphasizes the importance of getting good grades, making the honor roll, and producing mistake-free papers, these students would see themselves as deficient and different. With the focus on the self that is inherent in a performance-focused learning environment, they are put in a situation where comparisons with others are inevitable and demeaning. It is not difficult to understand why they would feel negatively about their school experiences and disconnected from learning and schooling. Although many students may be affected negatively by a performance goal structure, it is certainly those who are not performing well who are the most vulnerable to disaffection. Indeed, the early experimental studies by Dweck and her colleagues (e.g., Dweck & Leggett, 1988) indicated that the individuals in the performance goal condition who exhibited a maladaptive pattern of affect and behavior were those who were low in perceived ability and not those who were high in perceived ability.

We do not believe that it is just low-achieving students who are at risk for disaffection in a performance goal structure. Even students who feel that their ability is high may not always feel that they can get recognition for their high ability in a performance-oriented environment. In a class where a number of students receive high grades, getting high grades may not be enough to demonstrate high ability. High ability is confirmed only when the grade is higher than that of many others, or when high grades are earned with a lower expenditure of effort than that of other students. Thus, even students who perceive their ability as high may be not want to be perceived as investing a great deal of effort in their schoolwork (cf. Jagacinski & Nicholls, 1987). Students may engage in strategies such as devaluing the subject matter or the task, avoiding seeking help or taking on challenge in class, or engaging in disruptive behavior (e.g., Gheen & Midgley, 1999; Kaplan, Gheen, & Midgley, 2001; A. M. Ryan, Gheen, & Midgley, 1998) in order to protect their self-worth and maintain their image as high-performing students.

In contrast, a learning environment with a mastery goal structure emphasizes to students that what is valued is effort, hard work, challenge seeking, and real understanding. Every young person can aspire to that, regardless of his or her achievement history. In environments with a mastery goal structure, success is defined in self-referenced terms—how much the student has improved and learned. The more effort students invest in the task, the more likely they are to improve and master the skills. Jagacinski and Nicholls (1987) reported that when students were engaged in tasks in a mastery environment, they felt proud of the amount of effort that they invested in the task. Thus, in environments with a mastery goal structure, students are less likely to feel threatened, more likely to be oriented toward investing effort in the academic tasks, and more likely to feel successful and therefore good about themselves in school (Kaplan & Maehr, 1999a; Roeser, Midgley, & Urdan, 1996).

RESEARCH EXAMINING THE RELATION BETWEEN THE GOAL STRUCTURE AND INDICES OF STUDENT DISAFFECTION

We now describe studies that have looked at the relation between the goal structure in classrooms and schools and indicators of student disaffection from school. Many of these studies were conducted as part of the Patterns of Adaptive Learning Study. Acknowledging that there are other indicators of disaffection, we focus here on affect toward school and subject matter, a lack of connectedness to school, the use of ineffective coping strategies to deal with failure, engagement in disruptive behavior, and home–school dissonance.

The Goal Structure and Student Affect at School

Of the various indicators of disaffection that we consider in this chapter, affect toward learning, subject matter, and school is the one included most frequently in studies using a goal theory framework. Certainly students' positive and negative affect toward school is a clear indicator of their engagement in or disaffection from learning and schooling. Studies by Dweck and her colleagues provide evidence of the link between performance goals and negative affect for students low in perceived ability. For example, Elliott and Dweck (1988) experimentally induced a performance condition (emphasizing evaluation) and a mastery condition (emphasizing the value of the skill to be learned), and recorded the affect that children verbalized in each condition. Children who perceived that their ability to do the task was low expressed negative affect in the performance condition, whereas both high- and low-ability children expressed positive affect in the mastery condition. Studies by Bandura and Dweck (1985) and Leggett and Dweck (1986) in which individuals' existing goal preferences were measured (rather than manipulated) showed a similar pattern. Dweck described the mechanisms through which the different goals produce patterns of affect as follows:

> Within a performance goal, experiencing failure or effort exertion warns of a low-ability judgment and thus poses a threat to self-esteem. Such a threat might first engender anxiety (Sarason, 1975; Wine, 1971), and then if the negative judgment appears increasingly likely, depressed affect (Seligman, Abramson, Semmel, & von Baeyer, 1979) and a sense of shame (Sohn, 1977; Weiner & Graham, 1984) may set it. Alternatively, individuals could adopt a more defensive, self-protective posture, devaluing the task and expressing boredom or disdain toward it (Tesser & Campbell, 1983; cf. Berglas & Jones, 1978). Within learning (mastery) goal, the occurrence of failure simply signals that the task will require more effort and ingenuity for mastery. This creates, for some, the opportunity for a more satisfying mastery experience, producing the heightened positive affect noted earlier. (Dweck & Leggett, 1988, p. 261)

In a number of studies using survey methodology, researchers have examined the relation between personal goals or perceived goal structures and indicators of affect. In general, mastery goals have been related to positive affect and performance goals have been either negatively related or unrelated to affect. Meece and her colleagues (Meece, Blumenfeld, & Hoyle, 1988) found that mastery goals were positively related to attitudes toward science (e.g., "Science is an enjoyable subject"), whereas ego–social (performance) goals were negatively (but not significantly) related to these attitudes. Nolen and Haladyna (1990), in a study examining college-bound and non-college-bound 9th-, 11th-, and 12th-grade high school students, found the same pattern for attitudes toward science, as did Ames and Archer (1988) in a sample of stu-

dents attending a secondary school for academically advanced students. Using a scale that included items assessing both positive and negative (reversed) affect toward school, Kaplan and Maehr (1999a) found that the perceived mastery goal structure in school was related positively, and the perceived performance goal structure was related negatively to affect. Nicholls, Patashnick, and Nolen (1985), across four different samples of high school students, found that mastery goals were positively related, and ego–social goals were unrelated to satisfaction with learning ("At school I usually like thinking about schoolwork" and "At school I usually am bored"—reversed). Similarly, Roeser and his colleagues (1996) found that mastery goals were positively related, and performance goals were unrelated to affect at school ("Most of the time being in school puts me in a good mood" and "I like being in school") in a sample of eighth graders. In a sample of fifth graders, Seifert (1995) included measures of both positive affect ("When I am in school, I usually feel proud") and negative affect ("When I am in school, I usually feel frustrated"). Positive affect was more strongly correlated with a mastery orientation than with a performance orientation, although the correlations were positive in both cases. Negative affect was negatively related to mastery goals and unrelated to performance goals.

In our studies conducted in conjunction with the Patterns of Adaptive Learning Study, we have continued to examine the role of the goal structure in students' affective responses to school. Lynley Anderman (1999) used data collected from students when they were in the fifth grade in elementary school and a year later when they were in the sixth grade in middle school. Perceiving an emphasis on mastery goals in the sixth grade was associated with an increase in positive affect toward school from fifth to sixth grade, whereas perceiving an emphasis on performance goals in the sixth grade was associated with an increase in negative affect from fifth to sixth grade. In another study, students were divided into groups depending on whether they perceived an increase, decrease, or no change in the mastery and performance goals structure both across the transition to middle school and during the middle school years (Urdan & Midgley, 2000). Students who perceived a decrease in the emphasis on mastery goals when they moved to middle school experienced a decline in positive affect toward school and an increase in negative affect. Students who perceived an increase in the emphasis on mastery goals experienced an increase in positive affect. In general, the same patterns of change in affect found across the transition were found as students moved from sixth to seventh grade in the middle school.

Kaplan and Midgley (1999) investigated whether the perceived mastery and performance goal structures in the learning environment were associated with students' use of different coping strategies when they encountered difficulty in school, and in turn with their positive and negative affect. A mastery goal struc-

ture focuses students on the possibility of investing effort and using learning strategies in order to improve. In such an environment, experiencing difficulty is likely to be interpreted as an indication that more effort needs to be invested and that different learning strategies should be employed. In contrast, when students experience difficulty in an environment with a performance goal structure, they are likely to feel threatened, and may engage in coping strategies to protect their self-worth. Though some coping strategies may be adaptive, alleviate the stress, and contribute to well-being, other coping strategies may not be adaptive, may exacerbate negative emotions, and in the long run may interfere with students' development and well-being (Folkman & Lazarus, 1988; Phelps & Jarvis, 1994). Thus, when students respond to stressful events in school, like failing on a test, by trying to figure out what went wrong and attempting to make sure that it does not reoccur, they are more likely to have positive feelings about school and schoolwork. In contrast, when they blame their teacher for giving an unfair test or for not teaching the material well, they are likely to feel angry and alienated from school. Further, coping with failure by denying that it was important could contribute to students' perception that school is not important, leading to less engagement in schoolwork.

We used longitudinal data to examine students' perceptions of the goal structure in their classrooms, their coping strategies when dealing with an academic set back, and their affect in school as they made the transition from fifth grade in elementary school to sixth grade in middle school (Kaplan & Midgley, 1999). Using *structural equation modeling* (SEM), we found that perceiving an emphasis on mastery goals in the classroom was indeed related to positive ways of coping such as figuring out what went wrong, trying to make sure that it would not happen again, and telling oneself that it will be better next time. This way of coping in turn related to students' positive affect toward school. The classroom performance goal structure was related to coping strategies such as blaming the teacher for the failure and denying that the failure was important. Coping by blaming the teacher was in turn related to students' negative affect in school. Thus, this study provided further support for the role that an emphasis on besting others in the classroom plays in students' disaffection from school. It also provided support for the beneficial role that an emphasis on learning and personal improvement plays in enhancing adaptive coping and positive affect in school.

THE GOAL STRUCTURE AND STUDENTS' SENSE OF SCHOOL BELONGING

In the Patterns of Adaptive Learning Study, we have included a scale assessing students' sense of school belonging. A positive relation between students' sense of school belonging and levels of academic engagement and achieve-

ment has been well established (Finn, 1989; Goodenow, 1993; Goodenow & Grady, 1993; Wehlage, Rutter, Smith, Lesko, & Fernandez, 1989). A sense of school belonging is related to students' expectancy for success, positive feelings about themselves, and their motivation in general (Finn, 1989; Goodenow, 1993; Voelkl, 1996). Students who do not identify with school are less likely to succeed (Goodenow 1993; Voelkl, 1996) and more likely to drop out (Finn, 1989). They are also more likely to engage in negative behaviors (e.g., Brook, Nomura, & Cohen, 1989; Garmezy, 1983; Hoppe et al., 1998). We believe a low sense of school belonging is an important indicator of disaffection from school.

There is evidence that the achievement goal structure in school is related to students' feelings of belonging. Roeser and his colleagues (1996) found that students' perception of an emphasis on mastery goals in the school was related to their adoption of personal mastery goals, which in turn was related to their feelings of belonging to school. In another study, we found that middle school students' perceptions of an emphasis on performance goals in the school were negatively related to their feelings of belonging in school (Arunkumar & Maehr, 1997). In a study conducted when the students in the Patterns of Adaptive Learning Study were in the fifth grade in elementary school and the following year when they were in the sixth grade in middle school, we again examined how the goal structure in the school related to students' sense of school belonging (Arunkumar & Bryant, 1998). Sense of school belonging was assessed by an adapted version of the Psychological Sense of School Membership Scale developed by Goodenow (1991). This five-item scale assessed students' feeling of membership and belonging to the school community and included items such as "I feel like a real part of this school" and "I am proud of belonging to this school."

All of the teachers (kindergarten through Grade 5) in each of the 21 elementary schools responded to surveys that assessed their perceptions of the emphasis on performance goals in the school. They responded to items such as "In this school, students who get good grades are pointed out as an example to others" and "In this school, students hear a lot about the importance of making the honor roll or being recognized at honor assemblies." To get a sense of the overall performance goal structure of the school, we aggregated the teachers' reports within each school. Using *hierarchical linear modeling* (HLM), we examined these research questions: Is the performance goal structure related negatively to school belonging? Do schools differ in the level of school belonging reported by fifth-grade students? Does the performance goal structure account for the variation between schools in sense of belonging?

We found that the school performance goal structure, as reported by the teachers, was related negatively to students' sense of school belonging. We found that there was significant variation between schools in the sense of be-

longing that students reported. Furthermore, we found that teachers' report on an emphasis on performance goals in the school was a marginally significant predictor of the variation between schools in students' feelings of belonging. The relationship between the school performance goal structure and school belonging also varied by school.

Thus, there is growing evidence that the goal structure in the learning environment is related to students' sense of belonging in school. If students feel less connected to school when there is an emphasis on performance goals, and more connected when there is an emphasis on mastery goals, this speaks to the need to attend to the messages that are conveyed to students about the meaning and purpose of school.

The Goal Structure and Disruptive Behavior in School

Disruptive behavior is another indicator of disengagement from learning and disaffection from school. Recent studies suggest that disruptive behavior in the classroom is a growing problem and that it is one of the most serious concerns of teachers and parents (Bear, 1998; Elam, Rose, & Gallup, 1996). Teachers often find that they are required to take time away from teaching to deal with such behaviors as teasing, talking out of turn, moving around the classroom inappropriately, and disrespecting others. Sometimes teachers are also called upon to deal with more serious behavior problems like violence and vandalism.

Disruptive behavior was traditionally considered to be a characteristic of the student or a problem of classroom management. We believe that the classroom motivational environment may affect the level of students' disruptive behavior (see Kaplan et al., in press). First, in environments with a mastery goal structure, students are more likely to feel that tasks are interesting, that teachers afford them opportunities for success, and that they can learn and progress. These feelings are likely to lead to more on-task behavior, and to a diminished inclination among students to use disruptive behavior as a strategy to distract classmates and teachers from the work. Second, in learning environments with a performance goal structure, students do not want to be perceived as expending too much effort on their schoolwork because such perceptions threaten their self-worth in the eyes of others. Engaging in disruptive behavior may thus send the message that they are not putting much effort into studying and that their possible failures should not be attributed to low ability.

In one study with an ethnically diverse sample of sixth-grade students (Kaplan & Maehr, 1999a), we found that Euro-American students' perception of the emphasis on mastery goals in the school was related to their adoption of personal mastery goals, which in turn was negatively related to their level of disruptive behavior. In addition, the school mastery goal structure was related

to lower levels of disruptive behavior among African American students, and the school performance goal structure was related to their adoption of performance goals which, in turn, were related to higher levels of disruptive behavior. A performance goal structure was directly related to higher disruptive behavior among Euro-American students, although for this group personal performance goals were related to lower disruptive behavior.

In a more recent study that used data from the Patterns of Adaptive Learning Study (Kaplan et al., in press), we used HLM to further investigate the relations between the goal structure and the level of disruptive behavior in the classroom. Using data from students in ninth grade in high school, we first found that the level of disruptive behavior differed among the various classrooms. That is, the incidence of disruptive behavior was significantly higher in some classrooms than in others. We then found that a classroom mastery goal structure was related to lower levels of disruptive behavior and that a classroom performance goal structure was related to higher levels of disruptive behavior among students in the classroom. These relations were found after taking into account the relations between gender, grades, self-efficacy, and students' personal achievement goals and disruptive behavior. These findings suggest that disruptive behavior is not only an outgrowth of students' own motivational and academic "deficits," but that there is an important environmental component. Furthermore, the findings suggest that a classroom mastery goal structure may have a beneficial effect on the level of disruptive behavior over and above the positive impact of a de-emphasis on performance goals in the classroom. Another interesting finding was that students' personal performance goals were positively related to disruptive behavior, suggesting that even when students are oriented to demonstrating high ability in the classroom, they may engage in behavior that will send the message that they are not investing effort in their schoolwork—behavior that may hinder their learning and lead to feelings of disaffection from school.

In a study following students from the spring of seventh grade to the fall of eighth grade, A. M. Ryan and Patrick (2001) looked at students' perceptions of four aspects of the classroom social environment in predicting change in disruptive behavior: the extent to which the teacher promoted positive student–teacher relationships, encouraged interactions among peers, promoted mutual respect among classmates, and emphasized performance goals in the classroom. The performance goal structure emerged as the strongest predictor of an increase in disruptive behavior from Grades 7 to 8.

Thus far we have argued for the central role of achievement goals in students' disaffection from learning and schooling. We now turn to studies that focus on a group of students that may be particularly at risk for disaffection, and consider the role that the goal structure plays in exacerbating or ameliorating

that risk. These are students who sense a dissonance between their lives at home and at school.

The Goal Structure and Home–School Dissonance

In this section we begin by describing home–school dissonance, and discussing its role as a risk factor for student disengagement. Next, we describe four studies from the Patterns of Adaptive Learning Study that examined issues related to home–school dissonance. The first two studies illustrate empirically that dissonance is associated with a host of other emotional and academic risks. The third study illustrates how feelings of dissonance change over time, and how the goal structure in the learning environment is related to these changes. The last study describes, through students' own voices, how their school experiences, conceptualized in terms of an emphasis on mastery and performance goals, ameliorate or exacerbate their feelings of dissonance.

Home–School Dissonance.   For some students, the daily transition from home to school is an alienating experience. Phelan and her colleagues have developed a comprehensive model to identify the various risk factors that are associated with students' disaffection from school. They defined these risks in terms of borders between students' selves—their thoughts, feelings, and adaptation strategies—and the multiple worlds of home, school, and peers, all located within the larger community in which they live. Each of these "worlds" or "contexts" is characterized by values, beliefs, expectations, actions, and emotional responses that may be consistent across contexts or dissonant across contexts (Phelan, Davidson, & Yu, 1996).

The literature on home–school dissonance is based largely on ethnographic studies. We wanted to expand on this research by creating a psychometrically sound measure of home–school dissonance. Drawing from the ethnographic studies in this field, Kumar and her colleagues on the Patterns of Adaptive Learning Study created a survey measure for students that tapped these feelings of dissonance between home and school (Arunkumar, Midgley, & Urdan, 1999). The scale consists of five items, each on a 5-point scale ranging from 1 *(not at all true)* to 3 *(somewhat true)* to 5 *(very true)*. Sample items include "I feel troubled because my home life and school life are like two different worlds" and "I don't like my parents coming to school because their ideas are very different from my teachers' ideas." The items assess students' discomfort or negative feelings resulting from differences in beliefs, values, and behavioral expectations between their parents and home life, and their teachers and school life. We found that the scale demonstrated good internal consistency

with an alpha that averaged .75 across the samples and years, and factored separately from other measures of disengagement and disaffection from school.

Correlates of Home–School Dissonance: Empirical Evidence.

What characterizes students who feel a discord between home and school? Using survey data, we examined the relation between experiencing home–school dissonance and students' academic and emotional well-being, as well as their beliefs about the value of school. Not surprisingly, we found that perceiving home–school dissonance was related to a negative pattern of beliefs and behaviors.

In the first study (Arunkumar et al., 1999), we used survey responses from 475 students who participated in the Patterns of Adaptive Learning Study when they were in the fifth grade in elementary school and the following year when they were in sixth grade in middle school. We then focused on students who reported they experienced either high dissonance (top third on the dissonance scale) or low dissonance (bottom third on the scale) on the home–school dissonance scale. We found that high-dissonance students were angrier and more self-deprecating, had lower self-esteem, were less hopeful, felt less academically efficacious, and had a lower grade point average (GPA) than did low-dissonance students. Additionally, high-dissonance students experienced a greater decline in GPA, and less of a decline in anger than did low-dissonance students when they moved into middle school.

In a second study (Gheen, Arunkumar, & Midgley, 1999), we explored the relation between home–school dissonance and students' skeptical beliefs about the value and relevance of education to their lives. Feeling that school has little meaning for one's future life is a sign of disaffection from learning and schooling. To assess skepticism, we included items such as "Even if I do well in school, it's not going to help me get ahead in life" and "My chances of succeeding later in life don't depend on doing well in my school." We were interested in assessing whether feelings of home–school dissonance might be associated with students' skeptical beliefs about the value of schooling. Turning to self-worth theory (Covington, 1992), we reasoned that the psychological toll of dissonance might lead students to motivationally withdraw from school. Students who experience home–school dissonance may disidentify with school and adopt beliefs that question the utility of educational success for their own lives.

In a sample of 378 eighth graders, we examined the relation between home-school dissonance and skepticism, over and above the association of home–school dissonance with ethnicity, gender, prior achievement (seventh-grade GPA), positive attitudes toward school, and ways of coping with academic failure (denial, projective, and positive coping strategies). We found that experiencing dissonance between home and school was a significant pre-

dictor of holding skeptical beliefs about the value of schooling, controlling for these other factors. Interestingly, we did not find any differences between African American and Euro-American students in their level of skepticism. Research has suggested that African Americans are more vulnerable to these beliefs than are Euro-Americans (e.g., Mickelson, 1990). Our study indicates that it is not ethnicity per se that is associated with skepticism, rather the perception that home and school are like two different worlds. Feeling that home and school are like two different worlds, and believing that school is not going to contribute to the quality of one's future life likely takes a toll on students. Over time, these students may be at increased risk of distancing themselves from learning and schooling.

In conjunction with the Patterns of Adaptive Learning Study, we also examined factors associated with changes in dissonance as students made the transition from fifth grade in elementary school to sixth and then seventh grade in middle school (Kumar & Midgley, 2001). Students moved from 21 elementary schools to 10 middle schools in the sixth grade. Students filled out a survey each year, and 74% of the teachers in the 10 middle schools completed surveys as well.

We examined whether student characteristics such as ethnicity, socioeconomic status (measured in terms of students' participation in the free- and reduced-fee-lunch program), gender, and GPA were associated with changes in dissonance as they moved from elementary to middle school. We also investigated whether changes in students' feelings of dissonance when they moved from elementary to middle school were related to changes in their perception of the goal structure in the classroom and to changes in their feelings of school belonging. Finally, an important purpose of this study was to identify whether moving into schools that had more or less of an emphasis on mastery goals (based on teachers' perceptions of their schools) was related to changes in students' feelings of dissonance after their transition into middle school. The results proved to be very interesting and again point to the role of the goal structure in classrooms and schools in exacerbating or ameliorating indicators of dissonance. The paper describing this study is under review, so the results are not presented here. Information regarding the publication of the paper can be obtained from Revathy Kumar.

Home–School Dissonance: Listening to Middle School Students. We went beyond survey reports to ask the students themselves about the reasons they experienced a discord between home and school, and how their teachers and schools contributed to or ameliorated these feelings. When students were in seventh grade, one-on-one interviews were conducted with a sample of 49 students who had reported high levels of dissonance on the survey (Arunkumar, 1999). All the interviews were conducted during school hours in a

separate room or private area in the school. The students were assured of complete confidentiality. They were also told that they did not need to answer any questions that made them feel uncomfortable and that they could request to have the tape recorder turned off at any time during the interview process. The length of the interviews ranged from an hour to an hour and a half. All the interviews were audio taped and transcribed. The interviews included specific questions to elicit reasons for dissonance, feelings associated with dissonance, and the link between dissonance and the learning environment. The interviews also included open-ended questions that allowed students to discuss what was salient to them regarding their feelings of dissonance.

Many of the codes created during data analysis were deduced based on themes that were identified in the literature as reasons for experiencing dissonance. Other codes emerged during the process of coding and analyzing the data. The interviews were first coded for broad themes and patterns that emerged. For example, in this study the two broad themes that first emerged were "factors ameliorating dissonance" and "factors causing or heightening dissonance." These two factors were based on an initial reading of the interviews, which suggested that students talked about both issues or features within school and home that were related to their feelings of dissonance and those that decreased their experiences of dissonance.

More fine-grained coding and clustering within the broader themes followed this. Whereas in some instances the more detailed and fine-grained categories were retained, in other instances these finer categories were again collapsed, if they did not lend themselves to meaningful interpretation. Miles and Huberman (1994) referred to this process of pulling together codes that go together and collapsing them into a single code as "factoring." Data were analyzed using the software program NUD*IST (Richards & Richards, 1990). This program was useful in creating and assigning codes and categories to the interview transcripts.

In some cases, it was difficult to ascertain whether students' comments related specifically to their feelings of dissonance between home and school or related to their feelings of disconnection from school. Inferences about the link to feelings of home–school dissonance were based on the way the sample was selected. These students had indicated on a survey that their home life and school life were like "two different worlds," that they were "upset because their teachers and parents had different ideas about what they should learn in school," and that they thought a lot about how their life at home was "different from the home life of many of the students in the school." Almost all the students who were interviewed mentioned feeling different from others when they were at school. Many described occasions when the behavioral norms between home and school were in conflict. Some of the reasons articulated by students for feeling dissonant were tied closely to their ethnicity and others cut

across racial lines. The study presented here is limited to factors related to dissonance that were common across ethnic groups.

Across ethnic groups, some students mentioned that their low socioeconomic status (SES) or religious affiliation contributed to their feelings of dissonance. Students from all ethnic groups talked at length about experiences in school that they associated with feeling different. Not surprisingly, students provided examples of policies and practices that we would label as "performance-focused" and said they often made them feel different and deficient, especially in the case of students who did not perform well on their schoolwork. Students were asked: "Have you ever felt, when you are in the classroom or anywhere else in the school, that you were very different from your classmates?" Shaun[1] said that it was very embarrassing to perform less well on tests than friends and other classmates:

I: Have you ever felt, when you are in the classroom or anywhere
        else in the school, that you are very different from your class-
        mates?
Shaun: Sometimes. Like when I am in class and I get a different grade
        from them. A test, if I get a C and they get an A, I feel that they are
        better than me.
I: Do you know who does well in this class and who does not?
Shaun: Yes, the smart people in my class usually get As.

Shaun indicated over the course of the interview that there were multiple reasons for his feelings of dissonance in school. His parents' lack of fluency in English was a source of embarrassment to him. His poor performance on schoolwork added to his discomfort and unhappiness in school. Ford voiced his unhappiness at being criticized for performing poorly by his teachers in front of his peers:

I: Why did you say you did not like these teachers?
Ford: Because they keep criticizing me at the negative end. If she
        would quit criticizing me in front of the whole class I think I
        would feel better. I don't like them because they criticize me
        and are always embarrassing me in front of my friends and ev-
        erything. I feel different because I get an easy question in class
        and I get it wrong, and another kid gets it. That makes me feel
        different.

Vin voiced his frustration that he could never be as smart as his classmates:

---
[1]All names are pseudonyms.

I: Are there ever times when you feel you are different from your classmates?

Vin: Yes, when most of them know the questions and they don't even be studying. I know—I be studying and I don't know the questions and stuff. And I just, I be studying really hard, and I don't ever get it right.

In comparing the amount of effort he expended on his schoolwork with the amount of effort expended by some of his classmates, Vin was describing a negative belief sometimes associated with a performance-focused learning environment—"You are not smart if you have to put in a lot of effort into your schoolwork."

Whereas for some students, feeling dissonant was restricted to certain teachers and certain classrooms, others described their experience in school in general as a dissonant one. This was the plight of Barnie, who at the beginning of the interview described himself as a "hillbilly." He felt he was different from other students on many fronts. He said he received little help at home with his work. His final sixth-grade GPA was a D–. He said he disliked school more than anything else:

I: Are there times when you feel you are really different from your classmates?

Barnie: Yeah, all the time.

I: All the time? Why?

Barnie: Because they all answer the questions, when I raise my hand I always get it wrong. Last week I was in a group, a smart group and I am not that smart. And I mostly get all the wrong answers and they yell at me.

I: What do they say?

Barnie: "You're dumb! You're stupid!"

I: What do you tell them?

Barnie: That's the way I am.

I: Can you tell me about any other times when you felt different?

Barnie: When I am in the gym, I cannot run as fast as everybody and they all laugh at me.

I: How does this make you feel?

Barnie: It feels like I am the worst student ever.

Barnie's description of his experience in a group activity raises questions about mixed ability cooperative group activities in our schools. There is much to be said about the benefits of cooperative learning (Johnson & Johnson, 1984; Slavin, 1983), but as Barnie's comments indicate, merely having students work

in mixed-ability groups does not necessarily diminish the emphasis on performance goals. Although one of the advantages of cooperative learning is the opportunity to de-emphasize relative ability and promote equal status among students, there is increasing concern that it is being used in a way that exacerbates status problems (e.g., Cohen, 1986). In the situation described earlier by Barnie, individual ability still seemed to be the focus of the group activity.

Performance goals can also be made salient by ability grouping and tracking. A number of students indicated that being in the lower ability groups was stigmatizing. Ceci had opted out of the advanced math class because she felt she could not do the work:

I: Are you still in that?
Ceci: Uh uh. I quit. I thought that it was too hard and too much stress on
        me, so I quit it and now everybody is calling me a quitter. Well,
        they don't anymore but they used to.... Because I used to be in
        the higher math class, and now that I am in the lower math class
        and I have to ask a question I feel kind of stupid, because I was
        smart enough to be in it.

Ceci's comments about how she felt about asking questions illustrate some of the findings reported in chapter 3 (this volume). That is, when students are in a classroom where relative ability is salient, they may feel threatened by seeking help, and avoid asking for it even when they need it (A. M. Ryan & Pintrich, 1997).

Some students mentioned that they felt more comfortable in classrooms in which their ability was not called into question. For example, when asked why he liked his science class, Ford said:

Ford: Like if I don't understand anything in class, she'll take time out
        in class and show me how to do it and give me good criticism in-
        stead of bad criticism and embarrassing me in front of the class-
        room.

Students were asked if they had ever had a teacher they liked a lot, and if they did, whether that teacher had made a difference in their lives in school. They were also asked if they had ever had a teacher they did not like and whether this made a difference in their lives in school. Some students described teachers who were unwilling to help them with their schoolwork. For example, Ashley described teachers as unsympathetic and unresponsive to her academic needs. Ashley was already experiencing dissonance because she felt that her peers devalued her religious beliefs. She remarked several times during the course of

the interview that she disliked coming to school and said that the thought of getting up everyday to go to school made her miserable:

Ashley: Like if I need special training, some teachers don't like to go over things over and over again. Sometimes that is what I really need to understand and they don't realize that. With a lot of students they do that. Mr. C doesn't like to go over things, and Mrs. B doesn't. I am not very good at math and she doesn't like to go over things with me, and I get Ds and stuff in her class.

Ronnie, a high-achieving student, talked at length about the lack of communication between her mother and her teachers because of her mother's lack of fluency in English. This made her unhappy, particularly because she felt her mother could not help her when she had problems in school. She also described some teachers who seemed unwilling to provide help when if was needed:

Ronnie: My math teacher, she's like boring. She does not try to make things fun. She will just teach and that's it. I don't like how she acts. If we ask a question about a problem, she will look really frustrated. And I don't like that because she is a teacher and she should be happy that we are asking questions because if we did not she would not have a class.

Sandie was very unhappy that her science teacher did not like her and treated her unfairly. She felt her science teacher was unfair in rating her performance as poor because she had done well in science in sixth grade, and she perceived herself as a "good science student." The question "is there a teacher you do not like?" brought forth this angry outburst from her:

Sandie: She [science teacher] doesn't teach right, she doesn't treat me right, I don't like her. I don't feel that my teacher really teaches well in science class and I feel like she doesn't like me cuz I don't even think that she does. And when she passes tests out, I'm always getting the low score and everybody else is getting the high score. But I'm good in science cuz last year in sixth grade I had been doing good. And she doesn't have control over the class. And almost everyday she'll kick me out of class for nothing and then I won't even know anything. She'll tell me "get out of class, get out of class" if I just say like something, if she doesn't like it she'll just be like "get out of class," she's like "go out in the hall."

Sandie's comments implied that her teacher was making unfair use of the power differential between herself and her students. Withdrawal of support by teachers, who have power over them, can be a difficult and alienating experience for students.

Occasionally some of these students talked about caring teachers who seemed to lessen their feelings of dissonance. Steve, for example, had disclosed early in the interview that he was facing problems both at home and at school. He did not want to divulge the exact nature of his problems at home, but he said that his home life was unhappy and that it was weighing him down. The one class he said he felt happy and comfortable in was his special education class because that teacher understood his problems. Other students also said that they liked teachers who were considerate of their feelings, did not put them down, had a sense of humor, and tried to bridge the gap between their students and themselves:

> Shaun: Mr. W, my science teacher, I like him a lot. He always helps with tests and stuff. He never makes fun of people. He is a good teacher. Some teachers joke around and make the student feel bad. But Mr. W he never cracks jokes on students. He always cracks jokes on himself.

Students were asked a series of questions regarding their parents' involvement in school and the extent and quality of their interaction with teachers and other school personnel. The interviews provided evidence that it is the quality of home–school communication, not the quantity that is related to students' feelings of identification with or disaffection from school. Some students mentioned that teachers and school personnel frequently called home or asked parents to come to school because they were dissatisfied with the student's behavior. Jamal said that the only time his grandpa came to school was when Jamal got into fights:

> I: Has your grandpa come to school?
> Jamal: Yup, when the teachers call him.
> I: What did they call him for?
> Jamal: The only time they call him is when I am being bad, the teacher will call him, he will come up here and have a meeting with the teacher.
> I: If you are being good do the teachers call?
> Jamal: No.

Chuck's response was similar to Jamal's when he was asked in what way his parents were involved in school:

Chuck: They monitor my grades and how my behavior is and if I don't show up in school any time, the school would call my parents and they would straighten me up.

I: Can you tell me about a time when that happened?

Chuck: One time, my father and mother came here because I got kicked out of class and then I got kicked out of school, they came up here, talked and tried to straighten it out.

Later in the interview, Chuck said that he was like his father who was always getting into trouble with the authorities when he was in school. Chuck also said that his father felt it was okay to get into trouble in school, but that he should keep it within limits. This is illustrative of the differences in norms and expectations and home and at school that may be problematic for students.

The interviews revealed that multiple factors contributed to students' feelings of dissonance in school. No two students experienced dissonance for all the same reasons. Interviews indicated that lack of material resources and religious affiliation led to feelings of dissonance in some students. However, students described factors at school, more than factors at home, as contributing to dissonance, including the emphasis on relative ability in the classroom and school, and the nature of their interpersonal relationships with teachers.

Our review of the research that examines causes and consequences of home–school dissonance concurs with the research on students' affect in school, their sense of school belonging, and their reports of disruptive behavior to suggest that a learning environment with a performance goal structure is likely to elicit emotions and behaviors that put students at risk for disengagement from learning and disaffection for school. However, the research also suggests that learning environments with a mastery goal structure are likely to ameliorate feelings of dissonance and contribute to positive emotions, engagement in learning, and resilience in the face of stressful events.

IMPLICATIONS FOR TEACHERS AND SCHOOLS

The studies cited previously suggest that attempts to alleviate students' sense of disaffection through interventions that focus narrowly on one aspect of students' experience in school may not be enough. Principals and teachers may need to focus their reform efforts on comprehensive school wide attempts to strengthen the mastery goal structure and reduce the emphasis on performance goals. The teachers we have collaborated with have expressed a particular concern for students who are disengaged from learning and schooling. We have written a number of papers suggesting how teachers can reduce the emphasis on performance goals and increase the emphasis on mastery goals (e.g., Midgley, 1993). Table 5.1 in chapter 5 (this volume) includes strategies that

were generated by teachers during a 3-year coalition with principals and teachers in an elementary school and a middle school (Anderman, Maehr, & Midgley, 1999; Midgley & Maehr, 1999; Midgley & Urdan, 1992).

Teachers seem better able to move away from an emphasis on performance goals than to move toward an emphasis on mastery goals (Bergin, 1995; Midgley & Edelin, 1998). What can schools and classrooms do to convey mastery goals? A detailed description of our 3-year collaboration is described in Maehr and Midgley (1996). In addition, Carole Ames (1990) collaborated with elementary teachers to use ideas from research on motivation to create a learning environment with a mastery goal structure. This collaborative program is described briefly in chapter 9 (this volume). Ames (1992a) used the acronym TARGET, originally used by Epstein (1988), to represent six manipulable classroom structures, namely, the nature of academic Tasks, the Authority assumed by teachers or granted to students, the bases for student Recognition, Grouping practices, the Evaluation system, and the way Time is used. Ames (1992b) suggested ways in which each of these aspects of the classroom environment can be structured to emphasize task mastery. Recently, we (Kaplan & Maehr, 1999b) used this framework to articulate principles that could guide educators as they attempt to implement these structure in schools with African American students. In particular, we pointed to practices such as building on students' cultural knowledge in designing tasks, valuing culturally relevant skills, and providing opportunities for equal status in collaborative groups. These practices should communicate to students that the purpose of schooling is learning and understanding, rather than demonstrating how smart one is or competing favorably with others on academic tasks and tests.

THE CURRENT EMPHASIS ON HIGH-STAKES TESTING AND ACCOUNTABILITY

Attempts to reform schools in a way that will emphasize mastery goals and de-emphasize performance goals can be successful, but take time, dedication, and thoughtful discussion among principals, teachers, and parents. Some may fear that policies such as de-emphasizing grades, eliminating honor rolls and tracking policies, and encouraging alternative assessments over frequent multiple-choice factual testing somehow undermines high standards and sets the stage for a "less rigorous" learning environment. During our collaboration with teachers, these issues surfaced frequently and were discussed in depth. Principals and teachers grappled with these issues and ended up making some remarkable changes to create a mastery-oriented learning environment. Teachers, parents, students, and the district at large agreed that at-risk students were more engaged in school and were learning more as a result of the changes.

The elementary school was later recognized for these efforts by being named an "Exemplary Title One School."

However, the emphasis on high-stakes testing has escalated since that time. In our recent conversations with the teachers with whom we collaborated, they talk about how the testing and accountability movement has influenced their teaching. Rather than promoting thinking, understanding, and creativity, many feel pressured to teach facts and test-taking strategies. When we present our results from the Patterns of Adaptive Learning Study to participating schools, we increasingly hear teachers and administrators express their frustration with the negative impact that statewide testing has had on the academic climate of their schools, and their skepticism about their ability to consider changes consistent with promoting an emphasis on mastery goals, given the current educational climate. Our anecdotal evidence is mirrored in the empirical work of Urdan and Paris (1994) who found that many teachers feel negatively about standardized tests.

Of particular importance to the focus of this chapter, this approach is often touted especially for children who are low achieving and disaffected. "Accountability" and "incentives" are suggested as the motivational mechanisms by which testing will operate to increase the performance of these students. We believe that students who are at risk for disengagement from school will suffer the most from this emphasis on high-stakes testing. Some may disengage from the tests altogether, proclaiming that they "don't care" about the scores and fail to give their best effort. For others, this may be another indicator that school is not for them. A large-scale evaluation of Texas standards-based educational reform found that a disproportionately high number of minority students were assigned to special education programs (which eliminated them from schools' accountability ratings) and dropped out of high school upon the introduction of these high-stakes reform policies (Haney, 2000). The Coalition for Authentic Reform in Education recently released a report on high-stakes testing in Massachusetts (*http://www.fairtest.org/care/MCAS%20Alert%20Sept.html*). This report indicated that the most vulnerable students were being left behind in the wake of a policy that links high school graduation to test scores. A review of the state's dropout data for the past 4 years shows that since the introduction of high-stakes testing:

1. More students are dropping out of Massachusetts high schools, with an increasingly large proportion coming from urban districts.
2. A greater proportion of students who drop out are African American and Latino (now 40% compared to 34% three years ago).
3. More students are dropping out in earlier grades, including the middle grades.
4. A lower percentage of dropouts are reenrolling in school.

In the recent controversy regarding whether performance goals are "good," (Harackiewicz, Barron, & Elliot, 1998; Midgley et al., 2001; Pintrich, 2000), there is little mention of students who are disaffected from learning and schooling. Indeed, the opposite case is made; that an emphasis on demonstrating ability may be facilitative in some cases for students who are high in the motive to achieve. The evidence reviewed here would indicate that students who are disengaged from learning and schooling are particularly vulnerable to an emphasis on performance goals. This is sobering, given the growing emphasis on performance goals that is communicated through the testing and accountability movement. It appears we are setting the stage for even greater gaps in achievement between the "haves" and the "have nots."

REFERENCES

Ames, C. (1990, April). *The relationship of achievement goals to student motivation in classroom settings.* Paper presented at the annual meeting of the American Educational Research Association, Boston.

Ames, C. (1992a). Achievement goals and the classroom motivational climate. In D. Schunk & J. Meece (Eds.), *Student perceptions in the classroom* (pp. 327–348). Hillsdale, NJ: Lawrence Erlbaum Associates.

Ames, C. (1992b). Classrooms: Goals, structures, and student motivation. *Journal of Educational Psychology, 84,* 261–271.

Ames, C., & Archer, J. (1988). Achievement goals in the classroom: Student learning strategies and motivation processes. *Journal of Educational Psychology, 80,* 260–267.

Anderman, E. M., & Maehr, M. L. (1994). Motivation and schooling in the middle grades. *Review of Educational Research, 64,* 287–309.

Anderman, E., Maehr, M. L., & Midgley, C. (1999). Declining motivation after the transition to middle school: Schools can make a difference. *Journal of Research and Development in Education, 32,* 131–147.

Anderman, L. H. (1999). Classroom goal orientation, school belonging and social goals as predictors of students' positive and negative affect following the transition to middle school. *Journal of Research and Development in Education, 32,* 90–103.

Arunkumar, R. (1999, April). *Listening to students' voices: Reasons for experiencing a cultural dissonance between home and school.* Paper presented at the biennial meeting of the society for Research in Child Development, Albuquerque, NM.

Arunkumar, R., & Bryant, A. (1998, April). *The negative effects of ability-focused schools: Undermining students' school belonging.* Paper presented at the annual meeting of the American Educational Research Association, San Diego.

Arunkumar, R., & Maehr, M. L. (1997, March). *School "psychological climate" and student self esteem.* Paper presented at the annual meeting of the American Educational Research Association, San Francisco.

Arunkumar, R., Midgley, C., & Urdan, T. (1999). Perceiving high or low home–school dissonance: Longitudinal effects on adolescent emotional and academic well-being. *Journal of Research on Adolescence, 9,* 441–467.

Bandura, M., & Dweck, C. S. (1985). *The relationship of conceptions of intelligence and achievement goals to achievement-related cognition, affect, and behavior.* Unpublished manuscript, Harvard University, Cambridge, MA.

Bear, G. G. (1998). School discipline in the United States: Prevention, correction, and long-term social development. *School Psychology Review, 27,* 14–32.

Bergin, D. (1995). Effects of mastery versus competitive motivation situation on learning. *Journal of Experimental Education, 63,* 303–314.

Berglas, S., & Jones, E. (1978). Drug choice as a self-handicapping strategy in response to non-contingent success. *Journal of Personality and Social Psychology, 36,* 405–417.

Berndt, T. J., & Keefe, K. (1995). Friends' influence on adolescents' adjustment to school. *Child Development, 66,* 1312–1329.

Biafora, F. A., Jr., Warheit, G. J., Zimmerman, R. S., Gil, A. G., Apospori, E., & Taylor, D. (1993). Racial mistrust and deviant behaviors among ethnically diverse Black adolescent boys. *Journal of Applied Social Psychology, 23,* 891–910.

Brook, J. S., Nomura, C., & Cohen, P. (1989). A network of influences on adolescent drug involvement: Neighborhood, school, peer, and family. *Genetic, Social, and General Psychology Monographs, 118,* 419–438.

Carnegie Task Force on the Education of Young Adolescents. (1989). *Turning points: Preparing American youth for the 21st century.* New York: Carnegie Corporation.

Cohen, E. G. (1986). *Designing group work: Strategies for the heterogeneous classroom.* New York: Teachers College Press.

Comer, J. P. (1987). Black family stress and school achievement. In D. S. Strickland & E. J. Cooper (Eds.), *Educating Black children: America's challenge* (pp. 77–84). Washington, DC: Howard University, Bureau of Educational Research.

Comer, J. (1988). Educating poor minority children. *Scientific American, 259,* 42.

Covington, M. V. (1992). *Making the grade: A self-worth perspective on motivation and school reform.* Cambridge, England: Cambridge University Press.

Deci, E., Vallerand, R. J., Pelletier, L. G., & Ryan, R. M. (1991). Motivation and education: The self-determination perspective. *Educational Psychologist: Special Issue: Current issues and new directions in motivational theory and research, 26,* 325–346.

Dryfoos, J. G. (1990). *Adolescents at risk: Prevalence and prevention.* New York: Oxford University Press.

Dryfoos, J. G. (1994). *Full-service schools: A revolution in heath and health services for children. Youth, and families.* San Francisco: Jossey-Bass.

Dweck, C. S., & Leggett, E. L. (1988). A social-cognitive approach to motivation and personality. *Psychological Review, 95,* 256–273.

Elam, S. M., Rose, L. C., & Gallup, A. M. (1996, September). The 28th annual Phi Delta Kappa/Gallup poll of the public's attitudes toward the public schools. *Phi Delta Kappan,* pp. 41–58.

Elliot, A. J. (1999). Approach and avoidance achievement goals. *Educational Psychologist, 34,* 169–189.

Elliott, E. S., & Dweck, C. S. (1988). Goals: An approach to motivation and achievement. *Journal of Personality and Social Psychology, 54,* 5–12.

Epstein, J. L. (1988). Effective schools or effective students: Dealing with diversity. In R. Haskins (Ed.), *Policies for America's public schools: Teachers, equity, and indicators* (pp. 89–126). Norwood, NJ: Ablex.

Finn, J. (1989). Withdrawing from school. *Review of Educational Research, 59,* 117–142.

Folkman, S., & Lazarus, R. S. (1988). Coping as a mediator of emotion. *Journal of Personality and Social Psychology, 54,* 466–475.

Garmezy, N. (1983). Stressors of childhood. In N. Garmezy & M. Rutter (Eds.), *Stress, coping, and development in children* (pp. 43–84). New York: McGraw-Hill.

Gheen, M. H., Arunkumar, R., & Midgley, C. (1999, April). *"This school's not going to get me anywhere"*: Correlates *of students' skeptical beliefs in middle school.* Paper pre-

sented at the biennial meeting of the Society for Research in Child Development, Albuquerque, NM.

Gheen, M. H., & Midgley, C. (1999, April). *"I'd rather not do it the hard way": Student and classroom characteristics relating to eighth graders' avoidance of academic challenge.* Paper presented at the annual meeting of the American Educational Research Association, Montreal.

Goodenow, C. (1991). The psychological sense of school membership among adolescents: Scale development and educational correlates. *Psychology in the Schools, 30,* 79–90.

Goodenow, C. (1993). Classroom belonging among early adolescent students: Relationships to motivation and achievement. *Journal of Early Adolescence, 13,* 21–43.

Goodenow, C., & Grady K. E. (1993). The relationship of school belonging and friends' values to academic motivation among urban adolescent students. *Journal of Experimental Education, 62,* 60–71.

Haney, W. (2000). The myth of the Texas miracle in education. *Education Policy Analysis Archives, 8*(41). Available: http://epaa/asu.edu/epaa/v8n41.

Harackiewicz, J. M., Barron, K. E., & Elliot, A. J. (1998). Rethinking achievement goals: When are they adaptive for college students and why? *Educational Psychologist, 33,* 1–21.

Harley, L. P., & Lustbader, L. L. (1997). Project support: Engaging children and families in the educational process. *Adolescence, 32,* 523–531.

Haynes, N. H., Comer, J. P., & Hamilton-Lee, M. (1988). School climate enhancement through parental involvement. *Journal of School Psychology, 27,* 87–90.

Hoppe, M. J., Wells, E. A., Haggerty, K. P., Simpson, E. E., Gainey, R. R., & Catalano, R. F. (1998). Bonding in a high-risk and general sample of children: Comparison of measures of attachment and their relationship to smoking and drinking. *Journal of Youth and Adolescence, 27,* 59–81.

Ianni, F. A. J. (1989). *The search for structure: A report on American youth today.* New York: The Free Press.

Jagacinski, C. M., & Nicholls, J. G. (1987). Competence and affect in task involvement and ego involvement: The impact of social comparison information. *Journal of Educational Psychology, 79,* 107–114.

Johnson, D. W., & Johnson, R. (1984). Building of differences between handicapped and non-handicapped students. *Journal of Social Psychology, 122,* 257–267.

Kaplan, A., Gheen, M., & Midgley, C. (2001). *The classroom goal structure and student disruptive behavior.* Manuscript submitted for publication.

Kaplan, A., Gheen, M., & Midgley, C. (in press). Classroom goal structure and student disruptive behavior. *British Journal of Psychology.*

Kaplan, A., & Maehr, M. L. (1997). School cultures. In H. Walberg & G. Haertel (Eds.) *Psychology and educational practice* (pp. 342–355). Berkeley, CA: McCutchan.

Kaplan, A., & Maehr, M. L. (1999a). Achievement goals and student well-being. *Contemporary Educational Psychology, 24,* 330–358.

Kaplan, A., & Maehr, M. L. (1999b). Enhancing the motivation of African American students: An achievement goal theory perspective. *Journal of Negro Education, 68,* 23–35.

Kaplan, A., & Midgley, C. (1999). The relationship between perceptions of the classroom environment and early adolescents' affect in school: The role of coping strategies. *Learning and Individual Differences, 11,* 187–212.

Kerckhoff, A. C., & Bell, L. (1997–1998). Early adult outcomes of students at "risk." *Social Psychology of Education, Special Issue: Student disadvantage and educational outcomes, 2,* 81–102.

Krohn, M. D., Lizotte, A. J., Perez, C. M. (1997). The interrelationship between substance use and precocious transitions to adult statuses. *Journal of Health and Social Behavior, 38,* 87–103.

Kumar, R., & Midgley, C. (2001). *The interplay of individual and contextual factors on change in dissonance between home and school across the transition from elementary to middle school.* Manuscript submitted for publication.

LeCompte, M. D., & Dworkin, A. G. (1991). *Giving up on school: Student dropouts and teacher burnouts.* Newbury Park, CA: Corwin Press.

Leggett, E. L., & Dweck, C. S. (1986). *Goals and inference rules: Sources of causal judgments.* Unpublished manuscript.

Maehr, M. L., & Midgley, C. (1991). Enhancing student motivation: A school-wide approach. *Educational Psychologist, 26,* 399–427.

Maehr, M. L., & Midgley, C. (1996). *Transforming school cultures.* Boulder, CO: Westview Press.

Meece, J. L., Blumenfeld, P. C., & Hoyle, R. H. (1988). Students' goal orientation and cognitive engagement in classroom activities. *Journal of Educational Psychology, 80,* 514–523.

Meece, J. L., & Miller, S. D. (1999). Changes in elementary school children's achievement goals for reading and writing: Results of a longitudinal and an intervention study. *Scientific Studies of Reading: Special issue: How motivation fits into the science of reading, 3,* 207–229.

Mickelson, R. A. (1990). The attitude-achievement paradox among Black adolescents. *Sociology of Education, 63,* 44–61.

Middleton, M., Kaplan, A., Midgley, C., & Anderman, E. (2001). *Classroom goal structure: Perceiving an emphasis on multiple goals.* Manuscript in preparation.

Midgley, C. (1993). Motivation and middle level schools. In P. Pintrich & M. L. Maehr (Eds.), *Advances in motivation and achievement: Vol. 8. Motivation in the adolescent years* (pp. 219–276). Greenwich, CT: JAI.

Midgley, C., & Edelin, K. (1998). Middle school reform and early adolescent well-being: The good news and the bad. *Educational Psychologist, 33,* 195–206.

Midgley, C., Kaplan, A., & Middleton, M. J. (2001). Performance-approach goals: Good for what, for whom, under what circumstances, and at what cost? *Journal of Educational Psychology, 93,* 77–86.

Midgley, C., & Maehr, M. L. (1999). Using motivational theory to guide school reform. In A. J. Reynolds, H. J. Walberg, & R. P. Weissberg (Eds.), *Promoting positive outcomes: Issues in children's and families' lives* (pp. 129–159). Washington, DC: Child Welfare League of America, Inc.

Midgley, C., & Urdan, T. (1992). The transition to middle level schools: Making it a good experience for all students. *Middle School Journal, 24,* 5–14.

Miles, M. B., & Huberman, A. M. (1994). *Qualitative data analysis: An expanded source book* (2nd ed.). Thousand Oaks, CA: Sage.

Nicholls, J. G. (1984). Achievement motivation: Conceptions of ability, subjective experience, task choice, and performance. *Psychological Review, 91,* 328–346.

Nicholls, J. G., Patashnick, M., & Nolen, S. B. (1985). Adolescents' theories of education. *Journal of Educational Psychology, 77,* 683–692.

Nolen, S. B., & Haladyna, T. M. (1990). Motivation and studying in high school science. *Journal of Research in Science Education, 27,* 115–126.

O'Donnell, J., Hawkins, J. D., Catalano, R. F., Abbott, R. D. (1995). Preventing school failure, drug use, and delinquency among low-income children: Long-term intervention in elementary schools. *American Journal of Orthopsychiatry, 65,* 87–100.

Ogbu, J. U. (1987). Variability in minority responses to schooling: Nonimmigrants vs. immigrants. In G. Spindler & L. Spindler (Eds.), *Interpretive ethnography of education: At home and abroad* (pp. 255–280). Hillsdale, NJ: Lawrence Erlbaum Associates.

Phelan, P., Davidson, A. L., & Yu, H. C. (1996). *Adolescents' worlds: Negotiating family, peers, and school.* New York: Teachers College Press.

Phelps, S. B., & Jarvis, P. A. (1994). Coping in adolescence: Empirical evidence for a theoretically based approach to assessing coping. *Journal of Youth and Adolescence, 23,* 359–371.

Pintrich, P. R. (1994). Continuities and discontinuities: Future directions for research in educational psychology. *Educational Psychologist, 29,* 137–148.

Pintrich, P. R. (2000). Multiple goals, multiple pathways: The role of goal orientation in learning and achievement. *Journal of Educational Psychology, 92,* 544–555.

Richards, T., & Richards, L. (1990). *NUDIST 2.0: User's manual.* Melbourne, Australia: Riplee.

Roeser, R., Midgley, C., & Urdan, T. (1996). Perceptions of the school psychological climate and early adolescents' self-appraisals and academic engagement. *Journal of Educational Psychology, 88,* 408–422.

Ryan, A. M., Gheen, M. H., & Midgley, C. (1998). Why do some students avoid asking for help? An examination of the interplay among students' academic efficacy, teachers' social-emotional role, and the classroom goal structure. *Journal of Educational Psychology, 90,* 528–535.

Ryan, A. M., & Pintrich, P. R. (1997). "Should I ask for help?" The role of motivation and attitudes in adolescents' help seeking in math class. *Journal of Educational Psychology, 89,* 329–341.

Ryan, A. M., & Patrick, H. (2001). The classroom social environment and changes in adolescents' motivation and engagement during middle school. *American Educational Research Journal, 38,* 437–460.

Sarason, I. G. (1975). Anxiety and self-preoccupation. In I. G. Sarason & C. D. Spielberger (Eds.), *Stress and anxiety* (Vol. 2, pp. 27–44). Washington, DC: Hemisphere.

Seifert, T. L. (1995). Academic goals and emotions: A test of two models. *The Journal of Psychology, 129,* 543–552.

Seligman, M. E. P., Abramson, L. Y., Semmel, A., & von Baeyer, C. (1979). Depressive attributional style. *Journal of Abnormal Psychology, 88,* 242–247.

Slavin, R. (1983). *Cooperative learning.* New York: Longman.

Sohn, D. (1977). Affect-generating powers of effort and ability self attributions of academic success and failure. *Journal of Educational Psychology, 69,* 500–505.

Steinberg, L., Blinde, P. L., & Chan, K. S. (1984). Dropping out among language minority youth. *Review of Educational Research, 54,* 113–132.

Tesser, A., & Campbell, J. (1983). Self-definition and self-evaluation maintenance. In. J. Suls & A. Greenwald (Eds.), *Social psychological perspectives on the self* (Vol. 2, pp. 123–149). Hillsdale, NJ: Lawrence Erlbaum Associates.

Urdan, T., & Midgley, C. (2000, May). *Developmental changes in the relations among goal structures, motivational beliefs, affect, and performance.* Paper presented at the 7th Workshop on Achievement and Task Motivation, Leuven, Belgium.

Urdan, T. C., & Paris, S. G. (1994). Teachers' perceptions of standardized achievement tests. *Educational Policy, 8,* 137–56.

Voelkl, K. E. (1996). Measuring students' identification with school. *Educational and Psychological Measurement, 56,* 760–770.

Wang, M. C., & Walberg, H. J. (1987). Evaluating educational programs: An integrative, causal-modeling approach. In *Evaluation studies: Review annual* (Vol. 11, pp. 534–553). Thousand Oaks, CA: Sage.

Wehlage, G. G., Rutter, R. A., Smith, G. A., Lesko, N., & Fernandez, R. R. (1989). *Reducing the risk: Schools as communities of support.* New York: Falmer Press.

Weiner, B. (1990). History of motivational research in education. *Journal of Educational Psychology, 82,* 616–622.

Weiner, B., & Graham, S. (1984). An attributional approach to emotional development. In C. Izard, J. Kagan, & R. Zajonc (Eds.), *Emotions, cognitions, and behavior* (pp. 167–191). New York: Cambridge University Press.

Wigfield, A., & Eccles, J. S. (1994). Children's competence beliefs, achievement values, and general self-esteem: Change across elementary to middle school. *Journal of Early Adolescence: Special Issue: Middle grades schooling and early adolescent development; I. Early adolescents' psychological characteristics, relationships with others, and school performance, 14,* 107–138.

Wine, J. (1971). Test anxiety and direction of attention. *Psychological Bulletin, 76,* 92–104.

Zimmerman, B. J., Bandura, A., & Martinez-Pons, M. (1992). Self-motivation for academic attainment: The role of self-efficacy beliefs and personal goal setting. *American Educational Research Journal, 29,* 663–676.

7

Can Achievement Goal Theory Enhance Our Understanding of the Motivation and Performance of African American Young Adolescents?

Kimberley Edelin Freeman
Frederick D. Patterson Research Institute, Fairfax, Virginia

Leslie Morrison Gutman
University of Michigan

Carol Midgley
University of Michigan

The study of the motivational characteristics of African American students has a long history in psychological research, in an attempt to determine the origins of this group's persistent underachievement in school. Although the achievement motivation of African Americans has undergone extensive investigation in psychological research, the theories, assumptions, and explanations offered have not received consistent support (Kaplan & Maehr, 1999). Early studies narrowly defined the achievement motivation of African Americans as lacking and negative, whereas contemporary research often takes a more holistic approach and views their motivation in context and as positive and adaptive.

Many of the early explanations of the achievement motivation of African Americans can be characterized as "deficit" theories, or theories that blame the victim for his or her failures. These perspectives view the African American child (and family) as the problem and fail to consider characteristics of schools and classrooms that might contribute to the seemingly poor motivational orientation of African American students (Maehr & Midgley, 1999). Some researchers posit that African American learners are "culturally deprived" and not prepared to succeed academically because of inadequate parental socialization and disadvantaged backgrounds (e.g., Moynihan, 1965). Other researchers suggest that because of societal racism and discrimination, African American students have low self-esteem, and feel hopeless and defeated, resulting in little motivation for school (Cummings, 1997). Finally, some researchers examining the motivational characteristics of African American students assert that these learners have little intrinsic drive for learning, and are externally motivated and in need of reinforcement to maintain their engagement in schoolwork (see Banks, McQuater, & Hubbard, 1978; Banks, Ward, McQuater, & DeBritto, 1991, for reviews). This body of research has also consistently compared the motivational characteristics of African Americans to Whites and has classified African Americans as inferior (see Banks et al., 1978; Graham, 1994, for reviews).

Cultural and structural theories have dissented from deficit perspectives and have focused instead on the cultural strengths of African American learners, and the societal and school factors that may be related to their lower school achievement (Boykin, 1986; Delpit, 1988; Ladson-Billings, 1994; McLoyd, 1991; Ogbu, 1988; Steele, 1997). These researchers recognize the cultural integrity of African American students and/or the structural barriers that they confront in society and in the school system. Delpit and Boykin both focused on the "cultural capital" that White students are afforded in the classroom because American education is predicated upon a White, middle-class cultural frame of reference, and White students are members of this culture of power. They posited that African American students, especially those who are poor, are not participants in the culture of power, and thus are disadvantaged and placed at risk for failure in the classroom. Success in school, then, is dependent on the acquisition of White, middle-class culture (Delpit, 1988). Delpit asserted, however, that African American students (and other students outside the culture of power) are not given sufficient access to the rules and codes of the dominant culture.

Another thread of research on structural characteristics focuses on the specific inequities in access to knowledge and resources that exist in schools and classrooms. Darling-Hammond (1995) suggested that African American and poor students receive a substandard education and do not have the same access to high-quality teachers and curricula that other students do. In schools where

the majority of students are African American, compared to schools in which no African American students are enrolled, there is a greater percentage of students in remedial reading (24.9% vs. 15%) and remedial math (22% vs. 12%) programs (Nettles & Perna, 1997). Additionally, in schools with high minority enrollments, the odds are less than one in two that students will get a science or math teacher who is licensed or who holds a degree in the field he or she teaches (Darling-Hammond, 1997).

African American students may experience another kind of inequity in the classroom via teacher expectations. The classic Pygmalion studies demonstrate the powerful effect that teacher expectations have on student outcomes. Research on teachers and in classrooms has documented the lower expectations that teachers hold for (poor) African American students (Glasgow, 1980; Rist, 1970; Winfield, 1986). When teachers hold low expectations for students, they often provide them with fewer and less meaningful interactions in the classroom, fewer opportunities to demonstrate competence, and less time to develop ideas (Rist, 1970). Ethnographic studies of African American students' classrooms and teachers suggest that teachers of African American students do not expect or support these students to excel academically, which contributes to their poor school performance (e.g., Fine, 1991; Glasgow, 1980; Rist, 1970).

How African American students respond to school and societal conditions is another component of this body of research. Ogbu (1988, 1992) suggested that African American students oppose White mainstream culture and associate success in school with this culture. As a response to discrimination and subordination, African American students oppose doing well in school because doing well is associated with the dominant culture and giving up one's own identity and culture. Steele (1997) suggested that African American students "disidentify" with school as a response to their treatment in school and their status in the broader society. Steele posited that schools do not value African American students or expect them to perform well. Consequently, African American students disidentify with schooling or separate school achievement from their sense of self-worth.

Other research on the academic motivation of African American students, however, provides evidence of positive, healthy motivational characteristics, and relatively little disengagement from school. For example, there is evidence that African Americans have always valued education, and still do, especially as a means of social mobility (Dubois, 1973; Mickelson, 1990). In addition, studies of self-perceptions indicate that African American students hold positive views of themselves and their academic ability, including high self-efficacy and self-concept of academic ability (Edelin & Paris, 1995; Gutman & Midgley, 2000; Lindsey, Edelin, & A. Ryan, 1997; Stevenson, Chen, & Uttal, 1990; Winston, DeBritto, & Eccles, 1997; Winston & Edelin,

1996). In our work on the Patterns of Adaptive Learning Study, we also find that African American students consistently report feeling more academically efficacious than do White students. Moreover, research has shown that African American youngsters hold positive expectancies for success at a task, even following failure (Graham & Long, 1986).

Although there is a plethora of research investigating the motivational characteristics of African American learners, there is no consensus on the motivational orientation of these students (e.g., extrinsic/intrinsic; positive/negative), or on what types of learning environments are most facilitative of their academic achievement. Goal theory is a preeminent, social-cognitive perspective on achievement motivation that may offer some insight into the motivation of African American students that other theories have not. Rather than focusing on individual characteristics such as needs and outcomes, achievement goal theory examines the meanings that students make of their learning contexts and how they perceive and pursue various goals in these contexts. Achievement goal theory focuses on students' reasons for engaging in schoolwork and how students perceive the purposes for work that are emphasized in the learning environment. This social-cognitive perspective should be especially informative with respect to how meanings vary across (and within) diverse groups (Kaplan & Maehr, 1999). The question that we attempt to answer in this chapter is, how does achievement goal theory help us to understand the achievement motivation and performance of African American young adolescents?

Research on goals has flourished over the past decade. Nonetheless, there has been very little attention given to the achievement goals of African American students (Graham, 1994; Pintrich & Schunk, 1996), or how the environments in which they learn shape their goals. Graham, in an extensive review of studies of the motivation of African American students, concluded that "some of the current themes that dominate the study of motivation—such as ... the goals to which individuals strive—have been too sparsely examined among African Americans to make a review of findings possible" (p. 56). It may be that some researchers have looked for race effects, and finding none, have not reported them. Or it may be that the participants included in goal theory research have largely been White. Given the importance of goals for students' engagement in or disengagement from learning, and the persistent underachievement of African American students, this is a serious omission.

One aim of the Patterns of Adaptive Learning Study was to examine how goals operate for racially diverse students. In particular, we recruited a large sample that included both African American and White young adolescents. In this chapter, we describe what we have learned about how African American young adolescents perceive and pursue achievement goals in classrooms, and how goal processes operate differently for African American and White students. We first describe some of our earlier studies that shed light on the

achievement goals of African American students. We follow that with a report of new analyses run with the data from the Patterns of Adaptive Learning Study that provide some limited evidence of interactions between race and goals for selected outcomes. We then describe in some detail a qualitative study conducted by the first author of this chapter based on interviews with 24 African American middle school students in a poor neighborhood regarding their achievement goals and the goals they perceived in their classrooms. Finally, we consider whether these results help us to understand the achievement motivation and performance of African American young adolescents.

OUR PREVIOUS RESEARCH

For over a decade we have been using goal theory as the framework within which to examine the antecedents and consequences of personal and perceived goals. Four different samples of young adolescents have participated in these studies. In almost all of these studies, we have looked for race differences. That is, we have looked for mean differences in African American and White students' personal and perceived goals, for interactions between race and independent variables in predicting dependent variables, and for different relations among variables for African American and White students. Here we describe one study in which there was an interaction between performance-approach goals and race in predicting the use of self-handicapping (Midgley, Arunkumar, & Urdan, 1996), and a second study in which we found some differences between the two racial groups in the role of academic self-efficacy in mediating the relations between performance-approach goals and outcomes (Kaplan & Maehr, 1999).

These two studies were conducted in a small working-class school district in southeastern Michigan. The first study included a sample of 112 eighth-grade students (51% African American) in the only middle school in the district. We have become very interested in the role of personal and perceived goals in students' use of avoidance strategies (see chap. 3, this volume). In this study we looked at an avoidance behavior that has been labeled *self-handicapping*. It has been suggested that some students procrastinate, fool around, reduce effort, and use other self-handicapping strategies so that if subsequent performance is low, these circumstances (rather than lack of ability) will be seen as the cause. Self-handicapping is a proactive attempt to manipulate others' perceptions of the causes of performance outcomes. For example, saying that you did not do well because you were tired is an attribution; whereas deliberately staying up late in order to use lack of sleep as an excuse in case you should do poorly is a self-handicapping strategy. These strategies are called self-handicapping because they often result in a decrement in performance.

We examined predictors of self-handicapping including race, grade point average (GPA), positive and negative attitudes toward school, and an orientation to performance-approach goals (the goal to demonstrate ability). There were no mean differences by race in handicapping. However, an orientation to performance-approach goals was a significant positive predictor of handicapping for African American students but not for White students. We pointed to the work of Steele and his colleagues (e.g., Steele, 1997; Steele & Aronson, 1995) in interpreting these results. Steele has suggested that in a setting where relative achievement is salient, African American students must deal with the stereotype that students of their racial background perform less well than do other students. We suggested that African American students who want to demonstrate that they are able (oriented to performance-approach goals) use self-handicapping as a self-protection mechanism. "If I don't perform well, it's not that I'm African American, it's that I fooled around last night instead of studying." It is even possible that self-handicapping plays a role in the suggested relationship between stereotype threat and lowered performance. If African American students react to this stereotype by engaging in activities that are associated with less academic effort, then lower performance is likely to occur (Midgley et al., 1996).

The second study was conducted in the same school with a sample of 168 sixth-grade students, 34% African American and 66% White (Kaplan & Maehr, 1999). This study examined personal and perceived mastery and performance-approach goals as predictors of students' well-being and reports of engagement in disruptive behavior. Generally, mastery goals and perceptions of the school as emphasizing mastery goals were related positively to well-being, and performance-approach goals and perceiving the school as emphasizing performance goals were related negatively to well-being. There was some evidence, however, that different processes were involved for African American and White students. In particular, the role of perceived self-efficacy in mediating the relation between performance-approach goals and outcomes differed for the two racial groups. Academic self-efficacy served as a mediator for White students but not for African American students. The authors pointed to a review by Graham (1994) that suggests that self-hood plays a different role among African American adolescents than among White adolescents. They also urged caution in interpreting these findings due to the relatively small number of African American students in the sample.

THE PATTERNS OF ADAPTIVE LEARNING STUDY

When we began the Patterns of Adaptive Learning Study, we made a special effort to recruit districts that included both African American and White students (see chap. 1, this volume). In the many studies that have been conducted with that

sample over a period of 6 years, we found very little evidence of race differences in the relations between goals and outcomes, or interactions between variables based on race. An exception is the study by A. M. Ryan and Patrick (2001) that is described in detail in chapter 4, this volume. Once again perceptions of efficacy seemed to operate differently for African American and White students, though in this case the focus was on efficacy for relating positively with the classroom teacher. Being an African American boy was related to lower efficacy for relating positively to the teacher in eighth grade. Furthermore, there was a significant interaction between race and gender on changes in social efficacy from seventh to eighth grade. Being an African American boy was related to decreased efficacy for relating effectively to the eighth-grade teacher. Furthermore, African American boys' efficacy for relating to their teacher declined more than any other groups' from seventh to eighth grade.

Because we agree that the role of race has largely been ignored in studies using a goal theory framework, in writing this chapter we decided to look carefully at the data from the Patterns of Adaptive Learning Study to see first, if there was evidence of mean differences in goals or perceptions of the goal structure by race, and second, to determine if there were different relations between goals and outcomes for African American and White students.

Mean Level Differences by Race

At all eight waves of the study, an investigation of mean-level differences in personal goals by race revealed that African American students espoused personal mastery goals and extrinsic goals significantly more than did White students. That is, African American young adolescents were more likely than White young adolescents to report that they engaged in their schoolwork with the purpose of learning and task mastery. They were also more likely than White students to report that they did their work for the purpose of getting extrinsic incentives such as good grades or passing to the next grade. At most waves, African American students were also more likely than White students to perceive their classrooms as emphasizing mastery and extrinsic goals. At no wave, however, did African Americans espouse personal performance goals significantly more than did their White counterparts. African American students perceived their classrooms as significantly more performance focused, however, than did White students at all four waves in the fifth and sixth grades, but there were no significant differences between African American and White students in perceived performance goals in the seventh, eighth, or ninth grades.

These mean-level differences point to a fairly consistent finding concerning the achievement motivation of African American students that has been found in numerous studies—an "attitude–achievement paradox" (Mickelson, 1990).

In a number of studies, African American students' self-concept of ability, expectancies for success, and perceptions of their educational competence were equal to and often higher than their White counterparts'. These positive beliefs, however, do not translate into a comparable (high) level of academic performance—thus, the demonstration of an attitude–achievement paradox. It is not clear why or how African American students maintain such optimistic beliefs in spite of their lower academic performance. In the data from the Patterns of Adaptive Learning Study, we see more evidence of this paradox. African American students endorse personal mastery goals more and feel more academically efficacious than do White students, but consistently receive lower average grades than do White students. The question remains, why is it that the adoption of positive motivational characteristics (i.e., mastery goals) does not lead to higher achievement for African American students?

The finding that African American students also espouse personal extrinsic goals more than do White students may provide one answer to why their adoption of personal mastery goals does not necessarily translate into higher performance. There is evidence that students do not hold only one goal, but multiple goals as they approach and engage in their schoolwork (Ainley, 1993; Dowson & McInerney, 1997; Meece & Holt, 1993; Pintrich & Garcia, 1990; Wentzel, 1991; Wolters, Yu, & Pintrich, 1996). Most of the studies investigating multiple goals have not included extrinsic goals, however. It could be that the combination of high mastery and high extrinsic goals is associated with lower performance. Or, if extrinsic goals are a predominant goal for African American students, then perhaps this contributes in some way to their lower academic performance. In several studies that have included mastery, performance, and extrinsic goals, extrinsic goals have emerged as particularly maladaptive (Urdan, 1997; Wolters et al., 1996). Further research on the attitude–achievement paradox and how students coordinate multiple and different goals is warranted and necessary to shed light on this very important issue.

Mean differences tell us very little about race effects and may be used by some to suggest that minority groups are somehow deviant from the majority group (Graham, 1992; McLoyd, 1990). An examination of simple group differences on outcomes will not explain the mechanisms and factors underlying differences between groups. Thus, we turn to evidence of different relations between goals and outcomes for African American and White students.

Interactions With Race

Using the data from the Patterns of Adaptive Learning Study, we selected five outcome variables that assessed both beliefs and behaviors, and that we felt might shed light on race differences that have emerged in other studies. We in-

cluded self-handicapping because of the results described earlier in the study by Midgley and her colleagues (1996). Self-handicapping is an avoidance behavior, and we decided to include the avoidance of help seeking in the classroom to see if we would find similar results for another type of avoidance behavior. We included academic self-efficacy and GPA because of the studies, cited previously, that have documented both an achievement gap and an efficacy gap between African American and White students. Additionally, the studies described previously conducted by Kaplan and Maehr (1999) and A. M. Ryan and Patrick (2001) included academic and social efficacy. Finally, we included self-regulated learning because it has been modestly related to achievement in studies using survey research (e.g., Meece & Holt, 1993; Pintrich & De Groot, 1990). Information about the research design, the sample, the scales, and the procedures used to collect the data is presented in chapter 1, this volume.

Many of the scales assessing personal goals, perceived goals, and students' beliefs and behaviors were asked generally in elementary school and in the math domain in middle and high school. We decided to limit our analyses to math-specific scales at the middle school level (Grades 6, 7, and 8). Although we gathered data in both the fall and spring at some grade levels, in the analyses conducted for this study we included the data collected in the spring, with the exception of extrinsic goals, which we did not assess in the spring of seventh grade, and therefore data from the fall of eighth grade were included. Although we have focused in particular on mastery and performance goals in the other studies emanating from this study, we decided to include extrinsic goals because they had emerged as important influences on African American students in a qualitative interview study undertaken by the first author of this chapter, which is described later in this chapter. At that point in time, we had not yet developed a scale to assess the performance-avoid goal structure in the classroom, so we did not include personal performance-avoid goals.

We first used each of the three personal goals (performance, mastery, extrinsic), and second we used each of the three perceived goals (performance, mastery, extrinsic) as predictors of each of the five outcomes (self-handicapping, avoiding help seeking, academic efficacy, self-regulated learning, and GPA). Using regression analyses, we examined how each of the three personal goals and each of the three perceived classroom goal structure variables related to each of the five outcomes. For each regression, we included free/reduced-fee lunch status (as a proxy for socioeconomic status, see chap. 1, this volume), the goal variable (personal or perceived), and race, and a multiplicative interaction term of goal by race. To interpret significant interactions, we used an approach suggested by Jaccard, Turrisi, and Wan (1990). This approach involves calculating the slope of the outcome on race as high and low values of the goal,

where "low" is defined as one standard deviation below the mean, and "high" as one standard deviation above the mean (see Figs. 7.1 through 7.6).

In the case of personal performance goals and the perceived performance goal structure in the classroom, so few interactions emerged that we do not report them here. We have to conclude that in our data set and for these outcome variables, performance goals appeared to operate similarly for African American and White students. This was unanticipated, because in the studies described earlier, race effects were generally found only for performance goals.

In the case of mastery goals, we ran 30 regressions and a significant interaction with race emerged in 6. For extrinsic goals, we ran 28 regressions and 6 interactions with race emerged as significant. We summarize our findings here, but emphasize that these interactions were significant at some waves and not at others, and should be considered exploratory. We hope that they will provide useful information to others who wish to design studies to examine achievement goals in samples of African American students, or samples that include both African American and White students.

Mastery Goals. Significant interactions between personal mastery goals and race, or between perceived mastery goals and race emerged for four of the five outcome variables. No significant interactions were found when predicting self-regulated learning. The main effects mirrored those reported in other studies. That is, mastery goals were related positively to self-efficacy and grades, and were related negatively to the use of avoidance strategies (avoiding help seeking and self-handicapping). However, in some cases the effects were stronger for African American students and in some cases they were stronger for White students. For GPA at the eighth-grade level and the avoidance of help seeking at the sixth-grade level, mastery goals had a stronger effect for White students than for African American students. As an example, see Fig. 7.1, which indicates that White and African American students had similar grades when they perceived the classroom as low in the emphasis on mastery goals, whereas White students had higher grades than African American students when they perceived that the classroom was high in the emphasis on mastery goals. It is troubling that perceiving an emphasis on mastery, effort, and improvement in the classroom does not translate into higher grades for African American students as it does for White students.

For self-efficacy, the use of handicapping strategies, and the avoidance of help seeking at the seventh-grade level, mastery goals had a stronger effect on African American students than on White students. When African American young adolescents perceived an emphasis on mastery goals in the classrooms, their beliefs about their own efficacy were higher than when they perceived a low emphasis on mastery goals. Although the trend was similar for White students, it was weaker (see Fig. 7.2). A somewhat similar pattern emerged for re-

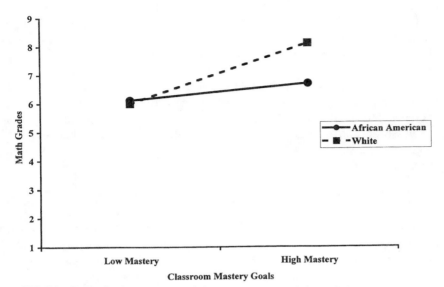

FIG. 7.1. Interaction between race and classroom mastery goals in predicting math grades in eighth grade.

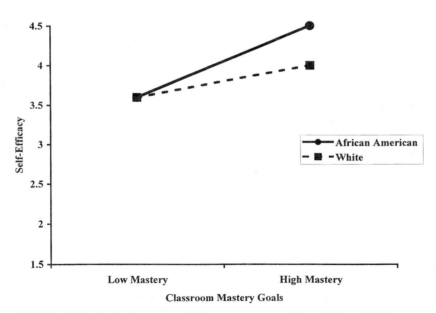

FIG. 7.2. Interaction between race and classroom mastery goals in predicting self-efficacy in seventh grade.

ports of using handicapping strategies (see Fig. 7.3). When African American students perceived a low emphasis on mastery goals in the classroom, they used handicapping more than when they perceived a high emphasis on mastery goals; whereas the handicapping reported by White students did not seem to be related to the high or low emphasis on mastery goals in the classroom.

Although these results are interesting, the interactions predicting the avoidance of help seeking showed different patterns at different grade levels. That is, at Grade 6, the relationship between a perceived emphasis on mastery goals in the classroom and avoiding help was stronger for White students than for African American students, whereas at the seventh-grade level, the relation was stronger for African American than for White students.

Extrinsic Goals.   Significant interactions between personal or perceived extrinsic goals and race emerged for four of the five outcome variables. No significant interactions were found when predicting grades. The six significant interactions with race that occurred between personal and perceived extrinsic goals and the four dependent variables provide some evidence that extrinsic goals may be more facilitative of positive outcomes for African American students than for White students. For example, espousing personal extrinsic goals and perceiving an emphasis on extrinsic goals in the classroom were more strongly related to self-efficacy for African American students than for White

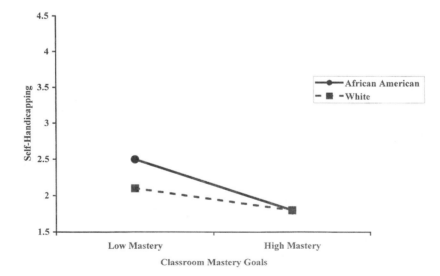

FIG. 7.3.   Interaction between race and classroom mastery goals in predicting self-handicapping in seventh grade.

students. As illustrated by Fig. 7.4, eighth-grade African American and White students did not differ in their academic efficacy when they perceived a low emphasis on getting good grades or on doing work to pass or to get a good job. However, when they perceived a strong emphasis on extrinsic reasons for doing work in their classrooms, African American students' academic efficacy was higher, whereas White students' efficacy was not.

Similarly, the relation between perceiving an emphasis on extrinsic goals in the classroom and self-regulated learning at the eighth-grade level was stronger for African American than for White students (see Fig. 7.5). For African American students, a higher emphasis on extrinsic goals was associated with reports of greater self-regulated learning. For White students, perceiving a high or low emphasis on extrinsic goals in the classroom was unrelated to their reports of engaging in self-regulation. There was also some evidence that a perceived emphasis on extrinsic goals was associated with a small reduction in the use of handicapping for African American students, whereas that was not the case for White students.

Regarding the avoidance of help seeking, a different pattern emerged. The relation between personal and perceived extrinsic goals and the avoidance of help seeking in the eighth grade was stronger for White students than for African can American students. For White students, high personal and perceived ex-

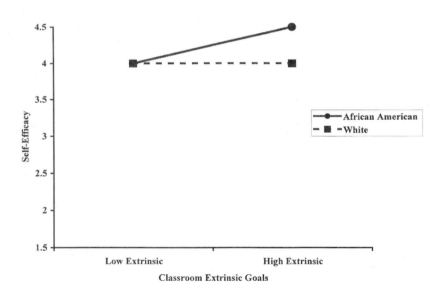

FIG. 7.4.   Interaction between race and classroom extrinsic goals in predicting self-efficacy in eighth grade.

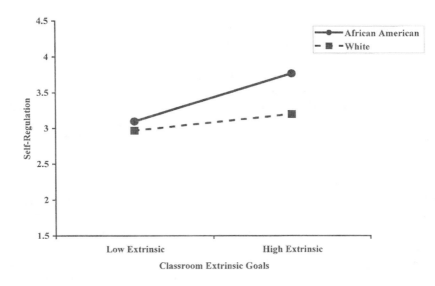

FIG. 7.5.   Interaction between race and classroom extrinsic goals in predicting
self-regulation in eighth grade.

trinsic goals were associated with a greater avoidance of help seeking, whereas
for African American students, the level of personal and perceived extrinsic
goals appeared to make little difference in the avoidance of help seeking (e.g.,
see Fig. 7.6). It may be that extrinsic goals are related positively to outcomes
such as self-efficacy and self-regulated learning for African American students, but have little effect on their use of avoidance strategies. But given the
exploratory nature of these analyses, no definitive conclusions can be drawn.
These relations will need to be examined in other samples of White and African American students. We do believe it is important to look at both "positive"
(e.g., perceived efficacy) and "negative" (avoidance behaviors) outcomes, and
both beliefs and reported behaviors.

   We found it interesting that African American students reported higher personal extrinsic goals than did White students at every wave and that there was
some evidence of a more positive effect of extrinsic goals on the academic efficacy, self-regulated learning, and use of handicapping for African American
students than for White students. As part of the Patterns of Adaptive Learning
Study, the first author of this chapter conducted interviews with 24 African
American students when they were in the sixth grade in middle school. These
students frequently mentioned espousing extrinsic goals and perceiving an
emphasis on extrinsic goals in their classrooms. To provide additional insight

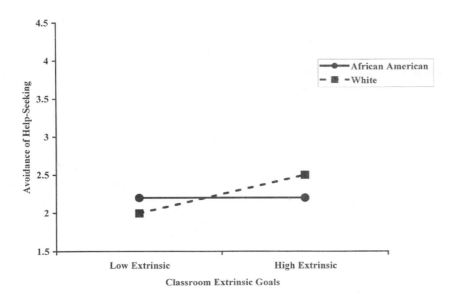

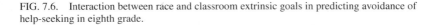

FIG. 7.6.   Interaction between race and classroom extrinsic goals in predicting avoidance of help-seeking in eighth grade.

into the role of extrinsic goals in the achievement motivation of African American young adolescents, an overview of that study is presented next.

A QUALITATIVE INVESTIGATION OF THE ACHIEVEMENT GOALS THAT AFRICAN AMERICAN STUDENTS PURSUE AND PERCEIVE IN THE MIDDLE SCHOOL LEARNING CONTEXT

As described in chapter 1 (this volume), there were 10 middle schools involved in the Patterns of Adaptive Learning Study. The study described here was conducted in the middle school with the largest percentage of African American students (93%) and the lowest average family income. The principal informed me that about 70% of the students were on free or reduced-fee lunch, and that most came from single-parent families. He commented that it was "tough" and that I should "get involved." (This section of the chapter is written in the first person, to reflect that the interview study was conducted by Kimberley Edelin Freeman.) There were 210 students in the sixth grade during the 1995–1996 school year. All 24 participants in this study were African American. There

were 14 boys and 10 girls ranging in age from 11 to 13. Most (15) of the respondents had cumulative GPAs between 2.0 and 3.0. Four respondents had GPAs greater than 3.0, and five held GPA's below 2.0.

During the 4 months prior to the interviews, I spent at least 1 day per week in the school as a participant observer. During this time, I rotated among the eight sixth-grade classrooms. My purposes were to establish rapport with teachers and especially with students, and to familiarize myself with the school setting. The sixth grade was organized into teams. The same teacher taught math and science to students; a different teacher taught them language arts and social studies. During my time as a participant observer, I selected the 24 students who would be interviewed. I selected students to ensure that my sample included significant variation (Weiss, 1994). Though respondents were all asked the same basic questions, I let each interview take its particular course depending on what the respondent said, what issues were salient, or what additional information the student wanted to convey to me. In this way, the interviews were a combination of fixed and open-ended questions.

The primary aim of the interviews was to assess students' personal achievement goals and their perceptions of the goal structures in place in their classrooms (via their teachers' practices). I used the work of Ames (1992) to define characteristics of classroom practices that convey different achievement goals to students. I structured questions to assess whether students perceived that their teachers used practices that were mastery focused, performance focused, and/or extrinsic focused. In particular, I questioned students about the nature of academic tasks, opportunities for autonomy, and the nature of evaluation in the classroom. Each question was specific to either the student's language arts and social studies teacher or the student's math and science teacher. Examples of questions that assessed the classroom goal structure included:

1. Does the teacher want you to really work hard on your math and science work, or just work to get it done and get a grade on it?
2. Does the teacher tell you how you compare to other students on your work in language arts and social studies?
3. Does the teacher say a lot that you're going to get graded on this so you need to finish?
4. Does the teacher ever let you decide what work you will do in class?
5. What are your grades based on? What counts for your grade?

To assess students' personal achievement goals, I asked them about their purposes for engaging in their schoolwork. Questions were framed to assess whether students' achievement goals reflected mastery, performance, and/or extrinsic reasons for engaging in academic work. I used questions that were parallel to the questions I asked students about their teacher's practices. Near

the end of the interview, I asked respondents in general *why* they did their schoolwork. Examples of questions that assessed students' achievement goals included:

1. Students have different reasons for why they do their work. In general, when you sit down to do your work in class, why do you do it?
2. Do you feel like you should always get a reward when you do your work?
3. Is it important to you to make honor roll or merit roll?
4. Do you think it's okay to make a mistake on your work?

Most interviews took place at school during the school day. Each interview lasted about 80 minutes and was tape-recorded. Upon completion, each respondent was given a $15 retail store gift certificate. Each interview was transcribed. I utilized issue-focused analysis as described by Weiss (1994) in order to uncover patterns in students' perceptions of the goal emphases in their classrooms and students' own purposes for engaging in schoolwork. Four components are involved in issue-focused analysis (Weiss, 1994): coding, sorting, local integration, and inclusive integration. I used coding and sorting in the early phases of analysis to classify meaningful segments of interview data and to group them. I grouped interview material according to the different classes of personal achievement goals (e.g., mastery, performance, extrinsic). Additionally, I categorized interview text that described characteristics of the goal structure into the three classroom dimensions (task, autonomy, and evaluation). I labeled segments of data with codes that I had developed a priori from the work of Ames (1992) as well as with new codes that emerged during analysis. To group similarly coded segments of data, I entered the coded interview text into HyperResearch (Hesse-Biber, Kinder, Dupis, Dupis, & Tornabene, 1994), a software program that aids in the management of qualitative data. I used HyperResearch to sort, group, and count all instances of each relevant code.

Step 3 in issue-focused analysis, local integration, involved interpreting each group of interview segments. This step focuses on extracting emerging themes from the data. In particular, I developed "mini theories" about which achievement goals were being made salient to students through different characteristics of task, autonomy, and evaluation structures. In addition, I sought to interpret students' reasons for engaging in their schoolwork based on traditional goal theory and the recent theoretical refinements that have been made. Thus, I first interpreted students' achievement goals using the conventional definitions of goals as mastery, performance, or extrinsically oriented. I then further delineated between relative ability and extrinsic goals, approach and avoidance goals, and single versus multiple goals. During coding, sorting, and local integration, I used memoing (Miles & Huberman, 1994) extensively to

record my ideas and thoughts about the data and to link the data into themes and theories. Finally, during inclusive integration, I organized the interpreted data segments into a logical sequence that would coherently depict students' personal goals and perceptions of the classroom goal structure.

In presenting the results, I use students' own words to describe their purposes for engaging in their schoolwork. I then examine, from the student's perspective, the task, autonomy, and evaluation structures of the classroom contexts in which they engaged in their academic work. The students mentioned personal achievement goals similar to those identified in the literature. For example, students said they did their work so they would learn and understand (mastery goals), so that they could show that they were smart (performance), and so that they would get good grades or avoid getting bad grades (extrinsic). Although each individual seemed to have a particular goal orientation, many students articulated multiple goals during the interviews. Overwhelmingly, however, respondents reported doing their work for extrinsic reasons. Mastery goals were mentioned less often, and performance goals were mentioned only rarely. Social reasons for engaging in academic work were not expressed at all.

Personal Mastery Goals

Some students did mention that they engaged in schoolwork in order to learn, to understand, or to experience challenge. This was particularly true for high-achievers. I asked one student if he wanted to understand the work in his language arts class or if he just wanted to memorize it: *"I want to understand it.... If you just memorize it, you probably don't know what it mean or nothing. If you understand it, you know what it means too."* Another student mentioned that she did not have to do any work in her language arts class, but still got good grades. I asked her if she liked that: *"Not really. 'Cause I want to learn how, I want to know things about the world, and I ain't learning it.... I want to learn."* Although one of the students told me he did not enjoy being at school, and mentioned many negative encounters with teachers, clearly he was mastery focused in math. When I asked him why he liked math even though he was often frustrated with the with the work and his math teacher he said: *"That's what I like about it, it's challenging.... I want to do something that you gotta find the answer out by yourself."*

Personal Performance Goals

Only four students articulated performance goals at any time during the interviews. These students, who mentioned engaging in their work in order to demonstrate that they were one of the smartest in the class, were all high-achievers.

They stated that most of the other students were "dumb" or "bad" and they did not want to be seen as similar to them. For example, when I asked one student about making the honor roll she said: *"I think that's a good thing because I know my name is up there.... And you know bad students look up there, oh she think she so smart. You know, but they ain't making A's and B's."* Similarly, another student indicated that he liked his math teacher's emphasis on grades because: *"[It] shows how smart I am. Because some people get uh, below average, some people get average, some people get real high grades."* One student said he liked to compete, so I asked him why: *"Cause you want to be the best. You want to know is you the best in your, competing, like if I get the answer right and he get the answer wrong, you better, you know that, you know you can get the answer faster than he can."*

Personal Extrinsic Goals

Almost all the students gave extrinsic reasons for doing their work. Some students mentioned extrinsic goals frequently during the course of the interview, even when we were not discussing goals or purposes for doing work. In most cases, the extrinsic reasons were not tied to the demonstration of ability. Grades and being evaluated were very salient to students as they approached and engaged in their work. Students often mentioned that they "needed" acceptable grades and that this was why they did their work in class. In particular, students indicated that they needed passing grades so that they could move onto the next grade. For some students the extrinsic reasons for engaging in academic work could be characterized as "approach" tendencies. That is, students were oriented to positive extrinsic incentives (I want to get good grades, I want to pass). In other cases, these extrinsic reasons could be characterized as "avoidance" tendencies. Students seemed to be driven by fear of failure (I don't want to get bad grades, I don't want to fail). The pervasive nature of students' extrinsic goals was made salient when students were asked the broad question: "In general, when you sit down to do your work, why do you do it?" Several students stated the following:

To get good grades.... 'Cause I want to get money from my auntie.

Because I don't want to get bad grades. I want to do the best that I can. Get all A's sometimes.

'Cause she tell me to, and I need the credits and the grade.

'Cause she tell us to, and 'cause if I don't I get an E. I want to pass to the next grade so I got to work.

Multiple Goals

Finally, many students mentioned more than one achievement goal. Some students seemed to adopt mastery goals as primary goals, and extrinsic goals as the ultimate goal. Often students said they wanted to master their work to get good grades and pass the sixth grade.

Perceptions of the Classroom

The academic tasks that students engaged in, the autonomy they were given, and, in particular, how they were evaluated were salient dimensions of the classroom that students discussed in detail, and that reflected a classroom emphasis on different goals. In this section, I describe each of these features of the academic context, including quotes from the students.

Academic Tasks.   For the most part, students reported being given academic tasks that were typical of the conventional, low-level work done in many public middle and high schools (Midgley, 1993; Steinberg, 1996). Students mentioned filling in worksheets, solving math problems and answering reading comprehension questions in textbooks, memorizing spelling and vocabulary words, and taking many quizzes and tests. Many students mentioned that the work they were doing was easy and boring. One student complained: *"I don't like science either, it's boring. We don't do anything in there. We just read. And we do a couple of science tests and write vocabulary words."* I asked one student if the work he was doing in middle school was harder than his work in elementary school:

> Nope, it ain't nothing but what you used to do in elementary except more added on to it to me. Like when you do math, they 2 + 4, and 5 + 5, and 6 + 6, then they do nothing but add more numbers, like on division. They just add more numbers to it.... Everything in middle school is easier to me.

Students often mentioned doing work to prepare for standardized tests. Students also indicated that teachers frequently referred to schoolwork in the context of needing to do it in order to be ready for the next grade. *"Like, today he worked on the um, on the, we did some stuff and he said that we are doing this to get ready for the seventh grade. That's why we doing it, to get ready for the seventh grade."* Students reported that teachers said they needed to do their schoolwork so that they could "be something" in the future, go to college, or be able to get a job. Students reported that math teachers often told them that it was important that they learn math so they would not get cheated out of their

money in the future. Asked if her math teacher wanted students to memorize or understand their work, one student stated:

> I can tell Ms. B wants us to memorize. I don't know how, but I know she wants us to memorize because she tells us that we might need it in the future and stuff. Seventh grade. And like, if you get a job or something, somebody won't cheat you out your money. You'll know how many gallons and pounds and stuff, and you'll know your times.

Although there was very little evidence that teachers emphasized the intrinsic value of academic tasks, one student mentioned that his teacher wanted him to enjoy his schoolwork and provided students with a variety of academic tasks.

> Enjoy it.... Because how she be giving it to us, she be explaining it out to us and everything. Show us the, show us the fun way of doing it, let us work with other people. Like when we be on the board, like if we have spelling words, she'll put it on the board. Like we playing a game, Jeopardy or something, and we have to spell it.

Autonomy.   Students rarely reported any choice about the nature of work they had to do in class. Sometimes students reported that they could choose partners to work with, and could decide which subject to work on first (i.e., math vs. science; language arts vs. social studies). In some cases, students could choose to do their work in the way that was easiest for them. I asked one student if his teacher let him decide what work he would do in class:

> Not really, she just give us the work herself, because she think that's the work what we need to learn. We don't have to like the work, we just have to do it. She say what's the best way for us to do it, the easiest way for us to learn it and that's the way she let us do it. If we writing a paper and we got to do the information about it she just, some people she just let write lists, some people she let [do charts] 'cause that's [what] they are used to doing. And that's the easiest way for them to learn and do it so that's the way she let them do it.

Evaluation.   Students described an overwhelming emphasis on grades and being evaluated. They rarely mentioned being evaluated on the basis of effort, improvement, or the willingness to take on difficult work. In particular, they pointed out that teachers used the threat of failure as a controlling strategy to get them to do their work and behave. Indeed, in many situations the orientation toward engaging in work was "do it or fail." Students' grades frequently were tied to their classroom behavior. Respondents indicated that teachers often made public statements about the likelihood of failure, especially to and about students who were misbehaving. One student described this scenario: *"One day he told Tom, he told Tom, Tom said something smart to him and he said you just made your E*

for the year." Another student described how grades were based on behavior in her language arts class. She said that the teacher did not require students to do any work in the class to get a good grade. All she needed to do was behave: *"I just don't do it. I just behave and then I get a good grade."*

Feedback to students about their work mostly came in the form of grades. Respondents indicated that two teachers in particular rarely provided them with feedback about the quality of their class and homework assignments. Students in these classes said that they were unsure about the criteria their teachers used in grading their work and were disappointed that their teachers were not providing them with feedback. Students commented:

> When he check papers he don't put them back out. He never gives papers back. I don't know. I don't know how he check 'em or what.

> When we put it in our folder, she say, I guess she grade it. They be in the folder. She take them out the folder, but I don't know if they been did or not.... I don't think she be grading it, that's why I don't know what she doing. I'm wasting my time, doing the work....

SUMMARY OF FINDINGS FROM THE INTERVIEW STUDY

Evidence of personal mastery, performance, and extrinsic goals was found in this study of 24 sixth-grade African American students. Students frequently articulated multiple goals. A number of students mentioned mastery reasons for engaging in schoolwork, expressing especially that they wanted "to learn." The only students who espoused performance goals were high-achievers. This was somewhat surprising and may be related to what has been described as the "communalism" of African American culture (Boykin, 1986). Communalism is a "commitment to social connectedness which includes an awareness that social bonds and responsibilities transcend individual privileges" (Boykin, 1986, p. 61). Whereas schools typically value competition and individuality, there is evidence that African Americans are more oriented toward seeking assistance from and providing assistance to others in accomplishing tasks (Boykin, 1986; Gay, 1975). Perhaps the relative absence in this study of evidence that students espoused performance goals supports this view of the cooperative culture of African Americans.

What was most striking in the interviews was how often these students mentioned extrinsic reasons for their academic behavior. Even students who talked about engaging in their schoolwork to learn and to improve also emphasized the importance of getting good grades and continuing through school and graduating. Indeed, it appeared that the primary goal for many respondents was to pass each grade and graduate.

Students' overwhelming extrinsic motivational orientation may be linked to two factors: (a) their social status in society, and (b) the task, autonomy, and evaluation structures of their middle school learning context. All respondents in this study were African American and all but three of them were poor. Further, the school and neighborhood surroundings were scarred by poverty as evidenced by abandoned, dilapidated, and vandalized buildings, and high rates of drug use and crime. Education and schooling in this context clearly means something very different than it does in an affluent, suburban context where most students experience a very different social status. The goals that students adopt in school may be linked to their experiences in the larger neighborhood, and their status relative to other groups in society.

The experience of many African Americans in this country is characterized by racism and second-class status. In particular, poor African Americans are often trapped into the lowest classes of society. Education has always been important to African Americans, especially as a means of personal growth and social mobility. When African American people were slaves in this country, many risked death so that they or their children could learn to read and write, even though it was illegal. Further, African American high school students risked their lives when they fought for and attended integrated schools because they believed they would receive a better education. For many African Americans, education symbolizes a vehicle for achieving political, economic, and social equality (Edelin & Winston, 1997). Thus, many African Americans value education for extrinsic reasons, such as better future economic and employment outcomes.

As evidenced in this study, teachers of African American low-income youngsters may send messages to them about the purposes for engaging and being successful in schoolwork that are extrinsic, and related to the cultural, historical, and socioeconomic circumstances of these youth. Though it is important for students and teachers to recognize that school success is related positively to later employment and economic outcomes, goal theory research would suggest that this should not be promoted as the primary purpose for engaging in schoolwork and school. The importance of learning, understanding, working hard, and taking on challenging work should also be emphasized. Although teachers' beliefs were not investigated in this study, other studies have found that teachers often hold lower expectations for poor African American students than for White students (Glasgow, 1980; Ladson-Billings, 1994; Rist, 1970; Winfield, 1986). Some teachers may believe that poor African American students cannot learn the higher level work that other students can learn (Darling-Hammond, 1995; Giroux, 1983). In addition, there is evidence that teachers of low-income students believe that these students lack the inner controls necessary to regulate their own learning (Solomon, Battistich, & Hom, 1996). Thus, teachers of poor children make greater use of extrinsic controls than do teachers of more affluent children.

How teachers (and schools) shape the learning context may be the most important influence on students' personal goals and patterns of learning. Indeed, it is the classroom context that students experience when they engage in schoolwork. Although this study provides supporting evidence for earlier studies that documented an extrinsic motivational orientation in African American students (see Graham, 1994, for a review), the African American young adolescents in this study may have had little choice but to be extrinsically focused in their schoolwork. That is, students reported little evidence that the learning context fostered intrinsic or mastery motivation.

There was considerable evidence in the qualitative study that many of the teacher practices reported by students were those identified in the research literature as leading to maladaptive patterns of learning. Providing students with low-level, often boring academic tasks, failing to provide opportunities for student autonomy, and using evaluation to control rather than to inform have all been documented as undermining motivation.

Many students reported that schoolwork was boring and lacked variety or challenge. The work of Banks et al. (1978) provides evidence that when African American students are *interested* in the task they are doing, they are just as intrinsically motivated as are White students. Students provided little evidence that teachers expected or provided opportunities for students to engage in high levels of learning. Furthermore, many teachers were described by students as being controlling and not supporting their desire for autonomy or allowing them to become the directors of their learning. The large number of respondents (over half) who said that they engaged in their schoolwork because they "had to" or because they were told that they had to by their teachers seems to indicate that these students were in a controlling learning environment. The work of Deci and Ryan and their colleagues provides evidence of the deleterious effects of controlling classroom events on student outcomes. R. M. Ryan, Connell, and Deci (1985) concluded from classroom research:

> Increased pressure or control in the classroom is likely to deny self-determination and to be deleterious to intrinsic motivation. And while strong controls may bring immediate behavioral results, every indication is that they will impair learning and be deleterious to autonomy, enduring motivation, and self-esteem. (p. 27)

Steele (1997) characterized a "threat in the air" as a fear that African American students endure in school settings because they are vulnerable to confirming the stereotype that they are intellectually inferior. The findings from this study suggest that it is another type of threat that is salient to these youngsters—the threat that their teachers will fail them. In particular, students reported that teachers used grades to control them; often stressing that students must complete their work in order to pass. Indeed, the achievement goal that was made salient by teachers seemed to be "do it or fail."

CONCLUSIONS

Our work using achievement goal theory has provided additional insight into the achievement motivation of African American young adolescents. Both the new analyses from the Patterns of Adaptive Learning Study and the qualitative findings from the interview study provide evidence that African American students endorse mastery and extrinsic goals, but rarely performance goals. Moreover, and contrary to other research using a goal theory framework with White students (e.g., Urdan, 1997; Wolters et al., 1996), data from the Patterns of Adaptive Learning Study provide evidence that extrinsic goals may have some benefit for African American students. Given the overwhelming emphasis on extrinsic goals in the learning environment of the African American students in the qualitative study, perhaps endorsing extrinsic goals is *adaptive* for African American students and thus leads to more facilitative patterns of learning. Endorsing extrinsic goals may also be adaptive for African American students because of the socioeconomic realities of these students—education is a tool for advancement.

Nonetheless, there may be positive and negative aspects of extrinsic goals and further research is warranted to unpack the different types of extrinsic goals and their influence on student outcomes. In the qualitative study, we saw evidence of both "approach" extrinsic goals (to pass) and "avoid" extrinsic goals (to avoid failure). Other research has concluded the performance-avoid goals (an orientation to avoiding the demonstration of low ability) are related to more maladaptive student outcomes than are performance-approach goals (an orientation to demonstrating high ability; Middleton & Midgley, 1997; Midgley & Urdan, 2001; Rawsthorne & Elliot, 1999). It may be that extrinsic-avoid goals are detrimental, whereas extrinsic-approach goals are beneficial. Nonetheless, researchers agree that mastery goals are the most adaptive for all students and should be fostered in schools and classrooms nationwide (Urdan, 1997).

Lastly, our research shows that achievement goals are not related to the academic performance of African American students. This is disappointing. Though mastery and extrinsic goals often lead to positive behaviors, self-beliefs, and learning strategies for African Americans, they are not associated with higher performance. Evidence from the qualitative study seems to indicate that the grades of African American students may in some cases be based on their behavior—not on their work. There is other, international, evidence that supports this finding. Eggleston, Dunn, Anjali, and Wright (1986) showed that the grades of Black youngsters in England are based not on the quality of their schoolwork, but instead on how they behave.

Though we do not support misbehavior in classrooms, using grades to control students' behavior and motivation is damaging socially and academically and may unfairly punish African American students. Currently there is a national focus on the disproportionate numbers of African American students

who are sent to the principal's office or suspended and expelled from school because of disciplinary problems. More often than White students, African American students are punished for "subjective" offenses such as insubordination (The Advancement Project and the Civil Rights Project, 2000). Teachers may be misunderstanding the behavior, speech patterns, and interpersonal styles of (low-income) African American students (Gay, 1975). More than 85% of all public school teachers are White and only 9% are African American, whereas 16% of all public school students are African American (U.S. Department of Education, 1997). Indeed, a cultural clash or conflict may be occurring in the classroom between African American youngsters and their mostly White teachers.

The author of the qualitative study witnessed several negative encounters between African American students and White teachers in school. Students made comments to the author that described racial conflict with White teachers. After a confrontation with a teacher, a female student remarked, "I don't like them. They don't like us. They act like they prejudice." Other students informed the author that some students deliberately misbehaved in White teachers' classrooms, because the teachers were White. Students may be responding to larger power structures and inequities by misbehaving in the classroom. Critical theorists assert that power struggles reflective of the larger society are mirrored on a microlevel in classrooms (e.g., Giroux, 1983, 1992). Further, if schoolwork is low-level and boring then students will be more likely to misbehave. Using the threat of failure to get students to be engaged, however, is not an effective solution. Mastery approaches to learning and schoolwork can perhaps keep students on-task. In addition, teachers of diverse students must become familiar with the experiences and culture of their students in order to be effective and culturally responsive instructors.

Additional research is needed to determine what other variables impact the performance of African American students. Perhaps social variables, such as the relationship with the teacher, play a more important role in African American young adolescents' school performance than do the goal emphases in the classroom or the personal goals that students hold. Finally, motivational research, including research using a goal theory framework, should continue to include diverse groups of students in its samples. The purposes that students adopt for doing their work and the goals that teachers make salient in the classroom may depend heavily on the type of school, teachers, and students under consideration. Though most processes operate the same for all children, there is solid evidence that many motivational processes differ based on student background and these distinctions may make all the difference between the worst and best outcomes.

REFERENCES

The Advancement Project and the Civil Rights Project. (2000). *Opportunities suspended: The devastating consequences of zero tolerance and school discipline policies.* Cambridge, MA: Harvard University.

Ainley, M. D. (1993). Styles of engagement with learning: Multidimensional assessment of their relationship with strategy use and school achievement. *Journal of Educational Psychology, 85,* 395–405.

Ames, C. (1992). Classrooms: Goals, structures, and student motivation. *Journal of Educational Psychology, 84,* 261–271.

Banks, W. C., McQuater, G. V., & Hubbard, J. L. (1978). Toward a reconceptualization of the social-cognitive bases of achievement orientation in blacks. *Review of Educational Research, 48,* 381–397.

Banks, W. C., Ward, W. E., McQuater, G. V., & DeBritto, A. M. (1991). Are Blacks external: On the state of locus on control in black populations. In R. Jones (Ed.), Black psychology (3rd ed., pp. 181–192). Berkeley, CA: Cobb & Henry.

Boykin, A. W. (1986). The triple quandary and the schooling of Afro-American children. In U. Neisser (Ed.), *The school achievement of minority children* (pp. 57–92). Hillsdale, NJ: Lawrence Erlbaum Associates.

Cummings, S. (1997). Explaining poor academic performance among Black children. *The Educational Forum, Winter,* 335–346.

Darling-Hammond, L. (1995). Inequality and access to knowledge. In J. A. Banks & C. A. M. Banks (Eds.), *Handbook of research on multi-cultural education* (pp. 465–483). New York: Macmillan.

Darling-Hammond, L. (1997). *Doing what matters most: Investing in quality teaching.* New York: National Commission on Teaching and America's Future.

Delpit, L. D. (1988). The silenced dialogue: Power and pedagogy in educating other people's children. *Harvard Educational Review, 58,* 280–298.

Dowson, M., & McInerney, D. M. (1997, March). *Psychological parameters of students' social and academic goals: A qualitative investigation.* Paper presented at the annual meeting of the American Educational Research Association, Chicago.

Dubois, W. E. B. (1973). *The education of Black people.* New York: Monthly Review Press.

Edelin, K. C., & Paris, S. G. (1995, April). *Black students' efficacy beliefs and the match between beliefs and performance.* Paper presented at the annual meeting of the American Educational Research Association, San Francisco.

Edelin, K. C., & Winston, C. E. (1997). *Cultural justice for the Black student.* Unpublished manuscript, University of Michigan, Ann Arbor.

Eggleston, J., Dunn, D., Anjali, M., & Wright, C. (1986). *Education for some: The educational and vocational experiences of 15–18 year old members of minority ethnic groups.* Stoke-On-Trent, England: Trentham Books.

Fine, M. (1991). *Framing dropouts.* Albany: State University of New York Press.

Gay, G. (1975). The education of Black children. *Momentum, 6,* 30–33.

Giroux, H. A. (1983). Theories of reproduction and resistance in the new sociology of education: A critical analysis. *Harvard Educational Review, 53,* 257–293.

Giroux, H. A. (1992). *Cultural studies, resisting difference, and the return of critical pedagogy.* New York: Routledge.

Glasgow, D. (1980). *The Black underclass.* San Francisco: Jossey-Bass.

Graham, S. (1992). Most of the subjects were White and middle class: Trends in published research on African Americans in selected APA journals, 1970–1989. *American Psychologist, 47,* 629–639

Graham, S. (1994). Motivation in Blacks. *Review of Educational Research, 64,* 55–117.

Graham, S., & Long, A. (1986). Race, class, and the attributional process. *Journal of Educational Psychology, 78,* 4–13.

Gutman, L. M., & Midgley, C. (2000). The role of protective factors in supporting the academic achievement of poor African American students during the middle school transition. *Journal of Youth and Adolescence, 29,* 223–248.

Hesse-Biber, S., Kinder, I. S., Dupis, P. R., Dupis, A., & Tornabene, E. (1994). *HyperResearch: A content analysis tool for the qualitative researcher.* Randolph, MA: Researchware, Inc.

Jaccard, J., Turrisi, R., & Wan, C. K. (1990). *Interaction effects in multiple regression.* Newbury Park, CA: Sage.

Kaplan, A., & Maehr, M. L. (1999). Enhancing the motivation of African American students: An achievement goal theory perspective. *The Journal of Negro Education, 68,* 23–41.

Ladson-Billings, G. (1994). *The dreamkeepers.* San Francisco: Jossey-Bass.

Lindsey, T., Edelin, K. C., & Ryan, A. (1997, March). *Group differences in academic self-efficacy during the transition to middle school.* Poster session presented at the annual meeting of the American Educational Research Association, Chicago.

Maehr, M. L., & Midgley, C. (1999). Creating optimum learning environments for students of diverse socio cultural backgrounds. In J. Block, S. T. Everson, & T. R. Guskey (Eds.), *Comprehensive school reform: A program perspective* (pp. 355–375). Dubuque, IA: Kendall/Hunt.

McLoyd, V. C. (1990). The impact of economic hardship on Black families and children: Psychological distress, parenting, and socioeconomic development, *Child Development, 61,* 311–346.

McLoyd, V. C. (1991). What is the study of African American children the study of? In R. Jones (Ed.), *Black psychology* (3rd ed., pp. 419–440). Berkeley, CA: Cobb & Henry.

Meece, J., & Holt, K. (1993). A pattern analysis of students' achievement goals. *Journal of Educational Psychology, 85,* 582–590.

Mickelson, R. (1990). The attitude-achievement paradox among black adolescents. *Sociology of Education, 63,* 44–61.

Middleton, M. J., & Midgley, C. (1997). Avoiding the demonstration of lack of ability: An unexplored aspect of goal theory. *Journal of Educational Psychology, 89,* 710–718.

Midgley, C. (1993). Motivation and middle level schools. In P. Pintrich & M. L. Maehr, (Eds.), *Advances in motivation and achievement: Vol. 8. Motivation in the adolescent years* (pp. 219–276). Greenwich, CT: JAI.

Midgley, C., Arunkumar, R., & Urdan, T. (1996). "If I don't do well tomorrow there's a reason": Predictors of adolescents' use of academic self-handicapping strategies. *Journal of Educational Psychology, 88,* 423–434.

Midgley, C., & Urdan, T. (2001). Academic self-handicapping and achievement goals. A further examination. *Contemporary Educational Psychology, 26,* 61–75.

Miles, M. B., & Huberman, A. M. (1994). *Qualitative data analysis.* Thousand Oaks, CA: Sage.

Moynihan, D. P. (1965). *The Negro family: A case for national action.* Washington, DC: U.S. Department of Labor.

Nettles, M., & Perna, L. (1997). *The African American education data book: Vol. 2. Preschool through high school Education.* Fairfax, VA: Frederick D. Patterson Research Institute.

Ogbu, J. U. (1988). Cultural diversity and human development. *New Directions for Child Development, 42,* 11–28.

Ogbu, J. U. (1992). Understanding cultural diversity and learning. *Educational Researcher, 21,* 5–14.

Pintrich, P. R., & De Groot, E. V. (1990). Motivational and self-regulated learning components of classroom academic performance. *Journal of Educational Psychology, 82,* 33–40.

Pintrich, P. R., & Garcia, T. (1990). Student goal orientation and self-regulation in the college classroom. In M. Maehr & P. Pintrich (Eds.), *Advances in motivation and achievement* (Vol. 7, pp. 371–402). Greenwich, CT: JAI.

Pintrich, P. R., & Schunk, D. H. (1996). *Motivation in education: Theory, research, and application.* Englewood Cliffs, NJ: Prentice-Hall.

Rawsthorne, L. J., & Eliot, A. J. (1999). Achievement goals and intrinsic motivation: A meta-analytic review. *Personality and Social Psychology Review, 3,* 326–344.

Rist, R. (1970). Student social class and teacher expectations: The self-fulfilling prophecy in ghetto education. *Harvard Educational Review, 40,* 411–450.

Ryan, A. M., & Patrick, H. (2001). The classroom social environment and changes in adolescents' motivation and engagement during middle school. *American Educational Research Journal, 38,* 437–460.

Ryan, R. M., Connell, J. P., & Deci, E. L. (1985). A motivational analysis of self-determination and self-regulation in education. In C. Ames & R. Ames (Eds.), *Research on motivation in education: Vol. 2. The classroom milieu* (pp. 13–51). San Diego: Academic Press.

Solomon, D., Battistich, V., & Hom, A. (1996). Teacher beliefs and practices in schools serving communities that differ in socioeconomic level. *Journal of Experimental Education, 64,* 327–347.

Steele, C. M. (1997). A threat in the air: How stereotypes shape intellectual identity and performance. *American Psychologist, 52,* 613–629.

Steele, C. M., & Aronson, J. (1995). Stereotype threat and the intellectual test performance of African Americans. *Journal of Personality and Social Psychology, 69,* 797–811.

Steinberg, L. D. (1996). *Beyond the classroom: Why school reform has failed and what parents need to do.* New York: Simon & Schuster.

Stevenson, H., Chen, C., & Uttal, D. (1990). Beliefs and achievement: A study of Black, White, and Hispanic children. *Child Development, 61,* 508–523.

Urdan, T. (1997). Achievement goal theory: Past results, future directions. In M. L. Maehr & P. R. Pintrich (Eds.), *Advances in motivation and achievement* (Vol. 10, pp. 99–141). Greenwich, CT: JAI.

U.S. Department of Education, National Center for Education Statistics. (1997). *America's teachers: Profile of a profession, 1993–1994.* Washington, DC: Authors.

Weiss, R. S. (1994). *Learning from strangers: The art and method of qualitative interview studies.* New York: The Free Press.

Wentzel, K. R. (1991). Social and academic goals at school: Motivation and achievement in context. In M. L. Maehr & P. R. Pintrich (Eds.), *Advances in motivation and achievement* (Vol. 7, pp. 185–212). Greenwich, CT: JAI.

Winfield, L. F. (1986). Teacher beliefs toward academic at risk students in inner urban schools. *The Urban Review, 18,* 253–268.

Winston, C. E., DeBritto, A. M., & Eccles, J. (1997). The utility of an expectancy/value model and disidentification models for understanding race differences in academic performance and self-esteem. *Zeitschrift Fur Padagogische Psychologie, 11,* pp. 177–186.

Winston, C. E., & Edelin, K. C. (1996, April). *Academic beliefs and performance of Black students: Evidence from two studies.* Paper presented at the annual meeting of the American Educational Research Association, New York.

Wolters, C. A., Yu, S. L., & Pintrich, P. R. (1996). The relation between goal orientation and students' motivational beliefs and self-regulated learning. *Learning and Individual Differences, 8,* 211–238.

8

A Goal Theory Perspective on Teachers' Professional Identities and the Contexts of Teaching

Robert W. Roeser, Ph.D.
Stanford University

Roxana Marachi
University of Michigan

Hunter Gehlbach
Stanford University

Teachers are at the center of efforts to motivate students to learn in school. Understanding teachers' professional identities and the contexts of their work is important for understanding their pedagogical choices and practices, and the effect these can have on students' motivation to learn (e.g., Talbert & McLaughlin, 1993). By adopting a comprehensive view of schooling that attends explicitly to teachers' professional identities and work contexts, researchers may gain new insights into the multiply determined factors in school that cultivate positive motivational orientations and achievement among some students, or potentiate motivational and learning difficulties among others (Maehr & Midgley, 1991, 1996).

Unfortunately, despite decades of research on "school effects" and "effective schools," the role of teachers' professional identities and pedagogy has remained in the shadows of this work, though clearly teachers mediate many of the effects of schooling on student outcomes (Cuban, 1990; Talbert &

McLaughlin, 1993, 1999). This lack of attention to teachers has also characterized research on students' motivation to learn in formal educational settings
that takes an achievement goal theoretical orientation. Research on teachers'
goal-oriented approaches to instruction and the contexts of teaching is considerably less well developed than research on students' goal-oriented approaches
to learning and their perceptions of learning contexts despite the important interdependencies between the two.

In this chapter, we attempt to bring teachers out of the shadows in goal theory research by exploring three main issues and by providing some related,
empirical analyses. First, we use goal theory as a general framework within
which to discuss the kinds of teaching-related beliefs and approaches to instruction that, in part, constitute important components of teachers' "professional identities." Second, we explore how the multilevel contexts of teachers'
work shape aspects of their professional identities, and how goal theory can
provide one way of conceptualizing the contexts of teaching and learning in
schools. Third, we illustrate some of the complex relations that link aspects of
teachers' work environments and professional identities with students' motivation to learn in the classroom. We conclude with some thoughts on future directions for research in this area.

CONCEPTUALIZING TEACHERS' PROFESSIONAL IDENTITIES

Teachers' professional identities can be defined in terms of social, psychological, and behavioral factors. Such factors include teachers' participation in various professional communities, their subject matter and pedagogical content
knowledge, their beliefs and attitudes concerning teaching, and their repertoire
of pedagogical skills and techniques (Shulman, 1986; Talbert & McLaughlin,
1993). In this chapter, we focus on a subset of identity processes that are motivational in nature—those that give direction to the kinds of decisions teachers
make and the kinds of instruction they enact in their classrooms. Paralleling
work on motivated patterns of learning in students, we propose that teachers'
pedagogical goals and goal-oriented approaches to instruction, their perceived
self-efficacy in enacting and accomplishing their goals, and their feelings about
their role as a teacher all represent important motivational components of their
professional identities. Goal theory provides one fruitful way of beginning to
frame and understand such identities (Ames, 1992a, 1992b; Midgley, 1993).

Components of Teachers' Professional Identities

Achievement Goal Theory.   Achievement goal theory is a social-cognitive
approach to the study of students' motivated behavior in achievement settings

that defines personal motives (called goal orientations) and situational affordances (called goal structures) in the same conceptual terms. As such, the theory is useful for understanding linkages between different forms of personal motivation and different types of learning environments. Goal theorists are interested in understanding the "super-ordinate classes of goals that are behind the particular outcomes individuals strive for" in learning situations (Dweck, 1992, p. 165) as well as the social affordances that tend to promote different achievement-related goals (Ames, 1992b). In particular, goal theorists posit that cognitive *purposes* or goals associated with the approach or avoidance of learning activities organize the quality of students' attention, emotion, cognition, and consequently, behavior in learning situations. Additionally, goal theorists who study actual educational settings assume that students' goals and their psychological and behavioral correlates are shaped in large part by the social-contextual features of the classroom and the school as a whole (Ames, 1992b; Maehr & Midgley, 1991). Figure 8.1 depicts this model of student motivation. Assumptions of this model include (a) that contextual affordances and activities in a learning environment emphasize certain implicit achievement-related goals ("goal structures"); (b) that these goal structures are perceived and evaluated by students; (c) that subjective perceptions (appraisals) of the environment shape students' own goals in the classroom; and (d) that students' adoption of certain goals, in conjunction with their relevant cognitive abilities, knowledge, and self-regulatory processes, shape their cognitive, emotional, and behavioral engagement or disaffection in that environment. Reciprocal causal relations are thought to exist between the different factors in the model, such that motivational beliefs both affect and are affected by perceptions of the environment, behavior both affects and is affected by motivation, and so on (see Bandura, 1993; Connell, Spencer, & Aber, 1994; Eccles, 1983; Ford, 1992). Research on students' perceptions of classroom and school goal structures as well as their personal achievement goals, including goals associated with task mastery (mastery goals) and the demonstration of or hiding of one's ability rela-

Objective Environment	*Subjective Environment*	*Motivation*	*Behavior*
Learning Activities & Contexts → (Goal Structures)	Perceived Goal Structures →	Personal Goals →	Patterns of Behavioral Engagement and Disaffection related to Learning

FIG. 8.1. Description of a goal theory perspective on *student* motivation in educational settings.

tive to others (performance goals), has documented the predictive power of goals in explaining patterns of engagement and disaffection among students in actual educational settings (see Ames, 1992b; Midgley, 1993; Urdan, 1997, for reviews). As noted earlier, however, much of the research that applies goal theory to actual educational settings has been concerned with students' perceptions of the environment, their personal goals, and the psychological and behavioral consequences of their espousal of various goals. Less research has been conducted on teachers' pedagogical goals and goal-related approaches to instruction that form the contexts in which these student-level variables are embedded.

Teachers' Pedagogical Approaches to Instruction.   Paralleling a focus on students' achievement goals have been theoretical discussions of teachers' practices that create either mastery- or performance-oriented learning environments. Ames (1992a, 1992b) used goal theory to describe how mastery- or performance-oriented classrooms can emerge from the ways that teachers use time in their classrooms; distribute authority; recognize, group, and evaluate students; and design classroom tasks. Rather than examining teachers' own instructional goal orientations per se, Ames' analysis focuses on how teachers' overall constellation of practices reflect mastery or performance goals—goals that parallel those used to conceptualize students' motivation to learn.

A performance orientation is thought to emerge through teachers' use of practices that implicitly or explicitly promote the idea to students that proving their abilities relative to classmates is what is valued, expected, and rewarded. Use of within-class ability grouping, rewards for superior achievement, public evaluative feedback, and uni-dimensional tasks in which student-to-student comparisons are easy to make are examples of performance-oriented instructional practices. A mastery orientation is thought to emerge in classrooms where teachers use practices that implicitly or explicitly promote the idea to students that progressively mastering content and improving skills through hard work is what is valued, expected, and rewarded. Provisions of challenging and meaningful tasks, acknowledgment of student effort and improvement, use of nonpublic formative and summative feedback, opportunities for revision of work, and use of multidimensional tasks in which different students work on different aspects of the task are examples of mastery-oriented instructional practices (Ames, 1992b; Midgley, 1993).

To date, few studies using goal theory concepts with teacher data exist. In one study, Meece (1991) observed fifth- and sixth-grade science teachers and compared teachers who seemed to promote more or less of a mastery orientation in their students. Observations revealed that teachers with students with the highest mastery orientations were more likely to promote meaningful learning, adapt instruction to the developmental levels and interests of students, support student

autonomy and peer collaboration, and emphasize the intrinsic value of learning. Urdan, Midgley, and Anderman (1998), using teacher and student survey data, found that fifth-grade teachers' reports of their performance-oriented approaches to instruction (e.g., helping students see how their performance compares to others, pointing out students who do well academically as models for other students) were positively associated with students' reported use of self-handicapping in the classroom (purposefully withdrawing effort in order to protect self-worth). Kaplan, Gheen, and Midgley (2001), using teacher and student survey data from the Patterns of Adaptive Learning Study, found that ninth-grade teachers' mastery-oriented approaches to instruction (e.g., emphasizing to students the importance of understanding work and not just memorizing it, making an effort to provide students with work that has meaning in their everyday lives) were positively associated with students' aggregate perceptions of their classrooms as mastery oriented. These aggregate perceptions were related, in turn, to lower incidences of student-reported disruptive behavior in the classroom. In chapter 9 (this volume), additional observational studies from the Patterns of Adaptive Learning Study are described that point to instructional practices that are associated with students' perceptions of an emphasis on mastery and/or performance goals in the classroom. Thus, evidence is gradually accumulating that teachers' goal-oriented approaches to instruction are associated with students' perceptions of the goal structure in their classrooms as well as consequential psychological and behavioral outcomes. However, little is known about how teachers' goal-oriented approaches to instruction are associated with other aspects of their professional identities. Such research could contribute to our growing understanding of beliefs and behaviors that underlie effective, motivating instruction in the classroom.

Teacher Efficacy. Teachers' teaching-related efficacy beliefs are also an important component of their professional identities. Studies have demonstrated that teachers who feel they can teach even the most difficult students and who believe they can affect students' intellectual development above and beyond other influences such as the family tend to communicate these positive expectations and beliefs to their students. In this way, such teachers enhance students' own beliefs about their capacities to master academic material, and thereby promote students' investment of effort in learning and achievement (Ashton, 1985; Bandura, 1993; Midgley, Feldlaufer, & Eccles, 1989). Teachers' efficacy beliefs are also related to the amount of effort they put into, and satisfaction they derive from, teaching. Tschannen-Moran, Woolfolk-Hoy A., and Hoy (1998) reported that teachers' efficacy was positively related to their investment of effort in teaching, their persistence in working with students with academic difficulties, and their willingness to experiment with new teaching strategies. Finally, teachers' efficacy beliefs are related to their role percep-

tions and the kinds of goals they see as central to learning. Roeser and Midgley (1997) found that elementary school teachers' efficacy was negatively related to feelings of burden due to students' mental health needs and positively to their endorsement of the idea that attending to such needs was part of their professional role. Midgley, Anderman, and Hicks (1995) found a positive relationship between middle school teachers' efficacy beliefs and their endorsement of mastery-oriented goals for students (getting students to focus on their own improvement, to do challenging tasks or projects, etc.).

Role-Related Perceptions.   Teachers' beliefs about what their professional role entails are another important component of their professional identities. Two common role definitions that teachers identify with are that of the "academic instructor" (oriented toward teaching academic content) and that of the "socializer" (oriented toward addressing children's social-emotional and behavioral needs; fosterer of the "good citizen"). In one study of 98 elementary school teachers, Brophy (1985) found that an endorsement of the "instructor" role was critical for teachers' ability to ensure student achievement, but that some of the most effective teachers were those who blended an academic with a socializing focus.

These studies of teachers' efficacy and role beliefs lead us to believe that the most effective teachers are those who simultaneously press for achievement and attend to students' social-emotional needs. But just how do such teachers press for achievement? In one study, Roeser, Midgley, and Urdan (1996) found that middle school students' perceptions of a school mastery goal structure were positively correlated with their perceptions of caring, respectful teachers; whereas their perceptions of a school performance goal structure were negatively correlated with perceptions of caring teachers. In another study, Roeser and Midgley (1997) found that teachers' mastery orientations were positively associated with their sense that attending to students' social-emotional needs was part of their role. It may well be that teachers who are more mastery oriented, because of their attention to individual effort and improvement as valued purposes of learning, are also those who attend to students' broader needs and are therefore perceived as the most caring by students. In the next section, we describe a study from the Patterns of Adaptive Learning Study that tests our hypotheses concerning the interrelations among teachers' goal-oriented instructional approaches, efficacy beliefs, and role beliefs.

An Empirical Examination of Components of Teachers' Professional Identities

Variable- and person-centered data analytic techniques were used to examine the interrelations between these three components of elementary, middle, and high

school teachers' professional identities. Variable-centered techniques address the relations among variables across persons in a sample, whereas person-centered techniques address the patterning of variables within subgroups of individuals in a sample (Magnusson & Bergman, 1988). A correlational analysis is an example of a variable-centered technique and a q-type cluster analysis is an example of a person-centered technique. Whereas correlational analyses yield information on the interrelations of variables across all persons in a sample, q-type cluster analysis is a technique that considers the interdependence among variables within persons and thereby classifies them into relatively homogenous groups based on their similarity across a series of measures (Aldenderfer & Blashfield, 1984; Magnusson & Bergman, 1988).

Overview of the Teacher Study.   Data used in this chapter come from the Patterns of Adaptive Learning Study. Some of the results using variable-centered analyses are from a study by Marachi, Gheen, and Midgley (2001). In this chapter we add to this study by including teachers' perceptions of their own work environment (mastery or performance oriented) and principals' reports of the use of mastery and performance practices in the school. We also present the results from new analyses using person-centered analyses. When students in the longitudinal sample were in the fifth (1994), sixth (1995), and ninth (1998) grades, all of the classroom teachers in their elementary, middle, and high schools, respectively, were given surveys. Teachers answered questions about their professional background, their teaching-related beliefs, and their perceptions of the learning environment for students and the work environment for teachers in their school. All participating teachers were given surveys at the school site and asked to fill them out and return them at their own convenience. Participation rates for elementary, middle, and high school teachers were 70%, 74%, and 93%, respectively. During 1994, the sample included 217 teachers from 20 elementary schools. In 1995, the sample included 179 teachers in 10 middle schools. In 1998, the sample included 250 teachers in five high schools. Seventy-two percent and 68% of teachers in the elementary and middle school samples, respectively, had a master's degree or higher (no information on educational level was collected for the high school sample). Due to missing data and study design factors, the samples of teachers used in different analyses vary. Such variation is noted in the text, tables, and figures.

Measures.   Surveys assessed teachers' performance- and mastery-oriented approaches to instruction, their efficacy beliefs, and their beliefs about whether or not attending to students' social-emotional needs was part of their professional role. The performance-oriented approach to instruction scale measured teachers' self-reported use of teaching practices that emphasized competition and social comparison. The mastery-oriented approach to instruction scale assessed

teachers' self-reported use of teaching practices that emphasized the importance of understanding material, giving tasks that are creative and imaginative, and connecting with salient issues in the lives of students. The personal teaching efficacy scale assessed the degree to which teachers reported feeling effective in promoting the educational progress of their students. The role in student mental health scale assessed teachers' belief that their role includes addressing social-emotional needs of students.

Teachers also rated the extent to which the learning culture of the school for students and the work culture of the school for teachers were performance and mastery oriented. The perceived performance goal structure for students scale assessed teachers' perceptions that competition, a focus on extrinsic outcomes and test scores, and the recognition of superior achievement were salient aspects of the school's academic culture for students. The perceived mastery goal structure for students scale assessed teachers' perceptions that a focus on investing effort in learning, learning from mistakes, and connecting learning with students' lives were salient aspects of the school's academic culture for students. The perceived performance goal structure for teachers scale assessed teachers' perceptions of competition among teachers, differential treatment of teachers by administration, and status differentials among teachers in the school. The perceived mastery goal structure for teachers scale assessed teachers' perceptions of support for innovation, improvement, and hard work in the school. Items for each of these scales are presented in the Appendix to this chapter and on our Web site (http://www.umich.edu/~pals/; see Midgley et al., 2000).

In addition, "objective" principal reports of school-level policies and practices reflective of performance and mastery goals for students were used. The principal performance practices scale included five items that assessed whether the school used a public honor roll and specific rewards for high-achievers, provided bumper stickers to parents of the highest achieving students, had a "gifted and talented" program, and recognized achievement in public assemblies. The principal mastery practices scale was much more difficult to create because the actual school-level practices that give rise to this orientation are less well understood. The four items in this scale assessed whether the school used portfolio assessments, provided grades for effort, recognized student improvement, and provided extracurricular and enrichment activities in which all students, regardless of their ability level, could participate.

A Variable-Centered Approach to Teachers' Identities.   Table 8.1 is adapted from Marachi et al. (2001) and presents the correlations among aspects of elementary, middle, and high school teachers' professional identities. Results showed that teachers' performance- and mastery-oriented approaches to instruction were uncorrelated at each of the school levels. These results suggest that rather than being antithetical approaches to instruction, teachers may

TABLE 8.1

Means, Standard Deviations, and Bivariate Correlations for Elementary, Middle, and High School Teachers' Professional Identity Components and Demographic Characteristics

	M (SD)	1	2	3	4	5	6
1. Performance-Oriented Approach to Instruction	**2.58 (.90)**						
Elementary School Teachers	2.19 (.87)	—					
Middle School Teachers	2.66 (.84)	—					
High School Teachers	2.88 (.83)	—					
2. Mastery-Oriented Approach to Instruction	**4.25 (.59)**	**.00**	—				
Elementary School Teachers	4.36 (.55)	–.06	—				
Middle School Teachers	4.26 (.58)	.10	—				
High School Teachers	4.14 (.62)	.12	—				
3. Personal Teaching Efficacy	**3.48 (.71)**	**–.10**[*]	**.42**[**]	—			
Elementary School Teachers	3.76 (.60)	.06	.32[**]	—			
Middle School Teachers	3.55 (.70)	–.05	.48[**]	—			
High School Teachers	3.19 (.69)	.01	.37[**]	—			

continued on next page

213

TABLE 8.1 (*continued*)

Means, Standard Deviations, and Bivariate Correlations for Elementary, Middle, and High School Teachers' Professional Identity Components and Demographic Characteristics

	M (SD)	1	2	3	4	5	6
4. Role in Students' Mental Health	**4.30 (.66)**	**-.17****	**.47****	**.56****			
Elementary School Teachers	4.58 (.45)	-.17*	.46**	.43**	—		
Middle School Teachers	4.27 (.63)	-.09	.48**	.52**	—		
High School Teachers	4.08 (.74)	.00	.43**	.54**	—		
5. Total Years Teaching Experience	**18.09 (10.08)**	**.06**	**-.08***	**-.01**	**-.13****		
Elementary School Teachers	18.06 (9.02)	.07	-.08	.09	-.06	—	
Middle School Teachers	17.96 (10.09)	.09	-.10	-.13	-.18*	—	
High School Teachers	18.21 (10.95)	.05	-.06	.01	-.16*	—	
6. Teacher Is Female	**71%**	**-.26****	**.22****	**.23****	**.29****	**-.14****	
Elementary School Teachers	89%	-.23**	.05	.00	.05	-.15*	—
Middle School Teachers	71%	-.24**	.25**	.22**	.26**	-.25**	—
High School Teachers	56%	-.15*	.20**	.15*	.25**	-.09	—

Note. Adapted from Marachi, Gheen, and Midgley (2001). Pairwise deletion of cases used in these analyses. Number of teachers: Elementary ($n = 217$), middle ($n = 250$), and high school ($n = 179$). $^*p < .05$. $^{**}p < .01$.

emphasize one, the other, or both goals in their instruction. Next, results showed that teachers' performance-oriented approach to instruction was unrelated to their efficacy and role beliefs concerning students' social-emotional needs. The one exception was a negative relation between a performance-oriented instructional approach and perceiving a role in students' mental health at the elementary level. In contrast, teachers' mastery-oriented approach to instruction, efficacy, and role beliefs were positively correlated at each school level. These results suggest that teachers who feel efficacious also believe that emphasizing student effort, improvement, and mastery, and attending to the needs of the "whole child" are important. Finally, results showed that at the middle and high school levels, female teachers used mastery approaches more and perceived a greater role for themselves in the mental health of their students than did male teachers; and at all three school levels, male teachers used performance approaches more than did female teachers. These results parallel findings that show male students tend to endorse the pursuit of performance goals more than do female students (see Urdan, 1997).

A Person-Centered Approach.   Although instructive for understanding general trends, correlations are in some sense "statistical abstractions" that do not aid our understanding of "types of teachers" who may hold particular configurations of identity beliefs. As a means of identifying such "types," we clustered together subgroups of elementary teachers based on their similarities across their goal-oriented approaches to instruction and efficacy beliefs. We assumed teachers could be high in efficacy and performance or mastery oriented in their pedagogy, efficacious and oriented to both goals, or low in efficacy and performance or mastery oriented. We focused on the elementary school sample because, as we discuss later, this sample provided us with the most students to link with the teacher data. We purposefully did not include teachers' beliefs about their role in students' mental health in the clustering procedure. This allowed us to "validate" the emergent clusters by seeing if a substantively related scale differentiated the emergent groups in meaningful ways. Based on the correlational results, we expected that high-efficacy and/or mastery-oriented teachers would be more likely than low-efficacy and/or performance-oriented teachers to see students' mental health needs as part of their role.

Based on the emergent structure of our data, on our initial hypotheses concerning plausible patterns of teacher "types," and on considerations of parsimony, a five-cluster solution was extracted using Ward's method and Euclidean distance as the measure of similarity among the three measures. Clusters were conceptualized as different "types of professional identities." We emphasize, however, that these "types" are more fluid than fixed and represent teachers' status on these particular indicators relative to that of their peers in this particular sample at a particular moment in time (e.g., 1994).

The types that emerged are presented in Fig. 8.2. They were labeled as follows: Type I = a multiple-goal, efficacious type ($n = 27$, 12%); Type II = a performance-oriented, efficacious type ($n = 24$, 11%); Type III = a mastery-oriented, efficacious type ($n = 19$, 9%); Type IV = a performance-oriented, low-efficacy type ($n = 30$, 14%); and Type V = a mastery-oriented, low-efficacy type ($n = 34$, 16%). Approximately one third of the teachers were not characterized by a conceptually recognizable "type" using this procedure, thus eventuating in five types that characterized 134 teachers. Because this was largely an exploratory analysis, this proportion of unclassified cases was deemed acceptable though not optimal.

The graph portion of Fig. 8.2 depicts the profile for each subgroup on the clustering variables and the table below displays the means and the results of the group comparisons. Analyses of variance (ANOVAs) and post-hoc Tukey honestly significant difference (HSD) comparisons for all possible pairs were used to assess group differences. Note in the graph portion of Fig. 8.2 that the emergent clusters support the idea that teachers, like students in relation to their learning, can endorse a performance, a mastery, or a multigoal orientation. Note also in the table portion of Fig. 8.2 that the clustering procedure itself clearly differentiates the groups on the clustering variables. Finally, note that the groups differed on the validation variable in the expected ways. Performance-oriented, low-efficacy teachers (Type IV) were the least likely, and efficacious, mastery-oriented teachers (Type III) were the most likely to endorse the idea that attending to students' social-emotional needs was part of their role. These findings complement and extend the variable-centered results by documenting that there exist several "types of teachers" who believe students' mental health needs are important—those who are mastery oriented and efficacious, those who are mastery oriented and not as efficacious, and those who endorse both pedagogical approaches to instruction and feel efficacious. No significant group differences in gender composition or in the years of teaching service were noted. We return to these types in subsequent sections to illustrate how teachers' perceptions of their school and students' personal goal orientations in the classroom are related to them.

A CONTEXTUALIST PERSPECTIVE
ON THE CONTEXTS OF TEACHERS' WORK

Teachers' professional identities are embedded within and influenced by the contexts of their work in the same manner that students' motivation is embedded within and influenced by the contexts of their learning. In this section, we describe a causal predictive and a causal descriptive model that, individually and together, are useful for understanding the contexts of teachers' work and the relation of these contexts to their professional identities.

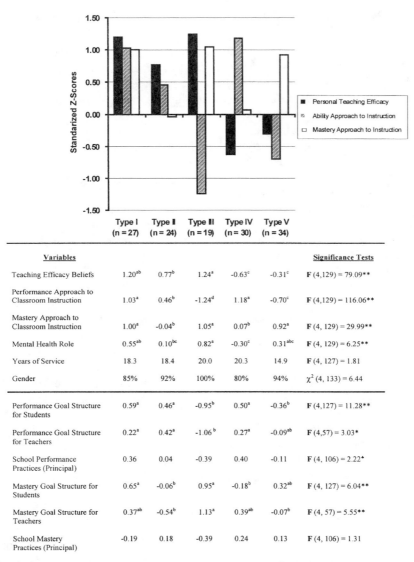

Variables	Type I (n = 27)	Type II (n = 24)	Type III (n = 19)	Type IV (n = 30)	Type V (n = 34)	Significance Tests
Teaching Efficacy Beliefs	1.20^{ab}	0.77^{b}	1.24^{a}	-0.63^{c}	-0.31^{c}	$F_{(4,129)} = 79.09**$
Performance Approach to Classroom Instruction	1.03^{a}	0.46^{b}	-1.24^{d}	1.18^{a}	-0.70^{c}	$F_{(4,129)} = 116.06**$
Mastery Approach to Classroom Instruction	1.00^{a}	-0.04^{b}	1.05^{a}	0.07^{b}	0.92^{a}	$F_{(4, 129)} = 29.99**$
Mental Health Role	0.55^{ab}	0.10^{bc}	0.82^{a}	-0.30^{c}	0.31^{abc}	$F_{(4, 129)} = 6.25**$
Years of Service	18.3	18.4	20.0	20.3	14.9	$F_{(4, 127)} = 1.81$
Gender	85%	92%	100%	80%	94%	$\chi^{2}_{(4, 133)} = 6.44$
Performance Goal Structure for Students	0.59^{a}	0.46^{a}	-0.95^{b}	0.50^{a}	-0.36^{b}	$F_{(4,127)} = 11.28**$
Performance Goal Structure for Teachers	0.22^{a}	0.42^{a}	-1.06^{b}	0.27^{a}	-0.09^{ab}	$F_{(4,57)} = 3.03*$
School Performance Practices (Principal)	0.36	0.04	-0.39	0.40	-0.11	$F_{(4, 106)} = 2.22^{\clubsuit}$
Mastery Goal Structure for Students	0.65^{a}	-0.06^{b}	0.95^{a}	-0.18^{b}	0.32^{ab}	$F_{(4, 127)} = 6.04**$
Mastery Goal Structure for Teachers	0.37^{ab}	-0.54^{b}	1.13^{a}	0.39^{ab}	-0.07^{b}	$F_{(4, 57)} = 5.55**$
School Mastery Practices (Principal)	-0.19	0.18	-0.39	0.24	0.13	$F_{(4, 106)} = 1.31$

Note: Means for each group on efficacy beliefs, ability, and mastery-oriented approaches to classroom instruction, and role in students' mental health are expressed in standard z-score units; years of teaching service are presented in years, and gender composition is expressed as the percentage of female teachers. The first three measures in the table were used to create identity types.[abc] Groups that do not share a superscript are significantly different from one another at the .05 level using Tukey's HSD comparisons for all possible pairs.

$\clubsuit$ $p \le .075$; $^{*}p \le .05$; $^{**}p \le .01$

FIG. 8.2   Group comparisons on teacher beliefs, approaches to instruction, and demography by elementary school teacher professional identity types.

General Predictive Model of Teachers' Identity and Pedagogy

Teachers' professional identities are affected by the social and organizational features of their work settings (Lee, Bryk, & J. B. Smith, 1993; Talbert & McLaughlin, 1993). Figure 8.3 depicts a hypothesized causal motivational model that is parallel to the model of student motivation discussed earlier (see Fig. 8.1). This model depicts a "flow" from teachers' work contexts to their context perceptions, beliefs, and enacted pedagogy. Assumptions of the model include (a) that the contexts of teaching influence teachers' identities; (b) that these contexts are perceived and evaluated by teachers in terms of their own needs and goals; (c) that context perceptions shape teachers' goals, efficacy beliefs, and role-related beliefs; and (d) that teachers' goals, efficacy, and role beliefs constitute important motivational processes that shape their pedagogy in the classroom. Consistent with motivational approaches more generally (see Eccles, Wigfield, & Schiefele, 1998), we assume that teachers' subjective perceptions of their work environments are stronger determinants of their identities than are more "objective" context features. Feedback loops and reciprocal causal processes are hypothesized to characterize each stage of the model such that contexts affect teachers' identities, teachers' identities affect their work environments, and so on. Though the model appears to be highly deterministic, it is really probabilistic given the important agentic role teachers can play in interpreting the contexts of their work environment and in choosing to act in concert with or in altogether unique ways from those contexts.

The prescriptive model in Fig. 8.3 raises fundamental questions like: What are the specific contexts that define the work environment of teachers? What are the processes by which aspects of teachers' work environments influence their beliefs and practices? How does the nature of these contexts differ for teachers in elementary, middle, and high school settings? A descriptive model of the "embedded contexts of teaching" is needed to address these issues in a more systematic manner.

Objective Environment	*Subjective Environment*	*Motivation* *(Professional Identity)*		*Behavior*
Work Activities & Contexts →	Perceived Work Activities & Contexts →	Personal Goals Efficacy Beliefs Role Beliefs →		Pedagogy

FIG. 8.3.   General motivational model for understanding teachers' professional identities.

General Descriptive Model of Teachers' Work Environments

Based on work by Talbert and McLaughlin (1993, 1999), Fig. 8.4 depicts the work environments of teachers as a series of embedded contexts involving characteristics associated with students and the subject matter of the classroom, academic departments, the culture of the school as a whole, the level of the institution (elementary, middle, or high school), school governance structures and sector (public or private school), and the families and communities the school serves. Each of these levels of context can impact on teachers' professional identities and pedagogy. We discuss only a few relevant assumptions here (see Eccles & Roeser, 1999; Talbert & McLaughlin, 1993, 1999).

First, each level of teachers' work environments can be characterized by both "objective" and "subjective" features. For instance, we have depicted a "right-hand, objective dimension" of these contexts to denote the explicit features of each level such as the social class backgrounds of students, the curricular content of the different subject matters, the existence of departments as organizational units in a school, the size and resources of different schools, district wide policies, and so on (Lee et al., 1993; Talbert & McLaughlin, 1993). These right-hand dimensions can be observed by those who do not work in the setting on a daily basis (an "etic" perspective). Each of the right-hand dimen-

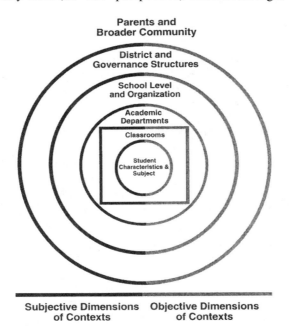

FIG. 8.4. Embedded contexts of teaching.

sions is assumed to have a "left-hand, subjective dimension." These dimensions are implicit and include things like the motivational attitudes and mental health of students; the sequence and structure of the different subject matters; the power of departmental structures in decision-making processes; the culture of the school in terms of norms, roles, and rules; the culture of the district; and the values of parents and the community (e.g., Lee et al., 1993; Maehr & Midgley, 1991, 1996; Stodolsky & Grossman, 1995). The left-hand dimensions are not readily apparent to outsiders and are usually assessed via the perceptions of students, teachers, and educational leaders who inhabit these settings (an "emic" perspective).

Another assumption of this model is that interactions in these different subcontexts vary in their relevance for teachers' professional identities depending on the nature of the specific school and the level of institution in which they work. For example, although students affect teachers' identities and pedagogy at all levels (Lee et al., 1993), subject matter departments clearly matter more for high school teachers than for those who teach at the earlier grades (Talbert & McLaughlin, 1993).

Finally, we assume that the influences of these levels on teachers can be direct or indirect and need not "travel through" the intervening levels (Talbert & McLaughlin, 1993). For instance, federally or state-mandated testing can directly encourage teachers' use of particular classroom instructional methods, such as drill and practice, independent of district and departmental structures (M. L. Smith, 1991). The main point we want to emphasize here is that whatever the causal chains of influence may be by which objective and subjective dimensions of schools exert "effects" on students, these effects more often than not come through teachers' professional identities and pedagogy (Cuban, 1990).

Integrating the Prescriptive and Descriptive Models

A comprehensive view of schooling that attends explicitly to teachers' professional identities and work contexts is ultimately one, we believe, that encompasses both the prescriptive and descriptive models presented in Figs. 8.3 and 8.4. In the next section, we pursue a more modest goal by selectively reviewing studies that document associations between some of the contextual levels depicted in Fig. 8.4 and particular aspects of teachers' professional identities. The contexts we focus on here include the level of institution (elementary, middle, high school), the learning and work cultures of the school, teachers' subject matter, and characteristics of students. Empirical findings documenting associations between teachers' goal-related approaches to instruction, efficacy beliefs, and the goal structures in their schools are also presented in this section.

School Level

Research has documented school-level differences in aspects of teachers' professional identities. Marachi and her colleagues (2001), for example, found linear declines in sense of efficacy and beliefs that attending to students' social-emotional needs was part of the teacher role among groups of high school, middle school, and elementary school teachers. Other studies have also reported that secondary teachers feel less efficacious than their do elementary school colleagues (Fuller & Izu, 1986; Midgley et al., 1989). Furthermore, Marachi et al. found that teachers reported using performance-oriented approaches to instruction more in middle and high school than in elementary school, and fewer mastery-oriented approaches to instruction in high school than in middle or elementary schools.

Several authors have described objective, organizational factors that differ across these institutional levels that may account for these findings (Eccles & Midgley, 1989; Eccles et al., 1998; Maehr & Anderman, 1993; Midgley, 1993). First, there is an increase in school size when one compares middle and high schools with elementary schools. Increased school size is correlated with departmentalization and increased teaching loads—middle and high school teachers typically teach many more students than do elementary teachers. Larger teaching loads and fewer contact hours with students make it harder for secondary school teachers to develop personal relationships with students, to feel like they can teach all of their students, and perhaps to endorse mastery-oriented pedagogical practices. When teachers do not feel efficacious or know and trust their students, they may abandon the use of mastery- and autonomy-supportive practices in favor of extrinsic motivators and other forms of teacher control (Eccles & Midgley, 1989).

Studies also document an intensification in the use of between-class ability grouping and increased pressures for content coverage in secondary as compared to elementary schools (see Good, 2000; Oakes, Gamoran, & Page, 1992). Such features may make issues of relative ability, quantity rather than quality of coverage, and performance on standardized tests salient in secondary schools. Teachers, in turn, may come to endorse these kind of academic goals through their own instructional practices in the classroom.

Schoolwide Goal Structures or "Cultures"

Not only is the objective level of the institution in which a teacher works associated with aspects of their professional identities, but so too is the subjective culture for teaching and learning that exists in a school (Maehr, 1991; Sarason, 1990). Whereas much of the research within goal theory has focused on the na-

ture of goal structures in classrooms and their relations to student motivation (Ames, 1992a, 1992b), others have utilized goal theory to describe the goal structure of the school as a whole in relation to students' motivation and learning (Maehr, 1991; Maehr & Fyans, 1989; Roeser et al., 1996) and teachers' motivation and pedagogy (Maehr & Buck, 1993; Maehr & Midgley, 1991, 1996).

A focus on school-level in addition to classroom-level goal structures arose out of insights gleaned from early intervention work in elementary schools conducted by Carole Ames. In her collaborative reform work in Illinois, Ames (1990) found that efforts to help teachers move their classrooms toward a greater mastery orientation were often hampered by school-level policies and practices that were more performance oriented. For instance, helping teachers to devise new strategies that recognize the value of student effort and self-improvement and that normalized mistakes as part of the learning process were sometimes undermined by school-level practices in which public recognition of students for superior achievement or "perfect performance" was granted through school-level honor rolls and assemblies.

Based on these insights and others, Maehr and Midgley (1991, 1996) suggested that it was important for researchers and reformers to acknowledge how particular school-level practices, in addition to classroom-level practices, could reflect and promote a performance or mastery goal emphasis in a school. Specifically, they suggested that school-level decisions concerning the nature of the tasks to which students were exposed (e.g., textbook selection), norms associated with the empowerment of students (e.g., student government programs), means of recognizing students for various behaviors (e.g., honor rolls and public assemblies), approaches to grouping students (e.g., tracking policies), formats for formally evaluating students (e.g., portfolio assessments), and the use of time (e.g., block scheduling) could all eventuate in a culture at the school level that was more or less performance or mastery oriented.

An assumption of this early work was that such school wide policies and practices could influence not only students' motivation and achievement, but also teachers' professional identities and pedagogy. As many studies have shown, competent leadership and a sense of mutual support among school staff are two important features of effective schools (Good & Weinstein, 1986). However, not all schools have work environments in which there is equitable treatment of teachers, democratic decision-making processes, a spirit of innovation, and opportunities for the professional development of all teachers. From a goal theory perspective, it is hypothetically possible to describe the work environment of a school as emphasizing competition, social comparison, and differential treatment of teachers (e.g., a performance goal structure); cooperation, equity, and a spirit of innovation (e.g., a mastery goal structure); or to some degree, both.

Data collected from elementary and middle school teachers during the first years of the Patterns of Adaptive Learning Study allowed us to assess the relations between school policies and practices reflective of different goals for students (based on principal reports), teachers' perceptions of the learning and work culture of their school, and teachers' own goal-oriented instructional approaches. Again, both variable-centered correlational analyses and person-centered, cluster analyses were used to examine these relations. We hypothesized that to the extent principals rated their school as performance oriented for students, and to the extent teachers rated their school as performance oriented for teachers, teachers would also report a greater performance orientation in their classroom pedagogy. This prediction is based on our assumption that the school culture both affects teachers' identity beliefs and reflects, in part, how teachers teach in their classrooms. We expected a similar set of relations among the mastery-oriented scales for these same reasons. Results of the partial correlations in which years of teaching was controlled are presented in Table 8.2. The number of cases included in each analysis varies due to the study design (see chap. 1, this volume) and is noted in the table.

By and large, the partial correlational results supported our hypotheses. Teachers at both the elementary and middle school level who were more performance oriented in their approach to classroom instruction also worked in schools where principals reported a greater use of performance-oriented practices and policies, and where there was greater competition among staff and inequitable treatment of teachers by the administration (school performance goal structure for teachers). Similarly, teachers who reported a greater mastery orientation in their approach to instruction also perceived a greater emphasis on innovation and improvement for teachers among the staff and administration and, at the middle school level, had principals who reported slightly more use of mastery-oriented practices and policies. The correlation of principal reports of mastery-oriented practices and teachers' mastery-oriented approaches to instruction was not significant at the elementary level. These findings extend the work of Marachi et al. (2001) in which teachers' goal-oriented instructional approaches were found to be correlated with their perceptions of whether the wider school environment emphasized performance or mastery goals for students.

We also examined the partial correlations between teachers' efficacy beliefs and their perceptions of the work-related goal structures in their school, controlling for their years of teaching. We found that teachers who perceived an emphasis on mastery goals for teachers in their school felt more efficacious—partial r $(263) = .31; p \leq .001$—whereas efficacy was uncorrelated with perceptions of an emphasis on performance goals for teachers. Perhaps this latter, nonsignificant relation reflects the fact that "favored teachers" in performance-oriented work environments feel efficacious, whereas those who are granted less status and attention do not. These remain speculations at this time.

TABLE 8.2

Partial Correlations Between Teachers' Approaches to Instruction, Principals' Reports of School Goal Practices for Students, and Teachers' Perceptions of the School Goal Structure for Teachers

Teachers' Approach to Classroom Instruction	Principal Reports of School-Level Performance Practices for Students	Principal Reports of School-Level Mastery Practices for Students	Teachers' Perceptions School Performance Goal Structure for Teachers	Teachers' Perceptions of School Mastery Goal Structure for Teachers
Performance-Oriented Approach				
Elementary School Teachers	.19**	.04	.27**	.02
(Number of cases)	(167)	(167)	(90)	(90)
Middle School Teachers	.23**	.04	.18*	.00
(Number of cases)	(173)	(173)	(170)	(173)
Mastery-Oriented Approach				
Elementary School Teachers	.10	–.06	–.11	.28**
(Number of cases)	(167)	(167)	(90)	(90)
Middle School Teachers	.00	.18*	.07	.30**
(Number of cases)	(173)	(173)	(170)	(173)

Note. Teachers' years of teaching service are partialed out of these relations. Pairwise deletion of cases used for each analysis; number of cases in each analysis is presented in table. Two-tailed significance tests.
$*p < .05$; $**p < .01$.

In order to complement these variable-centered analyses, we conducted another person-centered analysis. We examined how these objective and subjective reports of the school work environments differed across the five different types of elementary school teachers identified earlier (see Fig. 8.2). Group differences in these measures across types were assessed with ANOVAs and Tukey's HSD comparisons. Results are presented in the lower portion of the table at the bottom of Fig. 8.2. In these analyses, we included teachers' reports of whether they perceived the wider school environment as performance oriented or mastery oriented for students.

Results for the performance goal structure scales showed that the high-efficacy, multi-goal-oriented (Type I); high-efficacy, performance-oriented (Type II); and low-efficacy, performance-oriented teachers (Type IV) tended to perceive their school as more performance oriented for both students and teachers compared to those teachers who were less performance oriented (Types III and V). In addition, teachers who were the most performance oriented (Types I and IV) worked in schools where principals reported the greatest use of performance-oriented learning practices, though these were trends rather than statistically significant differences.

Results for the mastery goal structure scales revealed a similar, though less differentiated pattern of results. Teachers who were efficacious and mastery oriented (Type III) perceived their school culture as the most mastery oriented for students and teachers alike compared to the other groups. In contrast, high-efficacy, performance-oriented teachers (Type II) perceived the least emphasis on mastery goals in the school for both students and teachers. No group differences were found in principals' reports of the number of mastery-oriented practices currently in use at the school.

Results from the variable- and person-centered analyses suggest that the school goal structure, both in terms of the school learning culture for students and the school work culture for teachers, is related in conceptually consistent ways with teachers' own instructional approaches in the classroom. To the extent the school culture was characterized by an emphasis on competition and comparison among students and teachers, teachers were more likely to emphasize these things in their classroom instruction; to the extent the school was perceived by teachers as emphasizing mastery and improvement for teachers and students alike, they were more likely to be mastery oriented in their classroom instruction. These results likely reflect the fact that teachers are both shaped by, and contribute to, the kinds of implicit goals that characterize the learning and teaching cultures in their schools. We also found that teachers who worked in schools where they perceived support for innovation and professional development (mastery goal structure) were more likely to feel efficacious. Again, it may be that efficacious teachers tend to perceive their schools more in these ways, that such school cultures actually nurture the development of efficacious teachers, or

both (Bandura, 1993; Good & Weinstein, 1986). Determining issues of causal direction in these findings necessitates further research.

Subject Matter

Subject matter and departmental affiliations are another important context of teachers' work. In fact, teachers' professional identities at the secondary level are often defined almost exclusively in reference to their subject matter (Talbert & McLaughlin, 1993). Studies have linked teachers' subject matter affiliations to their perceptions of students' capacities and their preferences for particular pedagogical approaches. For instance, because the curriculum is more sequential and well defined in math and science than it is in English and social studies, math and science teachers tend to agree more on standards, be concerned more with imparting basic skills, and more strongly endorse the use of ability grouping than do humanities teachers. In contrast, because of the ill-defined nature and lack of sequence in their subject areas, humanities teachers tend to report more autonomy in choosing curricula, agree less on standards, and feel less committed to ability grouping compared to math and science teachers (Stodolsky & Grossman, 1995).

These findings raise the possibility that math and science teachers may be more performance oriented than are English and social studies teachers in that the relative ability of students and a preference for teacher-controlled curriculum where the acquisition of basic skills is central seems to be more likely in these disciplines. On the other hand, English and social studies teachers may be more mastery oriented than are their math and science colleagues given that a focus on effort, improvement, and student autonomy may be easier to enact in classes where the curriculum is not so well defined and highly sequential in nature.

To examine these hypotheses, we compared middle and high school math, science, English, and social studies teachers on their goal-oriented approaches to instruction. A multivariate analysis of variance (MANOVA) was conducted with school level and subject matter as the between-subjects factors, total years teaching as a covariate, and goal-oriented approaches to instruction as the dependent measures. Because school-level differences were described earlier using these samples (see Marachi et al., 2001), we concentrate here on describing subject matter and subject matter by school-level interaction effects that are significant after accounting for the main effects of school level.

Results revealed no differences in teachers' performance approaches to instruction by subject matter and no interaction between subject matter and level. This was contrary to our expectations. On the other hand, we did find an overall

subject matter effect for teachers' mastery approaches to instruction, $F(2, 332) =$ 6.42, $p < .001$, $\eta^2 = .06$. Confirming our predictions, English and social studies teachers were more mastery-oriented than were math and science teachers at both the middle and high school levels. No significant interactions were found. These findings suggest that although teachers of different subject areas may use similar practices reflective of a performance orientation (increasingly so with school level), it is in their emphasis on self-improvement, on providing meaningful activities that connect with students' lives outside of school, and on creativity and enjoyment of learning that humanities teachers differ most from their math and science teacher colleagues at the secondary level.

Student Characteristics

One final, understudied aspect of teachers' work contexts that can influence their identities and pedagogy is the characteristics of the students they teach (Lee et al., 1993). For instance, Solomon, Battistich, and Hom (1996) conducted observational and survey studies with a sample of elementary teachers in 24 urban and suburban schools throughout the United States that served either high- or low-income students. They found that teachers in low-income communities were more likely to endorse the use of extrinsic controls and social comparison, and less likely to encourage student autonomy and interaction than teachers in schools serving higher income populations (see additional discussion of this issue in chap. 7, this volume). They attributed these differences to perceptions of teachers in the low-income districts of their students as lacking the necessary inner controls to regulate their own learning. Bandura (1993) has discussed how the collective efficacy of teachers in schools serving high proportions of poor students can be undermined by the pervasive educational and noneducational needs of such students. Confronted with a certain "critical mass" of high-needs students, many faculty can begin to feel demoralized and unable to counteract the forces that affect their students outside of school.

Few goal theory studies have examined how students affect their teachers. In our own work, we have found that students identified by their fifth-grade elementary teachers as socially withdrawn or rebellious also show motivational and achievement problems (Roeser, Lau, & Midgley, 1999). That is not surprising, but we also found that such students also perceive their classrooms as more performance oriented than do a group of non-nominated controls. Do teachers respond to vulnerable students by using more controlling practices because they view them as lacking the necessary inner resources and controls for learning as Solomon and his colleagues (1996) found? These questions require future research and may provide insights into how the design of classroom environments can potentiate or remediate social-emotional and behavioral problems in the most vulnerable members of a classroom.

LINKING CONTEXT, TEACHERS' IDENTITIES, AND STUDENT MOTIVATION: AN ILLUSTRATION

Perhaps the most comprehensive motivational perspective on schooling is one that connects the contextual antecedents and personal consequences of both teachers' and students' motivation to teach and motivation to learn, respectively. Here we present a single empirical illustration of what such an integration of the models depicted in Figs. 8.1, 8.3, and 8.4 would look like by linking variables assessing the contexts of teaching and teachers' goal orientations with the goal orientations of students. Data collected from fifth-grade elementary school teachers and their students during the first wave of the study were used for purposes of illustration. During this wave, we had data from more than 80% of the students in the elementary school teachers' classrooms. This provided ample numbers of students for such an analysis. Data were collected at the beginning and the end of the 1994–1995 school year. This allowed us to examine the association of teachers' goal-oriented approaches to instruction and students' personal achievement goals after controlling for students' achievement goals and performance at the beginning of the year.

To examine linkages between teacher types and student motivation, we conducted two analyses of covariance (ANCOVAs)—one with students' year-end performance goals as the outcome, and the other with students' year-end mastery goals as the outcome. The between-subjects factors in these analyses were teacher type (see Fig. 8.2) and students' gender. Students' gender was included because previous studies have shown gender differences in students' personal goals, with boys endorsing performance goals more than do girls (Urdan, 1997). Covariates in these analyses included students' grade point average (GPA) and personal achievement goals (performance and mastery) assessed at the beginning of the school year. The outcome measures were assessed at the end of the school year (see chap. 1, this volume, for the research design). Thus, these analyses assess differences in students' personal goals by teacher type at the end of the school year after accounting for students' personal goals and academic achievement at the beginning of the school year. The student rather than the teacher was used as the unit of analysis for this final set of comparisons.

Teacher Types and Students' Performance Goals

Results for students' year-end performance goals revealed several significant effects. First, we found that both prior performance goals—$F(1, 342) = 61.58, p < .001, \eta^2 = .15$—and prior GPA in the core academic subjects—$F(1, 342) = 3.60, p < .059, \eta^2 = .01$—were significantly related to students' year-end performance goals. Both of these factors had significant, positive relations with the outcome.

There was also a main effect by gender showing that boys endorsed performance goals more than did girls, $F(1, 342) = 5.77, p < .05, \eta^2 = .02$. There was no significant effect for teacher type—$F(4, 342) = 0.88, p = .48, \eta^2 = .01$—but we did find a significant gender by teacher type interaction, $F(4, 342) = 2.40, p < .05, \eta^2 = .03$. The nature of this interaction is presented in Fig. 8.5. As one can see, female students' performance goals "tracked" more closely on their teachers' performance orientations compared to those of male students. This was especially true when the teacher tended to emphasize only performance goals (Types II or IV) or mastery goals in their instruction (Types III and V) rather than both. Girls in the former classrooms showed higher performance goals and those in the latter lower performance goals. It may be that female elementary school students are more sensitive than are male students at this age to their teachers' performance-oriented pedagogy, especially if it is the predominant orientation of the teacher. Although our data suggest that girls are more likely to attempt, initially, to mirror their teachers' performance goal orientations in their own motivational strivings during elementary school, we would expect this to be less the case during middle school when such environments are antithetical to adolescents' need for a safe, noncomparative school setting (Dweck & Leggett, 1988). These speculations warrant investigation in future studies.

One other point deserves mention concerning these results. If one integrates the findings presented in Figs. 8.2 and 8.5, one can see that a consistent set of school- and teacher-level variables are associated with female students' performance goals. Recall that teachers characterized as Types II and IV perceived a school goal structure for teachers and students alike that was particularly performance oriented; they worked in schools where the principals reported more use of performance-oriented practices; and they reported the greatest endorsement of performance-oriented approaches to instruction in the classroom themselves. It was in these classrooms in particular that girls also showed the greatest endorsement of performance goals. These findings raise the possibility that such teachers are both affected by and reflect a performance-oriented school culture, and this in turn affects the quality of their female students' motivation to learn in the classroom. However, we want to note that these results should be regarded as preliminary given the small effect size of the teacher by gender interaction and the small number of cases represented by some of the teacher types.

Teacher Types and Students' Mastery Goals

Results for analyses assessing students' year-end mastery goals as the outcome yielded only one significant effect. Students' prior mastery goals—$F(1, 343) = 196.18, p < .001, \eta^2 = .36$—were significantly related to their year-end mastery goals. No significant main effects or interactions involving teacher type and gender were found. These results were unexpected. It may be that scales assessing

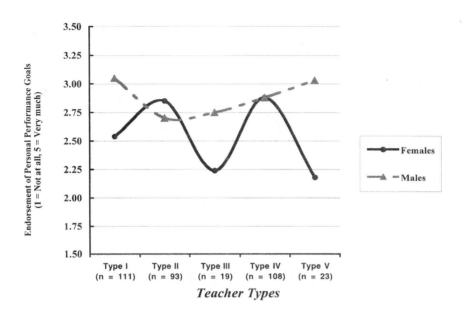

FIG. 8.5.   Interaction of elementary school teacher type and gender for students'
performance goals.

mastery goals in students are more socially desirable than those assessing performance goals and thus prove less fruitful in differentiating different individuals (Roeser et al., 1999).

CONCLUSIONS

Teachers are at the center of efforts to motivate students to learn in school. In
this chapter we outlined how understanding the contexts of teachers' work is
important for understanding their professional identities, their pedagogical
orientations, and thereby their potential influences on student motivation. In
particular, we emphasized the need in motivational research for studies that
adopt a multilevel, embedded contexts view of teachers' work environments—contexts associated with student characteristics, the subject matter,
the school culture, and the level of the institution in which teachers work. We
attempted to illustrate how such a perspective could lead to new insights about
the multilevel factors by which schools can "effect" students' motivation to
learn. Such insights can lead to the identification of "levers for change" at dif-

ferent levels of school systems that then become the logical targets of school reform efforts (Talbert & McLaughlin, 1993).

One set of findings discussed in this chapter that we believe has important implications for school reform was concerned with teachers' perceptions of the work culture in their school. We presented some evidence that when teachers perceived differential treatment of teachers by school leaders and a sense of competitiveness among colleagues, they were also more likely to endorse classroom practices that highlighted competition and ability differences between students. Furthermore, person-centered analyses showed that for some elementary teachers (e.g., Types II and IV), a performance orientation seemed to extend all the way from the school work culture to their pedagogical orientation "down to" the kinds of achievement goals that female students were likely to endorse in their classrooms. These findings underscore how interdependencies between school and classroom cultures may effect students' motivation to learn in the classroom, though the data presented here do not allow us to draw definitive causal inferences. On the other hand, our results showed that when teachers in elementary and middle schools perceived support for innovation and experimentation from school leaders and colleagues, they were more likely to emphasize these things in their own classroom pedagogy and to feel more efficacious as a teacher. Together, these findings underscore the possibility that real change in students' motivation and learning through reform efforts may turn on whether or not a supportive work culture for teachers in which cooperation, innovation, and experimentation are valued exists in a school (Good & Weinstein, 1986; Maehr, 1991; Maehr & Midgley, 1996; Sarason, 1990). Reforms that are most likely to be successful and successfully integrated into the ongoing life of a school are likely those that create a safe, supportive, and motivating climate for teachers and students *alike* (Deci & Ryan, 1985; Sarason, 1990). This is a tall order, and goal theory provides one theoretical framework that can justify and guide such efforts (Maehr & Midgley, 1996).

Another potential set of implications for reform arising from the research reviewed in this chapter may not be obvious at first. It concerns the kinds of teachers and pedagogy that students experience as they move through progressively larger and more anonymous school environments across their development. From a students' perspective, the findings we reviewed and reported on here can be interpreted as a developmental sketch of the kinds of teachers they encounter as they move through the school system. The results suggest that students increasingly encounter teachers who feel less efficacious, who are less inclined to attend to their social-emotional needs, and who increasingly use practices that emphasize social comparison and competition rather than task mastery, improvement, and effort. Such changes may account, in part, for the declines in students' motivation to learn that occur as students move from elementary to middle to high school (e.g., Eccles & Midgley, 1989; Eccles et al.,

1998). Finding ways to reduce teacher work loads by creating teacher teams and schools within schools is one important reform that can create more caring environments for adolescents in middle and high schools. Finding symbolic and communal ways to reward all students around a diversity of abilities rather than just those with superior intellectual performance are also important reform strategies. Providing a learning environment in which teachers can emphasize mastery-oriented messages in their instruction is a third. This would include providing support for teachers in learning how to use alternative assessment strategies (e.g., portfolios), how to teach learning strategies, and how to create developmentally meaningful and challenging curricula.

On more of a research note, we think it is important to acknowledge that the statistical relations between teacher variables and motivational outcomes in students are often small to modest in size. This was true of the findings presented in this chapter. Why might this be the case? Rather than seeing this exclusively as a problem of research methodology and design (which it can be!), we think it is important to explore whether or not this may reflect the reality that both teachers and students, as agentic individuals, do not mechanically adopt and espouse the goals, norms, and values of their social surroundings. Researchers who adopt a goal perspective, including the first author (e.g., Roeser et al., 1996), sometimes depict theoretical models that imply a one-to-one correspondence of goal structures and the personal goals and beliefs individuals adopt in that context. This is too simplistic of an accounting of "school effects" because such models fail to address the agency of individuals to choose to adopt or not to adopt the norms, values, roles, and goals of the settings in which they live, learn, and work (e.g., Deci & Ryan, 1985). Others have discussed this as a persistent "problem" with school reform efforts in that higher level mandates, policies, and practices are not necessarily adopted by teachers and therefore never reach students (Cuban, 1990). Appreciating that modest relations between context variables and teacher or student variables are often as instructive as strong effects is an important goal to keep in mind among those who would attempt to link the contexts of teaching and the contexts of learning with students' motivation. As we discuss later, such modest effects often point to a need to understand those processes that facilitate or undermine such "interlevel" effects within classrooms and schools.

On a more theoretical note, we believe at least three important expansions of goal theory arise from the present discussion. First, we believe that studies within a goal theory tradition could benefit from a broader focus on the multiple contexts in which teaching and learning are embedded. Indeed, if we had broadened our perspective in this chapter even more, we might well have found that performance-oriented demands from "higher up" in the educational hierarchy and out in the community today (e.g., district and state testing requirements, parental pressures for particular types of instruction) are affecting

teachers' pedagogical orientations and students' motivation in important ways (e.g., Ryan & LaGuardia, 1999; Talbert & McLaughlin, 1993).

Second, little attention in goal theory research has been devoted to understanding those processes that explain the conditions under which environmental presses toward different achievement goals eventuate in goal adoption or not among teachers and students. Is it possible that the nature of social relationships that permeate schools may provide some insight into the conditions that facilitate or hinder the adoption of goals, roles, and values among members of the school community? This seems like a real possibility but requires further research (e.g., Deci & Ryan, 1985). Finally, little attention in goal theory research has been given to the consequential effects that the absence of goal structures in classrooms and schools can have on teachers and students alike. It is clear that some of the most debilitating work and learning environments are those in which chaos, rather than any definable goal structure, is the norm. Understanding how the lack of goal structures, in addition to different kinds of goal structures, affects teachers and students is another needed direction in this work.

Future Directions

Future studies linking the contexts of teaching and learning with teachers' identities and students' motivation will require attention to several of the challenging issues just mentioned. We discuss three such issues in more depth here. The first concerns a theory-into-practice problem—how can motivational researchers use theory to directly assist educators in the field as they struggle to make positive changes in their schools? The second concerns a perspectival problem—how to get researchers into the habit of thinking contextually in a manner that matches the complexity of the settings they study. The third is a conceptual problem—how to think about the process of integrating information from multiple sources when studying the contexts of teaching and learning.

The Theory-to-Practice Problem.   Researchers interested in motivational processes and education have long confronted the problem of developing conceptual tools that faithfully capture the complex environments of schools in ways that are also useful to educators. Recent advances in motivational theory generally (Eccles et al., 1998), and in goal theory in particular, have provided a powerful set of conceptual tools that can inform both research and practice (Maehr & Anderman, 1993; Midgley, 1993; Urdan, 1997). Goal theory, for example, provides a means of describing personal motivation and learning environments in congruent terms. The functional utility of an approach that begins with the question: "What are teachers (or students) trying to do in their classrooms?" (e.g., what are their goals?), and then follows up with the question of

"Why are they trying to accomplish that goal?" is clear. Such an approach can both promote reflective practice and potentially explain linkages between teachers' intentions and the actions (or inaction) of their students (Maehr & Midgley, 1996). Though goal theory has proven useful in addressing issues of research and practice (e.g., Urdan, 1997), we want to note here that other motivational theories, including stage–environment fit theory (Eccles & Midgley, 1989) and self-determination theory (Deci & Ryan, 1985) are equally viable approaches in this regard. Both of these theories ask slightly different but related questions such as "What are teachers' (and students') needs?" and "How are the environments we are creating in schools (classrooms) fulfilling or frustrating those needs?" Indeed, it may not really matter which theory is employed to make the theory-into-practice leap as long as the theory can address the complexity of individuals, systems, and the realities of everyday practice in the schools. Though it is hard to know, we suspect that theories, not a particular theory, are what Lewin (1936) thought so eminently useful in addressing practical issues and problems. These three motivational theories seem to be particularly useful in translating theory and research into practice and reform.

A Perspective Problem.   A second issue that deserves attention in future motivational research on teaching and learning concerns perspective. Motivational researchers, in order to address pressing educational issues, must increasingly attend to the multilevel contexts of teaching and learning in their research designs. This is a complex issue and has been labeled the "vertical problem" in research on teaching and public policy (Talbert & McLaughlin, 1993). The question is how to attend to the complex levels of analysis that impinge on the outcome of interest in a study. An initial step in addressing such interlevel effects is for researchers to develop an appreciation for the contexts in which the particular outcome of interest is embedded. For instance, if one studies classrooms and motivation, it may be well to consider in one's research design how school-level policies and practices, community characteristics, and state and federal education mandates affect the classroom and motivational processes that are of focal concern (e.g., Maehr & Midgley, 1991; Talbert & McLaughlin, 1993, 1999).

Another aspect of the vertical problem is how to capture the transactional processes that occur across different contextual levels and that affect teachers' and students' motivation and behavior. The most notable example of such a transaction concerns how teachers and students mutually influence one another in the classroom. At the present time, we know little about, and seem to pay very little attention to, how students shape aspects of their learning environments, including the motivation and instructional practices of their teachers (see Skinner & Belmont, 1993 for an exception). Documenting transactional influences in future studies of the classroom will extend our ability to understand school-related

outcomes for what they really are, a function of transactions between students' personal characteristics, the curriculum, and their teachers and classmates (Sameroff, 1983). Perhaps the easiest way to think through this challenge when designing future studies is to imagine the hypothesized causal flow of the context and outcome variables in reverse.

The Informant Challenge. One final challenge that confronts those of us interested in linking the study of teaching and learning concerns the issue of informants—who is to tell us what the classroom or school environment is "really" like? Should we expect the experiential realities of different parties to cohere? Usually we extol the virtues of triangulating data based on student or teacher perceptions with the use of observations, third-party raters, and so on. But if we accept the etic–emic distinction seriously, then a quest for correspondences rather than "consensual" realities between informants becomes a more realistic goal. Continuing to struggle with how to integrate information from multiple sources, acknowledging that there may not be a so-called objective reality to certain aspects of school environments (e.g., Is this a fair place for teachers? Is the curriculum meaningful?), will remain a challenge in research that attempts to integrate the worlds inhabited and perceived by teachers and the worlds inhabited and perceived by students in school. Thankfully, newer statistical approaches such as hierarchical linear modeling and the use of person-centered techniques such as those employed in this chapter provide some fresh, though still only partial, statistical solutions to these persistent and pressing problems. Arguably, more important than these techniques for firmly establishing the role of motivational research in understanding teaching and learning and guiding school change efforts will be case studies, observational studies, and intervention studies in which "thick" descriptions of actual learning environments are married with multiple sources of data that are collected often and over extended periods of time (e.g., Meece, 1991; see also chap. 9, this volume).

Summary

In sum, we have emphasized throughout this chapter that teachers' professional identities, much like students' motivation, are situated within specific contexts that both affect and reflect them. Furthermore, we have suggested that such identities give direction and focus to teachers' behavioral choices and actions. We reviewed evidence that supports these contentions and have provided some empirical findings that bear on these issues. Our goal has been to promote the idea that attending to teachers' professional identities and the contexts of their work can prove fruitful for understanding more fully the manifold factors that affect students' motivation to learn in school. Such a perspective is necessary, we have argued, for capturing more fully the complex spectrum of

organizational, instructional, and interpersonal processes in schools that, through their influences on teachers, also influence students' motivation to learn. In the end, if we are ever to create learning environments in which students take risks, seek creative solutions to problems, attempt challenging tasks, come to love learning, and help each other in the process, then what we have presented in this chapter suggests the importance of helping educational leaders and teachers to create environments that nurture these same habits of heart and mind among and within themselves.

REFERENCES

Aldenderfer, M. S., & Blashfield, R. K. (1984). *Cluster analysis.* Newbury Park, CA: Sage.

Ames, C. (1990, April). *Achievement goals and classroom structure: Developing a learning orientation.* Paper presented at the annual meeting of the American Educational Research Association, Boston.

Ames, C. (1992a). Achievement goals and the classroom motivational climate. In D. H. Schunk & J. L. Meece (Eds.), *Student perceptions in the classroom* (pp. 327–348). Hillsdale, NJ: Lawrence Erlbaum Associates.

Ames, C. (1992b). Classrooms: Goals, structures, and student motivation. *Journal of Educational Psychology, 84,* 261–271.

Ashton, P. (1985). Motivation and the teacher's sense of efficacy. In C. Ames & R. Ames (Eds.), *Research on motivation in education: Vol. 2. The classroom milieu* (pp. 141–171). Orlando, FL: Academic Press.

Bandura, A. (1993). Perceived self-efficacy in cognitive development and functioning. *Educational Psychologist, 28,* 117–148.

Brophy, J. (1985). Teachers' expectations, motives, and goals for working with problem students. In C. Ames & R. Ames (Eds.), *Research on motivation in education: Vol. 2. The classroom milieu* (pp. 175–213). New York: Academic Press.

Connell, J. P., Spencer, M. B., & Aber, J. L. (1994). Education risk and resilience in African-American youth: Context, self, action, and outcomes in school. *Child Development, 65,* 493–506.

Cuban, L. (1990). Reforming again, again, and again. *Educational Researcher, 19,* 3–13.

Deci, E., & Ryan, R. (1985). *Intrinsic motivation and self-determination in human behavior.* New York: Academic Press.

Dweck, C. S. (1992). The study of goals in psychology. *Psychological Science, 3,* 165–166.

Dweck, C. S., & Leggett, E. (1988). A social-cognitive approach to motivation and personality. *Psychological Review, 95,* 256–273.

Eccles, J. S. (1983). Expectancies, values and academic behaviors. In J. T. Spence (Ed.), *The development of achievement motivation* (pp. 283–331). Greenwich, CT: JAI.

Eccles, J. S., & Midgley, C. (1989). Stage–environment fit: Developmentally appropriate classrooms for young adolescents. In C. Ames & R. Ames (Eds.), *Research on motivation in education: Vol. 3, Goals and cognitions* (pp. 13–44). New York: Academic Press.

Eccles, J. S., & Roeser, R. W. (1999). School and community influences on human development. In M. H. Boorstein & M. E. Lamb (Eds.), *Developmental psychology: An advanced textbook* (2nd ed., pp. 503–554). Hillsdale, NJ: Lawrence Erlbaum Associates.

Eccles, J. S., Wigfield, A., & Schiefele, U. (1998). Motivation. In N. Eisenberg (Ed.), *Handbook of child psychology* (Vol. 3, 5th ed., pp. 1017–1095). New York: Wiley.

Ford, M. E. (1992). *Motivating humans: Goals, emotions, and personal agency beliefs.* Newbury Park, CA: Sage.

Fuller, B., & Izu, J. (1986). Explaining school cohesion: What shapes the organizational beliefs of teachers. *American Journal of Education, 94,* 501–535.

Good, T. L. (2000). Introduction to the special issue on non-subject matter outcomes of schooling. *Elementary School Journal, 100,* 405–408.

Good, T. L., & Weinstein, R. S. (1986). Schools make a difference: Evidence, Criticisms, and New Directions. *American Psychologist, 41,* 1090–1097.

Kaplan, A., Gheen, M., & Midgley, C. (2001). *Individual and classroom level predictors of disruptive behavior in the classroom.* Manuscript under review.

Lee, V. E., Bryk, A. S., & Smith, J. B. (1993). The organization of effective secondary schools. In L. Darling-Hammond (Ed.), *Review of research in education* (Vol. 19, pp. 171–267). Washington, DC: American Educational Research Association.

Lewin, K. (1936). *Principles of a topological psychology.* New York: McGraw-Hill.

Maehr, M. L. (1991). The "psychological environment" of the school: A focus for school leadership. In P. Thurstone & P. Zodhiates (Eds.), *Advances in educational administration* (Vol. 2, pp. 51–81). Greenwich, CT: JAI.

Maehr, M. L., & Anderman, E. M. (1993). Reinventing schools for early adolescents: Emphasizing task goals. *Elementary School Journal, 93,* 593–610.

Maehr, M. L., & Buck, R. (1993). Transforming school culture. In M. Sashkin & H. Walberg (Eds.), *Educational leadership and school culture* (pp. 40–57). Berkeley, CA: McCutchan.

Maehr, M. L., & Fyans, L. J., Jr. (1989). School culture, motivation, and achievement. In M. L. Maehr & C. Ames (Eds.), *Advances in motivation and achievement* (Vol. 6, pp. 215–247). Greenwich, CT: JAI.

Maehr, M. L., & Midgley, C. (1991). Enhancing student motivation: A school-wide approach. *Educational Psychologist, 26,* 399–427.

Maehr, M. L., & Midgley, C. (1996). *Transforming school cultures to enhance student motivation and learning.* Boulder, CO: Westview Press.

Magnusson, D., & Bergman, L. R. (1988). Individual and variable-based approaches to longitudinal research on early risk factors. In M. Rutter (Ed.), *Studies of psychosocial risk: The power of longitudinal data* (pp. 45–61). New York: Cambridge University Press.

Marachi, R., Gheen, M. H., & Midgley, C. (2001). *An examination of elementary, middle, and high school teachers' beliefs and approaches to instruction using a goal theory framework.* Manuscript under review.

Meece, J. L. (1991). The classroom context and students' motivational goals. In M. L. Maehr & P. Pintrich (Eds.), *Advances in motivation and achievement: Vol. 7,* (pp. 261–285). Greenwich, CT: JAI.

Midgley, C. (1993). Motivation and middle level schools. In M. L. Maehr & P. Pintrich (Eds.), *Advances in motivation and achievement: Vol. 7, Motivation and adolescent development* (pp. 217–274). Greenwich, CT: JAI.

Midgley, C., Anderman, E., & Hicks, L. (1995). Differences between elementary and middle school teachers and students: A goal theory approach. *Journal of Early Adolescence, 15,* 90–113.

Midgley, C., Feldlaufer, H., & Eccles, J. S. (1989). Change in teacher efficacy and student self- and task-related beliefs during the transition to junior high school. *Journal of Educational Psychology, 81,* 247–258.

Midgley, C., Maehr, M. L., Hruda, L. Z., Anderman, E., Anderman, L., Freeman, K. E., Gheen, M., Kaplan, A., Kumar, R., Middleton, M. J., Nelson, J., Roeser, R., & Urdan, T. (2000). *Manual for the Patterns of Adaptive Learning Scales (PALS)*. Ann Arbor: University of Michigan.

Oakes, J., Gamoran, A., & Page, R. N. (1992). Curriculum differentiation: Opportunities, outcomes, and meanings. In P. Jackson (Ed.), *Handbook of research on curriculum* (pp. 570–608). New York: Macmillan.

Roeser, R. W., Lau, S., & Midgley, C. M. (1999, April). *On studying academic motivation and mental health in early adolescents: Individual and contextual-level processes.* Paper presented as part of a symposium at the biennial meeting of the European Association for Research on Learning and Instruction, Gotenburg, Sweden.

Roeser, R. W., & Midgley, C. (1997). Teachers' views of issues involving students' mental health. *Elementary School Journal, 98,* 115–133.

Roeser, R. W., Midgley, C. M., & Urdan, T. C. (1996). Perceptions of the school psychological environment and early adolescents' psychological and behavioral functioning in school: The mediating role of goals and belonging. *Journal of Educational Psychology, 88,* 408–422.

Ryan, R. M., & La Guardia, J. (1999). Achievement motivation within a pressured society: Intrinsic and extrinsic motivations to learn and the politics of school reform. In T. Urdan (Ed.), *Advances in motivation and achievement: Vol. 11. The role of context* (pp. 45–85). Stamford, CT: JAI.

Sameroff, A. (1983). Developmental systems: Contexts and evolution. In W. Kessen (Ed.), *Handbook of child psychology* (Vol. 1, pp. 237–294). New York: Wiley.

Sarason, S. (1990). *The predictable failure of educational reform.* San Francisco: Jossey-Bass.

Shulman, L. S. (1986). Those who understand: Knowledge growth in teaching. *Educational Researcher, 15,* 4–14.

Skinner, E. A., & Belmont, M. J. (1993). Motivation in the classroom: Reciprocal effects of teacher behavior and student engagement across the school year. *Journal of Educational Psychology, 85,* 571–581.

Smith, M. L. (1991). Put to the test: The effects of external testing on teachers. *Educational Researchers, 20,* 8–11.

Solomon, D., Battistich, V., & Hom, A. (1996). Teacher beliefs and practices in schools serving communities that differ in socioeconomic level. *Journal of Experimental Education, 64,* 327–347.

Stodolsky, S. S., & Grossman, P. L. (1995). The impact of subject matter on curricular activity: An analysis of five academic subjects. *American Educational Research Journal, 32,* 227–249.

Talbert, J. E., & McLaughlin, M. W. (1993). Understanding teaching in context. In D. Cohen, M. W. McLaughlin, & J. E. Talbert (Eds.), *Teaching for understanding: Challenges for policy and practice* (pp. 167–206). San Francisco: Jossey-Bass.

Talbert, J. E., & McLaughlin, M. W. (1999). Assessing the school environment: Embedded contexts and bottom-up research strategies. In S. L. Friedman & T. D. Wachs (Eds.), *Measuring environment across the life span: Emerging methods and concepts* (pp. 197–227). Washington, DC: American Psychological Association.

Tschannen-Moran, M., Woolfolk-Hoy, A., & Hoy, W. (1998). Teacher efficacy: Its meaning and measure. *Review of Educational Research, 68,* 202–248.

Urdan, T. (1997). Achievement goal theory: Past results, future directions. In P. R. Pintrich & M. L. Maehr (Eds.), *Advances in motivation and achievement: Vol. 10* (pp. 99–142). Greenwich, CT: JAI.

Urdan, T., Midgley, C., & Anderman, E. (1998). The role of classroom goal structure in students' use of self-handicapping strategies. *American Educational Research Journal, 35,* 101–122.

APPENDIX

Teachers' Performance-Oriented
Approach to Classroom Instruction

In my classroom:

I display the work of the highest achieving students as an example.

I help students understand how their performance compares to others.

I point out those students who do well academically as a model for the other students.

I encourage students to compete with each other academically.

Teachers' Mastery-Oriented
Approach to Classroom Instruction

In my classroom:

I make a special effort to give my students work that is creative and imaginative.

I stress to students that I want them to understand the work, not just memorize it.

I frequently tell my students that I want them to enjoy learning.

I make a special effort to give my students work that has meaning in their everyday lives.

Teachers' Personal Teaching Efficacy

Some students are not going to make a lot of progress this year, no matter what I do (reversed).

There is little I can do to ensure that all my students make significant progress this year (reversed).

I can deal with almost any learning problem.

If I try really hard, I can get through to even the most difficult student.

I am good at helping all the students in my classes make significant improvement.

Factors beyond my control have a greater influence on my students' achievement than I do (reversed).

Teachers' Perceptions of their
Role in Students' Mental Health

I believe I must be both a teacher and a counselor to my students.

My primary role is to teach students, not to attend to their feelings and emotions (reversed).

I cannot teach my students effectively unless I also consider their social and emotional needs.

I play an important role not only in my students' learning, but also in the way they feel about themselves and life in general.

I frequently think about my students' mental health and well-being.

Teachers' Perceptions of a School Performance
Goal Structure for Students

In this school:

Students hear a lot about the importance of making the honor roll or being recognized at honor assemblies.

Students are encouraged to compete with each other academically.

Students hear a lot about the importance of getting high test scores.

Students who get good grades are pointed out as an example to others.

Teachers' Perceptions of a School Mastery
Goal Structure for Students

In this school:

Students are frequently told that learning should be fun.

A lot of the work students do is boring and repetitious (reversed).

Students are told that making mistakes is OK as long as they are learning and improving.

The emphasis is on really understanding schoolwork, not just memorizing it.

The importance of trying hard is really stressed to students.

A real effort is made to show students how the work they do in school is related to their lives outside of school.

Teachers' Reports of a School
Performance Goal Structure for Teachers

Some teachers have more influence than other teachers.

The administration shows favoritism to some teachers.

Some teachers have greater access to resources than others.
Teachers compete with one another.
Teachers try to outdo each other.
Power and influence count a lot around this school.
The administration actively encourages competition among teachers.

Teachers' Reports of a School
Mastery Goal Structure for Teachers

This school makes teachers want to work hard.
Teachers have many opportunities to learn new things.
If someone has a good idea or project, the administration in this school listens and supports it.
The administration is always working to improve teaching.
This school supports instructional innovations.
Practical restraints severely limit teachers' ability to implement new ideas (reversed).

9

Observing Classroom Goal Structures to Clarify and Expand Goal Theory

Lynley H. Anderman
University of Kentucky

Helen Patrick
Northern Illinois University

Ludmila Z. Hruda
University of Michigan

Elizabeth A. Linnenbrink
University of Michigan

Survey research on personal goal orientations and classroom goal structures has been important in showing associations between academic goals and a wide range of achievement-related outcomes. Little is known, however, about what specific teacher behaviors and characteristics actually influence their students' perceptions of the goal structures that are emphasized in the classroom. In this chapter we outline an observational project that was developed within the larger, survey-based Patterns of Adaptive Learning Study. The aim of this project was to investigate variations in teachers' instruction and management in relation to students' perceptions of various aspects of the classroom environment, particularly classroom goal structures. We present briefly the development of an instrument to guide these observations, and then review three studies that came from the observation data collected. We conclude by discuss-

ing implications of our findings for both goal theory and practice, in terms of teaching and teacher education.

As discussed in other chapters, a growing body of research emphasizes the importance of students' personal goal orientations in relation to a number of important achievement-related outcomes. Furthermore, one of the strengths of goal orientation theory in understanding student motivation is that it explicitly considers the role of teachers and instructional contexts in shaping students' personal goal orientations. That is, a central tenet of goal theory is that students' adoption of personal goals is influenced, at least in part, by the goal structures present in and promoted by the classroom and broader school environments within which they work (e.g., E. M. Anderman & Maehr, 1994). Recently, there has been a growing call for research in educational psychology in general, and in motivation specifically, to consider the role of context in shaping individuals' cognitions and affect (L. H. Anderman & E. M. Anderman, 2000; Blumenfeld, 1992). Thus, understanding the interplay between characteristics of a particular instructional setting, and students' achievement-related perceptions and beliefs is an important direction for motivational research.

Typically, classroom goal structures have been assessed by measuring students' perceptions of the motivational environments of their classrooms (see chap. 2, this volume). That is, students are asked the extent to which they perceive mastery and performance-related purposes and values as being characteristic of their class instructional environment. For example, items might ask about the extent to which effort is valued, whether mistakes are "okay as long as you are learning," and whether the teacher tells students how they compare with each other (see the *Manual for the Patterns of Adaptive Learning Scales* on the Web at http://www.umich.edu/~pals/). Whereas this method has been shown to provide measures of students' perceptions that are psychometrically robust and that predict theoretically related outcomes (e.g., L. H. Anderman & E. M. Anderman, 1999; E. M. Anderman & Young, 1994; Urdan, Midgley, & E. M. Anderman, 1998), it does not describe particular instructional practices and teacher–student relational characteristics that are fundamental to shaping those perceptions.

In contrast, earlier studies of achievement goals did specify various classroom instructional practices as making different types of goals salient and, consequently, eliciting different patterns of motivation (e.g., C. Ames, 1992b; E. M. Anderman & Maehr, 1994; Maehr & Midgley, 1991). C. Ames (1992a) outlined particular classroom structures that can make different achievement goals salient. Drawing on a large literature on classroom motivational environments (e.g., Marshall & Weinstein, 1984; Meece, 1991; Rosenholtz & Rosenholtz, 1981; Stipek & Daniels, 1988), Ames focused on six categories that contribute to the classroom motivational environment. These categories, represented by the acronym TARGET and described originally by Epstein (1983), include task, au-

thority, recognition, grouping, evaluation, and time. This framework has been utilized and adapted by other goal theorists working within classroom and school contexts (e.g., Maehr & Anderman, 1993; Midgley, 1993). Furthermore, the importance of some of these dimensions has been supported by experimental studies (e.g., C. Ames & R. Ames, 1981; Butler, 1987; Covington & Omelich, 1984; Elliott & Dweck, 1988; Jagacinski & Nicholls, 1984) that have demonstrated that different personal goal orientations can be induced by manipulating factors such as levels of interpersonal competition, self- or norm-referenced standards of evaluation, or providing retest opportunities.

Despite the apparent utility of this list of classroom practices, however, very few studies have examined specific practices in relation to students' perceptions of goal structures in the ecology of the regular classroom. There is a need for clarification in terms of which teacher behaviors and classroom structures are most important in influencing students' perceptions and personal goal orientations. For example, as noted by Blumenfeld (1992), we need to know the range of typical practice within each of the TARGET categories. In terms of informing practice, we also need to know "how much is enough?". That is, will even a small amount of student autonomy pay large dividends in terms of student motivation? How can teachers provide flexibility in task content and the use of time, within the sometimes-rigid policies of their schools and districts? In addition, describing practice may include questions about "how" as well as "how much." That is, there may be qualitative differences in the way in which, for example, rewards or social comparison information are utilized in classrooms. Another important question for both theory and practice is whether instructional categories interact in important ways to either bolster or counteract one another. For example, if a teacher provides interesting and relevant tasks but then assesses students solely in comparative terms, does the effect of the latter "wipe out" the effects of the former? Finally, there is the question of whether the categories included in TARGET are the only, or the most important characteristics of classrooms in terms of shaping goal structures. Are there other aspects of the instructional context of classrooms that also need to be considered in creating an adaptive motivational environment? Answering such questions requires a range of methodological approaches, particularly those that can provide a richer description of teachers' actual practices in relation to students' perceptions.

OBSERVATIONAL STUDIES OF CLASSROOM MOTIVATIONAL CLIMATE

Early studies of classroom climate and of teacher behaviors in relation to student learning often utilized observational methodologies (e.g., Brophy & Evertson, 1987; Flanders, 1970; Stallings, 1975). As cognitive perspectives have come to dominate the field, however, and emphasis has been placed on

students' *perceptions* of classroom events, self-report methods have been used increasingly. Few studies of students' motivation have incorporated both classroom observations and students' self-reported motivational characteristics. Exceptions include Blumenfeld, Puro, and Mergendoller (1992), Meece (1991), Marshall and Weinstein (1986), and Feldlaufer, Midgley, and Eccles (1988); for a review of studies in this area see Turner and Meyer (2000). Even fewer observational studies have been framed in terms of achievement goal theory. One example of such work, however, was conducted by Meece (1991).

Meece's (1991) study combined survey and observational methodologies in examining fifth- and sixth-grade science classrooms taught by teachers who had been identified by their principal as exemplary. Using student survey data, Meece found that students in 2 of her 10 classes, on average, had a stronger personal mastery goal orientation than did students in 2 other classes. She then utilized observational data from those classrooms to identify differences in teacher practices between these two kinds of classrooms. She found little variation among classrooms in terms of the cognitive demands made on students or in teachers' questioning patterns, however the classes did vary in other instructional characteristics. Students whose teachers used an active instructional approach, adapted instruction to the developmental levels and personal interests of their students, supported student autonomy and peer collaboration, and emphasized the intrinsic value of learning adopted a greater personal mastery goal orientation than did those whose teachers did not. Meece's study clearly demonstrated that differences in teachers' instructional practices were indeed associated with students' endorsement of personal mastery goals. In addition to these findings, however, there is a need to understand the explicit and implicit ways in which teachers create a mastery and/or performance goal structure in their classrooms. It also is important to understand the ways in which classroom motivational climate is constructed at the beginning of the school year and the extent to which this is stable or can be modified as the year progresses. For the purposes of expanding and refining goal theory, it may also be important to consider social-relational dimensions of the classroom and their impact on students' motivation (Blumenfeld, 1992).

Thus, the aim of our observational project was to clarify and expand goal orientation theory by examining variations in teachers' instruction and management practices, particularly in terms of communicating goal structures, and to relate those practices to students' survey reports of their classroom's mastery and performance goal structures.

DESCRIPTION OF OBSERVATIONAL PROJECT

The major question guiding our observational project centered around understanding and describing the ways in which teachers emphasized mastery

and/or performance goals in their classrooms. That is, we examined the associations between teachers' behaviors and practices and their students' perceptions of the goal structure of their classes. We were interested, in particular, in how classroom goal structures, or the overall motivational climate, were established at the beginning of the school year. Our goal was to provide rich, detailed descriptions of teacher and student classroom behaviors related to classroom goal structures, and to examine variations in classroom practices that were related to students' perceptions of different goal emphases.

Two methodological issues were particularly important during the design phase of this project. First, we needed to use mixed methods so that we could link students' perceptions of their classroom environment to direct observations made in that setting. Second, we decided to use a narrative system for observation rather than checklists or other low-inference systems (see Turner & Meyer, 2000, for discussion of these issues). This approach was appropriate to our aims of providing a rich description of typical classroom practices as well as allowing us to consider dimensions beyond those usually included in goal orientation theory.

Development of OPAL

To systematize data collection we developed an observational protocol that became known as Observing Patterns of Adaptive Learning (OPAL; Patrick et al., 1997). This protocol was designed for use by nonparticipant observers making narrative running records of teacher and student behavior during regular classroom instruction. In addition to being grounded in goal orientation theory, the protocol was guided by theories and research on social-cognitive views of learning strategies, social relationships and classroom interactions, and help seeking and help giving in the classroom.

The observation protocol was developed and piloted before data collection began, during the period when observers were being trained. We wrote a list of questions that referred to eight categories that we believed might provide an important focus for our observations: the six TARGET categories, the social-relational context, and help seeking in the classroom. These questions served as a guide during the development of the protocol. We piloted iterative versions of the protocol, first with videotapes of middle-grade classrooms and later in summer school. During data collection we wrote continuous running records recording details about behaviors and speech that related to the following classroom features: the nature of tasks; the locus of authority in the classroom; methods of recognition, grouping, and evaluation; the use of time, social interactions, and students' approaches to seeking help when needed. Because we were interested in the communication of goal structures to the class as a

whole, our primary focus was on the teacher and his or her comments and behaviors. However, observers also recorded students' behaviors and comments, to the extent that they illuminated the interpretation of the motivational climate. More extensive details of the development of OPAL and training of observers are outlined in Patrick, L. H. Anderman, A. M. Ryan, Edelin, and Midgley (2001).

We experimented with two different data reduction and analytic methods for the running records. Both involved generating themes, then coding records according to those themes, and summarizing data across classrooms (Miles & Huberman, 1994). One approach was to use the computer program HyperResearch (Hesse-Biber, Kinder, Dupis, Dupis, & Tornabene, 1994) to code the running records. The codes used with this program were developed during extensive group discussions, and related closely to the OPAL categories but were more highly differentiated. The second approach was to pencil code the running records, then create data matrices, and summarize and stack those matrices into a meta-matrix.

Project Design

Participating Classrooms.   We conducted observations in 10 fifth-grade classrooms in two school districts in southeastern Michigan. All six fifth-grade teachers at the three elementary schools in one school district participated. In the second district we randomly selected two fifth-grade teachers from each of the two schools identified by the district superintendent as being the most economically and ethnically diverse.

Procedures.   Research on other aspects of classroom climate has indicated that classroom norms and practices tend to become established relatively early in the school year and then remain quite stable (Deci, Schwartz, Sheinman, & R. M. Ryan, 1981; Evertson & Emmer, 1982). Thus, we reasoned that instructional practices established during the early part of the school year would be especially salient in contributing to the motivational climate of the classroom. We also believed that teachers would be most likely to make explicit statements about the meaning and purpose of academic tasks and achievement at the beginning of the school year. Given these assumptions, we arranged to observe classrooms for the entire morning on each of the first 3 days of the school year. We then observed in each classroom for an additional five sessions, spread throughout the remainder of the first 3 weeks of classes. Each of these sessions lasted for 90 minutes and included math and/or language arts lessons. Other subject areas were observed if they were scheduled during our visits. Finally, we conducted three additional 90-minute observation sessions in each classroom within a 1-week period, during the spring semester. These observa-

tions were conducted to assess the extent to which teachers' practices were stable or changed during the school year.

Study 1: Case Studies of Teachers Communicating Classroom Goal Orientations

The first study (Patrick et al., 2001) addressed our initial goal of linking rich descriptions of teacher practices and student behavior to students' perceptions of the classroom goal structure. We therefore used students' survey data from the larger project to select 4 classrooms from the original 10 for more detailed analysis using the observational data. Using analyses of variance, we compared the 10 classes in terms of students' perceptions of the mastery and performance goal structures in their classes, for both fall and spring semesters. Post-hoc tests allowed us to identify four classrooms with significantly different motivational environments: high mastery and low performance, low mastery and high performance, high mastery and high performance, and low mastery and low performance. These classrooms did not necessarily represent the most extreme perceptions of these goal structures but they met our criteria of (a) demonstrating significant differences between the two classrooms high and low in each goal structure, but no significant differences between those in the same category, and (b) demonstrating a consistent pattern in both fall and spring data. We then analyzed the observational data to identify commonalities and differences in teacher behaviors and instructional practices (see Patrick et al. for a detailed description of the classrooms and analysis methodology).

Summary of Findings

In the published paper we presented detailed descriptions of teachers' practices according to each of the OPAL categories. This enabled us to show an explicit "paper trail," from our observation protocol, through the extensive coded data matrices and summary meta-matrix, to our findings. However, by laying out the data so carefully for each category, we felt we lost somewhat the holistic, interconnected portrayal of the classrooms. Therefore, in this chapter we take a different focus by presenting the more holistic themes we identified that differentiated between the motivational environments. Readers interested in findings specific to the different observational categories are referred to the published paper.

There were similarities across all four classrooms. For example, all teachers used rewards. These included giving out candy, pencils, or homework passes to excuse the student from doing a homework assignment, identifying a student each week as a "Super Citizen," and giving students special tasks and responsi-

bilities. Further, the practice of making individual students' performance public within the classroom was not in itself related to the classroom goal structures as perceived by the students. For example, the two low-performance-focused teachers posted students' homework grades on the board, asked students to raise their hands to indicate whether or not they understood the lesson, and read students' grades aloud. The two high-performance-focused teachers also made students' performance public and read their work aloud. In light of common recommendations against such practices, these findings were surprising to us. It may be that making students' performance public is so ubiquitous in students' experience of schooling that such events are not especially salient in shaping their perceptions of the goal structures in a particular class.

Interestingly, there were considerable differences between the high- and low-mastery-focused classrooms, and many fewer differences between the high- and low-performance-focused classrooms. Looking across these differences, we identified two clear themes that distinguished the high- and low-mastery-focused teachers. We present these themes next, with examples from the case studies.

Theme 1: Teachers' Implicit Theories of How Students Learn.
One general theme that differentiated between the classrooms perceived by students to be high and low in the emphasis on mastery goals was the teachers' apparent theories of how students learn. Each teacher made explicit statements to students that indicated his or her beliefs about learning. In addition, their actual practices were consistent with these stated beliefs, including behaviors and comments about the role of mistakes, class participation structures, interaction patterns among students, seatwork procedures, informal evaluation, and recognition practices.

The two teachers who were perceived as being low-mastery-focused (Ms. Peters and Mr. Laurey) made statements consistent with a transmission model of learning. For them, learning appeared to be viewed as an individual process that is achieved by listening to information given by the teacher and doing what they are told. For example, the importance of listening and following directions was evident when Ms. Peters told the class on the first day:

> "Learning, understanding and following instructions—that's basically what fifth grade will be for you this year. Understanding and following rules. Understanding and following rules ... My goals as a teacher are that you are to listen [she writes "Listen" on the board] and follow directions [writes "Follow directions" on the board]. If you understand what I'm saying to you and you follow what I'm telling you, you will be a high-achiever. There's no way around it. How do you understand? One way is by what?" A few students respond with, "Listening" and she replies, "Listening."

A few days later Ms. Peters also seemed to suggest that experience, though another route to learning, is not usually as good as being told. She said to her class:

"It seems like learning and listening may come hand in hand. Can learning come without listening?" Some students called out in response, "No." Ms. Peters countered with, "Yes, we can learn something without listening but it's not always the best way to learn." She elaborated by giving an example of a person riding a bike through a stop sign without stopping and said, "We can learn from experience but it's not always pleasant."

With regard to teacher talk about tasks, neither of the low-mastery-focused teachers made comments about the students' level of understanding or asked them to give reasons for their answers. Rather, Ms. Peters seemed most interested in students' mistakes, whereas Mr. Laurey's comments typically expressed his desire that students got the answer correct. These teachers' statements and behaviors about students' mistakes and perfect performance seemed to reflect their apparent views about learning. If learning is believed to involve a relatively uncomplicated transmission of knowledge from the teacher to the student, then errors generally indicate deficiencies either in ability or in effort-related factors such as paying attention or following directions. In addition, Mr. Laurey frequently made statements that indicated a belief that mistakes would be upsetting for the students. He frequently encouraged students to work slowly, not to "get tricked," and to focus on getting answers correct. He also tended to take away challenges, reduce pressure, and encourage students not to expend full effort, perhaps to ensure they could work error-free. For example, during a math lesson he said, "I am not expecting a perfect paper. I am happy with about half. Don't put pressure on yourself." Similarly, during a language arts lesson he told the class he only wanted them to write notes and not perfect sentences, to which some students responded by crumpling up their papers and starting over.

The low-mastery-focused teachers' practices and statements about participation and interaction, help seeking, informal evaluation, and recognition also were consistent with their apparent beliefs that learning is an individual activity, best achieved by listening and following directions. From the procedures they established about students' verbal participation in lessons, the teachers did not seem to consider student talk during lessons to be potentially helpful to learning. For example, on the second day Mr. Laurey assured students he would only have volunteers answer questions, saying, "I don't want you to worry that I am going to call on you." The only time he was observed to call on a student who had not volunteered, he gave her an excuse for not participating. He said, "Do you want to try or are you still waking up like me?" She declined to give an answer. Ms. Peters discouraged students' talk during her instruction. Rather than student participation being viewed positively, Ms. Peters used calling on students to answer questions as a punishment for not paying attention. For example, on the first day of school she told the class that if she found they were not paying attention, then she would call on them to answer a question.

She later warned Chenise, "Remember to pay attention because I will call on you at any time," and said to the class, "That means if I call your name, you know you probably were not paying attention."

There was very little interaction among students during seatwork in either of the low-mastery-focused classes. The individual nature of learning was underscored when both teachers actively encouraged students to keep their work covered and not to look at others' papers during regular class tasks. Students were admonished not to get or "steal" ideas from one another. The teachers' practices relevant to student help seeking also were consistent with a view that learning is individually situated, and that access to others is not necessary. Both teachers were available to answer students' questions only at designated times during the day. Although students in Ms. Peters' class were allowed to ask a classmate if they had a work-related question, they could ask only one specific peer—their "buddy" who was designated by the teacher. Her explanation of the purpose of buddy pairings revealed that she expected students' questions to be largely procedural; their questions would be about what they were supposed to be doing. Therefore all information sources would be equally useful.

The student behaviors the teachers monitored in class, and the behaviors they recognized students for, were consistent with the high importance they placed on following directions and doing what they were told. Mr. Laurey directed praise almost exclusively toward students who adhered to procedural requests and exhibited social responsibility norms, and it appeared to serve primarily a management function. Ms. Peters' recognition practices also tended to focus on procedural issues rather than the task. Instead of praising behavior that conformed to her expectations, she tended to use punishment or threats of punishment with students who did not do what they were told. For example, she made comments to the class such as, "Ms. Peters has her way of treating certain people who follow directions. I also have a way of treating those who don't."

In contrast to the two low-mastery-focused teachers, the two high-mastery-focused teachers (Ms. Miller and Ms. Hillman) spoke about learning as an active process that requires student involvement; that understanding, rather than memorization and replication, is important; and that interaction is a key feature. There was acknowledgment of more than passive transmission when Ms. Miller said to her class, "There are three ways to learn: from seeing, hearing, doing. I will try to use all of those ways." Ms. Hillman, too, advocated active views of learning. For example, she told the class, "I don't have a problem when you talk. You are learning while you are discussing." Later she said to a student who was writing in his journal, "You've got to think, be creative, use your mind. You get ideas from meeting people, talking to your peers. Don't stay cooped up in your little box. Use your judgment."

These teachers focused on student understanding and improvement considerably more than on getting the answer correct. Unlike the low-mastery-focused teachers, both Ms. Miller and Ms. Hillman mentioned repeatedly that mistakes are a natural part of the learning process. For example, Ms. Hillman said to her class, "You have to practice. It is OK if you make mistakes, if you are learning. And soon you are going to have a fantastic handwriting." This was in contrast to the more summative notion of errors that the low-mastery-focused teachers appeared to hold. Both teachers also seemed to take a rather matter-of-fact approach to student errors, identifying them but not responding as if they were an indicator of ability or effort. This was evident also when they gave students feedback about how to improve their work. For example, during journal writing Ms. Hillman said to a boy, "This is one very long sentence. Can you rewrite this so you don't have one long sentence? Have you ever in your life read a book that had a sentence that long? I don't think so." She then told him to rewrite that portion, breaking the sentence into shorter sentences by using periods. The conversation was supportive, constructive, and mastery focused, and did not imply that either his effort or ability was lacking.

The high-mastery-focused teachers' practices and statements about participation and interaction, informal evaluation, and recognition also were consistent with their apparent views about active learning. It appeared important to both teachers that all students participated actively in classroom talk and academic activities. In these classrooms anyone could have been called on to answer. Students who answered questions were not limited to volunteers or to those not paying attention, as in the low-mastery-focused classrooms. In Ms. Miller's class, equal student participation was established by her procedure of assigning each student a number, and then drawing numbers from a basket to determine who would answer questions (this same procedure was used also for nonacademic tasks, such as selecting crossing monitors). Ms. Hillman routinely called on students to participate, and called on many different students.

Both high-mastery-focused teachers allowed students to talk among themselves during seatwork. In fact, as noted previously, Ms. Hillman actively encouraged students to interact with each other, although she insisted that their conversations be focused on the task in hand. Ms. Miller also encouraged students to help each other: "When we are in [math] groups, your group members can help. We are all here to help one another. It does not bother me at all if you ask your neighbor for help when we are in groups."

In addition to these teachers allowing or encouraging students to view each other as resources, both teachers made explicit comments about their own availability to help students understand the content. For example, Ms. Miller said to her class, "Math is an essential part of life. I want you to get math. Don't ever hesitate to ask me for help"; and, "I love to answer questions. Don't let me get paid for standing here and doing nothing. Don't hold your questions." Fur-

ther, we did not observe any instance when either teacher was unavailable to answer questions, as was the case with the low-mastery-focused teachers.

The strong emphasis on task content and students' understanding of the material, rather than on procedures, was evident also by the way in which the high-mastery-focused teachers monitored their students when working, and by the ways in which students were recognized. For example, Ms. Hillman said, "Chris, are you talking spelling? I hear some neat things going on, but some are not on task." While her students were working individually on math problems Ms. Miller said, "Let me come around and see if you all have got the concept."

Theme 2: The Interface of Social, Affective, and Academic Dimensions in the Classroom.

The second theme that differentiated between the high- and low-mastery-focused classrooms related to the social and affective environment of the classroom, and the interface of those dimensions with academic dimensions of the classroom. This theme was evident particularly from comments and behaviors regarding the teacher–student relationship, affect, recognition practices, authority, and autonomy.

One difference between the high- and low-mastery-focused teachers concerned their observed affect regarding academics. Although all teachers made comments about academic subjects as being fun, only the two teachers who were perceived as being high-mastery-focused exhibited consistently high levels of enthusiasm for learning and academic content. Both of these teachers consistently showed pleasure, interest, and enthusiasm about inherent aspects of academic tasks and engagement in learning activities. For example, the following extract was taken from field notes during a science lesson in Ms. Hillman's class. Students had collected insects and "bugs" the previous day on a field trip, and were now noting observations about the animals. There was considerable enjoyment and interest evident from the teacher and students:

> The teacher takes a slug out of the tank, saying to the group of four boys, "Here's the slug—look—look—he's wonderful." She places it onto a paper towel, saying, "Watch how he's crawling! Watch how he's stretching his body! You should be writing this down [i.e., their observations]." The boys study it intently. After a minute or so the teacher puts the slug back into the tank, and attention moves to a grasshopper in the tank. The grasshopper is walking upside-down on the lid, avoiding the breathing holes that have been punched in. The teacher encourages them to look hard at the underside of the grasshopper, and then to count the number of legs. She then asks them, "Do insects communicate with each other?"

Another aspect relevant to the social and affective theme involved features of the relationship between the teacher and his or her students. The high- and low-mastery-focused teachers appeared to differ from each other in the respect and eagerness they showed regarding their students' progress and the confi-

dence they exhibited in their students' ability to learn the material, conveyed often through their recognition practices. The two high-mastery-focused teachers repeatedly made comments that indicated they believed their students could do the work, even if they were currently having difficulties. Their interactions with students were characterized by giving warm praise that was also mastery related, clear, contingent, and credible. Ms. Hillman tended to direct her praise to specific students, but her attention was not confined to just a small group of students. For example, while Jared was reading a passage from the text aloud he came to a word he did not recognize, struggled, and finally read it correctly. Ms. Hillman commended him for not giving up and for trying to pronounce it, and called him a good reader. She said, "Nobody helped, you tried it on your own. You are learning," and she clapped. On another day, while reading students' science reports, Ms. Hillman looked at Carlos' report and then read it aloud to the class. She noted approvingly to everyone that he had put a comma between each of the "critters" he listed. "Yesterday I told them not to put 'I saw a slug and a spider *and* a grasshopper *and* a beetle,' and he paid attention." In contrast to Ms. Hillman singling out students for praise, Ms. Miller, also a high-mastery-focused teacher, tended to direct praise to the whole class. For example, when many students raised their hands to answer a question she had asked she exclaimed, "Boy, look at all the hands! What a bright class!" and, "Do you know how long it takes most classes to catch on to this? You catch on fast!"

Both high-mastery-focused teachers publicly identified specific students when they appeared to need help or reminding to stay on task. The feedback, though, was focused consistently on the academic activity, included suggestions for improving their performance, and generally conveyed positive expectations. Both also gave some autonomy to students about academics. These included some choice about the order in which they worked on morning activities, whether students worked alone or with others of their choosing, if they used a microphone while reading to the class, and what to include in creative writing activities. Additionally, the teachers gave students considerable behavioral freedom within the classroom (e.g., talking to classmates, eating snacks) provided they did not get distracted from the academic tasks at hand or distract others.

The two low-mastery-focused teachers did not appear to convey the palpable interest and enthusiasm for academic tasks that we saw from the high-mastery-focused teachers. Without exception, Mr. Laurey appeared quiet and calm, and demonstrated little affect or energy. Ms. Peters made general statements to the class in the first few days that learning would be "fabulous and fun and exciting," but may have lost credibility when she concurrently made statements that tests were fun. Furthermore, we saw no evidence to suggest that either she or the students found any aspect of academics exciting. In fact, during an activity on the first day she said, "You may find this to be boring and I don't

disagree with you. This information is important. It may be boring but when the time comes you will need to know it."

Regarding teacher–student relationships, the low-mastery-focused teachers did not convey, through their recognition practices, a sense of respect for students' intellect or confidence in students' abilities to learn the material. However, Mr. Laurey did appear to create a positive, warm, and nurturing environment, and to be concerned with students' comfort, both physical and psychological. He often expressed interest in students' lives, and frequently encouraged them to share things that happened outside of school. Mr. Laurey treated his students with considerable respect on a personal level, frequently making comments such as, "Thank you for your cooperation" and "I have been talking for half an hour and you have been kind enough to be patient." However, he did not express high expectations for his students' learning, and his frequent comments to students about not pushing themselves appeared to actively discourage effort. For example, after a language arts lesson he read aloud the number of lines of text students had written. Most students had written between five and seven lines; when he came to a paper with eight lines he commented, "I didn't ask for anything that long." Mr. Laurey specifically said at times that he was not interested in the content of students' work, but in the form, such as neatness or if they were doing what they were asked to do. For example, he said, "When I looked at your work, I looked at whether you're expressing yourself in a complete sentence. I did not look at whether or not you had complete thoughts." In contrast to Mr. Laurey's low expression of expectations for students, Ms. Peters typically expressed criticism and negative expectations for students, both as a group and particularly toward individuals. For example, she told her students that, given a chance, they would cheat:

"Usually I won't allow you to correct your own papers. Why do you think that is? Rolando, you look like you know." Rolando says he doesn't know. Ashley volunteers, "Because we might get the scoring wrong?" Ms. Peters replies, "That's a nice way of putting it. Yes, because you will cheat."

In the low-mastery-focused classrooms there was considerably less student autonomy and more teacher direction, with a focus on following rigid procedures, compared to those perceived as high-mastery-focused. Both teachers indicated to students when they could and could not be approached to answer questions. When a boy in Mr. Laurey's class did not walk down the designated aisle to leave the room he was told to return to his desk and do it again; he walked down the correct aisle. Ms. Peters retained a sense of control throughout the lessons, and she expected students to stay with her cognitively and not ask questions about other things. This sense of authority is illustrated when Ms. Peters talked about an imminent math test and Philip asked her a question

about what problems would be on the test. She replied, "I am not on that yet. I am still on 'Heading.' People are not following directions and you are one of them because you are thinking about the problems. We are on 'Directions.'"

In contrast to the considerable differences between high- and low-mastery-focused teachers, there were strikingly fewer differences between teachers who were perceived by students as being high on performance goals (Ms. Hillman and Ms. Peters) and low in the emphasis on performance goals (Ms. Miller and Mr. Laurey).

Theme 3: Differential Performance and Formal Evaluation.   The theme that differentiated between the high- and low-performance-focused classrooms involved indicators of differential student performance, particularly in terms of formal evaluation. Formal assessments, grades, and students' relative performance appeared to have a strong focus within the high-performance-focused teachers' classrooms. At the beginning of the year Ms. Peters mentioned tests and grades on each of the 8 days we were in her class, including the Michigan Educational Assessment Program (MEAP) tests (i.e., state-standardized assessments) on 2 of those days. Similarly, Ms. Hillman talked about grades on 7 of the 8 days we observed in her class. Ms. Peters' students took math tests on 3 different days and completed a handwriting sample. She told the class she would form math and reading groups on the basis of their classroom test scores, and indicated that she expected students would show differential performance. For example, on one occasion when she mentioned reading groups, her comments appeared to indicate that although she wished they all were good readers she knew that some students were better than others. One comment to students was, "Hopefully there will only be one reading group but I know better than that. Everyone reads on a different level." In answer to a student's request about whether they would receive a grade on a math test, Ms. Peters told them they would not, but "this [test] will determine where your math abilities are." She then linked the math test to the MEAP and California Achievement Test, saying, "They are important for some people and this test is important for me."

Ms. Hillman also tended to emphasize students' performance, and she talked frequently about test scores, relative performance, and differential prestige. For example, when talking about the upcoming spelling program she said:

> We will have a classroom bee and the best two people from here [i.e., the classroom] and the two best from Ms. Granger's room [i.e., other fifth-grade class] will have a spelling countdown. And the top person from that will compete against all the other district schools, and then the best there will go all the way to the district spelling bee. Last year the two top people from this class [her fifth-grade class last year] were the top two girls in the district. And they got a plaque, and winnings, and a lovely dictionary.

Students seemed very aware of whether their work would be graded in both Ms. Hillman's and Ms. Peters' classes. They tended to ask if particular assignments or worksheets would be graded, and asked about receiving extra credit.

In contrast to the pervasive mentioning of tests and the implications of test scores, the low-performance-focused teachers did not emphasize test scores and grades or students' differential performance on tasks. In fact, there was very little mention of formal assessments by these two teachers even though they also conducted assessments at the beginning of the year and often made aspects of students' performance public. Ms Miller explained that students would have pretests and tests weekly, but this was mentioned in a matter-of-fact manner and was not linked to other factors such as their ability, differential grouping, or prestige. Mr. Laurey also conducted tests, but he played down their importance in what appeared to be an attempt to decrease student anxiety or concern. For example, when introducing a math test he said, "Oh, this isn't a test. I shouldn't have even said that—this is to let me know the things that I need to highlight in the fifth grade." He then went on to tell students it was a "kind of worksheet."

Summary

Overall, the findings of this study both supported and elaborated on previous literature about goal structures in classrooms. As expected, some of the categories of practice summarized in the TARGET framework were found to differ among teachers who were perceived differently by their students. In particular, teachers' provision of autonomy for students distinguished between high- and low-mastery-oriented classes, whereas the emphasis on formal evaluation differentiated high- and low-performance-oriented classes. In terms of other TARGET categories, however, we observed few differences between teachers. All of the teachers in this study provided students with rewards, there was very little use of small-group instruction, and there were no apparent differences in the use of time. It is important to note that these findings do not mean that, if teachers had designed their instruction to be more flexible and mastery oriented in these ways, that students would not have perceived a mastery environment. Rather, they suggest that teachers can create a mastery-oriented environment without instantiating every one of the TARGET categories. It may be that some characteristics of instruction, such as the explicit focus on evaluation, are more salient and powerful in terms of influencing the goal emphasis of a context, than are others.

The findings of this study also add to traditional conceptions of classroom goal structures in that two general themes were identified that differentiated between high- and low-mastery-oriented practices. Teachers' apparent views

about the nature of learning, particularly with relation to the role of errors and collaboration, seemed to explain many of the specific practices linked with a high-mastery or low-mastery environment. Similarly, the nature of student–teacher relationships in the class distinguished between different patterns of perceived goal structure. Summarizing across the four cases, it appears that teachers who communicated a combination of both interpersonal warmth and intellectual respect for their students were those who created a mastery-oriented environment. Thus, it may be that definitions of a mastery environment need to be expanded to include aspects of the social-relational context of classrooms.

Study 2: Teachers' Use of Social Comparison in Classrooms

The second study (Middleton, Hruda, & Linnenbrink, 1998) examined teacher's use of social comparison using all 10 classrooms. The purpose of this study was to take an in-depth look at the way in which social comparison is used in elementary classrooms and to examine how these practices are linked to students' perceptions of the classroom goal environment as well as to other instructional practices. Although not included as a distinct dimension in the TARGET framework, social comparison practices are important to consider given the emphasis on performance goals that can be communicated through ability comparisons. Within the literature on goal orientation theory, social comparison is generally thought of in terms of its emphasis on relative ability (i.e., using comparisons to judge one's own work, behavior, or ability in relation to others) (e.g., C. Ames & Archer, 1988; Nicholls, 1984.). Several researchers (Butler, 1995; Ruble & Frey, 1991), however, note that social comparison can also serve a self-improvement, learning-related function. That is, social comparisons may be made for the purpose of gathering ideas, assistance, or strategies for improving one's own work, comparative information perhaps more in keeping with a mastery goal orientation. These two types of social comparison have been labeled *relative ability comparison,* and *informational comparison,* respectively.

Butler's (1995) experimental research suggested that it is indeed important to consider both relative ability and informational comparisons when examining how social comparison relates to achievement goals. In particular, she found that students working under performance-focused conditions used only relative ability comparison, whereas those in mastery-focused conditions used both informational and relative ability comparisons. These results have important implications for teachers' use of social comparison but remain to be supported by research conducted within actual classrooms. Thus, in the present study, we sought to describe the various ways in which comparisons occurred in the class-

room, as well as to examine how social comparison related to teachers' instructional practices and students' perceptions of classroom goal structures.

Using the narratives from all 10 classrooms in the observation project, we began by coding incidents representing social comparison, recognition, and help seeking (see OPAL; Patrick et al., 1997). From these data, we developed fine-tuned categories of social comparison and then examined patterns relating the social comparison categories to the perceived goal structure of the classroom as well as the teachers' use of recognition and help seeking.

Social Comparison Practices

Our observations confirmed teachers' use of both relative ability and informational comparisons in the classroom. However, we noted that in addition to distinguishing between the purpose of the comparison (relative ability vs. informational), the domain in which the comparisons occurred varied. In particular, we found that teachers' comments regarding social comparison could be categorized into the following four domains: (a) academic achievement: comments regarding students' performance on an academic task; (b) academic procedure: comments regarding students' behavior related to preparation and completion of an academic task; (c) behavior: comments regarding compliance with nonacademic rules; (d) ability: comments regarding students' innate academic ability or prior achievement. Furthermore, within each domain, examples of teachers' use of social comparison were judged as being either positive (recognizing good performance or behavior) or negative (recognizing poor performance or behavior). Thus, 16 potential categories of social comparison were generated (four domains × relative ability/informational × positive/negative). Not all of these possible combinations, however, were observed with equal frequency in classrooms. From the 16 potential dimensions generated, 9 patterns were more prevalent than others in the classrooms observed. These are described next.

For relative ability comparisons, positive comparisons were made about students' academic achievement, academic procedures, nonacademic behavior, and ability. In terms of academic achievement, students' grades were often made salient. For example, in relation to scores on a test, Ms. Peters asked her class, "How many did above 35?" Students raised their hands and were then praised for their performance. In other instances, the names of students receiving A's were displayed on the wall. Teachers also used relative ability comparisons to comment on both academic behaviors and nonacademic behaviors. For example, Ms. Garrett pointed out correct behavior by saying, "Some of you have done a really fine job and numbered each one on the left; this is what I want all of you to do." Finally, academic ability was also referenced in positive relative ability comparisons. For example, when a group of boys was struggling on an assignment, Ms. Hillman told them, "You guys should listen to John, he is good at reasoning. Listen to your peer.

You are good at problem solving, John." In another example, Mr. Hughes noted that some students had higher ability than others did in reading by saying, "Remember, with oral reading, some are faster than others."

Negative relative ability comparisons also played a prominent role in some classrooms. These comparisons were generally made in the domains of academic achievement, academic procedures, and nonacademic behaviors. Examples of negative relative ability comparisons in the domain of academic achievement generally focused on a student not knowing the answer or turning in lower quality work than others. For instance, in one class a boy was informed that his essay was the worst in his group. Teachers also used negative relative ability comparisons to point out ways in which students were not correctly following directions or other academic procedures. One example occurred in Ms. Peters' class when a student (April) was asked to make corrections to a sentence written on the blackboard. When April was not following the correct procedures, Ms. Peters said, "Wait a minute, April. Class, what is April doing wrong?" The class responded that April was crossing out words instead of circling them and Ms. Peters continued, "Little simple things like that. You may not think they are important but they are."

In contrast to relative ability comparisons, almost all of the informational comparisons teachers made were positive. These comparisons most frequently occurred in the domains of academic achievement and academic procedures. For example, students' papers were often held up as examples of good work. Teachers also pointed out students' work to demonstrate the correct way to follow academic procedures. This is shown in an episode from Ms. Garrett's class when students were working on a final draft of a paper. In this instance, Susan showed her final draft to Ms. Garrett who in turn said to the class, "See how nice and neat it is. See how she has indented. Excellent job."

These findings reinforce the utility of observational methods for examining motivational questions in that the narrative data allowed for a more fine-grained analysis of teachers' use of social comparison. That is, our research suggests that social comparison practices are more diverse and complex than was suggested by earlier research. Furthermore, the classroom study was able to distinguish between categories of social comparison that exist theoretically and those that teachers actually use in regular classroom settings.

Associations Between Social Comparison and Classroom Goal Structures

In addition to describing how social comparison was used in elementary classrooms, we also were interested in how social comparison related to students' perceptions of classroom goal structures. In doing so, we sought to elaborate on Butler's (1995) finding that students used different types of social

comparison in settings that emphasized mastery or performance goals. Rather than examining students' use of social comparison, however, we focused on relating teachers' use of social comparison to students' perceptions of the goal structures in their classrooms. Students' scores on survey measures assessing their perceptions of the classroom goal structure were used to identify classrooms as either high or low on both mastery and performance goals. Each classroom was also rated on a 3-point scale in terms of the frequency with which teachers used each of the 16 potential categories of social comparison. Several patterns of practice emerged.

First, in classrooms in which students reported a strong emphasis on performance goals, teachers were observed making negative relative ability comparisons for academic achievement. That is, teachers would make implicit or explicit negative judgments about students' performance on academic tasks in comparison to others in the class. In contrast, in classrooms that were perceived as being high in the emphasis on both mastery and performance goals, teachers were more likely to use positive social comparison for informational purposes. That is, teachers would draw attention to examples of students' academic work that were particularly well done. Finally, it is important to note that teachers in classes that were perceived as high in the emphasis on mastery goals and low in the emphasis on performance goals demonstrated very few examples of social comparison in any category.

Associations Between Social Comparison and Other Classroom Practices

In addition to describing the various categories of social comparison used by teachers, we also examined associations between social comparison and other classroom practices. We found that in some cases teachers' recognition of students was tied to their use of social comparison. That is, when teachers wanted to provide students with feedback or praise in the class setting, they often did so by pointing out how those students compared to others in the class. Second, teachers' routines and support for students' help seeking in class were related to their use of social comparison. When students needed help with an academic task, some teachers would refer them explicitly to a more capable peer, thus communicating their judgment of the relative skills of each student. In contrast, other teachers created an instructional environment in which collaborative work was viewed as commonplace and in which any student could seek help from any other peer, thus avoiding public acknowledgment by the teacher of differing ability. Finally, routine instructional practices sometimes made social comparisons salient, even when this did not appear to be the teacher's purpose. For example, teachers often monitored students' progress

on a task by asking them to raise their hands when they were finished. Although not explicitly intended to make relative ability comparisons among students, such practices tend to draw attention to differences between students' performance. In other examples, some teachers supported informational social comparison, for example by asking students to model successful work or to demonstrate a method of problem solving. In these examples, attention was drawn less to relative ability judgments and more to the ways in which students could gain ideas or strategies to improve their own learning.

Summary

This study, examining social comparison practices, is useful for understanding the diversity of practices linked to social comparison and how these various socially comparative practices are linked to perceptions of the classroom goal structures. The fine-grained approach to analyzing teacher practices used here may be particularly important in linking social comparison to achievement goals. That is, considering the domain and valance of the comparison, in addition to its purpose (informational vs. relative ability), appears to be important when distinguishing between classrooms perceived as communicating only performance goals and those perceived as communicating both mastery and performance goals. In addition, the relation of teachers' use of recognition, help seeking, and more general instructional techniques with social comparison practices is important for helping teachers realize when they use social comparison in their classrooms. Illustrating the frequency and range of comparisons, both explicit and implicit, may help teachers recognize how much socially comparative information they provide to students. We found that social comparisons were often situated within other types of classroom practices, possibly obscuring them from the teacher's attention. Realizing this connection may help teachers to become more aware of the ways in which they use social comparison on a daily basis. And, being aware of the dimensions of social comparison that we examined here may also help situate social comparison more appropriately within a goal theory framework, not just theoretically or experimentally, but in keeping with what happens in typical learning situations.

Study 3: Classroom Management and Goal Theory

The third study (Hruda, Middleton, & Linnenbrink, 1999) examined teachers' facilitation of students' socioemotional development through classroom management. Teaching effectively requires that teachers establish sufficient order in the classroom to provide students with an environment conducive to learning. Although teachers undoubtedly differ in their beliefs about what is

required to provide an orderly environment, the primary purpose of class-room management is to engender a situation in which the focus can be on learning. In this way, an orderly classroom is one in which achievement goals that focus the student on learning can prosper. Classroom management is not itself a central aspect of the TARGET framework (described earlier), but does infuse itself into many of the TARGET dimensions, and is consequently linked to achievement goals. Some of the more obvious TARGET dimensions falling within a traditional definition of classroom management include pacing classroom events (Time), monitoring student behavior and progress (Evaluation), and organizing classroom groups (Grouping). In addition, setting up rules and procedures falls within the scope of the Authority/Autonomy dimension of TARGET, whereas reacting to misbehavior may invoke Recognition.

Even with these links to TARGET, there are no studies of classroom management that have used achievement goal theory as the organizing framework. In general, previous research has examined teachers' classroom management responsibilities in relation to students' academic achievement and learning. Some studies have also examined the association between teachers' classroom management techniques and students' abilities to reason socially, develop social competence, and internalize feelings of responsibility (e.g., Blumenfeld & Meece, 1985; Blumenfeld, Pintrich, & Hamilton, 1987; Rohrkemper, 1984). These socially relevant competencies were the focus of our third study. We examined the links between the TARGET categories, teachers' management styles, and students' social outcomes.

The foundation for our interest in this topic lay in how teachers' management of classroom routines, emphasis on values such as fairness and respect, praise and criticism of behaviors, and promotion of social responsibility through classroom management might influence students' perceptions of the social-relational environment of the classroom. Differences in how teachers handle rules, responsibility, and respect within the classroom reflect two broad approaches to classroom management. The older behavioral tradition frames management around controlling students through rewards and punishments (Bear, 1998). Here the focus is on the teacher's control of students' behavior and is, therefore, closely linked to the Authority/Autonomy dimension of TARGET. In contrast, the newer social cognitive approach to management places the teacher in the role of facilitator, as students develop appropriate ways of thinking socially. Within the social-cognitive arena there is a further distinction made between direct approaches, which teach specific social-cognitive skills, and discovery approaches, which adopt a constructivist paradigm (Bear, 1998). The direct social-cognitive approach relies heavily on the use of verbal instruction, modeling, and rehearsal in the teaching of prescribed skills for specific situations. It is a top-down transmission of social knowledge. Dis-

covery approaches, mirroring discovery learning in the academic areas, aim to develop the student's understanding of more general social processes and relationships. This latter method places the teacher in the role of coconstructor of social understanding with the student.

Mirroring the categories used to describe parents (Baumrind 1971, 1991; Grusec & Goodnow, 1994), teachers also can be categorized as authoritarian or authoritative in style based on their assertion of power and application of rules. And, in accordance with what has been found with parents, authoritative teaching styles that stress reasoning over power assertion, apply rules consistently, are receptive to students' attempts to communicate, and express approval may lead to more positive outcomes than do authoritarian teaching styles. Furthermore, the adoption and internalization of the goals and values of significant adults may be fostered by perceptions of caring that are more highly associated with an authoritative style (Noddings, 1992; Wentzel, 1997). Therefore, similar to the way in which parents influence their children's social practices, teachers' classroom management has implications for how students behave socially toward the teacher as well as with one another. And, just as was true with the different approaches to management, because these teaching styles reflect the teacher's assertion of power over students, they are closely linked to the Authority/Autonomy dimension of TARGET.

In the observational study of classroom management, we addressed ways in which teachers may influence the global social climate within the classroom as well as students' perceptions of aspects of their relationship with their teacher. We expected that an authoritative style that allows students a voice in rule setting, maintains high expectations of compliance, yet includes frequent expressions of approval would be associated with a more positive social climate. In contrast, we expected the authoritarian style to be associated with more negative outcomes due to its stress on power assertion rather than self-discipline. In addition, we expected authoritative teachers to rely on social-cognitive approaches to management, especially discovery approaches that encourage the development of self-discipline. We also expected that the use of these social-cognitive techniques would be associated with a more positive social climate in the classroom, as students began to reason independently about social responsibility and internalize positive standards for social interactions. Finally, because of similarities in instructional practices linked to the discovery approach to classroom management, and descriptions of a mastery environment (student autonomy, recognition for prosocial activities), we expected authoritative and discovery approaches to management to be more prevalent in mastery-focused classrooms. Authoritarian teachers, on the other hand, were expected to rely primarily on behavioral approaches to maintain discipline in their classrooms, and were expected to be associated with more negative social climates and more per-

formance-focused classrooms because of the stress authoritarian styles place on status and doing things correctly as determined by the teacher.

We investigated these possibilities using the observational data from all ten classrooms, as well as the students' survey data assessing their perceptions of the classroom quantitatively. Judgments about styles (authoritative or authoritarian) were based on profiles of the teachers' practices regarding classroom rules and student autonomy. Teachers' approach to management was categorized according to how compliance and noncompliance to rules and classroom conventions were handled by the teacher, and with the ways in which the teacher discussed social responsibility with students. Finally, the overall social climate in the classroom was described using categories related to teacher–student social relations and student–student social relations.

Teacher Styles and Management Approaches.   Field notes from the classroom observations indicated that the teachers were approximately evenly divided between authoritarian and authoritative styles. However, 9 of the 10 teachers used behavioral techniques in the classroom, such as rewards and punishments, frequently. Whereas the authoritarian teachers did rely almost exclusively on behavioral techniques, most of the authoritative teachers used a combination of behavioral and direct approaches. Only one teacher was observed using a discovery approach to classroom management. Thus, although half of the teachers exhibited some emphasis on social cognition, it was primarily through a direct top-down approach that relied heavily on modeling and verbal reminders of appropriate behavior.

We linked differences in teachers' management styles to observed patterns of social relationships in class. Teachers judged as being authoritarian in their approach implied that students were required to respect them and stressed this over any other aspect of student social responsibility or reasoning. For example, when some students were talking while Ms. Peters went over a worksheet, she explained the two rules for her classroom:

> Rule number one: You don't talk while I'm talking. I've been teaching now, this is my eleventh year and one rule I've always taken with me, you don't talk when I'm talking. When you hear that voice, stop immediately in your tracks. Rule number two: Follow directions. Not getting and understanding is missing out on learning. Other than that, you're free to explore and learn.

Though the students were told this on the first day of class, such assertion of power continued in this classroom throughout the year, indicating that the students required ongoing reminders of the teacher's authority over them. One day during the spring semester, after having a substitute cover her class the pre-

vious day, Ms. Peters commented, "I told her [referring to the substitute] to use tough love with this class. As you get older you will know what I mean." When some students began to discuss this statement, Ms. Peters reminded the class, "Did I give anyone permission to talk?"

This style of management was associated with negative interactions between teachers and students. Ms. Williams, another authoritarian teacher, repeatedly told students "do not argue with me" when it came to disagreements with her over what students were allowed to eat for a snack and whether discipline had been meted out fairly. She also conveyed a lack of warmth in her relationship with the students and a distancing of herself from them. For example, when she discussed detention with the class, Ms. Williams told the students that if they got detention it would not hurt her in any way. "I get paid, so it is not a problem for me." The negative tone that characterized these teacher–student relationships also appeared to carry over into negative student–student interactions, including name-calling, arguing, and tensions among students in classrooms of authoritarian teachers. At the end of the year, Ms. Williams spent much of her time arbitrating student disagreements over such things as talking to one another inappropriately, getting into someone else's personal space or desk, telling others to shut up, and insulting others. Although the teacher told the students what to do to settle each dispute, her commands were unaccompanied by any discussion of why the inappropriate behavior was not a suitable way to interact. This lack of an explanation may have contributed to a recurring need for the teacher to intervene and arbitrate disagreements. Students did not appear to be expected to understand why behaving in certain ways was or was not appropriate but rather were only expected to behave appropriately, with the teacher seemingly the only one who determined what is right or wrong. The following observation illustrates the teacher's intervention in two similar incidents within an hour of one another, with reference also made to the same problem occurring the day before:

> 8:42—Gigi tells Damien that he should shut up, and "Don't tell me to shut up." Ms. Williams says, "Excuse me, Damien! You don't tell people to shut up. Mind your own business." Ms. Williams then tells Gigi that she also should not say that, and that they talked about it yesterday.

> 9:40—Talia and Justin are kicking each other at the computers. Ms. Williams does not appear to notice. Talia tells Justin to "Shut up." Ms. Williams tells the couple that they should be busy, and that they waste too much time on trying to find out what to do.

Teachers categorized as authoritative in style, though generally not exhibiting strongly negative social climates, did not have consistently positive ones either. Rather, these classrooms were characterized as somewhat mixed when it came to social relations: some positive social interactions were observed, as

were some negative ones, and, interestingly, several of these classrooms minimized interactions entirely. However, in general and in contrast to the negative teacher–student interactions commonplace in the classrooms of authoritarian teachers, we observed more positive interactions between authoritative teachers and their students. These interactions seemed to reflect a combination of warmth and respect on the part of teachers toward their students:

> Charlie flies a paper airplane from his desk at the edge of the classroom; it flies toward the closest wall. Ms. Hillman asks him if he has finished his spelling, and goes over to check. She then announces to the class that "Charlie has a library book on paper art ... He's finished with all his spelling and all his journal writing." [Implicit message is that it's okay to do something fun if you have done all your assigned work.] She then encourages Charlie to fly his plane again; the class all watches. Ms. Hillman asks if he has ripped a little hole on the bottom, to help it fly better. He doesn't seem to know what she is talking about. Ms. Hillman explains that when she was young and used to make paper planes, she always ripped a little hole in the bottom to help it fly better. Ms. Hillman tells Charlie to fly his plane, then to make a hole in it and see if it flies better that time. He does this all, and it does fly better the second time. Ms. Hillman then directs her attention to the other students; most continue with their task again.
>
> Ms. Hillman is outside her classroom. One girl shows her something she has brought from home. Another stands quietly and waits until Ms. Hillman has finished talking to the observer, then asks Ms. Hillman for a hug, which is given. On the blackboard is written, "Have a nice day Ms. Hillman." This is signed by four students.

At the same time, some teachers categorized as authoritative because of their consistent application of rules, receptivity to students' attempts to communicate, and lack of reliance on power assertion as the primary means of control did not have classrooms where this style translated into benefits to student–student relationships. In most of these classrooms, the teachers created a context in which student interactions were kept to a minimum. For example, Mr. Laurey set up learning tasks that had students working either independently or as a whole class with him as the focal point, both situations minimizing the interaction among students. When working independently, the classroom was largely silent with little disruption from students, something encouraged by Mr. Laurey's frequent reminders of "Shhh." Though only one negative interaction was observed in this classroom and some positive interactions were seen during off-task times, as a whole the social climate between students was primarily neutral.

The sole classroom that appeared to have a consistently positive social climate was the one in which the authoritative teacher used a discovery approach to classroom management. In this classroom, headed by Ms. Miller, we observed no incidents of student–teacher conflict, few student–student conflicts, and a good deal of positive affect among class members. At the beginning of

the year, the teacher and students worked together to create rules that were then hung up on a classroom wall. More important than the writing of the rules themselves was the initial emphasis on making sure the rules were decided together and that the rules were understood by all. For example, Ms. Miller introduced the creation of rules by telling the class, "Let's get going on the rules. It is important to create rules so you understand what they are." As students contributed suggested rules, she wrote them on the board, and then later edited them to create a final version written on poster board (the final version included some, but not all, of the students' original suggestions).

In addition, the rules (e.g., "Be nice to others") and statements by Ms. Miller highlighted this classroom's emphasis on respect, fairness, and caring. Before heading out to recess one day Ms. Miller told her students:

> "Respect one another out there and in here ... remember you are fifth grade, top of the line. Now since you have been so understanding, so patient, let's go out and have some fun." She tells the students that in this class there will not be a boys' line and a girls' line. "You are all equal, you are all human."

On another day, the "quote of the day" led students into a discussion about respecting one's elders. Thus, in this classroom discussion about and reminders of respect toward others was a recurring theme. And it was the stress on respect that underscored how students should behave and why rules existed.

The social relations in this classroom appeared to benefit from this approach to classroom management. The social climate was warm and comfortable and, with few minor exceptions, everyone appeared to get along well. Students supported one another's efforts by clapping in appreciation. Laughter, excitement, and positive feelings were exhibited frequently. And, there was a good-natured (sometimes teasing) relationship between the teacher and students:

> Looking at a picture in a book, Garth remarks to the teacher, "They make better baskets than you." Ms. Miller replies, "I know ... art is not my strong point. I do my best. Leave me alone." She then laughs and adds, "I know what was wrong ..." Cynthia interrupts, "No everything was fine—except the basket!" Ms. Miller responds, "Well, at least I try! You have to give me credit." "I do! I do!" Cynthia tells her. Students laugh.

Though it is difficult to generalize from this one case, the negative and neutral climates found in so many of the classrooms, and the reliance on the discovery approach in the one classroom with a consistently positive social climate hints at some possibilities. It may be that an authoritative management style coupled with the discovery approach to promoting social responsibility and behavior are particularly supportive of a positive social climate. This hypothesis merits further research.

Links From Observed Management Practices to the Survey Data.
In order to explore associations between teachers' management practices and students' perceptions of their relationships with their teachers, we used analysis of variance to examine four student-reported measures: student–teacher disparity, student–teacher harmony, autonomy, and teacher support. Results indicated significant differences between classrooms on all these measures. Not surprisingly, students from the classroom that was observed to have the most positive social climate ranked highest overall on all of the teacher–student relationship measures (i.e., low student–teacher disparity, and high student–teacher harmony, autonomy, and teacher support). Data from the other classrooms, however, displayed no strong pattern of associations between the observational and survey data.

We also examined whether teachers' approaches to classroom management were associated with differences in students' perceptions of their classroom goal structures. Again, the one classroom in which the teacher used a discovery approach to management showed a clear and distinctive pattern. This classroom had the lowest student-reported performance classroom goal structure and the second highest mastery goal structure of the 10 classes included. Thus, not only did we receive support for our initial expectation that the TARGET dimensions would link to positive and negative social outcomes based on how teachers managed their classrooms, but these dimensions also linked back in expected ways to the goal structures we had assessed using quantitative survey data.

Summary

Overall, the warm social climate in the one classroom that employed a constructivist approach to management indicates that a more strongly reflective approach in managing student behavior may be necessary to establish classroom climates that are a positive experience for students. This approach to management also might be expected to promote social reasoning and responsibility on the part of students (Blumenfeld & Meece, 1985; Blumenfeld et al., 1987; Rohrkemper, 1984). This relation between discovery approaches to classroom management and positive outcomes suggests that the link between improving students' social understanding may entail more than teaching prescribed strategies or skills useful in particular situations, such as those employed by many social problem-solving skills programs. As is currently believed for academic knowledge, developing social understanding may require shared construction of this knowledge. Furthermore, the links between the TARGET dimensions and the social aspects of a classroom, along with the

quantitative links between the discovery approach to the classroom mastery and performance goal structures, raise the possibility that a high mastery–low performance classroom environment may support not only academic development but students' social development as well.

SUMMARY OF OBSERVATIONAL STUDIES: CLARIFYING AND EXPANDING GOAL THEORY

The three studies described in this chapter each examine the associations between teachers' instructional practices and different aspects of students' perceptions, especially their perceptions of the goal structures emphasized in their classrooms. The results of each study lend support to the extant literature (e.g., C. Ames, 1992b; E. M. Anderman & Maehr, 1994; Maehr & Midgley, 1991; Meece, 1991; Midgley, 1993), but also suggest ways in which thinking about classroom goal structures might be refined.

One important contribution of the observational studies is that they document the actual practices common among regular teachers, as opposed to those that are hypothetical. That is, the observational data allow us to describe the range of teachers' practices across a number of different categories. For example, Middleton et al. (1998) identified 16 potential patterns of social comparison that could be used by teachers but noted that only half of these actually occurred in the classrooms we observed. Similarly, Patrick et al. (2001) found that the teachers in the four classrooms they examined did not differ in several aspects of practice, such as their use of time or making students' performance public. Nevertheless, the teachers in both of these studies were perceived differently by their students. Thus, it may be that some characteristics of instructional practice are more salient in communicating goal structures to students than are others. For example, the degree of emphasis on formal evaluation and grading was the most important difference between classes that were perceived as high or low in a performance emphasis. Similarly, different patterns of teachers' use of social comparison were associated with different combinations of mastery and performance goal structures. According to our data, the positive or negative valence of social comparison may be more important for some students than whether or not comparisons are made. These findings illustrate Turner and Meyer's (2000) comment that classroom research must concentrate on the "how" and "why" questions and not just on the "what." Understanding the ways in which regular teachers use comparison, rewards, and provide autonomy, for example, may help to clarify the definition of a mastery goal structure.

A second contribution is that patterns of instructional practices in different categories of TARGET may reflect more global beliefs and personal theories of teachers. As discussed earlier, the patterns of practice that differentiated

teachers perceived as high and low in the emphasis on mastery seemed to reflect their beliefs about the nature of student learning. That is, practices across several of the TARGET categories were consistent with either a transmission or a constructivist view. Teachers' use of feedback and recognition, and their attitude toward students' errors, participation in class, and help seeking all tended to reflect these views. In addition, practices consistent with constructivist views of learning (e.g., Collins, Brown, & Newman, 1989) were associated with students' perceptions of a mastery goal structure. The study by Hruda et al. (1999) also provided evidence that a constructivist approach to teaching about classroom rules and behavior may be linked to a more positive social environment. This underscores Blumenfeld's (1992) observation that "more attention should be given to how the teacher as a person and as an instructor influences perceptions of classroom goal orientations" (p. 276).

A final and important finding was that the nature of teacher–student relationships and the general social-relational climate of the classroom emerged as associated consistently with students' perceptions of an emphasis on mastery goals. In our data, warm interpersonal relationships between teacher and students were a necessary but not sufficient component of a mastery goal structure. Teachers who were perceived as high in mastery orientation not only communicated interpersonal caring but also demonstrated respect for their students' intellect and ability to learn. This finding relates to Wentzel's (1997) research about perceived pedagogical caring. She found that adolescents evaluated teachers' caring most by the extent to which teachers recognized students as learners and focused on students' academic skills, problems, and contributions to the class. Other researchers also have begun to explore perceived teacher respect, caring, and commitment as important contributors to students' motivation (e.g., L. H. Anderman, Hughes, Tussey, & Savage, 2000; Murdock, L. H. Anderman, & Hodge, 2000; see also chap. 4, this volume). Taken together, these studies suggest that we may need to expand our definition of a mastery goal structure to include more affective and social-relational dimensions, which, to date, have been omitted from descriptions of goal structures in classrooms.

IMPLICATIONS FOR TEACHING AND TEACHER EDUCATION

In addition to raising theoretical issues, the observation project and its resultant studies highlight a number of findings of importance for both classroom teachers and teacher educators. The considerable stability we found from the beginning to the end of the school year in both teacher practices and student perceptions indicates that the classroom motivational climate is established early and does not change much. The notion that teachers should "start tough" at the beginning of the school year because they can always "loosen up later"

does not appear to hold, at least in terms of classroom goals. Teachers need to know that the messages they send early in the school year contribute a great deal to the creation of a new and specific context of learning for that group of students, which will affect students' beliefs about what is important and what counts as success for that class.

Another issue that is relevant for practitioners is that it is the nuances of practice, rather than more simply whether or not practices are present, that contribute to students' perceptions. For example, our findings showed that it was not whether or not teachers used rewards or made performance public per se that was related to motivational climate, but rather the ways in which those things were done. For example, how teachers use rewards may be more important than whether they use them. Many of the recommendations made in teacher education programs regarding facilitating motivation tend to be fairly simplistic lists of principles such as "minimize reliance on extrinsic reinforcers" (Ormrod, 1998, p. 483). Whereas such recommendations are not incorrect, they may be viewed as unrealistic, particularly when preservice teachers participate in practicum placements and observe teachers regularly providing rewards in class. Rather than providing prospective teachers with a "shopping list" of such principles, it may be more important for teacher educators to facilitate an attitude of reflecting on and analyzing practices in terms of the motivational messages they are communicating.

The finding that teachers' implicit theories of how students learn are integral to the motivational environment they help create in their classroom also has implications for teacher education. We found that teachers' practices were consistent with their stated beliefs about how students learn, and those beliefs and related practices differentiated between the high and low mastery-focused classrooms. Specifically, the belief that learning involves the successful transmission of intact and well-defined bodies of knowledge, indicated by following procedures correctly, mastering skills through direct instruction and independent practice, and remembering—a belief commonly held by teachers (e.g., Calderhead, 1996; Nespor, 1987)—is related to practices that foster a low perceived emphasis on mastery goals. Conversely, beliefs about learning that seem consistent with a social constructivist approach, wherein students are viewed as actively constructing their own understandings through questioning, reflection, and interaction (e.g., Collins et al., 1989), are related to practices that foster the perception of a high mastery focus. This implies that efforts to help teachers create the most adaptive motivational environments for their students should focus more strongly on teachers' underlying belief structures than on their overt behavior. The utility of attending to teachers' fundamental beliefs and cognitions about student learning is consistent with Richardson's (1990) recommendation that "the focus of a change effort should be teachers' cognitions and thought processes rather than or in addition to behavior" (p. 12). Maehr and Midgley (1996)

participated in a coalition with teachers in two schools to bring about school reform using goal orientation as the framework. They noted that a change in thinking about the purpose and meaning of schooling was necessary before real, long-term change in policies and practices could be implemented. Given findings that conceptual change appears to be promoted more effectively during the preservice and novice teaching periods than after teachers have gained years of teaching experience (Cronin-Jones & Shaw, 1992), the results of our study add support to recent recommendations that preservice teachers be encouraged to adopt social constructivist views of learning (e.g., Anderson et al., 1995; Borko & Putnam, 1996).

In addition, the suggestion that both interpersonal and pedagogical caring are necessary for creating optimal motivational environments also carries important implications for teachers. Preservice teachers typically are very concerned about the social and emotional dimensions of the classroom, and often are anxious that students like them (Hollingsworth, 1989; Weinstein, 1989). Our research indicated, however, that demonstrating caring by being involved in students' personal lives or being "warm and fuzzy" was insufficient to foster a high mastery focus. Rather, conveying intellectual respect by indicating both high expectations and confidence in students' ability to meet those expectations was crucial for promoting a high mastery-goal focus in the classroom. That is, *both* a warm, positive teacher–student relationship and communicating high academic standards are necessary for facilitating a mastery-goal focus. The challenge for novice (and experienced) teachers is to create an environment that is simultaneously comfortable on an interpersonal level and challenging intellectually (Midgley & Edelin, 1998).

Overall, observational studies, especially those that provide rich descriptions and case studies of classroom practices (as opposed to low-inference methods), are particularly helpful for practitioners, who tend to find contextualized information presented as cases, stories, or events to be most meaningful (Carter, 1993). These concrete illustrations facilitate teachers' understanding and assist them in bridging material that often is presented as decontextualized principles (Anderson et al., 1995). Indeed, we have found the rich and contextualized descriptions from our observations to be extremely useful in our own educational psychology classes, both for illustrating instantiations of theoretical principles and for generating stimulating discussions about classroom practices, implicit messages these practices may convey, and environments that may be unwittingly created.

Clearly, our research in this area to date is suggestive rather than definitive. Nevertheless, the descriptive data provided raise interesting and important issues for both theory and practice. Our hope is that this work will become part of a larger body of research using multiple methodologies to understand the principles involved in the creation of adaptive motivational environments in classrooms.

REFERENCES

Ames, C. (1992a). Achievement goals and the classroom motivational climate. In D. F. Schunk & J. L. Meece (Eds.), *Student perceptions in the classroom* (pp. 327–348). Hillsdale, NJ: Lawrence Erlbaum Associates.

Ames, C. (1992b). Classrooms: Goals, structures, and student motivation. *Journal of Educational Psychology, 84,* 261–271.

Ames, C., & Ames, R. (1981). Competitive and individualistic goal structures: The salience of past performance information for causal attributions and affect. *Journal of Educational Psychology, 73,* 411–418.

Ames, C., & Archer, J. (1988). Achievement goals in the classroom, students' learning strategies and motivation processes. *Journal of Educational Psychology, 80,* 260–267.

Anderman, E. M., & Maehr, M. L. (1994). Motivation and schooling in the middle grades. *Review of Educational Research, 64,* 287–309.

Anderman, E. M., & Young, A. J. (1994). Motivation and strategy use in science: Individual differences and classroom effects. *Journal of Research in Science Teaching, 31*(8), 811–831.

Anderman, L. H., & Anderman, E. M. (2000). Considering contexts in educational psychology: Introduction to the special issue. *Educational Psychologist, 35,* 67–68.

Anderman, L. H., & Anderman, E. M. (1999). Social predictors of changes in students' achievement goal orientations. *Contemporary Educational Psychology, 25,* 21–37.

Anderman, L. H., Hughes, H. K., Savage, T. A., & Tussey, J. (2000, April). *Promoting task orientation and self-regulated learning: The importance of social perceptions.* Poster session presented at the American Educational Research Association annual conference, New Orleans.

Anderson, L., Blumenfeld, P. C., Pintrich, P., Clark, C., Marx, R., & Peterson, P. (1995). Educational psychology for teachers: Reforming our courses, rethinking our roles. *Educational Psychologist, 30,* 143–157.

Baumrind, D. (1971). Current patterns of parental authority. *Developmental Psychology Monographs, 4*(1, Pt. 2).

Baumrind, D. (1991). Effective parenting during the early adolescent transition. In P. A. Cowan & M. Hetherington (Eds.), *Family transitions* (pp. 111–164). Hillsdale, NJ: Lawrence Erlbaum Associates.

Bear, G. (1998). School discipline in the United States: Prevention, correction, and long-term social development. *School Psychology Review, 27,* 14–32.

Blumenfeld, P. C. (1992). Classroom learning and motivation: Clarifying and expanding goal theory. *Journal of Educational Psychology, 84,* 272–281.

Blumenfeld, P. C., & Meece, J. L. (1985). Life in classrooms revisited. *Theory Into Practice, 24,* 50–56.

Blumenfeld, P. C., Pintrich, P. R., & Hamilton, V. L. (1987). Teacher talk and students' reasoning about morals, conventions, and achievement. *Child Development, 58,* 1389–1401.

Blumenfeld, P. C., Puro, P., & Mergendoller, J. (1992). Translating motivation into thoughtfulness. In H. H. Marshall (Ed.), *Redefining student learning* (pp. 297–239). Westport, CT: Ablex.

Borko, H., & Putnam, R. T. (1996). Learning to teach. In D. C. Berliner & R. C. Calfee (Eds.), *Handbook of educational psychology* (pp. 673–708). New York: Macmillan.

Brophy, J. E., & Evertson, C. (1987). *Learning from teaching: A developmental perspective.* Boston: Allyn & Bacon.

Butler, R. (1987). Task-involving and ego-involving properties of evaluation: Effects of different feedback conditions on motivational perceptions, interest, and performance. *Journal of Educational Psychology, 79,* 474–482.

Butler, R. (1995). Motivational and informational functions and consequences of children's attention to peers' work. *Journal of Educational Psychology, 87,* 347–360.

Calderhead, J. (1996). Teachers: Beliefs and knowledge. In D. C. Berliner & R. C. Calfee (Eds.), *Handbook of educational psychology* (pp. 709–725). New York: Macmillan.

Carter, K. (1993). The place of story in the study of teaching and teacher education. *Educational Researcher, 22*(1), 5–12, 18.

Collins, A., Brown, J. S., & Newman, S. E. (1989). Cognitive apprenticeship: Teaching the crafts of reading, writing, and mathematics. In L. B. Resnick (Ed.), *Knowing, learning, and instruction: Essays in honor of Robert Glaser* (pp. 453–494). Hillsdale, NJ: Lawrence Erlbaum Associates.

Covington, M. V., & Omelich, C. L. (1984). Task-oriented versus competitive learning structures: Motivational and performance consequences. *Journal of Educational Psychology, 76,* 1038–1050.

Cronin-Jones, L., & Shaw, E. L. (1992). The influence of methods instruction on the beliefs of preservice elementary and secondary science teachers: Preliminary comparative analyses. *School Science and Mathematics, 92,* 14–22.

Deci, E. L., Schwartz, A. J., Sheinman, L., & Ryan, R. M. (1981). An instrument to assess adults' orientations toward control versus autonomy with children: Reflections on intrinsic motivation and perceived competence. *Journal of Educational Psychology, 73,* 642–650.

Elliott, E. S., & Dweck, C. S. (1988). Goals: An approach to motivation and achievement. *Journal of Personality and Social Psychology, 54,* 5–12.

Epstein, J. L. (1983). Longitudinal effects of family-school-person interactions on student outcomes. *Research in sociology of education and socialization: Vol. 4. Personal change over the life course* (pp. 101–127). Greenwich, CT: JAI.

Evertson, C. M., & Emmer, E. T. (1982). Effective management of the beginning of the school year in junior high classes. *Journal of Educational Psychology, 74,* 485–498.

Feldlaufer, H., Midgley, C., & Eccles, J. S. (1988). Student, teacher, and observer perceptions of the classroom environment before and after the transition to junior high school. *Journal of Early Adolescence, 8,* 133–156.

Flanders, N. (1970). *Analyzing teacher behavior.* Reading, MA: Addison-Wesley.

Grusec, J. E., & Goodnow, J. J. (1994). Impact of parental discipline methods on the child's internalization of values: A reconceptualization of current points of view. *Developmental Psychology, 30,* 4–19.

Hesse-Biber, S., Kinder, I. S., Dupis, P. R., Dupis, A., & Tornabene, E. (1994). *HyperResearch: A content analysis tool for the qualitative researcher.* Randolph, MA: Researchware, Inc.

Hollingsworth, S. (1989). Prior beliefs and cognitive change in learning to teach. *American Educational Research Journal, 26,* 160–189.

Hruda, L., Middleton, M. L., & Linnenbrink, E. (1999). *Teachers' facilitation of students' socio-emotional development through classroom rules and management.* Poster session presented at the annual meeting of the American Educational Research Association, Montreal.

Jagacinski, C. M., & Nicholls, J. G. (1984). Conceptions of ability and related affects in task involvement and ego involvement. *Journal of Educational Psychology, 76,* 909–919.

Maehr, M. L., & Anderman, E. M. (1993). Reinventing schools for early adolescents: Emphasizing task goals. *Elementary School Journal, 93,* 593–610.

Maehr, M. L., & Midgley, C. (1991). Enhancing student's motivation: A school wide approach. *Educational Psychologist, 26,* 399–427.

Maehr, M. L., & Midgley, C. (1996). *Transforming school cultures.* Boulder, CO: Westview Press.

Marshall, H. H., & Weinstein, R. S. (1984). Classroom factors affecting students' self-evaluations: An interactional model. *Review of Educational Research, 54,* 301–325.

Marshall, H. H., & Weinstein, R. S. (1986). Classroom context of student-perceived differential teacher treatment. *Journal of Educational Psychology, 78,* 441–453.

Meece, J. L. (1991). The classroom context and students' motivational goals. In M. L. Maehr & P. R. Pintrich (Eds.), *Advances in motivation and achievement: Vol. 7. Goals and self-regulatory processes* (pp. 261–286). Greenwich, CT: JAI.

Middleton, M. J., Hruda, L., & Linnenbrink, L. (1998). *Teachers' use of social comparison in the classroom.* Poster session presented at the annual meeting of the Society for the Psychological Study of Social Issues, Ann Arbor.

Midgley, C. (1993). Motivation and middle level schools. In M. L. Maehr & P. R. Pintrich (Eds.), *Advances in motivation and achievement: Vol. 8. Motivation and adolescent development* (pp. 217–274). Greenwich, CT: JAI.

Midgley, C., & Edelin, K. (1998). Middle school reform and early adolescent well-being: The good news and the bad. *Educational Psychologist, 33,* 195–206.

Miles, M. B., & Huberman, A. M. (1994). *Qualitative data analysis: An expanded source book* (2nd ed.). Thousand Oaks, CA: Sage.

Murdock, T. B., Anderman, L. H., & Hodge, S. A. (2000). Middle-grade predictors of students' motivation and behavior in high school. *Journal of Adolescent Research, 15,* 327–351.

Nespor, J. (1987). The role of beliefs in the practice of teaching. *Journal of Curriculum Studies, 19,* 317–328.

Nicholls, J. G. (1984). Achievement motivation: Conceptions of ability, subjective experience, task choice and performance. *Psychological Review, 91,* 328–346.

Noddings, N. (1992). *The challenge to care in schools: An alternative approach to education.* New York: Teachers College Press.

Ormrod, J. E. (1998). *Educational psychology: Developing learners.* Upper Saddle River, NJ: Merrill.

Patrick, H., Anderman, L. H., Ryan, A. M., Edelin, K., & Midgley, C. (2001). Teachers' communication of goal orientations in four fifth-grade classrooms. *Elementary School Journal, 102*(1).

Patrick, H., Ryan, A. M., Anderman, L. H., Middleton, M., Linnenbrink, L., Hruda, L. Z., Edelin, K., Kaplan, A., & Midgley, C. (1997). *Manual for Observing Patterns of Adaptive Learning (OPAL): A protocol for classroom observations.* Ann Arbor: University of Michigan.

Richardson, V. (1990). Significant and worthwhile change in teaching practice. *Educational Researcher, 19*(7), 10–18.

Rohrkemper, M. (1984). The influence of teacher socialization style on students' social cognition and reported interpersonal classroom behavior. *Elementary School Journal, 85,* 245–275.

Rosenholtz, S. R., & Rosenholtz, S. J. (1981). Classroom organization and the perception of ability. *Sociology of Education, 54,* 132–140.

Ruble, D. N., & Frey, K. (1991). Changing patterns of comparative behavior as skills are acquired: A functional model of self-evaluation. In J. Suls & T. Wills (Eds.), *Social com-*

parison: Contemporary theory and research (pp. 79–113). Hillsdale, NJ: Lawrence Erlbaum Associates.

Stallings, J. (1975). Implementation and child effects of teaching practices in Follow Through classrooms. *Monographs of the Society for Research in Child Development, 40*(7–8, Serial No. 163).

Stipek, D. J., & Daniels, D. H. (1988). Declining perceptions of competence: A consequence of changes in the child or in the educational environment? *Journal of Educational Psychology, 80,* 352–356.

Turner, J., C., & Meyer, D. K. (2000). Studying and understanding the instructional contexts of classrooms: Using our past to forge our future. *Educational Psychologist, 35,* 69–86.

Urdan, T. C., Midgley, C., & Anderman, E. M. (1998). The role of classroom goal structure in students' use of self-handicapping. *American Educational Research Journal, 35,* 101–122.

Weinstein, C. S. (1989). Teacher education students' perceptions of teaching. *Journal of Teacher Education, 40,* 53–60.

Wentzel, K. R. (1997). Student motivation in middle school: The role of perceived pedagogical caring. *Journal of Educational Psychology, 89,* 411–419.

10 Patterns of Adaptive Learning Study: Where Do We Go From Here?

Martin V. Covington
University of California at Berkeley

Thanks to the tireless efforts of several generations of investigators, we now have in place a broad outline of the cognitive, motivational, and situational determinants of school achievement. This is not to say, of course, that the picture is complete. Much is left to do and to learn. But at least we understand enough to identify many of the current gaps in our knowledge, to determine with some clarity what next steps need be taken, and to contemplate the wider social and educational policy implications of our emerging science.

I am honored by the invitation to provide some perspective on this fluid, unfinished agenda, and in particular, to comment on the place of the *Patterns of Adaptive Learning Study* (PALS) in this ongoing enterprise.

I have organized my remarks around two interlocking observations. First, I ask what has the PALS consortium contributed additionally to our understanding of the dynamics of school achievement, and where do we go from here—in effect, how do we best capitalize on the inspired insights and informed speculation of the PALS consortium that move the educational mission forward. Second, in conclusion, I note that the matter of future research directions depends closely on how the educational mission is viewed by observers, and I hope to make my views clear.

CONTRIBUTIONS AND FUTURE INQUIRIES

As to the first observation regarding the contributions of the PALS consortium, two major themes emerge:

First, the PALS research is broadly confirmatory. In general the consortium findings confirm the general organizing principles that have found their way into the existing research literature on school achievement dynamics, most notably, the proposition that the kinds of personal academic goals that students bring to the classroom and the prevailing goal structures of these classrooms jointly influence the amount and quality of student learning. And, these are the most valuable kinds of confirmation; not simply a replication of previous research using strictly identical measures and methods, but a reaffirmation based largely on new instrumentation developed by the PALS group and the use of multimethod approaches that allow for a triangulation of findings among case study, survey, and interview techniques. Because of the PALS research we can be reassured that the broad outlines of our understanding of achievement dynamics derived from a goal theory perspective is not simply the product of a particular methodology or procedure.

At the same time, besides supporting key predictions, the PALS consortium also confirms the continued existence of various puzzles that still defy our expectations, such as the fact that the evidence for the relationship between student *performance* goals and the quality of self-regulated learning is less consistent than that between *mastery* goals and achievement behavior. Fortunately, however, failures to confirm expectations, if properly considered—far from impeaching theory, often become an opportunity to expand the conceptual reach of theory. The PALS consortium has performed yeoman duty in taking up the challenge in this particular case by exploring the possibility that performance goals may have both approach and avoidance components that were not previously differentiated by investigators.

Second, the consortium findings are not only confirmatory, but provocative as well—provocative in that they open new vistas for interpretation, challenge our present ways of thinking, and stimulate new research questions, especially as related to matters of educational reform. Consortium members have already suggested a number of fruitful directions for future research. Some of these suggestions involve a follow-up in detail along specific lines of investigation. Other suggestions provoke an interlocking series of questions on a grander scale. I will add mainly to this latter category, and in particular, comment on issues that I believe are best pursued—indeed, in some cases, approachable only through—an alliance with the many players in the drama of schooling: variously, teachers, students, parents, and community.

But before considering these future directions, one may wonder why the PALS consortium has accomplished so much that is worthy of our attention.

First, the massive scale of the research and the many design intricacies involved are part of the answer—intricacies as well as ambitiousness reflected in the participation of hundreds of students—most repeatedly observed, the involvement of scores of teachers and administrative staff, and analyses always nested within levels ranging from the individual learner, to classrooms, to entire schools. The answer also rests in the fact that a multimethod approach is featured in combination with repeated intra-individual measurements, a paradigm whose developmental scope can be counted not in months, but in years. All these attributes contribute substantially to the importance of this enterprise. But in the end, I believe the overarching reason for the profundity of the PALS research lies in the fact that the entire study was theoretically based. Everyone acknowledges the important role that theory plays in directing and coordinating research, but all too often theory is honored more in the breach than by its observance. As a consequence, the landscape of our field is littered with isolated facts, tantalizing but untested propositions, and commonsense answers, which in the words of Ernest Becker (1981) are "strewn all over the place, spoken in a thousand competitive voices ... insignificant fragments magnified out of all proportion while major insights lie around begging for attention. There is no throbbing vital center." In this case, however, there is a vital center: achievement goal theory. In the hands of these accomplished researchers, achievement goal theory has come of age, having been expanded far beyond its relatively narrow, original focus on the relationship between goals and the quality of self-regulation processes, to encompass now a host of phenomena and topics including social motivation, teacher identity, and avoidance behavior, to name only a few. Today, achievement goal theory stands as a major, if not arguably, the preeminent theoretical position in the field of school achievement dynamics.

Obviously, there is nothing new about the human issues taken up by the PALS consortium, issues that sorely vex our society, and schools in particular—student disaffection, indifference, discontent, and failure. But what *is* new—and this is the important point—is that a team of researchers representing many different interests and diverse methodological expertise have come to view a variety of far-flung and sometimes apparently unrelated topics through a single theoretical lens. In effect, they have put a number of vital issues on the same conceptual footing, and the results are impressive. This positive verdict rests on many specific examples to be found within the pages of this book. But one single, overriding bit of logic adopted by consortium members conveys how what is of importance here was accomplished: If the actions of students are given meaning and purpose by the goals they seek out, then these same goal-seeking dynamics also likely apply to teachers, administrators, and parents as well. This goal-seeking proposition is the progenitor of all the far-reaching research and policy implications of the PALS research.

Now what future research directions are inspired by the findings of the PALS consortium, directions that are important enough to sustain a new generation of research, and at the same time best explored through a partnership with teachers, students, and community?

Interdependency of Schooling

First, the goal-seeking proposition directs our attention to a profoundly important kind of analysis that is rarely acknowledged and little researched. It concerns the interdependency of the educational enterprise. Not only is each player in the drama of schooling propelled individually by multiple goals, but the goals, aspirations, and intentions of, say, students can interact either harmoniously or in conflict with the goals of teachers. Likewise, the curriculum objectives of teachers can complement or conflict with the hopes of parents for their youngsters. Understanding the dynamics involved in this open, plastic system of relationships is the key to truly effective educational change. Indeed, it is precisely at the intersects among these players where the battle for reform will be won or lost. According to consortium reasoning, these intersects are best represented by the common denominator of goals—student goals, teacher goals, and even the goals of the public. The consortium has done a great service in beginning to sketch out the broad outlines of the kinds and quality of relationships to be found at these junctures, and in particular to alert us to the kinds of mismatches and contradictions that inevitably arise. For instance, students may be eager to learn, but their willingness can be undercut if teachers have little autonomy to act in students' best interest; nor can students be encouraged to love learning, if they are punished for not learning. The only way such mismatches can be resolved, and mutually agreed-upon goals emerge at all levels, and among all players, is through good-faith bargaining, occasional concessions, compromise, and a substantial dose of reeducation. Yet, we know little about these dynamics, let alone how best to proceed toward establishing the necessary goal alliances.

It is increasingly clear from research on effective schooling that only the total environment can have a positive impact on student achievement. No single element—be it increased parent involvement or reduced class size—is enough to make the difference, but no element can be ignored. Children need to be immersed in a coordinated circle of positive, interlocking influences in the form of parental health education programs, community clinics, service organizations, and church-based outreach groups. This point has not been widely appreciated if we are to judge from the relative lack of research on the nature of such coordination, despite repeated calls for its implementation and a few pioneering efforts to do so (see, e.g., Ames, 1992; Maehr & Midgley, 1991; 1996; Weinstein, 1998).

Research on these partnership issues should have the highest priority, and obviously is best conducted in the cockpit of change itself at the school site, in neighborhoods, in union halls, and in legislatures. But the study of partnership dynamics implies far more than a refocusing of research priorities and a reconsideration of the context in which these dynamics occur. It demands a fundamental shift in the role of researchers. Basically, I believe that effective educational change will not occur unless it is guided by theory and informed by empirically derived principles of behavior. This is where psychology comes into its own—offering its expertise to teachers and community, but only at the invitation of the players. The matter of invitation is central. Part of the problem is that for years researchers all too often have invited themselves into the classroom, not as supplicants or even as guests, but to use classes as laboratories to pursue answers to questions that teachers and parents may see as arcane, distant, and often quite divorced from the practical realities of schooling. To quicken the process of productive change, researchers need to spend more time as observers of the classroom scene, informally testing the limits of their theories in the crucible of real life, learning from the players, and searching for new ways to frame old questions in the tradition of an earlier generation of astute observers including Philip Jackson (*Life in Classrooms,* 1968), John Holt (*How Children Fail,* 1964) and most recently John Nicholls (Nicholls & Hazzard, 1993).

Magnitude of Change

Not only do the PALS findings imply the importance of studying the interdependent nature of schooling, but their work also anticipates a corollary: Just *how much* change in teaching practices is necessary to tip the balance in a direction favorable to student creativity and the productive use of the mind? I have just argued for a vision of schools in multiple partnerships to create an interlocking, positive circle of influence on children. But the prospects for such a vision becoming reality will depend on how successfully society deals with another equally powerful, but unforgiving and dangerous circle of influence—malnutrition, homelessness, drugs, and exploitation of every kind—that confronts millions of schoolchildren today. For example, consider the corrosive effects of competition. Competition is more than a dubious way to arouse children to learn. Competition in our society is also an ethos that prescribes the manners, customs, ideals, and, above all, determines the rules by which people relate to each other—in this case, rules that set person against person and discourage cooperation. The chances for true reform would be bleak, indeed, if the renewed pursuit of excellence required the virtual absence of competition, a hugely improbable proposition. Put in the context of the

PALS inquiries, the question becomes more specifically, how much or how little an emphasis on, say, mastery goals is needed in order for the values of discovery and creativity to thrive in the face of society-sanctioned competitive sorting and a performance ethic based on scrambling for extrinsic rewards, such as high grades, and avoiding punishment in the form of failing grades? We have virtually no empirical basis on which to address such questions. Happily, however, what little we do know encourages some optimism. For example, Ames and Archer (1987) found that as long as mastery goals were in place in classrooms, the presence of competition, often encouraged by parents, seemed to do little to diminish those positive behaviors we have come to associate with intrinsic task engagement. For example, students focused on effort explanations for their accomplishments, used sophisticated planning strategies, and preferred problems where "you can learn a lot of new things but will also have some difficulty and make many mistakes." And, most important of all, student enthusiasm for such challenges did not depend on their self-perceived ability level. Perhaps far fewer and less radical changes in classroom practices are needed to make a positive difference than may have been generally assumed. But, at present we simply do not know.

Goals as Personality Dimensions

Whatever we eventually discover regarding the degree of change needed, these judgments will almost certainly depend closely on a classic issue raised anew by the PALS group. It concerns the fundamental nature of achievement goals themselves: simply put, whether goals are best thought of as stable, traitlike personality dimensions, or by contrast, as more volatile, situationally influenced reactions to prevailing and changeable environmental demands. The stakes implied by this query are enormous for educational reform. As only one example, if students who are disengaged from school are particularly vulnerable to performance goals—as consortium evidence suggests—then emphasizing classroom goal structures that reward mastery objectives would seem the preferred course of action. However, to the extent that, say, student failure-avoiding goals and their attendant feelings of suspicion and fear are stable, trait-related reactions to change, then the best intentions of teachers to improve the climate of learning for failure-threatened students may be subverted. Here again we have little information about the threat level of change, although we do know that change can cut both ways for good and ill, motivationally speaking. For instance, the infusion of novel, provocative elements into otherwise routine school assignments can stimulate curiosity, feelings of independence, and intellectual excitement, but only up to a point (Covington & Wiedenhaupt, 1997). When novelty becomes equated in the minds of students with unfamiliarity and lack of structure, then

curiosity can turn to anxiety, defensiveness, and a renewed grade focus at the expense of subject matter appreciation. And this trigger point is typically lower for students harboring failure-avoiding goals.

On a more optimistic note, situational factors may be more responsible for resistance to change than the presence of any underlying personality dispositions. Consider the potential conflict between intrinsic and extrinsic rewards such that a preoccupation with high grades may interfere with the satisfaction of personal curiosity. Our evidence (McEvoy & Covington, 2001) suggests that the degree of incompatibility experienced by students between pursuing performance goals and caring about learning is less a matter of being either success oriented or failure threatened than it is the demands of academic life that leave little room to pursue either goal fully, let alone both goals simultaneously. Given the pressure of schoolwork in the face of sometimes overwhelming personal and financial burdens, students must often choose between, say, narrowing the focus of their study, for efficiency's sake, to what they believe will be tested versus attending to the personal meaning of what they are studying. Students make it clear which choice they often feel forced to make. But they also lament what is lost in the bargain. In short, students typically prioritize their goals, in this case, acquisition over appreciation. But that does not necessarily mean that these goals are incompatible, and certainly not that any conflict between them is necessarily due to personality dispositions. These goals have merely been prioritized in response to situational forces, and priorities can be changed by modifying circumstances.

Much of the prevailing evidence suggests that at least approach–avoidance goal-seeking tendencies are laid down early in life and crystallized through differential child rearing mechanisms (e.g., Tomiki, 1997). This should make our concerns about the likelihood of achieving positive change all the more urgent. On the other hand, it is patently clear that goals are malleable. Goal setting stands as a practical surrogate for motives. By rewarding some goals and not others, teachers can change the reasons students learn, which is to say, their motives. And, we know that goals control behavior, especially self-regulation and the individual's intentions regarding future actions, and it is this applied knowledge that will allow reform to proceed. Research on individual responsiveness to change, flexibility, and spontaneity are needed both for making informed policy decisions at the highest public levels as well as to alert teachers to the potential promise as well as the pitfalls involved in initiating educational reform.

Multiple Goals

The research of the PALS consortium has also underscored the urgent need to investigate further the basic structure of students' achievement goals, that is,

the need to fashion a "periodic table," so to speak, of fundamental, irreducible personal objectives, as well as to identify the interactions among them, and their individual and joint relationships to school achievement. For far too long researchers have explored only a narrow arc of achievement-related goals exemplified by the performance–learning goal distinction. Although this has been a conspicuously successful beginning, I believe we now need to expand our investigations in at least four directions:

1. Though we are relatively well informed about the role of academic goals in motivating the achievement of individuals, our understanding of how social goals enter into the process lags behind. But it will not be enough simply to study prosocial motives in their own right, even though it is clear from PALS research that prosocial goals likely influence achievement independent of variations in academic goals. Perhaps more important, prosocial goals clearly interact with academic goals to influence achievement jointly, and it is at this juncture that we need to concentrate our inquiries. Whatever these interactive dynamics eventually prove to be, we can expect that various combinations of goals will exert negative as well as positive influences on academic achievement. For instance, whether the willingness to share with others becomes a positive factor in the achievement equation will almost certainly depend on which achievement goals predominate. In this connection, Wentzel (1996) reported that the tendency of students to pursue social goals, like sharing, is positively related to learning goals but not to performance goals. This reflects the fact that by their very nature, learning goals—exploring, experimenting, and discovering—depend heavily on the active cooperation of others, whereas the main objective of performance goals—doing better than others—is patently contrary to positive social values involving as they do sabotage, deception, and a reluctance to cooperate. Also, there is the possibility of a direct conflict between social and academic goals that presents painful dilemmas for youngsters, as in the classic example of minority students who must accept dominant Anglo achievement values (competition, independence) sufficiently to survive in school but not enough to incur the wrath of their minority peers and families as betrayers of their cultural heritage. Finally, not only will the quality of achievement likely depend on the composition of the various multiple goal patterns, but as the PALS consortium has anticipated, teachers almost certainly will emerge as key moderators of these dynamics.

2. Second, our previous study of achievement goals has been unnecessarily restricted to classroom situations where students are provided with relatively clear directions and explicit standards of excellence, usually relative in nature, that define success and failure. This is the realm of *presented* problems; that is, school tasks presented in a neatly packaged, highly structured form, with all the

information provided for a solution—no more, no less. Most presented problems are in themselves quite trivial, and their preset answers are already known to the teacher. Few people really care how old Ralphie is, if his age is one third that of Bob's age, except as evidence that someone has mastered fractions. By comparison, we are far less knowledgeable about achievement dynamics as they relate to exploratory learning, or the realm of *discovered* problems for which the presenter (who may actually be the student) usually does care about answers—sometimes passionately, even desperately so, and precisely because there is no known or preset solution, or at least no single answer on which everyone (not even one's teachers) can always agree. These are problems of enormous personal interest—how to convince others, through one's writing, not to do drugs; or how to paint a picture that creates a deep appreciation for the subject matter. Here interest is not simply the by-product of either social approval or academic success. At their core, these problems possess a deeply held and abiding interest that has a private, protected side in which the rewards that sustain them are largely undiminished even by a mediocre record of objective school performance. These alternative rewards involve surpassing one's own idiosyncratic standards of excellence, the playful discovery of hidden talents, and the personal freedom to pick and choose different ways of pursuing whatever invites one's attention. It is in this sense that one's learning goals can be intangible—but motivating nonetheless—and what counts as success and failure comes to be defined idiosyncratically, not by consensus or by comparison with the accomplishments of others.

It is time that we give more attention to these valuing aspects of goals and their motivational properties (Brophy, 1999; Covington, 1999). This is especially imperative because many observers have lamented the prospects of ever encouraging such intrinsic values as subject matter appreciation in a context in which many students are grade driven and a common motivational strategy of teachers involves the threat of poor grades.

3. As already remarked, multiple goal combinations within the individual student can be characterized variously as additive and uplifting, merely compatible, or even conflicting. PALS researchers have correctly recognized the theoretical importance of these interactive dynamics. I concur with their conclusion that more research is needed on the issue of intra individual, multiple goal alliances. I would only argue further the need to extend an appreciation of the significance of such hybrid goal combinations to matters of school change as well. In this regard perhaps the most provocative of these goal profiles is reflected by those students who approach success as a means to avoid failure—individuals whom I have labeled as *overstrivers* (Covington, 1998) and who likely share much in common with goal combinations described by consortium members as performance-approach (also, see Elliot & Harackiewicz, 1996).

Overstrivers stand as a kind of cautionary tale, warning us that more is at stake in the cause of reform than merely improving achievement, and that the reasons for achieving must also be set right. When we fail to consider motives and feelings, individuals may strive successfully—like overstrivers who typically achieve top grades—but for the wrong reasons with the result that the benefits of success may be largely illusory. Success for overstrivers is a dubious proposition. They feel they must always succeed, every time, and against ever-increasing odds in order to feel worthy. As a result, their primary reaction to success is one of relief at not having failed rather than feelings of deserved pride in their accomplishments. Such successes are a poor foundation on which to build a continuing commitment to learning and a vibrant life of the mind.

4. Fourth, and finally, research employing a goal theory framework has been criticized for not adequately addressing socioeconomic and ethnic differences, especially dynamics associated with African American youngsters. Vigorous efforts are needed to identify not only the universal goals that mobilize all individuals, but those goals that may be differentially salient across the socioeconomic spectrum as well as inquiries into the mechanisms by which these goals operate to affect performance. The work of the PALS consortium represents an important step in addressing these issues. Among their many findings, I believe the most provocative concerns the relationship between teachers as conveyors of socially valued goals and minority students as potential recipients of this collective wisdom. Herein may lie some of those subtle, yet powerfully influential mismatches of which I spoke earlier. Of the three personal goal orientations studied most extensively by the PALS group—mastery, performance, and extrinsic—the latter has proven to be associated with the most negative educational outcomes. Yet, many teachers interviewed by PALS members nonetheless stressed the message with their African American students that doing well later in life (a patently extrinsic goal) depended on doing well in school now. Obviously this is not wrong-headed advice. But it appears to be the only reason given by some of these teachers as well as often being presented in superficial and shallow forms such as urging compliance with a work ethic in order to pass to the next grade. The key question, correctly anticipated by the PALS group, becomes "Aren't there any other reasons to learn?" Yes, of course. And the natural candidate is mastery goals. Here too, however, I believe we have not fully exploited the motivational potential of mastery goals, a neglect that may be particularly detrimental to minority students. Becoming more skillful serves a host of selfless, but practical, objectives besides the intrinsic value of self-improvement, such as assuming adult work roles to care for one's family, a goal that has driven many young Hispanic refugees from war-torn Central America to do well in school in order eventually to support families left behind (Suarez-Orozco, 1989).

As things stand, the dominant value of American schools favors individualism, autonomy, and independence, typically in the service of goals dominated largely by a competitive, entrepreneurial spirit that fuels a scramble for improved social status, and a preoccupation with high standardized test scores. These are basically selfish goals. There is little room for academic goals that mobilize achievements around a commitment to sharing and maintaining family values and kinship roles for the sake of survival. These are the primary goals to which many minority youngsters aspire, yet they lie largely outside the more traditional realm of academics defined by individual excellence. This conflict of values likely intensifies for minority youngsters in the transition from the elementary years to middle school, when evaluation becomes more formal and competitive as the function of schools focuses more and more on the selection and sorting of talent. As a consequence, minority youngsters often must increasingly play by competitive rules, if they are to play at all, rules that for them are often foreign, frightening, and confusing. If schools in America today have become a foreign country for countless youngsters, then responsible attempts at school reform need to consider ways to change the rules of the academic game so that they are more compatible with the preferred achievement approaches of the disenfranchised and minorities.

A further caution needs to be sounded. In fostering these needed changes, we should not consider helping goals simply as a way to mobilize selected students, with the end being improved achievement scores. The commitment to helping others represents the deepest expression of the fundamental human need for approval and sharing among all people, and as such should be fostered in its own right along with spontaneity of spirit and creative expression.

Goal Theory and the Need–Achievement Tradition

Finally, the work of the PALS group holds important consequences for achievement goal theory itself. Theories imbue phenomena with meaning, but theories too are subject to change by the very process of making the inexplicable meaningful. Achievement goal theory is no exception. Goal theory has come of age not only as an organizing principle of great conceptual reach, but also because of the capacity of its adherents to accommodate other theoretical perspectives, an openness that leads to a richer portrayal of school achievement dynamics than would otherwise be possible. This process is well illustrated by the PALS consortium's embracing of the insights of the need–achievement tradition embodied in self-worth theory (Covington, 1998), which maintains that goals can also serve an adaptive, even survival purpose beyond their self-regu-

latory functions. This need component, which is reflected in the classic approach–avoidance distinction (see Elliot & Covington, 2001), complements the cognitive self-regulation aspects of goals by addressing such questions as why individuals choose to pursue some goals and not others, as well as clarifying why some students act against their own self-interest by sabotaging their chances for success by procrastinating in their studies or by setting unrealistically high goals that doom them to failure.

The time is now ripe to seek a rapprochement between need-based and social-cognitive approaches to achievement behavior. The agenda for such an undertaking comprises a nested set of inquiries of the following kind (Pintrich & Covington, 2001):

1. What are the relative roles of achievement needs, personality traits, and achievement goals as contributors to the quality of self-regulation and school achievement?
2. How can achievement goals and self-regulation theory be infused with motivational properties?
3. What are the important sources of interindividual differences in motivation, self-regulation, and achievement?
4. What role does context play as a source for motivation, self-regulation, and achievement? In effect, how do contextual factors moderate the relations between motives, needs, traits, and goals?
5. Given these relations, what are the implications for instruction and educational practice? For example, how might instruction in self-regulation mitigate the potential maladaptive aspects of motives (e.g., fear of failure) or personality traits such as avoidance tendencies that might hinder learning and achievement?

CONCLUSIONS

Here, then, is a proposed agenda for future research anticipated in large part by the work of the PALS consortium. Other observers may favor somewhat different agendas or assign different priorities to the one proposed here. Obviously, many views are possible and all are welcome. However, whatever the particular content of our strategic plans, we must never treat them as merely "laundry lists" of separate items to be pursued in relative isolation, one from the other. In matters of educational reform, the most significant findings often lie at the interface between the various lines of investigation, as well as where the lines overlap. The matter of issue interconnectedness also underscores the fact that the collective value of multiple programs of research depend on coordinating our efforts toward a mutually agreed-upon end—in this instance, the end being a shared vi-

sion of what school can and should become. Michael Polanyi put it this way, "we cannot comprehend the whole without seeing its parts, but we cannot see the parts without comprehending the whole" (quoted in Reich, 1989, p. 17). In this case, I take "comprehending the whole" to mean grasping the totality of all those circumstances and conditions that maximize the greatest common good for all our children. Descriptions of this "whole" vision have been offered by many observers over the years, and in some cases they are accompanied by a listing of the psychological principles thought necessary to bring a particular vision into being (e.g., see McCombs, 2001). My short list of guiding objectives that follows was heavily influenced by reflecting on the work of the PALS consortium:

1. First, schools should not necessarily be particularized as a *place,* but rather more properly as a *state of mind* where learning can occur at any time, under any circumstances. This implies tutoring our students in the continual readiness to find problems and answers everywhere, as well as to be puzzled by the obvious, to see the extraordinary in the ordinary, and to have the willingness to turn the familiar, prosaic event into a profound revelation.
2. Second, schools should challenge students incrementally, with the prospect of success maximized when students are allowed to set achievement goals and to modify them as needed so that when failure occurs, it serves to renew student effort.
3. Third, schools should be responsive to the proposition that students learn best and teachers feel most satisfied professionally when both are encouraged to become allies in the process of learning.
4. Fourth, schools should encourage motives for learning that are positive and uplifting—for the sake of curiosity, to help others, and to improve one's skills as well as to widen the circle of legitimate reasons for learning and the permissible means for learning, including cooperation and sharing.

Now what of the time frame for the changes necessary to approximate these or any other similar objectives, and what else is needed to pave the way toward substantial progress? My tentative thoughts on these lingering questions and the very fact that these queries come to mind at all, is part of the positive legacy of the PALS research team. Actually, the kinds of changes in schools of the magnitude ultimately needed must be worked out in terms of generations, not just decades, time enough, for example, to reshape public beliefs about the mission of schooling and to revitalize teacher training. In closing I address the matter of public belief.

Perhaps the most subtle but powerfully entrenched obstacle to educational change is a world view held by many policymakers and ordinary citizens

alike regarding the essential nature of the process of schooling. This view is best expressed metaphorically as "schools as factories" (see Marshall, 1988). First come children cast in the role of workers whose job it is to learn, followed by teachers in the role of supervisors whose task it is to guarantee quality control, capped off by school boards (akin to management) who wield ultimate authority over the entire process. Many beliefs and practices detrimental to positive educational change form the vanguard of this metaphor, not the least of which are the hardened institutional lines of authority that run top down from school boards to teachers, a practice that disenfranchises teachers and undercuts their ongoing struggle for professional status. Another fallout of this factory model is the misplaced yet surprisingly pervasive view of children as passive recipients of knowledge—akin to vessels to be filled, or blank slates to be etched, not at all reflective of the active, willful, ingenious human beings that psychological research has shown children to be. This deadening belief justifies the practice of preparing most youngsters for what Robert Reich (1989) called "cog" jobs—being trained to follow directions for relatively simple, routine tasks that can be repeated over and over, whereas we send only a small minority of students on to advanced tracks to become decision makers at the top of the heap.

Before true educational reform can fully occur, this outdated factory metaphor of schooling must be replaced with new metaphors that respond to the demands and opportunities of the 21st century. We need not look far for attractive possibilities, including an odds-on favorite: schooling as future building. In this connection, one is reminded of Harry Lauder's remark that, "The future is not a gift, it is an achievement." If the future is an achievement, as Lauder argued, then teachers are futurists, along with politicians, filmmakers, and journalists—those individuals who make other people's futures more real to them.

Educational researchers can aid in creating new, more useful public visions regarding the role and mission of schools, and in a variety of ways, not the least of which involves redoubling research into children's perceptions of the future and their place in it. Also, we need to intensify our investigations of the learner from a *constructionist* perspective, that is, viewing students as goal-seeking, self-regulating individuals who not only extract meaning from information to create their own subjective reality, but do so in ways that form an accurate assessment of their gifts and strengths as well as their limitations. In this connection, if I read correctly the general direction in which the momentum of the PALS research propels us, then the search for Becker's elusive center will eventually refocus our attention on the single most important, irreducible component of all human experience: the self. As Susan Harter (1986) prophesied, "the self will once again be resurrected as a legitimate psychological construct" (p. 137). The hope is, of course, that with each resurrection will come a

more scientifically sound and practically useful version of the construct of self as learner. The contributions of the PALS consortium have laid the groundwork for such a hope.

REFERENCES

Ames, C. (1992). Classrooms: Goals, structures, and student motivation. *Journal of Educational Psychology, 84,* 261–271.

Ames, C., & Archer, J. (1987, April). *Achievement goals in the classroom: Student learning strategies and motivation processes.* Paper presented at the annual meeting of the American Educational Research Association, Washington, DC.

Becker, E. (1981). *The denial of death.* New York: The Free Press.

Brophy, J. (1999). Toward a model of the value aspects of motivation in education: Developing appreciation for particular learning domains and activities. *Educational Psychologist* [Special Issue]: *The value aspects of motivation in education, 34,* 75–85

Covington, M. V. (1998). *The will to learn: A guide for motivating young people.* New York: Cambridge University Press.

Covington, M. V. (1999). Caring about learning: The nature and nurturing of subject-matter appreciation. *Educational Psychologist, 34,* 127–136.

Covington, M. V., & Wiedenhaupt, S. (1997). Turning work into play: The nature and nurturing of intrinsic task engagement. In R. Perry & J. C. Smart (Eds.), *Effective teaching in higher education: Research and practice* (Special ed., pp. 101–114). New York: Agathon Press.

Elliot, A. J., & Covington, M. V. (2001). Approach and avoidance motivation. *Educational Psychology Review, 13*(2), 73–92.

Elliot, A. J., & Harackiewicz, J. M. (1996). Approach and avoidance achievement goals and intrinsic motivation: A mediational analysis. *Journal of Personality and Social Psychology, 70,* 461–475.

Harter, S. (1986). Processes underlying the construction, maintenance and enhancement of the self-concept in children. In J. Suls & A. G. Greenwald (Eds.), *Psychological perspectives on the self* (Vol. 3). Hillsdale, NJ: Lawrence Erlbaum Associates.

Holt, J. (1964). *How children fail.* New York: Dell.

Jackson, P. W. (1968). *Life in classrooms.* New York: Holt, Rinehart & Winston.

Maehr, M. L., & Midgley, C. (1991). Enhancing student motivation: A school wide approach. *Educational Psychologist, 26,* 399–427.

Maehr, M. L., & Midgley, C. (1996). *Transforming school cultures.* Boulder, CO: Westview Press.

Marshall, H. H. (1988). Work or learning: Implications of classroom metaphors. *Educational Researcher, 9,* 9–16.

McCombs, B. L. (2001, April). *What do we know about learners and learning? The learner-centered framework.* Paper presented at the symposium, "Integrating what we know about learners and learning: A foundation for transforming preK–20 practices," at the annual meeting of the American Educational Research Association, Seattle.

McEvoy, A. P., & Covington, M. V. (2001, April). *Is there life after grades: The effects of grades, personal interest, and intellectual climate on appreciation for learning.* Paper

presented at the annual meeting of the American Educational Research Association, Seattle.

Nicholls, J. G., & Hazzard, S. P. (1993). *Education as adventure: Lessons from the second grade.* New York: Teachers College Press.

Pintrich, P., & Covington, M. (2001, April). *Goals, motives, and school achievement: Toward an integration.* Symposium presented at the annual meeting of the American Educational Research Association, Seattle.

Reich, R. B. (1989, January). Must new economic vigor mean making do with less? *NEA Today,* pp. 13–19.

Suarez-Orozco, M. M. (1989). *Central American refugees and U.S. high schools: A psychological study of motivation and achievement.* Stanford, CA: Stanford University Press.

Tomiki, K. (1997). *Influences of cultural values and perceived family environments on achievement motivation among college students.* Unpublished master's thesis, University of California, Berkeley.

Weinstein, R. S. (1998). Promoting positive expectations in schooling. In N. M. Lambert & B. L. McCombs (Eds.), *How students learn: Reforming schools through learner-centered education* (pp. 81–111). Washington, DC: American Psychological Association.

Wentzel, K. R. (1996). Social and academic motivation in middle school: Concurrent and long-term relations to academic effort. *Journal of Early Adolescence, 16,* 390–406.

Author Index

Note: Page numbers in italic indicate reference pages; italic *f* following page number indicates figure; italic *t* following page number indicates table.

Subject Index

Note: Italic *f* following page number indicates figure; italic *t* following page number indicates table.